FOXY FERDINAND

FOXY FERDINAND
TSAR OF BULGARIA

Stephen Constant

Franklin Watts
New York / London / Toronto / Sydney
1980

For information address the publisher:
Franklin Watts, Inc.
730 Fifth Avenue
New York, New York 10019

Library of Congress Cataloging in Publication Data
Constant, Stephen, 1931-
Foxy Ferdinand, Tsar of Bulgaria.
1. Ferdinand I, Czar of Bulgaria, 1861-1948.
2. Bulgaria—Kings and rulers—Biography.
3. Bulgaria—History—Ferdinand I, 1887-1918.
I. Title
DR87.C66 1980   949.7'702'0924 [B]   80-14716
ISBN 0-531-09930-X

Maps by Dan Kitts

Copyright © 1979 by Stephen Constant
First published in the United States by Franklin Watts, Inc., 1980
First published in Great Britain in1979
by Sidgwick and Jackson
Limited

FOR ROSE AND TIFF

Acknowledgements

My thanks are due to my sister, Liliana Brisby, who has been good enough to read this book in manuscript and has contributed valuable suggestions. I am further much indebted to those members of the Stancioff family who very kindly provided me with written and illustrative material.

Readers of Joachim von Königslöw's study *Ferdinand von Bulgarien*, covering Ferdinand's early years, will be aware of how much the early part of this book has gained from his researches.

I should also like to thank the following for permission to publish extracts from copyright material in their possession: Cassell for *The Story of My Life* by Marie, Queen of Romania (1934) and *Queen Victoria's Relations* and *The Ambassador's Daughter* by Meriel Buchanan (1954 and 1958). The Hamlyn Publishing Group for *The World Crisis* by W.S. Churchill (originally published by Odhams Press Ltd). Hutchinson for *Recollections of a Bulgarian Diplomatist's Wife* by Anna Stancioff (1930), *Storm Centres of the Near East* by Sir Robert Graves (1933) and *Diplomacy and Foreign Courts* by Meriel Buchanan (1928). John Murray for *Dimitri Stancioff* by Nadejda Muir (1957), *The Sword and the Olive* by Sir George Rendel (1957) and *Diplomatic Reminiscences* by A. Neklyudoff (1920). Nigel Nicholson for *Lord Carnock* by Harold Nicholson (Constable 1930) and Oxford University Press for *The Struggle for Mastery in Europe* by A.J.P. Taylor (1954).

Author's Note

In transliterating Bulgarian and other Slav sur-
names, I have retained the old form of the suffix:
-*off* and -*eff*. This has been done for the sake of
consistency, as several of the present-day bearers
of names mentioned in the book (e.g. Stancioff
and Daneff) still use the old form. I have also used
the rendering of place names which was current
during the period covered in the book: Adrianople rather than Edirne, Philippopolis rather than
Plovdiv and Constantinople rather than Istanbul.
Both versions are indicated on the maps.

Contents

—◦❧❦◦—

List of Plates

—∘❧❦∘—

Prince Augustus of Saxe-Coburg, from a painting by Winterhalter (Popperfoto)

Princess Clémentine with Ferdinand, in 1866 (Reproduced by gracious permission of Her Majesty the Queen)

Prince Ferdinand at the coronation of Tsar Alexander III (British Library)

Prince Ferdinand in 1887 (Stancioff Collection)

Prince Alexander of Battenberg (Broadlands Collection)

The enforced abdication of Prince Alexander of Battenberg (Popperfoto)

Prince Ferdinand, before his departure for Bulgaria (Stancioff Collection)

Prince Ferdinand, on his arrival in Bulgaria (Mansell Collection)

Prince Ferdinand of Bulgaria, from *The Russian Dagger* by Virginia Cowles

Prince Ferdinand with his Bulgarian tutor, Dimitri Stancioff (Stancioff Collection)

Prince Ferdinand with a Bulgarian peasant woman (British Library)

Prince Ferdinand and Princess Clémentine at the monastery of Tirnovo (British Library)

The Royal Palace in Sofia (British Library)

The Palace at Euxinograd (British Library)

Prince Ferdinand on the Black Sea coast, at Euxinograd (British Library)

Prince Ferdinand dressed in Montenegrin national costume (Popperfoto)

Prince Ferdinand shooting sea birds at Euxinograd (British Library)

Prince Ferdinand in the robes of a Byzantine Emperor, from a painting in Sofia Cathedral. From *Czar Ferdinand and his People* by John MacDonald

MAPS

THE FAMILY TREE OF TSAR FERDINAND OF BULGARIA

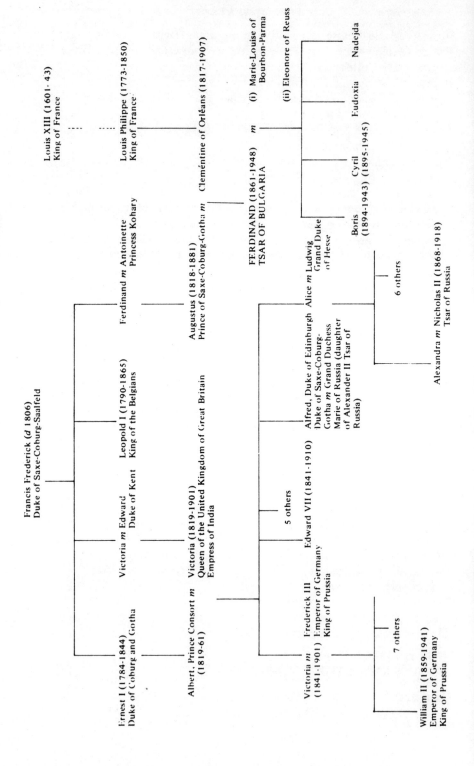

CHAPTER 1

A Night at the Opera

At the beginning of December 1886, just as the hard Balkan winter was about to settle, an official delegation of three young Bulgarians left Sofia to tour the major capitals of Europe. Their mission, as they were well aware, was of immense importance – not only as far as the independence of their country was concerned, but also for the sake of European peace.

Their brief was two-fold. First, they were to explain their country's difficult and dangerous position. For Bulgaria was threatened by invasion from Russia, which would in turn provoke Austria to attack Russia and so lead to the great war in Europe which so many then expected. Second, and more urgent, they were to find a European prince willing to occupy the vacant throne of Bulgaria, thus helping to remove the immediate Russian threat.

On arrival in Vienna, the three Bulgarians were acclaimed at the railway station by a great crowd of students. Earlier, when their train stopped in Budapest, an even greater crowd of young Hungarians had shouted anti-Russian slogans and 'Long live Bulgaria!' These expressions of support had encouraged the delegates. But they had no illusions about the difficulties and obstacles that lay ahead, chief among them the active ill-will of Russia.

On 13 December, the delegates were spending an evening at the opera, when, during the first interval, they received a message in their box telling them that an officer in the Austrian reserve, a Major von der Laaba, wished to see Konstantin Kalcheff, one of their number. Kalcheff went out into the foyer. The Major introduced himself to Kalcheff and then, with no preamble, made an unexpected proposal: 'There is here in Vienna a young prince of great family, related to all the courts in Europe. He is Ferdinand of Saxe-Coburg-Gotha. You won't find a better candidate.'[1] The Prince, added the Major, was at the opera and had expressed the wish to see him. In his private papers Kalcheff wrote:

> Since we welcomed every opportunity to contact persons of high rank who might be of help in our cause, I said that I would be delighted to pay my respects to the Prince and followed him to Ferdinand's box.
>
> The Prince got up to shake hands and expressed his pleasure at meeting one of Bulgaria's distinguished representatives. I repaid the compliment by thanking him for his interest in our people. We had a short talk, whereupon, as the curtain was about to go up I left him, however not without promising to go and call on him at his residence the following morning at 10 a.m.[2]

During their short talk at the opera, Prince Ferdinand confirmed that he was prepared to be elected as Prince of Bulgaria.

Europe's journalists were pleased by the incongruity of the first direct contact between Ferdinand and Bulgaria at the Vienna Opera and could not resist gilding the lily: the first meeting had taken place in a Viennese music-hall or circus, and Ferdinand had offered himself as a candidate for the Bulgarian throne 'over a marble-topped table' in either establishment.

As for Ferdinand, during the rest of his life he tried to draw a veil over the first stages of his candidacy and to encourage various legends: they came to a fine bloom in one version which had the Bulgarian 'king-seekers' coming to offer Ferdinand the Crown, while he, armed with a net, was hunting a butterfly along the embankment of the north Vienna railway line. These later legends had one point in common. In all of them Prince Ferdinand is quite oblivious of what is happening. It is the Bulgarians, having heard of him, who seek him out and beg him to undertake a difficult mission in an eastern land to save a troubled people. Prince Ferdinand, as he liked to see it and wanted it to be seen, was answering a summons by Fate.

Whether he had been summoned or not, Ferdinand's fate, and the fate of the country he felt that he was destined to rule, was not to be an easy one.

CHAPTER 2

The Liberators

—◦❦❦◦—

Bulgaria was the latest of the major countries of the Balkans to achieve independence from Turkish rule as a result of the 1877-8 war between Russia and Turkey. Russia, under Tsar Alexander II, had declared war on 24 April 1877, in the hope of dealing the *coup de grâce* to the 'sick man of Europe' and finally loosening the hand of the Turk from his last hold on Europe. The war was launched on a great swell of fervour and popular exaltation which seemed to mark the culmination of a new, restless Russian nationalism fanned by Panslav publicists. The Panslavists' call to action and to self-confidence, and their insistence on the mighty and historic role Russia was destined to play in the world, relieved some of the deep social frustration within her borders.

The overt aim of the war against Turkey was to free the Bulgarians, 'our Orthodox Slav brothers', from the Ottoman yoke which had been imposed in 1396, when the medieval Bulgarian Empire had finally collapsed.

Russia's Messianic zeal at the outset of the war, was almost entirely due to the 'Bulgarian Atrocities' of 1876, the massacre by Turkish irregular troops – *bashibazouks* and Circassians– of an estimated 30,000 Bulgarian men, women and children. The atrocities aroused the indignation of the whole Christian world, but nowhere did the events in the Balkans stir up emotions as violent as in Russia. The entire Russian Press called for war. All classes for once seemed united in a consciousness of Russia's mystical mission of liberation. William Gladstone's famous pamphlet *Bulgarian Horrors and the Question of the East* was translated into Russian and given the widest distribution possible. Excitement in Russia reached a climax in November 1876, when Tsar Alexander II declared publicly in Moscow that the 'honour of Russia' required the improvement in the life of the Christian inhabitants of the Balkans. He asked God's help to fulfil Russia's sacred mission.

The Tsar had only gradually and unwillingly agreed to wage war against Turkey. But during the course of 1876 Panslav and nationalist agitation for war in Court and military circles had become irresistible – even the Tsaritsa Maria Aleksandrovna was an ardent Panslav.

The great wave of Panslavist exaltation at the beginning of the war did not mean that there were not people in Russia who saw the war as the means of achieving precise military and political objectives. Some of the leading Panslavists had in fact worked hard and long to create the emotional atmosphere which would make it possible to achieve such specific aims.

In essence the aim was to gain total Russian control over the Balkans after the destruction of the remains of the Ottoman Empire, thus ensuring continued control of the straits – the Dardanelles and the Bosphorus – and Constantinople. These objectives were for the aggrandizement of the Russian Empire. The Slav nations of south-eastern Europe (and especially Bulgaria) – whatever the altruistic rhetoric of the Russian Press and the emotions of the public – were to become Russian dependencies. Chief among those Russians who encouraged Panslavist idealism (while privately despising it as nebulous and wishy-washy) in order to exploit it for what can be called Pan-Russianism, were Count Nikolai Ignatieff, Russia's Ambassador in Constantinople, and Rostislav Fadeyeff, a military man and publicist. Both wanted to extend the Russian Empire into Europe as the dominating power over a confederation of the Slav countries of Europe. Both men would have considered the emergence of Russian-dominated Eastern Europe after the Second World War as an approximate realization of their own dreams.

Men like Ignatieff and Fadeyeff had nothing but scorn for idealistic Panslavists who considered that Russia should make sacrifices in order to emancipate the Slavs under Turkish (or Austro-Hungarian) dominance for humanitarian reasons. Russia was only to make sacrifices in order to be able to free the Slavs – and then to dominate them. With the arrogance of a politician self-consciously and totally devoted to *Realpolitik,* Count Ignatieff had no doubt that the 'little Slav brothers' of Eastern Europe would readily accept the role which had been assigned to them. The Bulgarians, in particular, were to be so grateful to Russia for their liberation from the Turks, that they would willingly, even enthusiastically, become Russia's catspaw. In this assumption Ignatieff and his friends had totally abandoned the tenets of *Realpolitik* and floundered into wishful thinking. Once Bulgaria was freed from Turkish rule and welcomed her Russian liberators, she had no desire to exchange one despotism for another, for all that the latter was Orthodox and Slavonic.

The liberation of Bulgaria began in mid-June 1877, when the main body of the Russian army crossed the Danube southwards near the town of Svishtov. From there the Russians spread out in three directions. By the end of June, General Gurko had surprised Tirnovo, the medieval Bulgarian capital in the northern foothills of the Balkan range, and liberated it amid scenes of overwhelming popular enthusiasm. At that moment it seemed that the Russians could reach Constantinople within a month, having conquered what was left of Turkey-in-Europe. The threatening advance of the Tsar's armies was causing growing alarm to Austria-Hungary and Britain: to the former, because she saw her own claims to the western half of the Balkan peninsula endangered: and to Britain, especially to the Prime Minister Disraeli, by then Lord Beaconsfield, because Russia's presence and control of Constantinople were seen as a major threat to the road to India.

While Britain and Austria-Hungary unsuccessfully tried to set up some kind of anti-Russian alliance, the immediate threat presented by the spectacular initial Russian advance was removed when Turkey suddenly rallied and put up an unexpected defence at the Fortress of Plevna (Pleven) in northern Bulgaria. Repeated Russian attacks against the Turkish garrison were repulsed and crushingly defeated. The Turks under Osman Pasha only surrendered when their supplies ran out after a four month siege. The gallantry of the defenders of Plevna obliterated, especially in Britain, the memory of the Bulgarian massacres and turned the Turks into heroes. Russia's failure to gain a swift, easy and inexpensive victory over the 'sick man', the backward Asiatic Turk, created a profound feeling of national shame and frustration inside Russia and encouraged revolutionaries to try to topple their own 'sick men'. Nevertheless, Plevna fell on 10 December 1877, and the Russians continued to advance. They reached the outskirts of Constantinople at the end of January 1878.

By then Turkey had appealed to the European Powers for mediation and an armistice was concluded. Russian advance posts were within sight of Constantinople, but the victorious army was at the end of its tether. Russian forces were possibly just able to continue to fight the Turks and take panic-stricken Constantinople, but they were certainly in no condition to take on Britain or Austria-Hungary, and very possibly both. It was the mood in Britain which halted Russia within sight of her goal. For Lord Beaconsfield was ready to risk a war, with the support of the popular war-party in the streets of Britain's cities inflamed by music hall ditties; they did not want to fight but by jingo if they did...

Grand Duke Nicholas, brother of the Tsar and Commander-in-Chief on the Balkan front, had moved his headquarters to San Stefano, on the Sea of Marmara, only six miles from the walls of Constantinople. One day he and a party of Russian officers rode up to one of the heights from which he could see the dome of St Sofia, the skyline bristling with minarets. There were tears of frustration in his eyes – the Russians were not to have Constantinople. Only a few miles away from the Russian forces, off the island of Prinkipo, lay the British fleet.

The Tsar's desire to occupy Constantinople was to remain unfulfilled due to his impotence in the face of the British and Austro-Hungarian threat and the condition of the Russian army after the severe war. Yet Russia tried to reap the fruits of her victory by the terms of the peace treaty with Turkey signed at San Stefano on 3 March 1878. The Treaty of San Stefano was imposed on the Turks at pistol point by Count Ignatieff, who had rushed down from St Petersburg as the chief Russian negotiator. In his eagerness to secure the maximum gains from Turkey, Ignatieff made the Treaty of San Stefano look like a triumph of Panslavism.

The main provision of the Treaty was the creation of an autonomous Bulgarian Principality, which amounted to a restoration of the Bulgarian Empire of the Middle Ages. The frontiers drawn at San Stefano corresponded to the best ethnographical knowledge of the time. The Treaty gave Bulgaria a frontage both on the Black Sea, to the east, and the Aegean, to the south. Its inland frontier marched with the Danube to the north and comprised the Macedonian lakes of Ohrid and Prespa, whose shores were once the seat of the Bulgarian tsars.

The restoration of the Great Bulgaria of the Middle Ages was totally unacceptable to both Britain and Austria-Hungary. Lord Beaconsfield was convinced that Bulgaria would become a Russian satellite state (as Russia's militant Panslavists intended), giving Russia an overland route to the Mediterranean and a position allowing her to be a constant menace to Constantinople. Austria-Hungary saw her own interests in the western Balkans threatened by the extension of Bulgaria. The Bulgaria of San Stefano would have been an effective barrier to Vienna's eastward expansion by cutting Austria-Hungary off from the port of Salonika and the Aegean Sea.

London and Vienna insisted on the revision of the Treaty of San Stefano and Russia had to give in at the Congress of Berlin, held in June-July 1878 under the presidency of Bismarck. The Congress disregarded the ethnographic uniformity of the Bulgarians as expressed in the map drawn up at San Stefano, and carved up the country into three parts.

Only the north part of Bulgaria, between the Danube and the Balkans, bounded by the Black Sea, was to remain with some real degree of independence as an autonomous and tributary principality under the suzerainty of the Sultan. The Bulgarian lands south of the Balkans were artificially turned into an autonomous province, known

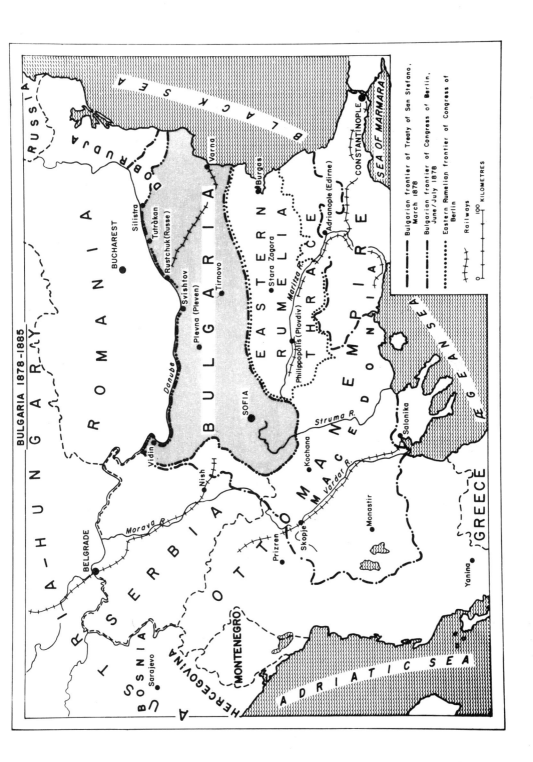

BULGARIA 1878-1885

Bulgarian frontier of Treaty of San Stefano,
March 1878

Bulgarian frontier of Congress of Berlin,
June/July 1878

Eastern Rumelian frontier of Congress of
Berlin

Railways

0   100
KILOMETRES

RUSSIA

BLACK SEA

Dobrudja

CONSTANTINOPLE

SEA OF MARMARA

Varna

Burgas

Adrianople (Edirne)

Silistra

Tutrakan

Rustchuk (Russe)

BUCHAREST

Svishtov

Plevna (Pleven)

Tirnovo

Stara Zagora

EASTERN RUMELIA

THRACE

ROMANIA

BULGARIA

Danube

SOFIA

Philippopolis (Plovdiv)

Maritza R.

OTTOMAN EMPIRE

MACEDONIA

Vidin

Struma R.

Salonika

AEGEAN SEA

Nish

Kochana

Vardar R.

Monastir

Morava R.

Skopje

Prizren

BELGRADE

SERBIA

AUSTRIA-HUNGARY

Yanina

GREECE

BOSNIA

HERCEGOVINA

Sarajevo

MONTENEGRO

ADRIATIC SEA

by the diplomatic name of 'Eastern Rumelia' and placed under the political and military authority of the Sultan, but administered by a Christian Governor-General named by the Porte, with the assent of the Powers, for a term of five years. The south-west part of Bulgaria, which it would be convenient to call Macedonia, was put back under Turkish rule. Lord Beaconsfield, as well as the Austrians, had determined to show that Russia did not dominate the Balkans. The dismemberment of Bulgaria and its artificial separation into north and south was considered a triumph of British statesmanship.

In reality, as was to become clear only a few years later, both Britain and Russia had acted mistakenly for the same reason. They had both failed to recognize the intense desire for national freedom of the Bulgarian people emerging from five centuries of foreign rule. The Bulgarians, whose national reawakening began towards the end of the eighteenth century, were determined to govern themselves and not to tolerate any interference in their internal affairs. Russia's failure to understand the intensity of Bulgarian nationalism made it possible for her to make plans to set up Bulgaria as a satellite or a trans-Danubian province. Britain's failure to understand the strength of Bulgarian nationalism naturally led to fears that Russia *would* be able to dominate the newly-liberated nation and use it as a springboard for furthering Russia's ambitions. The short-sightedness of Europe's diplomatists was such that when the north and south parts of Bulgaria proclaimed their union in 1885, it was the British Government that supported this violation of the Berlin Treaty and the Russian that condemned it. The two countries, in only seven years, had diametrically switched the roles they had played at the Congress of Berlin.

The predominating feeling in Russia about the Congress and its decisions was one of deep anger. Russia, it was felt, had been cheated of her due after her great sacrifices in lives and money. The only appeasement of this anger lay in a sullen self-righteousness directed against Britain, Austria-Hungary, and above all, although irrationally, against Germany, in whose capital Russia felt she had been cheated. And Bulgaria became a target of St Petersburg's ill-will and was accused of ingratitude when she began to resist the more blatant manifestations of Russian paternalism.

Bulgaria was to remain the centre of the European diplomatic struggle for many years following the Treaty of Berlin. During that time, Russia repeatedly tried to secure Bulgaria as a base for influence in the Balkans by means ranging from diplomacy and political intrigue to subversion and terrorism, all the time backed by the threat of a possible Russian military occupation of the country which she herself had freed from alien occupiers.

The pros and cons of the Treaty of Berlin have been much discussed by historians. Inevitably it has loomed large in all attempts to trace the root causes of the First World War. While it is a fact that the Berlin Treaty was followed by thirty-four years of European peace (except for two minor conflicts), it is also undeniable that the reasons for the assassination of the Austrian Archduke Francis Ferdinand at Sarajevo in June 1914 can be traced back in direct line to decisions reached at the Congress.

The rebirth of the Great Bulgaria of the Middle Ages at San Stefano, and its dismemberment in Berlin four months later, had a traumatic effect on the country's future development. Bulgaria was to begin her renewed national existence by trying to remedy that defect. Any remedy meant violating the *status quo* which the Great Powers were so loath to see disturbed. The future role of Bulgaria in the Balkans and in European politics as a whole was to be determined by the desire to revise the Treaty of Berlin and to restore the frontiers which were drawn up at San Stefano. If the Balkans were the 'powder keg of Europe', then Bulgaria's revisionist longings helped to shorten the fuse.

The Bulgaria which Europe's statesmen had carved out of the abortive Bulgaria of San Stefano, was to be headed by a prince. The Berlin Treaty specified that the country's ruler was to be 'freely elected by the population and confirmed by the Porte, with the consent of the Powers'. There had been no official discussion at the Congress as to who was to be the ruler of the new European state. But the Treaty was quite definite as to who it was not to be: no member of any reigning European dynasty would be eligible – which went to show how much they trusted one another.

The Treaty forced Russia to withdraw her armies from Bulgaria after a period of nine months. During that time a Russian Commissioner was to organize a provisional Bulgarian administration, work out a constitution for the country and once that had been passed by an Assembly of Notables, that body was to elect a prince. Russia wanted to see the Bulgarian ruler chosen within the nine-month period, while her authority in Bulgaria was complete. Ideally, Russia would have liked Bulgaria ruled by a Russian prince – but Britain and Austria-Hungary would, of course, have none of that.

A ruler had to be found who would be pliant to Russia and yet acceptable to London and Vienna.

CHAPTER 3

The Soldier Hero

—◦❧❧◦—

Prince Ferdinand of Saxe-Coburg-Gotha was not the first candidate for the Bulgarian throne. In 1878, eight years before Ferdinand approached the Bulgarian delegation at the Vienna Opera, the throne was about to be occupied by another German prince.

At that time Tsar Alexander II considered that there was no better candidate to be found than his young nephew, Prince Alexander of Battenberg, called Sandro, a son of the Tsaritsa's brother, Prince Alexander of Hesse. His qualifications seemed exactly right. As a German he was acceptable both to Bismarck and his Emperor. Even Queen Victoria was extremely fond of this very handsome young man, who was tall, slight, martial and charming. Her daughter Alice had married Sandro's cousin, Grand Duke Ludwig IV of Hesse, and a few years later Sandro's brother Henry married another of the Queen's daughters, Beatrice. Sandro's eldest brother, Louis of Battenberg (later Marquis of Milford Haven) was in the British Navy and later married one of Queen Victoria's granddaughters, Princess Victoria of Hesse. All this made Prince Alexander of Battenberg, then only twenty-one years old, totally acceptable to Britain.

As far as Russia was concerned, Sandro was the Tsar's favourite nephew, his godson, and best of all, had volunteered to take part in the war against Turkey and done well in the campaign. The Tsar urged him to accept the throne and when the young Prince expressed misgivings about his chances, cried: 'Don't make a lot of difficulties. You have always assured me that you are loyal to me, to my house and to Russia, and that you love us.'[1] The Tsar was so excited that tears ran down his cheeks. Bismarck, despite his strong dislike of Sandro's whole family, also urged him to accept the throne. When the young Prince told Bismarck that he did not wish to accept the offer, Bismarck shut the door of the room and said that he would not let him out until he promised to accept. Queen Victoria wrote in her diary: 'Sandro asked what would happen should he fail, as his whole future would be ruined, and he [Bismarck] answered, "You will at all events take away a pleasant recollection with you"'.[2]

Prince Alexander of Battenberg was elected Prince of Bulgaria in April 1879 After two months of considerable misgivings, but urged on by the interested European Powers and by his father's ambitions, he set foot in Bulgaria.

Seven years later, Prince Alexander left Bulgaria, almost a broken man though he had not yet reached his thirtieth birthday. He had to leave despite the fact that he had brought military glory to himself and to his young country. His going was accompanied by a surge of romantic pity and admiration throughout Europe – but no Power raised a hand to help. Queen Victoria agitated on his behalf in an almost feverish display of sympathy. 'The Queen is much attached to the dear, brave, and so cruelly used Prince of Bulgaria', she wrote. 'Such a heroic, noble young Sovereign.... We lose one of the bravest, wisest of rulers in Prince Alexander.'[3] But despite the Queen's demands, the British Government dropped Sandro, in common with the rest of the Powers.

Bismarck may not have been entirely cynical when he jollied Sandro into accepting the throne of Bulgaria with the promise that, even if he failed, he would have gained a 'pleasant recollection' for his old age. Even he, when he said this, could not have foreseen into what a cruel political mincer young Sandro was to fall.

Internationally, Sandro was a formal vassal of the Sultan of Turkey, a moral vassal of the Tsar of Russia, while his every move was jealously watched by Austria-Hungary. The essential insecurity of his position would have daunted the most able diplomatist, let alone a young man of twenty-two. While Prince Alexander's military experience and training fitted him for duties in open battle, he completely lacked political education and statesmanlike capacities. His lack of guile, his frankness and openness, his lack of and hatred of anything approaching cynicism and machiavellianism, his determination to speak his mind, his obstinacy even, foredoomed the young Prince.

The rapturous initial reception with which Prince Alexander was greeted on his arrival in Bulgaria concealed the reality of the situation with which he was faced. He soon grew more thoughtful as he walked through the streets of his capital. Sofia was then little more than a small town with twenty thousand inhabitants, one-storeyed wooden houses, unpaved the unlit streets, and, far worse, no drains: muddy in winter and dusty in summer. The squalor was unrelieved by the beautiful setting in a plain surrounded by mountains. The capital and the other cities in the Principality were eloquent, smelly monuments to five hundred years of Ottoman civil administration. Sandro's 'palace' was accepted by the good-natured Prince as a joke. It had been the *konak*, the former residence of the Sultan's representative in Bulgaria, a large one-storeyed building in an extensive garden. The Russian Commissioner in Bulgaria, Prince Dondukoff-Korsakoff, who had hoped and schemed to be appointed ruler of the country, had started to rebuild it as his future residence. But when it was realized that the Powers would not accept a Russian ruler of Bulgaria, the building was hastily completed with sole regard to the façade. The roof and ceilings let in the rain, the ceilings in three rooms had collapsed, and on the day of Sandro's arrival in Sofia, wooden scaffolding was erected over his bed, to protect him from any further collapse of the stuccoed ceiling.

The furnishings had been hastily bought in Vienna at a sale of the effects of a bankrupt lady singer, so that Prince Alexander's drawing room had a feminine *Biedermeier* raffishness. All this Sandro took fairly lightly as if he were on manoeuvres. But it was not the tumultuous welcome by the crowding peasants nor the lack of comforts which made the deepest impression on the Prince when he arrived. Almost immediately he realized that he was surrounded by the ill-will of those Russians who still remained in Bulgaria, many of them in important civil and military posts. The Prince's arrival had coincided with the departure of the great bulk of Russian occupation forces from Bulgaria, according to the terms of the Berlin Treaty. But some two hundred Russian officers stayed behind, to be joined by numerous officials from Russia who set up consulates and special agencies, and by businessmen and adventurers, all looking for lucrative employment in the new country. The resentment of the Russian officers, the majority of whom had Panslav leanings, towards Prince Alexander was deep and easily understood. Their predominant feeling was that they had not fought a hard and cruel war against Turkey and had not seen Russian blood spilt so that a German should rule in the land they had liberated. They had basked in the love and gratitude of the liberated Bulgarians and quickly assumed airs of swaggering proprietorship.

The arrival of 'the German' threatened to put an end to this. At first the Russians in Bulgaria expressed their hatred of Sandro more or less covertly. But no opportunity was lost to remind him that he owed his throne to Russia and that acting in Russia's interests was his paramount duty. Within a few weeks he wrote to his father: 'Can you believe it when I tell you that in the few days I have been here I have aged by ten years? All the scum of Russia has taken refuge here.'[4] He discovered that the footmen and lackeys left at the palace by the Russians were nearly all Russian agents.

Despite their provocative behaviour, the Russians could not act openly against the Prince who, after all, was the beloved nephew and godson of the Tsar. But the terrorist's bomb that killed Alexander II on 13 March 1881 also meant the beginning of the end for Sandro. On leaving for his uncle's funeral, the Prince said: 'My protector is dead: now all is lost for me.'

Alexander III, who succeeded his father, detested Sandro. Ever since he was a young boy he had maintained an attitude of deliberate contempt towards him and his brothers. Unlike his father, who only occasionally let himself be swayed by the supporters of Panslavism and ultra-nationalism, the new Tsar was entirely in sympathy with them. He reacted against the German orientation of his father and grandfather with a deep antipathy towards all things German. 'That *German*' was his way of referring to Sandro. To the new Tsar, Sandro was a living symbol of the disappointments of the Congress of Berlin.

The Panslav intrigue against Prince Alexander prospered under the new Tsar. His suspicious and mistrustful nature, his narrow outlook, indolence and lack of political and diplomatic education, were fertile soil in which accusations against Sandro readily took root. Increasingly Alexander III regarded the Prince as an ungrateful German upstart and a threat to Russia's territorial ambitions. Bulgaria's role, as he saw it, was to act as both vanguard and bridgehead for Russia. The occupation of Constantinople he declared, 'is in the interests of Russia and it ought to be our aspiration; everything in the Balkan peninsula is secondary for us. The Slavs must now serve Russia, and not we them.'[5] The idealistic Panslav sentiments which had led to the war against Turkey in 1877 had narrowed to a fine chauvinistic focus five years later.

An ever more dense web of Russian intrigues surrounded the Prince of Bulgaria. Russia was able to fish in the muddy, swirling waters of Bulgarian internal political life and so make life more difficult for the Prince by backing the party in opposition at any moment. Party life in the new country was roughly polarized into liberals and conservatives and conducted in an atmosphere of intense personal hatreds fanned by savage polemics. The Bulgarian constitution, drawn up under Russian guidance, was ultra-liberal, in fact one of the most liberal in Europe, and stimulated lack of restraint and discipline in public life.

The Tsar's hatred for his Battenberg cousin steadily grew with each new shift of the political kaleidoscope. As for Sandro, by 1884 he had become embittered enough to describe the Tsar as a 'mad dog'. When reports reached the Tsar of a possible marriage between Sandro and Princess Victoria of Prussia, a granddaughter of Queen Victoria, the Russian Government spread reports through its ambassadors in various European capitals that Prince Alexander had variously entertained prostitutes in his Sofia palace; had 'Turkish tastes' and was not interested in women, and had contracted venereal disease.

In the following year the Russian Press was openly discussing and
urging the Prince of Bulgaria's downfall. The Tsar made no effort to
conceal his malevolence. He talked to the Princess of Wales about
Sandro in a most sarcastic tone and told her that it amused him to watch
Prince Alexander writhing in his struggle against the inevitable. By that
time the Tsar was personally concerned in speeding up the 'inevitable'
by trying to engineer a *coup* against Sandro.

Prince Alexander's opponents in Russia, grouped around the Tsar,
had already elaborated plans to take over Bulgaria. After a *coup d'état*
against the Prince, a provisional military dictatorship was to be set up
prior to proclaiming the country a Russian protectorate on the lines of
Finland. Then, the union of the Bulgarian Principality (the north) with
Eastern Rumelia (southern Bulgaria) was to be achieved under the
aegis of the Tsar. But Russian plans were by no means concerted, due to
the deep rivalry in St Petersburg between the foreign ministry and the
war ministry. The former tended to back the conservatives in Bulgaria,
the latter the liberals. The conflicting aims and interests of Russian
agents of the two ministries in Bulgaria, allowed Bulgaria's politicians
to play them off against each other, occasionally to the advantage of
Bulgaria and to the increasing annoyance and frustration of the Tsar.

Relations between the two cousins deteriorated month by month
until September 1885, when an event took place which shook the whole
of Europe. A bloodless revolution in Philippopolis (Plovdiv), the capital
of Eastern Rumelia, resulted in a proclamation of the Union of the two
Bulgarias, north and south, under Prince Alexander. The Christian
Governor-General of Eastern Rumelia, the Sultan's appointee under
the terms of the Berlin Treaty, was sent packing to Constantinople after
being driven round the town in mock triumph, while a young school-
mistress sat by his side in the carriage holding an unsheathed sword.

Although he had been forewarned of the conspiratorial plans in
Philippopolis, Prince Alexander at first hesitated to back the *fait
accompli*. It would have meant tearing up that much of the Treaty of
Berlin and defying Turkey and the Powers. But Bulgarian opinion
ardently wanted the Union and would abandon a Prince who lacked the
courage to achieve the nation's deepest wish. Accordingly, Alexander
ordered the mobilization of the army and on 21 September entered
Philippopolis amid wild enthusiasm.

Turkey and the Powers reacted to this in quite unexpected ways. The
Sultan of Turkey contented himself with protests and merely defensive
preparations. Great Britain, with Lord Salisbury as Prime Minister,
strongly supported the re-unification of the two parts of Bulgaria which
she herself had torn asunder eight years earlier in Berlin. Salisbury now
saw the Union and re-creation of a bigger Bulgaria, in view of the

unhappy relations between the Tsar and Prince Alexander, as a means of undermining Russian efforts to dominate the Balkan peninsula and Constantinople.

The Union deeply angered the Tsar. It was galling to see his detested cousin hailed in all Bulgaria as a symbol of national union. It was even more infuriating that 'the German' had presided over the Union, an event the Tsar had been planning to bring about under his own aegis with the aim of turning Bulgaria into a Russian protectorate. Meanwhile, the Russian Press rejoiced over the Union as an act which had expunged the humiliating Treaty of Berlin. But, as was often the case in Russia, there was a split between popular opinion and official policy.

The sulking Tsar struck hard. A few days after the Union he sent a telegram to Bulgaria in which he recalled all Russian officers who had organized and were instructing Bulgaria's small new army. The order followed a previous negative reply from Russian officials in Bulgaria to a query from St Petersburg asking if Bulgaria's young officers would be able to command the army on their own. The Tsar's move was deliberately calculated to leave the Bulgarian army without a trained higher command at a critical moment, when Turkey was expected to attack.

A few weeks later the Tsar offered the Prince a public insult which could only be seen as a personal declaration of war. In an Order of the Day his name as an honorary officer was struck from the Russian army list. A telegram went out from Balmoral on receipt of the news: 'For Sandro, strictly secret, from highest source. Queen begs Sandro not to give in.'[6]

But to most people Prince Alexander's position appeared hopeless. He had placed himself at the head of a national movement to tear up the Treaty of Berlin, had not only lost the support but incurred the hostility of his country's 'protector', Russia, and had caused his country's young and hardly-trained army to lose its instructors and senior officers. Turkey, it was thought, as the interested party which had lost most by the Union, would attack Bulgaria.

The blow, immediately assumed to be the *coup de grâce*, came not from Turkey in the south, where Bulgaria's troops were massed in the expectation of an attack, but from the Principality's western neighbour, Serbia. King Milan of Serbia, whose internal difficulties were growing, needed a spectacular success to increase his prestige and that of his family, the Obrenovich. The Serbians were also afraid that the Union of northern and southern Bulgaria would spread to include Macedonia. The moment appeared propitious for a lightning attack in the direction of Sofia. With the new, untried Bulgarian army in the south, deprived of its Russian instructors and Russian support, the victory of the Serbian army, which had had the experience of two campaigns, seemed absolutely certain.

On 14 November 1885, King Milan declared war on Bulgaria with a manifesto in which he set himself up as the defender of the Treaty of Berlin. The Russian Tsar was delighted.

The war lasted two weeks. Within the first week Prince Alexander's troops, after a three-day forced march of about one hundred miles from the Turkish to the Serbian frontier, had won a stunning victory and annihilated the Serbs. Prince Alexander, who had at last found his true element, led his young army with a cool courage and firmness which turned him into a figure of heroic glamour in the eyes of Europe. The recall of the Russian officers had had quite the opposite effect from that hoped for by the Tsar. Young Bulgarian junior officers and NCOs had taken over from their Russian superiors and, eager for recognition and advancement, had efficiently channelled the burning enthusiasm of their untried men to secure victory.

The victory to which Prince Alexander had led his army was at the same time a necessary and appalling diplomatic blunder. In winning the war he had profoundly humiliated the Tsar of Russia. Alexander III's loss of face was gleefully anatomized by the newspapers of Europe. What hurt most was that those very actions by which the Tsar had wanted to humiliate his cousin, in fact enhanced the brilliance of his victory. The recall of the Russian officers showed up the Bulgarian victory as a genuine, national, unaided feat of arms. Worse still, perhaps, was the galling fact that the man whose name the Tsar had ordered to be erased as an honorary officer should, within a few days of this public humiliation be acclaimed as a military hero by Europe.

Apart from the loss of face, the Tsar was also bitterly disappointed. He had been so certain of Bulgaria's defeat that he had already seen Prince Alexander deposed. He had fondly imagined how the defeated Bulgarians would ask for Russia's intervention on their behalf. The Tsar had had his reply ready: Russia would not lift a finger to help Bulgaria as long as Prince Alexander remained on the throne.

The Russian Press and public had greeted the Bulgarian victory with no less enthusiasm than the rest of Europe. In this instance too, Russian public opinion and highest official policy were miles apart. Russia's Minister of Foreign Affairs, Giers, afraid that the Tsar's hostility towards the Prince of Bulgaria might drag Russia to the brink of a European war, encouraged some attempts towards a reconciliation. Prince Alexander was advised to express publicly his gratitude to the Russian officers who had brought Bulgaria's army into being. At considerable cost to his pride, he issued an Order of the Day which attributed the army's victory to the activities of its Russian instructors.

The Prince of Bulgaria also sent a personal letter to the Tsar. The autocrat's reaction was crushing. He said he would have nothing to do with Prince Alexander and added: 'Anyway, I think they will get rid of him within six months.'[7] Giers and other Russian officials stopped trying to bring about a reconciliation. The Tsar's feelings towards his cousin had turned from dislike to obsessive hatred.

The defeat of the Serbian invaders had consolidated the *de facto* union between the northern and southern parts of Bulgaria. But, obedient to the Tsar's wishes, Russia's diplomats worked hard all over Europe to prevent the official recognition of the Union. Russian agents inside Bulgaria hammered home the message: 'You shall never have the effective union of your country as long as the Battenberger remains on the throne!' The small group of Russophil politicians in Bulgaria who believed that the salvation of their country depended on close ties with Russia were provided with large sums of money to publish newspapers attacking the Prince as the obstacle in Bulgaria's path. Clandestine activity against the Prince, organized by the Tsarist equivalents of present-day agents of the KGB, was increased.

Two early attempts against Prince Alexander's life failed miserably. A heavily poisoned headache-powder plainly signalled a danger to the Prince by its colour and strong smell; it was totally different from the one he normally used. In May 1886, the local authorities in Burgas, the Bulgarian Black Sea port, uncovered a plot to kidnap and, in the event of resistance, to kill Prince Alexander. The plotters were led by a Russian officer, Captain Nabokoff, and included two Montenegrins, one of whom was a priest. Even before the police knew of any plot, they had warned the Russian Consul, whom Captain Nabokoff visited daily, that if the officer's provocative speech and behaviour went on, they would arrest him. Nabokoff, possibly one of nature's bad conspirators, as his later career will show, was arrested and denied the plot. As the Russian foreign ministry wanted to turn the arrest into a major diplomatic question, the authorities let the matter drop.

The Tsar's diplomatic agents in Sofia had meanwhile got in touch with a group of Bulgarian officers who felt that the Prince had deliberately overlooked their merits during the war against Serbia and not given them the promotion and rewards which were their due. Their resentful feelings against the Prince turned to hate under skilful manipulation by Bogdanoff, Russia's diplomatic agent in Sofia, and Sakharoff, his military attaché. Rumours that Serbia was preparing another invasion of Bulgaria in order to take advantage of the fact that the Bulgarian army was almost without ammunition and supplies, were rife and encouraged by Russian agents. The officers were told that Russia would not help Bulgaria, not even with military supplies, as long as the Prince remained on the Bulgarian throne. A conspiracy to kidnap the Prince, force him to sign his abdication and to take him to Russia was prepared. The Russian agents in Sofia pressed for action but were anxious to establish Russia's alibi. Europe had to see the *coup* as a purely Bulgarian action. Bogdanoff told the conspirators that there could be no question of killing the Prince: 'One day the truth will come out and Russia will have the heavy responsibility of having encouraged the assassination of a ruling prince. In any case, do not forget that the Prince is related to the Imperial family.'[8]

Just after three o'clock on the morning of 21 August 1886, the Prince's valet rushed into his bedroom. He woke him, handed him a revolver and shouted: 'Your Highness, you must get out! They want to kill you!' The Palace was surrounded by troops who, unlike their officers, had been told they were taking part in a special exercise to protect the palace. All regiments in or near Sofia, known by the conspirators to be loyal to Prince Alexander, had, a few days earlier, been sent to the Serbian frontier to take up defensive positions under the pretext of a possible Serbian attack.

The conspirators ordered a palace servant to call the Prince. When he appeared, dressed, he was accompanied by his youngest brother, Francis Joseph, a young boy. The head of the conspiracy, Captain Radko Dimitrieff, told the Prince that he would have to abdicate to save Bulgaria. The Prince refused to write out the abdication and only signed it after a young army cadet wrote it down under Captain Dimitrieff's dictation.

The Prince and his brother were escorted in a phaeton northwards to the Danube. A silent crowd of citizens had watched him leave Sofia at dawn, despite attempts by the conspirators to organize a popular demonstration against the Prince. At Orekhovo, the captives were put aboard the Prince's yacht, taken downstream to Reni, in Bessarabia, the first Russian town on the Danube. The Prince and his brother were there handed over to the local Russian military commander.

When Prince Alexander was first taken to his yacht, he had thought that the conspirators would merely send him to the opposite Romanian shore. Once he realized that he was being taken to Russia, the Prince became convinced that his Russian Imperial cousin's vengeance would only be complete once he was left to rot in Siberia. The hours since the *coup* had quite broken Alexander of Battenberg. The Bulgarian officers on the yacht, afraid that, driven by despair, he might throw himself into the swirling, muddy Danube, placed guards around his cabin.

The conspirators' *coup* in Sofia was typical of military palace revolts. The disloyal officers had made no preparations beyond their immediate tactical objectives regarding the person of the Prince. They had no

understanding of politics and affected to despise them. Once Prince
Alexander was out of Bulgaria they imagined that their action would be
welcomed and supported by the population and that they would bask in
the joint approval of the Bulgarian people and of Russia.

Various Bulgarian politicians, whom the conspirators approached
after the *coup,* refused their invitation to form a government. A wave of
disbelief, then revulsion, indignation and fury swept over the inhabitants of Bulgaria, when they realized what had happened. Within three
days of the Prince's kidnapping, a Provisional Government, scraped
together by the conspirators with Russian blessing and headed by a
churchman in the person of the Metropolitan Kliment, was dissolved
and its members declared traitors. The counter-revolution was led by
the President of the Sobranie (the National Assembly), Stefan Stamboloff, an intensely patriotic, passionate and highly intelligent young man
of thirty-two, whose short, brilliant political career later earned him
the sobriquet of 'Balkan Bismarck' in the British press. Stamboloff's
feelings were expressed in the corrosive telegram he sent to the
venerable Metropolitan Kliment on hearing that he had accepted to
head the Provisional Government: 'I congratulate you. Your political
career has reached new heights. All the best. The nation will not forget
that you stuck a knife in its heart. Best wishes!'[9]

The first news of the kidnapping created a European sensation.
Newspapers and public opinion in nearly all countries were totally in
sympathy with Prince Alexander, who only a few months earlier had
been hailed as a hero. But politically there was a unanimous feeling that
the *coup* in Sofia was a major diplomatic victory for the Tsar of Russia
and it was taken for granted that Bulgaria had become a virtual Russian
dependency. In Britain, it was seen as a diplomatic defeat. The Russian
Press wallowed in victorious self-congratulations and jeering editorials
asked: 'Where is all-powerful England now?'

A frantic search for Sandro by his brother Louis (directed by a
worried Queen Victoria), Stamboloff, and the European Press, ended
with the news of his arrival at Reni. The Russian authorities would not
let him return to Bulgaria, but did allow him to travel to Lemberg (the
present Lvov) in Austria-Hungary. Russia only let him go because the
news of the counter-revolution in Bulgaria was not believed by the Tsar
and his advisers. The Tsar's dislike of his cousin was such that he could
not bring himself to believe that the Prince enjoyed any real popularity.

When Prince Alexander arrived at Lemberg he received pressing
telegrams from Stamboloff urging him to return to Bulgaria. His
brother Louis joined him and told him of Queen Victoria's determination to support him and of her desire that he should return. She herself
pressed him by telegram from Balmoral urging his immediate return in

view of real temper of the people.

The Prince decided to return, although aware that he was risking his life. His motives were perfectly honourable. His honour as a sovereign and a soldier would not allow him to give in to a clique of traitors, he was deeply touched by his subjects' devotion and loyalty as expressed in the almost immediate counter-revolution – and he was aware of Queen Victoria's anxious support.

His return was a triumph. Thousands had come to Rustchuk, on the Danube, to welcome him, headed by Stamboloff, who declared: 'I assumed authority during your absence to preserve the honour of Bulgaria. Today I hand this power over to you so that you can save our country. The nation is with you; it loves you; it is ready to sacrifice itself for you.'[10]

The Prince looked pale and tired. Those around him were not sure whether the tremendous welcome had deeply moved or merely dazed him. He did notice suddenly that among the officials present was the local Russian Consul in full uniform. The Consul, Shatokhin, who had not received any instructions from St Petersburg, had joined his colleagues for the Prince's arrival. Prince Alexander fatally misinterpreted his presence in full uniform as an indication that the Tsar had had a change of heart. Why else, he thought, had the Russians allowed him to go free?

Prince Alexander talked to the young Russian Consul, who astutely advised him to try to conciliate the Tsar who alone could guarantee his throne. Acting on his advice later that day, Prince Alexander, together with his brother Louis, composed and sent a telegram to the Tsar. The telegram was abject in tone (the short text mentioned the imperial title *nine* times), astonishingly naive in its belief that there was any chance of conciliating the Tsar, and fatal for Sandro as ruler of Bulgaria. And yet Prince Louis of Battenberg described the telegram as 'masterly in conception' as it had built a 'golden bridge' for the Tsar. The telegram's last sentence was lethal for Sandro: 'As Russia gave me my Crown, I am prepared to give it back into the hands of its Sovereign.'[11] Not only was this abject and naive, but untrue: Alexander had been elected Prince of Bulgaria by the Bulgarian people, under the terms of the Berlin Treaty.

The Tsar, who had watched Sandro's return to Bulgaria and the triumphant proof of his popularity with loathing and fury, could hardly believe his eyes on reading the telegram. Was his sickening cousin affecting heavy irony in order to rub in his success? Or was he really offering his Crown on a platter?

Alexander III seized his chance and had the Prince's confidential telegram published together with his own reply before that had even reached Bulgaria. The reply was crushing. The Tsar said that he considered the Prince's return to Bulgaria as disastrous for that country. In view of the 'unhappy situation' to which Bulgaria was exposed as long as the Prince stayed there, the Tsar said the Prince would appreciate what he would have to do.

It was the language of melodrama, used towards the person who is being left alone with a loaded revolver. The Tsar was asking the Prince to kill himself politically, by abdicating. In effect, the publication of the telegrams demonstrated to the world the Prince's offer to give up his throne and the Tsar's immediate acceptance. It was quite clear that the Prince now had to abdicate.

Queen Victoria was deeply upset by what her protégé had done. She telegraphed immediately: 'I am speechless... After such triumphs this was unworthy of the great position you had won. You are blamed for having telegraphed to the Tsar instead of asking advice here first.'[12]

Stamboloff, who had known nothing about the telegram to the Tsar, shook with anger when he heard of it. To a close friend, he said: 'This is the man for whom we have roused the whole of Bulgaria, have put our necks into the noose and brother has raised sword against brother, and he takes such a momentous decision without even telling us of it beforehand: he throws his crown at the feet of a foreign ruler and keeps us in the dark about it.'[13]

On 7 September 1886, Prince Alexander announced his abdication and left Sofia that same day, escorted by a huge, sorrowing crowd. For seven years, the Prince had been on the anvil on which the major Powers of Europe were forging their national policies, doing his best to dodge the hammer-blows.

Russia's continued and unsuccessful bullying of small Bulgaria had produced denunciations by journalists and politicians all over Europe. This time the Tsar felt sure of complete victory. He made a determined but mistaken attempt to recover Russia's lost influence by sending to Bulgaria as his plenipotentiary the eccentric and extraordinarily undiplomatic General Nikolai Kaulbars, whose activities in a short time earned him the nickname 'General Sofiasco'.

Almost on arrival General Kaulbars made it clear that he saw himself as a dictator. He declared that he had no confidence in the three-man Regency, which included Stefan Stamboloff, and was appointed by Prince Alexander at his abdication. He also insisted, against the terms of the Bulgarian constitution, that the mandatory elections to the Grand Sobranie, which was to choose the new prince, should be postponed. On top of this, he demanded the release of all the arrested conspirators who had organized the *coup*.

General Kaulbars deluded himself into thinking that the great majority of Bulgarians were pro-Russian and even wanted the country to become a Russian protectorate and that only fear of the administration left behind by Prince Alexander prevented them from openly declaring their true feelings. He went on a barn-storming tour of the Principality and addressed open-air meetings at which he openly attacked the Bulgarian Government and the Regents. His total lack of sensitivity about the feelings of his audience had extraordinary results. Meetings which opened to well-meant shouts of 'Long Live Russia!' swiftly became hostile and ended with the crowd passing anti-Russian resolutions. His attempt to prevent the elections from taking place failed and the Grand Sobranie met to choose a new prince.

The election of a prince was the key to the whole crisis. Stamboloff, the other regents and the Government realized that once the principality's throne was filled, the country would return to a more stable political life, thus making it less easy for Russia to find an excuse for a military occupation. For these same reasons, Russia, through Kaulbars, was trying to leave the Bulgarian throne without an occupant. He had tried to prevent the Grand Sobranie from meeting until he had succeeded in installing a Russophil government in Bulgaria which would offer the throne to the Tsar. He let it be known that the Tsar would 'deign' to accept the title of 'Grand Duke of Bulgaria'.

The elections resulted in a massive victory for Stefan Stamboloff and his supporters. The Russophil party was heavily defeated – largely as a result of the speech-making efforts of General Kaulbars.

The Grand Sobranie would have liked to re-elect Prince Alexander of Battenberg, but the ex-ruler strongly advised the Bulgarians that such an action would have been an open provocation of Russia. The meeting elected Prince Waldemar of Denmark, the Tsar's brother-in-law and brother of Princess Alexandra of Wales. By electing and inviting a near-relation of the Russian Imperial family, Stamboloff wanted to demonstrate Bulgaria's good intentions. The Tsar vetoed the election, declared the elections and Grand Sobranie illegal, and under the circumstances Prince Waldemar declined the Bulgarian throne.

The ineffable General Kaulbars had meanwhile been busy contacting Bulgarian army officers in the hope of organizing a rising against the Regency. The arrival of two Russian warships off the Bulgarian coast seemed the prelude to an invasion. Faced by this supreme threat, Stamboloff released from prison the organizers of the coup against Prince Alexander. Just then, there reappeared on the scene the notorious Russian Captain Nabokoff, who had arranged the earlier unsuccessful attempt to kidnap or assassinate Prince Alexander in May 1886. Now, six months after he had been freed at the insistence of Russia, Nabokoff returned to the Black Sea port of Burgas, staged an uprising, declared himself master of the town, and proclaimed a 'provisional government'. General Kaulbars had hopes that this would set off a general uprising in Bulgaria. Instead, the *putsch* was easily put down, Nabokoff caught, sentenced to death, and on Kaulbars' insistence, deported to Russia where, naturally, he was released. It was not to be his last appearance in Bulgaria.

Kaulbars had tried to encourage other attempts at an uprising and approached several disaffected officers. The attempts came to nothing. He was mesmerized by his conviction that the Bulgarian nation asked for nothing better than to become a part of Russia. All that was needed, he considered, was a rallying point, such as a local *putsch,* for the people to rise as one against their government and declare for Russia. He had even got Russia's Foreign Minister, Giers, to believe this. Bismarck called it 'the Kaulbars myth'.

General Kaulbars' performance in Bulgaria was becoming the scandal of Europe. Even newspapers normally friendly towards Russia asked questions such as, 'Is there such a thing as international law in Europe?' If so, it was argued in editorial articles, why did the Powers permit the dictatorial antics of General Kaulbars?

The most powerful and effective attack on Russia was made by Lord Salisbury, the British Prime Minister. In an extraordinarily violent speech in London, he condemned Russia's policy towards Bulgaria. The Tsar was so incensed that he considered an immediate Russian invasion of India, until Giers, with considerable difficulty, managed to talk him out of it. Even after several years had passed, the Tsar, on meeting Lord Randolph Churchill, complained to him about the 'malice' Lord Salisbury had voiced in that speech.

All the Tsar's hopes about Bulgaria had come to nothing. He was reviled throughout Europe. Meanwhile, Russian newspapers stridently urged the occupation of Bulgaria by Russian armies. But the risk of a war with Britain was too great. In the margin of a despatch from Kaulbars urging the occupation of Bulgaria, the Tsar wrote : 'In my opinion, it would not be practical.'[14]

On 17 November 1886, General Kaulbars declared that the hostile attitude of the Bulgarian Government had made his task impossible and left the country, taking with him all Russia's official representatives, consuls and vice-consuls. It was at this point, when military intervention was expected daily, that the Sobranie appointed a delegation of three Bulgarians whose mission was to go round Europe to find a prince prepared to accept the throne of Bulgaria. But by breaking off diplomatic relations, Russia was not losing interest in Bulgaria. From now on, and for years to come, Russia would wage an undeclared war of subversion against Bulgaria – a cold war.

CHAPTER 4

My Effeminate Cousin

—◦❧❧◦—

When the news that Prince Ferdinand of Saxe-Coburg-Gotha had offered himself as candidate for the Bulgarian throne filtered through the courts of Europe, it caused much amusement. For Ferdinand was, on the face of it, a most unlikely candidate for such a hot seat.

There were two, very important people, however, who felt no such amusement. The first, Queen Victoria, was a cousin of Prince Ferdinand through her Coburg mother. On the morning of 16 December 1886, she rapped out a furious telegram to her Prime Minister, Lord Salisbury. 'Windsor Castle, 16 December 1886 – Hope no truth in respect of Prince Ferdinand of Coburg as candidate. He is totally unfit – delicate, eccentric and effeminate. Only seen it in *Times*. Should be stopped at once.'[1]

The next day Lord Salisbury received further evidence of her agitation: 'It is important that it should be known that I and my family have nothing to do with the absurd pretension of this foolish young cousin of mine.'[2]

The second opponent was far more implacable. Tsar Alexander III had by 1886 become obsessed with Bulgaria, and regarded with intense hostility almost any European prince who presented himself as a candidate for the vacant throne. When the Tsar was told that Prince Ferdinand had put himself forward as a candidate, his withering reaction surprised no one: '*La candidature est aussi ridicule que le personnage!* [The candidature is as ridiculous as the individual!]'[3]

The Tsar had already met Prince Ferdinand at his own coronation in 1883. Ferdinand, then aged twenty-two, had come to the coronation in Moscow as the official representative of the House of Coburg. Despite the vast number of guests from all over the world and from the Russian Empire, and despite the splendour of the occasion the new Tsar had managed to single out the young Ferdinand for instant dislike.

Even the sight of the young man seemed to irritate him. The

exaggerated dandyism of young Ferdinand, his immaculate uniform moulding his six-foot figure and wasp waist, the apparently affected nasal drawl just slightly high-pitched, the slight stoop of head and shoulders, gave an impression both of precociousness and condescension. Beneath the fair, wavy hair kept in perfect order, and a fine, high brow, the face itself was not reassuring. Ferdinand looked at the world through narrow, glittering, light blue eyes, a little too light and washed out. They were shrewd and often appeared mocking or sarcastic. Certainly, they were the eyes of an intelligent man. Ferdinand's eyes gave the misleading impression of smallness because of the contrast with his huge Bourbon nose, which surged out and curved downwards in a smooth arc.

The small-looking, bright eyes, the big nose, and, to complete the impression, his large ears, gave Ferdinand the air of an elephant. He knew this and that other people would be struck by the resemblance. Typically, he always pre-empted others from making the comparison by being the first to draw attention to it. He was self-conscious about his nose throughout his life. As God's gift to the political cartoonists of Europe for over thirty years, from his accession to the Bulgarian throne in 1887 to his fall in 1918, he was unlikely to forget about it.

Tsar Alexander III's antipathy towards Prince Ferdinand of Coburg during the coronation was made clear to those present. The German ambassador in Russia was later to report to Bismarck that the Tsar had made many jokes and 'disparaging remarks'[4] about Ferdinand's affected manner, his voice and, naturally enough, his nose. Ferdinand himself did not help matters. When he was asked by another princely guest why he wore no sword with his Austro-Hungarian military uniform, he replied that the skin on the lower part of his body was so delicate that his doctor had forbidden him to wear a sword belt. Worse still, he was afraid of horses and disliked riding. That sufficed to bring down on him the sarcasm of his peers who considered fine horsemanship the symbol of manliness. Ferdinand asked to be transferred from his Austrian Hussar regiment to an infantry unit for 'health reasons'. But it seems the taunts were too much for him, for he later returned to the cavalry as a first lieutenant in a Hungarian Honved regiment.

Prince Ferdinand earned his blackest mark from the Russian Tsar when courtesy orders and decorations were distributed to the coronation guests from abroad. Ferdinand expressed himself dissatisfied with the Order of St Alexander Nevski, and asked for the higher Order of St Andrew. When the Tsar heard of this, he said, devastatingly: 'Le Saint Alexandre est encore trop bon pour ce princillon. [Even the St Alexander is too good for this princeling.][5]

Lord Salisbury answered Queen Victoria's cross and irritated telegrams questioning the report in *The Times* about Prince Ferdinand's candidacy, and tried to soothe her. He assured her that it did not seem that the young Prince's move towards Bulgaria's empty throne was being taken seriously. He was right: Prince Ferdinand's candidacy for the dangerous throne of Bulgaria, in the teeth of a sullen and furious Tsar Alexander III of Russia, was not taken seriously because Ferdinand could not be taken seriously. To the world at large the contrast between the gravity to Europe of the Bulgarian Crisis and the personality of the Prince seemed merely comical.

Count Kálnoky, the Austro-Hungarian Foreign Minister, in speaking to the German Ambassador in Vienna on the day Ferdinand presented himself as a candidate, said he was baffled that 'this spoilt young gentleman, who lives an opulent, comfortable life, and, apart from that, has many intellectual interests and delights to move in intellectual circles, should be prepared to go to such a place of exile as Sofia'.[6]

Society had classified Ferdinand as a *Salon Prinz* – a drawing-room prince – considered by people who did not know him particularly well as a typical member of the troop of rich, aristocratic Viennese young men who did not allow their nominal military duties to interfere with the highly agreeable life and pleasures of the Austro-Hungarian capital.

To those who knew him better however, the fact that Prince Ferdinand, despite his dandyish airs and affectations, was not a 'chinless wonder', but very clever, caused unease. He was not a popular young man – indeed, he was actively disliked by many. Count Kálnoky found that he had too many of the 'airs and manners of a *vieille cocotte*'. He called him 'peculiar' and, as did Queen Victoria, 'effeminate'. Lady Paget, the wife of the British Ambassador in Vienna, wrote: 'His affectations are innumerable. He wears bracelets and powders his face. He sleeps in pink surah nightgowns, trimmed with Valenciennes lace. His constitution is so delicate and his nerves so finely strung, that he only consults ladies' doctors.'[7] Lady Paget was exaggerating, but her incredulity admirably conveys how people talked about Prince Ferdinand.

A Russian diplomat, A. Neklyudoff, gave a less sensational portrait of Ferdinand in those days:

> Prince Ferdinand cut a rather strange figure at the Austrian court and in high Viennese society. Remarks were made about his Bourbon nose, and everyone laughed at his effeminate manner, his exaggerated elegance, and his love for jewels and knick-knacks; he was supposed to possess inclinations which harmonized with his appearance and manner....
> Moreover he did not possess the gift of making himself liked. His

sly and suspicious expression prejudiced people against him. The more he became aware of his unpopularity, the more did he secretly indulge in venomous and bitter thoughts, and yet nurse in his heart ambitions and schemes which would have evoked shrieks of laughter if he had ever dared to disclose them.

It was only from his mother that he ever got encouragement and sympathy. And she was the only being that he ever really loved and who had any influence over him.[8]

Ferdinand was certainly unpopular, for his unfamiliar refinements and intellectual affectations did little to inspire confidence in other people. Even so, all his acquaintances were soon aware of his brilliant intellect, wide culture and remarkable gifts for the natural sciences. Ferdinand's scientific pursuits were by no means a princely hobby. At eighteen he had been made an honorary member of the German Ornithological Society in recognition of his success in breeding and rearing a rare bird species. He wrote a valuable scientific account of his explorations of the flora and fauna of Brazil and the coast of North-West Africa, forbiddingly entitled *Itinera principum S. Coburgi,* and regularly corresponded with some of the leading naturalists of Europe. Had his interests as a naturalist been those of a *curioso* or dilettante, they would not have provoked derision, but his serious interest and know-ledge sufficed to make him suspect and *infra dignitatem* in the eyes of male aristocratic contemporaries. Kaiser William II of Germany particularly resented this and he referred to him in his marginal notes to diplomatic dispatches as *Der Naseferdinand* (Noseferdinand).

A German diplomat expressed how Viennese Court society regarded the Prince and his scientific pursuits:

> His military duties did not bother him overmuch and if the Prince happened not to be busy stuffing some bird or other – he was very keen on this sport – one could see him airing his heels for hours on end in the region of the Graben, the Kohlmarkt and the Kärtnerstrasse [the most fashionable part of Vienna]. His figure was a well-known one in the town, the 'Prince with the long nose', as certain little ladies called him, and the 'bird-scholar', as his friends called him.[9]

Available opinions of Ferdinand as a young man are not all hostile or derisory. Mostly, people were puzzled by him and thought him odd. Some who knew him more intimately were often charmed by his amusing conversation and undoubtable wit. His peculiarities exerted a considerable fascination. When a startled Europe learnt that he had overnight become the centre of the biggest European diplomatic crisis since the Congress of Berlin, surmises about the twenty-five-year-old Prince of Saxe-Coburg-Gotha provided spice for the gossip of the courtiers and diplomats of the Continent.

CHAPTER 5

A Mother's Ambition

The single most important formative influence in Prince Ferdinand's life was his mother, Princess Clémentine of Orléans, the daughter of King Louis Philippe of France, born in 1817. It was she who instilled into her son the ambition to obtain a throne, anywhere in the world, and *to become a king.*

It now seems remarkable that the ambition to conquer a throne and found a new dynasty should burn so strongly in two people, mother and son, in the last years of the nineteenth century, when signs of the swift decline of the idea of monarchy were so widespread. Even in those days the sight of a prince preparing to set forth to conquer a throne for himself might have seemed an anachronism, startling in its naive simplicity. It could not be thought that Princess Clémentine was prompted by some kind of romantic, fundamentalist monarchism. She had a shrewd mind and a remarkable understanding of European politics and diplomacy. She knew or was related to many of the leading statesmen and rulers of Europe. An English diplomat said of her enthusiasms, interest, and persistence in learning about Europe's inner politics, that she was 'the Tsar's nightmare, the Austrian Emperor's bogey and Bismarck's sleeping draught'.[1]

The epigram, as is often the case, does not quite ring true. Bismarck may have thought Princess Clémentine tedious, but he had a healthy respect for this great-granddaughter of the Empress Maria Theresa of Austria. He was even worried by her, her wealth, her rigid Catholicism, her family and its efforts to bring about the restoration of the House of Orléans to the French throne. Moreover, as the daughter of King Louis Philippe, *le roi bourgeois,* she had received an education which allowed her to sympathize with some of the democratic tendencies of her time.

In her desire to obtain a throne for Ferdinand, her youngest child, Princess Clémentine was also trying to make up for her father's failure to retain the throne of France. The Paris revolution of 1848, triggered by her father's refusal to extend the franchise, had culminated in his abdication and the royal family's ignominious flight to England. Princess Clementine, a young woman of thirty-one, was at the Tuileries Palace and obstinately resisted to the last her father's signature to his abdication. While her father escaped from the palace in a common hackney carriage, hiding his face behind a loosely furled umbrella, she took her two sons by the hand and walked unafraid through the streets of Paris.

After the arrival of the French royal family in England, Queen Victoria wrote to her uncle Leopold, King of the Belgians: 'Poor Clém behaves beautifully, courageously, and calmly, and is full of resignation: but she can get no sleep, poor thing – and hears the horrid cries and sees those *fiend-like faces* before her!'[2]. But it was not only the memory of the Parisian mob that prevented the Princess from sleeping. A few days later Queen Victoria again wrote to her uncle and told him of Clémentine's feelings about the events in Paris and her father's abdication: she 'felt that *one* ought to have foreseen, and ought to have managed things better'.

Clémentine was outraged by her father's failure to prevent the fall of the monarchy. She could not help but blame him for lack of foresight, lack of what she considered to be the diplomatic instinct, for lack of political *finesse* and, possibly, for sheer lack of nerve. Of her own great gifts for statecraft, Ferdinand once said in his old age: 'My mother possessed the brains of a diplomat: she was shrewd to a degree – preternaturally far-seeing, and she was saved from disillusion by not possessing a grain of idealism in her composition.'[3]

Princess Clémentine's marriage to Ferdinand's father, Prince Augustus of Saxe-Coburg-Gotha, in 1843 when she was twenty-six, had owed more to realism than to romance. King Louis Philippe had for years been busy trying to secure thrones, through marriage, for his large family. In marrying a Coburg, Princess Clémentine thought that she stood a fair chance of some day sharing a throne with her husband. Her brother, the Duc d'Aumale, said she had chosen Prince Augustus 'because all the Coburgs became kings'.[4] In this, Princess Clémentine was to be disappointed.

Her husband was handsome. Queen Victoria, as a sixteen-year-old Princess, described Augustus in her journal as a tall young man with 'very fair hair, small blues eyes, a very pretty nose and likewise a very pretty mouth'.[5] Another entry ran 'Augustus was like a good affectionate child, quite unacquainted with the world, phlegmatic, and talking but very little'.[6] Gentle Augustus was eighteen at the time. Seven years later, when he married Princess Clémentine, he still had not become acquainted with the world. He was a Coburg who would not occupy a royal throne. However he was very rich. His mother was the only daughter and heiress of the fabulously wealthy Hungarian Prince Kohary.

Clémentine's thirty-eight years of married life with him were comfortable but not particularly happy. Her husband led the obscure life of an Austrian general. For Clémentine it was a narrow life, which her activities to restore the Orléans throne did not relieve. Her ferocious will urged her royal ambitions, but her intelligence and realism showed her that no means of satisfying them offered itself. By 1861 she had given birth to two sons and two daughters. To her critical eye neither son altogether satisfied her maternal ambitions. She was already in middle age and preparing to resign herself to an uneventful old age when, on 26 February 1861, she gave birth to Ferdinand (his full names were Ferdinand-Maximilian-Charles-Leopold-Marie) in the imposing Coburg Palace in Vienna.

All her will, her energy and her love were centred on her last born. She soon discerned in him proofs of intelligence and natural gifts which might lead to the fulfilment of her ambition: to see her son crowned as king. In him, her love and pride, she felt she could foresee the full bloom of his inheritance – the brilliance of her French ancestors combined with the intellectual gifts of the Coburgs.

She undertook his education with special care, engaged the best tutors available and spent much of her time with him. It was not the kind of intensive Coburg programme of education that Prince Albert, Queen Victoria's consort, tried to impose on his children. Princess Clémentine allowed her son to follow his natural bents and phantasies. These were never a cause of worry to her, especially as his remarkable gifts and aptitude for work allowed him to master the required disciplines. As quite a young man he knew five languages perfectly: German, French, English, Italian and Hungarian.

She kept him entirely under her wing. His father died in 1881, when Prince Ferdinand was twenty, without having had any decisive influence on his son. The wide age-gap between Ferdinand and his two brothers, Philip and Augustus – they were respectively seventeen and sixteen years his seniors – precluded them as companions of his childhood. By the time he was fourteen, they were both married. Philip, the eldest, was married to his cousin Louise, daughter of Leopold II of the Belgians also a Coburg. Augustus had married Léopoldine, daughter of Pedro II, the Emperor of Brazil. Ferdinand's sole companion from among his brothers and sisters was Amélie, a gifted painter. She was to marry the Bavarian Duke Maximilian, a brother of the Empress Elizabeth of Austria.

Ferdinand was thus to spend his youth in a predominantly feminine atmosphere. It was not what is usually implied by femininity. In Ferdinand's mother interests of State prevailed over those of the boudoir. The Duc d'Aumale called his sister 'Clémentine de Medici'. Yet the boudoir was not without its fascination for young Ferdinand. Very early he acquired a love for fine clothes and a passion for jewellery. Even as a young man his hands, of which he was proud, were 'luminous with rings' and all his life he carried cut precious stones like loose cash in his pocket. He said they soothed him. Queen Victoria's granddaughter, Queen Marie of Romania, described in her memoirs his passion for gems in middle age:

He would fondle them as though their touch gave him almost physical ecstasy. Considering me a worthy audience, he would bring out his little different stories for my benefit, knowing that I appreciated his subtleties, and thus he once drew a picture of himself which I have never forgotten, a picture where he is seated all by himself in a dimly lighted chamber, draped in a long black velvet dressing-gown fingering his priceless gems: *'Peux-tu me voir, tout de noir vêtu, laissant rubis, saphirs, éméraudes, perles et diamants couler entre mes doigts; drapé de velours, tout seul dans une demie-obscurité, très chère niéce, c'était je te l'assure, une vraie volupté.* [Can you see me, all in black, letting rubies, sapphires, emeralds, Pearls and diamonds cascade between my fingers; draped in Velvet, all alone in the half-dark – my very dear cousin, that was, I assure you, truly voluptuous.]

Uncle Ferdinand had beautifully kept, very white hands and wore his nails overlong, and looking at those pale fingers, ever afterwards it seemed to me that I saw the many-coloured gems slipping through them one by one.

In everyday life these pale fingers were covered with beautiful rings; his gestures were slow, and had about them something of a priest officiating in church; besides, he always wore a cross attached to a chain hidden beneath his coat or uniform, and he was continually toying with this cross, declaring that it gave him a venerable, almost a sacerdotal air. I think Uncle Ferdinand would have very much enjoyed being the Pope.[7]

Not surprisingly, the young boy's least favourite lessons were riding and gymnastics. His passionate interest in the natural sciences began very early. By the time he was ten years old he was already building up quite considerable collections of butterflies and beetles. Clémentine may well not have considered this a prerequisite for kingship; but on birthdays and at Christmas he would receive from his parents scholarly works on ornithology, entomology and botany. Clémentine, always an optimist, had decided that it was better to encourage rather than to frustrate.

Apart from the natural sciences, young Ferdinand showed great keenness for history. Here his mother was able to supplement his tutor's instruction. Of this, Ferdinand was to say after her death: 'My mother had the greatest influence on me, she was my guardian spirit, she took care of me, nursed me lovingly when I was ill, guided me through history and showed me its numerous wrong turnings, she had a deep understanding for everything, always supported the good and always wanted the best.'[8]

Ferdinand found history a subject of immense fascination. Even at the age of five, he realized he could relate it to himself through the study of genealogy. His ancestry on both sides enabled him to climb up family trees, frequently to move from tree to tree, with sudden dazzling atavistic discoveries of actual shared blood with legendary figures of the past. From those early beginnings he developed a most unscientific pride.

It was above all the consciousness of his Bourbon ancestry which he found exalting. While proposing a toast during the reception on the day of his first marriage in 1893 he marked the climax of his speech with the shout: 'In my veins too flows the blood of St Louis!'[9] St Louis was the canonized King Louis IX of France who died in Northern Africa in 1270 while leading the last Crusade to the Holy Land. When in 1912, Ferdinand, by then Tsar of Bulgaria, saw the victorious Bulgarian army almost on the point of entering Constantinople, he was acutely aware of the fact that he was leading another Crusade. Even in his formal proclamation of the First Balkan War against Turkey he spoke of this 'just, great and sacred struggle of the Cross against the Crescent'. His obsession with his ancestry and the intense imaginative pleasure he took in identifying with the personality of a dead forebear, had found its full expression. Thus the young boy's phantasies in the Vienna of the 1860s were destined to play a part in the history of Europe.

Perhaps related to Ferdinand's fascination with the history of kingship was his obsession with ritualism and the occult. Though he remained a faithful Catholic all his life, a constant and lively awareness of omens had an almost tyrannical hold on this man of quite outstanding intellectual gifts: he would not sign a major treaty of alliance with Serbia, the linchpin of the military league of Balkan nations against Turkey, on *13* March 1912. He did so on the 14th. In his sense of the occult he was really a man of his time. The revival of occultism, spiritualism and Satanism in Europe in the 1880s was an aspect of the so-called Decadent movement. Prince Ferdinand had, in his youth, consulted the celebrated clairvoyant Madame de Thèbes, in Paris, who had told his fortune: 'There is a hand between Vienna and Constantinople which is perhaps the most beautiful in Europe and whose importance is concealed by its delicate structure.'

Ferdinand's sister-in-law Princess Louise, the daughter of the King of the Belgians, has left a description of Ferdinand at the age of sixteen:

> I remember that in our palace at Vienna, Ferdinand would sometimes ask me to play to him when we were alone in the evening. He insisted upon the room being only dimly lit. He would then come near to the piano and listen in silence. At midnight he would stand up solemnly, his features drawn and contracted. He then looked at the clock and listened for the first of the twelve strokes, and when they were nearing the end he would say:
>
> 'Play the march from *Aida.*' Then, withdrawing to the middle of the room, he would strike à ceremonial attitude, and repeat incomprehensible words which frightened me.
>
> Ferdinand used to articulate cabbalistic formulas, stretching out his arms with his body bent and his head thrown backwards. Among the mysterious phrases a word which sounded like *Koptor, Kofte* or *Cophte* was often repeated. One day I asked him to write it down. He traced letters of which I could make nothing, excepting that I could recognize some kind of Greek characters.
>
> After these séances I questioned him, because while they were proceeding I had to be silent and play the march from *Aida.* He invariably answered: 'The Devil exists. I call on him and he comes.'[10]

Showing off to his attractive eighteen-year-old sister-in-law took on weirder aspects: 'Full of eccentricities, he would bury gloves and ties which he had worn. There was quite a ceremonial attached to this, at which I was sometimes obliged to assist. Ferdinand dug the hole himself, and repeated strange sentences with a mysterious air.'

Had Princess Clémentine known about these goings-on, her strict Catholicism might have caused her disquiet. On the other hand, maternal love for her favourite son would have probably dismissed them as harmless tomfoolery. Any fears that she might have had about her son's faith were in any case dispelled by his interest in all matters of Catholic Church ceremonial, liturgy and hierarchy. This interest was similar in kind to his knowledge of Court ceremonial, precedence of titles, rank, orders and decorations.

So far Prince Ferdinand's childhood and youth seem to suggest the hothouse, a somewhat exotic one. Yet his life was also worldly. When in Vienna, his parents lived a very active social life. They entertained often and lavishly in their palace in Vienna, where young Ferdinand could meet numerous members of Europe's aristocracy – to many of whom he was related – diplomats, statesmen, and some of the leading writers, artists and scholars. He had, as we have seen, the reputation of a 'drawing-room Prince' and frequently stayed at the country seats of his relations and his parents' friends. He also had a newspaper columnist's ear for gossip and his versions of scandal and anecdote were a fascinating blend of wit, mimicry and malice. He was certainly not dull and could, when he chose to, be indiscreet. His mother, too, had a reputation for a malicious tongue. Among some members of the Coburg family she was nicknamed 'Aunt Coffee-mill', a sobriquet cumbrously derived from the fact that the Princess, who was almost completely deaf, could only hear by means of a large chased silver ear trumpet, which resembled a type of coffee-mill. The idea was that she 'ground the reputation of others to powder by means of her coffee-mill'. In the last years of her life she could not hear even with the trumpet. Meriel Buchanan, the daughter of a British Minister in Sofia, later described an audience with the aged Princess Clémentine as a terrifying experience due to the conversation having to be conducted by writing on paper slips. Throughout the audience she was aware that 'all the slips of papers were kept so that he [Ferdinand] could see exactly what had been said, and amuse himself with the inanity of some of the remarks, or the bad French spelling and phrasing, and the thought of those mocking, sarcastic eyes of his deciphering one's feeble attempts was distinctly intimidating.'[11]

Prince Ferdinand's main residence was the huge Coburg Palace in Vienna. Its main façade, grey and severe, looked over the Ring, the impressive avenue recently constructed on the order of the Emperor Francis Joseph. A monumental colonnade on the other side overlooked gardens, which like the palace, were built on the site of an old bastion, known as the Coburg bastion. By the time he had reached early manhood, Ferdinand was given a separate apartment in the palace. A small door gave him independent access to the town and its pleasures.

For a large part of the year he lived at the palace of Ebenthal, his mother's favourite house, in beautiful country some twenty-five miles north-east of Vienna. Ebenthal was as simple, elegant and agreeable as the palace in Vienna was imposing and gloomy. It was a low, square, white, country house of the eighteenth century, in which Napoleon had stayed after his victory at Wagram, and was surrounded by miles of woods and vineyards. There as a child, Ferdinand netted the butterflies which were the start of his extensive collection.

Apart from Ebenthal, Ferdinand could give scope to his ever-growing love of nature in six different country castles and estates belonging to his father in Hungary. These included the 'eagle's nest' of Murany, which had resisted several Turkish sieges centuries earlier, and provided Ferdinand with his incognito, 'Count of Murany', during his later travels. In these surroundings he seemed quite free of his 'drawing-room' self. Here, in the eyes of his male contemporaries, he even made up for his appalling horsemanship by being an excellent shot. He was a greedy man – and a gourmet; if his dead quarry had wings and was a fine specimen, there was always the dilemma: to eat it or stuff it? Usually, the collector in him would win.

Prince Ferdinand's passion for travel began with his mother urging him to pay visits to his royal relatives all over the world. There was no lack of choice: on the paternal, Coburg side, his family had five thrones at the beginning of the century, and acquired four more in the course of it. The Coburgs were the royal stud farm of Europe. When the Duchess of Dino once asked a diplomat whom the young Queen of England would marry, the answer was: 'One of the royal stallions, of course! A prince of Saxe-Coburg and Gotha.'[12] Ferdinand's wide choice of visits to people on the paternal side of his family was, of course, supplemented by his mother's Orléans connections. In some cases he was doubly related to the same person on both his father's and mother's side. It was so in the case of King Leopold II of the Belgians who was both Princess Clémentine's nephew and her husband's first cousin. (With no attempt to simplify matters, let it be added that the Belgian King's daughter was Clémentine's daughter-in-law.)

Prince Ferdinand first visited Leopold II when he was fifteen years old. The King, born like Ferdinand of a Coburg/Orléans marriage, amassed a huge fortune from the Congo which he ran for twenty years as his private estate. His unquestionable mental power, allied to the profound business mind of the Coburgs, deeply impressed Ferdinand. At the royal palace of Laeken Ferdinand received an initiation in politics on a grand, world scale, which was to stimulate his royal ambitions along practical, realistic lines. These were to run parallel to his more fanciful royal urges rooted in the consciousness of his pedigree. When he was finally proclaimed Tsar of Bulgaria in 1908, he was deeply gratified that his Belgian royal cousin was still alive to witness his triumph.

One year his father took him on a cruise to Constantinople, the city that was to obsess him in later life. They sailed on the Austrian steamship *Orient*, the same ship which years later was to take Ferdinand on his first trip to Bulgaria and its dangerous throne. They then went on a tour of Asia Minor and Greece, during which Ferdinand, while adding to his natural science collections, became fascinated by the cult of the Cabeiri, mythical divinities whose origins and nature still remain mysterious.

In 1879, when he was eighteen, his mother sent him to Brazil with his brother Prince Augustus, the Emperor of Brazil's son-in-law. They first went to Lisbon, where their Coburg uncle Ferdinand had married the

Queen of Portugal. From Lisbon their steamship, the rapid *Niger* of the Méssageries Maritimes, took them to Brazil via Dakar. Ferdinand kept himself busy with the scientific observations which he published on his return to Europe.

In Brazil Ferdinand enjoyed meeting the kindly, philosophic and slightly eccentric Emperor Pedro, under whose rule Brazil enjoyed forty years of order, peace and economic progress. Ferdinand's comments to an American journalist shortly after Pedro II was deposed and exiled in 1889 are interesting as evidence of his constant self-consciousness, which frequently led him to condemn in others what he felt could be said against himself:

He had only himself to blame for his deposition and, later, his exile. The poor man was a savant. He devoted himself to the history of the dead past and to speculations about the future of science. He was surrounded by antiquarians conversant with what happened in the Middle Ages, and by star-gazers whose speculations as to what the world would look like in the twenty-second century fascinated him. But he absolutely ignored the living world. He did not consult the statesman and the editors who were shaping the destinies of his people; indeed, he did not even know them by name, and he paid the penalty. For this he forfeited his throne and lost his crown.[13]

This pitying sarcasm revealed far more than Ferdinand intended: the fact that he could be uneasy about the effect his own private preoccupations could have on his royal ambition. While ill-luck had often attended royal members of his family, *he* intended to avoid the pitfalls into which they had fallen.

CHAPTER 6

Public Relations

—◦❧◦—

The spectacle of the Bulgarian throne going a-begging was meat and drink to Europe's satirical Press and vaudeville stage. Graver voices, like that of *The Times*, declared that no man would accept the thankless task. There was every reason to think that Alexander of Battenberg was at least fortunate in that he had got out of Bulgaria alive and that his eventual successor would be risking his neck. Bismarck hypothesized about a Prince of Bulgaria, 'if there is in the world a being unfortunate enough to take that position'.[1]

Prince Ferdinand's first approach to the three Bulgarians in the Vienna Opera took place on 13 December 1886, exactly a week after they had left Sofia. When Konstantin Kalcheff rejoined the other two delegates after his talk with Ferdinand in the Prince's box, the three of them discussed the singularity of this bid for the throne of their country in the interval of an opera. Whatever their scepticism and amusement, they agreed that they could not afford to overlook any possibility. They decided that Kalcheff should call on Prince Ferdinand at the Coburg Palace the next morning at ten o'clock.

The Bulgarian delegate arrived at the Coburg Palace punctually. Kalcheff was somewhat taken aback to see the Prince at this early hour of the morning – for Vienna – waiting for him in full dress uniform 'resplendent in all his decorations'. Prominently displayed among them was the Russian order he had received at the coronation of Tsar Alexander III. Next to it was a Bulgarian order which he had received at the same coronation from Prince Alexander of Battenberg. Ferdinand was putting himself on show and a display of monarchic gravity came easily to the tall, just slightly portly twenty-five-year-old prince.

Almost the first question that Prince Ferdinand asked Kalcheff was whether there was any likelihood of Prince Alexander's return to Bulgaria. Kalcheff replied that were he to return, he would be greeted with enthusiasm by the whole nation. But, in view of Russia's attitude, and that of the Tsar in particular, a return seemed most unlikely.

Kalcheff then asked him outright whether he would be prepared to offer himself as a candidate for the Bulgarian throne. In his memoirs, the Bulgarian delegate wrote:

> I added that I was convinced the Regency would welcome him as Prince, once it had heard of his great qualities, his noble origin and his family connections with the ruling houses of some of the Great Powers, who could throw their influence behind Bulgaria's cause.
>
> As to the Bulgarian people, I said, who were so attached to Prince Alexander of Battenberg, they would be just as loyal to his successor, if they were given proof of his qualities.
>
> I could see that my words had made an impression – he shook my hand warmly, thanking me for my frankness, and said he would also like to meet my colleagues, so that we could discuss the matter further.[2]

Kalcheff was delighted and another meeting was arranged for the next morning.

With something like a definite offer from Kalcheff, Prince Ferdinand got busy that same day. He immediately called on Count Kálnoky, the Austrian Foreign Minister, to tell him that the Bulgarians had asked him to offer himself as a candidate for the Bulgarian throne. He then went to the hotel in which the Bulgarians were staying to leave his visiting cards.

Kálnoky sent a telegram to the Austro-Hungarian Ambassador in St Petersburg to tell him of Prince Ferdinand's 'unexpected' news. The Prince had appeared to be 'seriously determined to take on this difficult task'[3] and had told Kálnoky that he was *persona gratissima* at the Russian Court.

When the three Bulgarian delegates called at the Coburg palace the following day, Prince Ferdinand, this time in civilian dress, told them he had high hopes that his candidature would not be opposed by the Russians. He recalled his 'cordial reception' in Russia during the Tsar's coronation in 1883 and spoke about his 'personal acquaintance' with the Tsar. The Bulgarians were naturally very pleased. A European prince who said he was well liked in the Russian Court and who was also related by blood with the Austrian, German, Belgian and English royal houses seemed made to order to lead Bulgaria out of danger.

It is not easy to decide whether Prince Ferdinand's claim to be *persona gratissima* at the Russian Court was a case of self-delusion, or a deliberate attempt by the Prince to enhance his value as a future Prince of Bulgaria in the eyes of the Bulgarians. Pure self-delusion would have meant that

Prince Ferdinand had not noticed Alexander III's snubs and taunts during the coronation festivities. Throughout his life, Ferdinand showed remarkable sensitivity – and immediate resentment – to anything approaching a slight, be it real or imagined. Yet, as far as Russia was concerned, Ferdinand may have considered that his friendship with the Tsar's brother and sister-in-law, the Grand Duke and Grand Duchess Vladimir, had made up for the Tsar's earlier snubs. The Grand Duchess, *née* Mecklenburg-Schwerin, was a strong personality who played a leading role in St Petersburg society. She felt that she understood Ferdinand and his foibles and admired him for what she later called his 'instinct for greatness' and his 'royal bearing'. Ferdinand may well have over-estimated the value of this support, for a few months later Bismarck warned Ferdinand against the Bulgarian throne and urged him not to rely 'on the sanguine expectations of Russian grand duchesses which are out of step with the true mood of the Russian court'.[4]

Ferdinand's early optimism could not have lasted long. After his talks with the Bulgarians, he telegraphed the Tsar to tell him that the delegation of the Bulgarian Sobranie had offered him the throne of the Principality. Alexander III's reply was icy: he told the Prince that he knew of no delegation and of no Sobranie. There was no equivocation. The Tsar was determined to veto automatically any move by the Bulgarian national assembly, the Government, and the Regents on the grounds of his claim that they were all illegal. It was then that he said to Giers, his Foreign Minister: '*The candidature is as ridiculous as the individual.*'[5]

The Russian Press immediately published sharp attacks against Austria-Hungary, accusing her of contriving and supporting Prince Ferdinand's candidature. The leading newspaper, *Novoie Vremia*, said:

> It is self-evident that Russia will never agree to the election of this prince. As a Catholic, a relative of the Queen of England and of the Austrian imperial family, Prince Ferdinand has no recommendations which would allow our government to let him get to the Bulgarian throne. A formal, unconditional refusal is the only thing that this lieutenant in Austrian service can expect from St Petersburg.[6]

The icy Russian showers fell on Prince Ferdinand thick and fast. Once he had made the first move by button-holing the Bulgarian delegation at the opera, an embarrassment that he would be at pains to conceal for the rest of his life, he saw that his personal ambition to obtain a throne was beginning to approach a conceivable reality. However, Ferdinand never fooled himself about the problems that faced him; ambition and self-esteem at this time were in no sense at odds with his keen intelligence.

He was able to view his efforts to obtain a throne in a light that was satisfying both to his intellect and to the more exotic, romantic, *fin de siècle* side of his nature.

The erosion of Turkey in Europe in the nineteenth century, and the re-emergence of long-forgotten nations in the south-east corner of the continent meant that new lands and new markets had become available right next-door to the Major Powers, to be reached and exploited without the toil and sweat – and above all without the naval requirements – of a scramble for colonies overseas. The Panslavists of Russia had already made their bid with the war against Turkey, only to see Europe deny them the fruits of victory at the Congress of Berlin.

Austria-Hungary, on the other hand, having lost her influence in Italy and Germany, bolstered her self esteem with a growing conviction that she had a historic mission in the Balkan peninsula. Crown Prince Rudolf, a friend of Ferdinand, expressed this following a journey to Eastern Europe: 'I have always considered that Austria's mission in the east of Europe is a law of nature. Now, after my journey, my conviction is stronger than ever that we have a great future in these regions.'[7]

Crown Prince Rudolf's 'law of nature' for Austria had a curious – and ominous – parallel in the writings of Nikolai Danilevski, the Russian Panslavist and author of *Russia and Europe,* published in 1869 and subsequently styled 'the Bible of Panslavism'. Danilevski, who had studied the natural sciences, managed to combine Darwinism with Panslavism and from his botanical studies derived the idea that the struggle for existence was the dominating factor in relations between states. Force was justified as leading the development of a healthy species. Russia was bound by the laws of nature to defeat a 'diseased' Europe and form a Slav federation with its capital in Constantinople. Such parallel Russian and Austrian lines of thought were eventually to converge and cross in 1914.

Where Crown Prince Rudolf saw his country destined to fulfil its *Kulturmission,* Prince Ferdinand believed he himself had the ability and talents to restore Bulgaria to her former greatness. This greatness and standing would reflect his own qualities, and earn him a place in history. The Coburgs were royal material. His mother was the daughter of a King of France. A throne, though as yet only a princely one, was available in Europe. In moments when Ferdinand's natural pessimism took the upper hand and spelt out the dangers and difficulties that clearly lay ahead, Princess Clémentine was at his side to whisper 'Fortune Favours the Brave'. For that indomitable lady, her piety and her ambitions for Ferdinand went hand-in-hand. She vowed to buy a big golden crown for the statue of the Virgin Mary at Lourdes if it was granted that her son should obtain the throne of Bulgaria.

The seventy-year-old Princess was not the kind of woman to rely on votive offerings alone. She became her son's indefatigable public relations officer, which led to a tart exchange of letters with her 'very devoted cousin and faithful friend', Queen Victoria. The Queen wrote to tell her that she disapproved of Ferdinand offering himself as a candidate. Clémentine was stung into replying with a proud fib: her son had *not* put himself forward as a candidate, the Bulgarians had insisted that he should accept the candidature and 'many others' were in favour of this.

Ferdinand and his mother had, in fact, had their sights trained on Bulgaria for years before Prince Alexander's abdication. In 1883, while talking to General Kaulbars, at that time Russia's Military Attaché in Vienna, about Prince Alexander's latest conflict with St Petersburg following his dismissal of several Russian officers from his *entourage*, Prince Ferdinand said: Had I been in Battenberg's place, I would have settled the whole thing in quarter of an hour.'[8] Ferdinand was then only twenty-three, and his cockiness was partly the result of what he considered had been his highly successful stay in Russia for the coronation of the Tsar. His belief that he stood in high favour with the Russian Imperial family was, apart from his friendly relations with the Grand Duke Vladimir, also based on his family link with the Tsar's family: through his cousin Alfred, Duke of Edinburgh, Queen Victoria's son, who was married to the Tsar's only sister, Grand Duchess Marie of Russia.

Princess Clémentine's boast to Queen Victoria that Ferdinand's candidature was being desired by 'many others' beside the Bulgarian delegates, was not wholly dictated by pique and motherly pride. Ferdinand's and her own overestimate of his standing in St Petersburg was also due to their friendship with the Russian Ambassador in Vienna, Prince Lobanoff-Rostovsky, later a Minister of Foreign Affairs.

Prince Lobanoff, who was a close friend of the Princess and shared some of Ferdinand's scientific and artistic interests, upheld to a certain extent Ferdinand's nascent ambitions. In his despatches to St Petersburg he represented Ferdinand as possessing far more strength of personality than public opinion would have supposed. When the Bulgarian delegate Kalcheff called on Prince Lobanoff, at Ferdinand's insistence, to inform him of the latter's candidature, the Russian Ambassador told him that if Ferdinand succeeded in obtaining the approval of the Great Powers for his election as Prince of Bulgaria, that would be of 'great benefit to the Bulgarians'.[9] Lobanoff made it clear that he was not speaking officially, but merely as a private person. He also told the Bulgarian delegate that he disapproved of the Tsar's Slavophil entourage, especially those of his advisers who were urging him to occupy Bulgaria with Russian troops.

He told Kalcheff that Giers, his Foreign Minister, had been very much opposed to General Kaulbars being sent to Bulgaria, but that the appointment had been made over his head by the Tsar. Lobanoff's attitude to Ferdinand and the Bulgarian delegation was to annoy the Tsar greatly, when he eventually heard of it.

Lobanoff's friendly attitude in Vienna, Ferdinand's own wrong impressions of his stay in Russia three years earlier, and his tenuous connections with the Russian Imperial family, all helped to encourage the Prince and his mother. At the time they could not know of the contempt which Alexander III expressed about Ferdinand to Giers. In his letter to the Prince the Tsar had merely refused to recognize the legality of the Bulgarian Sobranie and its delegation.

If anything, the Prince and his mother felt flattered when the official *Journal de St Petersbourg,* while explaining that Russia had refused to countenance a candidature proposed by the 'illegal' Bulgarian delegation, added that the refusal was 'in no way connected with the person of Prince Ferdinand, who enjoys general respect'. But such a small crumb could not make up for Russia's evident opposition to the candidature. Lobanoff reported to St Petersburg that Ferdinand had been 'unpleasantly surprised' by the official newspaper article.

While Ferdinand and his mother quickly realized that their initial expectations of a Russian approval had been over-sanguine, Austria's attitude to the candidature was equivocal. After his initial meetings with the Bulgarian delegates, Ferdinand, as an officer in the Austrian army, went to ask the Emperor Francis Joseph for his consent to accept the Bulgarian offer. He appears to have received it without any difficulty. When he called on the Foreign Minister, Count Kálnoky, and asked him if he had any objections to his candidature, Kálnoky assured him that there was none.

Kálnoky at that time could not take Ferdinand seriously and was baffled by him. His dispatches, which speak of the Prince's 'unmanliness and singularity', also show that he was impressed by his 'great self-confidence', by his serious ambition for the Bulgarian throne and by his great wealth. Neither the Austrian Emperor nor Kálnoky could believe that this weird, rich, and decadent young Prince, who abominated horses and hunting and adored chasing butterflies, armed with a net and killing jar, could succeed in a position which had broken Alexander of Battenberg, that contemporary romantic model of martial valour.

While Kálnoky simply could not understand why a young man with Prince Ferdinand's tastes and money should want to bury himself in Sofia, he did not underestimate his intellectual gifts nor his astuteness. He told the German Ambassador in Vienna that Prince Ferdinand would fight no open battles, but was intelligent. Austria would have no objections if the Prince tried to reconcile Russia's policy demands with Bulgaria's own advance to complete independence.

The Austrian Foreign Minister's attitude towards Ferdinand was in keeping with his overall policy towards Russia. This consisted of securing Austria's position in the Balkans without, however, affronting Russia and incurring the risk of war. In view of the Tsar's well-known and almost pathological sensitivity about Bulgaria, it was essential that Austria should be seen as having nothing to do with the candidature of Ferdinand. If, as seemed likely, the Prince's adventure ended in disaster, Austria would have lost nothing. If, however, the Prince managed to stay on the Bulgarian throne against all the odds, then, in Austria's calculations, she would have found another means of increasing her influence in the Balkans. In any case, a positive move might help to solve the dangerous uncertainties of the present, as Kálnoky wrote to his ambassador in St Petersburg: 'We have nothing to do with this candidature but, if it has any real chance of success, we would like to support it. The reason for this is that we would consider the settling of the Bulgarian rulership issue as the quickest way of resolving the present crisis.'[10]

In that dispatch, the Austrian Foreign Minister wrote that Ferdinand's news was 'unexpected.' Kálnoky however was not telling his ambassador in St Petersburg the full truth about the Prince's candidature. He had, in fact, known about the possibility of Prince Ferdinand's candidature for some weeks before the Bulgarians reached Vienna. The Prince's name had come up during the meeting in November in Budapest of the Delegations, the body composed of Austrian and Hungarian representatives which met annually to discuss matters affecting the Dual Monarchy of Austria-Hungary. The meeting of the Delegations was always a testing time for the government, especially in steering through the foreign and military policies of the joint state. Kálnoky was particularly anxious to avoid heated debates about the Bulgarian Crisis which Russia would see as a provocation. He was worried about possible extreme anti-Russian outbursts by the hot-headed and temperamental Hungarian representatives.

Among them was Count Eugene Zichy, a rich Hungarian magnate and landowner, who was a friend of Prince Ferdinand's family. Count Zichy, who occasionally spoke on foreign affairs, saw the departure of General Kaulbars from Bulgaria and the break in diplomatic relations between Sofia and St Petersburg as a favourable opportunity for Austria-Hungary to steal a march on Russia in the Balkans. The best way to do this, he considered, was to present Europe with an Austro-Hungarian candidacy for the vacant Bulgarian throne.

Clearly no believer in half-measures, Count Zichy proceeded to blackmail Kálnoky. Knowing that at that moment the Foreign Minister was at all costs trying to avoid making a definite statement of Austrian policy on the Bulgarian Question, Zichy told Kálnoky that he intended to raise the issue at the following day's sitting. But, said Zichy, he would refrain from raising awkward questions about the Bulgarian Crisis, if Kálnoky promised him something in return. The outraged Foreign Minister asked what that might be, so Count Zichy simply asked him not to object if Prince Ferdinand of Coburg's name were to be put forward as candidate for the Bulgarian throne. Indignantly, Kálnoky agreed. An anti-Russian outburst or demonstration at the Delegations had to be avoided at all costs. He only stipulated that Prince Ferdinand had to resign his commission in the Austro-Hungarian army before he 'took decisions which would lead him to Bulgaria'.

The following day, pleased with his successful ploy, Zichy called on Archduke Joseph, Count Palatine of Hungary and brother-in-law of Prince Ferdinand (he was the husband of Ferdinand's sister Clotilde), and told him his news. The Archduke, who had not had any inkling of his brother-in-law's plans, was amazed. At first he refused to listen to what Zichy had to say, but finally exclaimed: 'You and your tales – he is a wretched coward, small [sic] and can't ride!'[11]

Count Zichy, much to Ferdinand's later regret, persuaded the Prince to let him act as a kind of Press and public relations officer. The Count, whose main source of income was the sale of grain from his Hungarian estates, had delivered great quantities of grain to Bulgaria during the Serbo-Bulgarian war of 1885, by means of his agent and right-hand man, one Philip Waldapfel. Because of the contacts Waldapfel had in Bulgaria as a result of the grain trade, Zichy recommended him to the Prince as an 'adroit and dependable' man to send there to make propaganda and agitate on Ferdinand's behalf. The Prince was not impressed by Waldapfel. He was a 'fixer', coarsely jovial, uneducated, given to violent outbursts and threats, real or assumed, in the pursuit of his one goal: money. Bribery, corruption and even blackmail were his stock-in-trade. The aesthete in Ferdinand shrank at the sight of him. Nevertheless, a few days after meeting the Bulgarian delegates, the Prince gave Waldapfel his instructions and sent him off to Bulgaria with a large sum of money.

On arriving in Sofia, Waldapfel received a letter from Count Zichy, telling him to go ahead and not to worry about finances: 'Expenses present no problem, since they will be reimbursed. I am convinced that His Royal Highness [sic], who is filled with ambition for his throne and feels that he is up to the fine task before him, will reward your expenditure and labours with princely generosity.'[12] He urged Waldapfel to support Prince Ferdinand's candidature for the throne and in doing so to put about the idea that Ferdinand was 'the one man who, through his connections, can bring about a compromise with and even have a conciliatory influence on Russia'.

Although richly endowed with rustic cunning, Waldapfel was not the ideal man to send on a delicate diplomatic mission closely connected with a grave European political crisis. On the day of his arrival in Sofia, he grinningly presented himself to the Austro-Hungarian Consul General, Stefan von Burian, as the 'house-Jew of the monkey Zichy'. As a result, Burian avoided all further contact with him.

Politics held no charms for Philip Waldapfel. As far as he was concerned, his mission in Bulgaria was an opportunity to make money. He managed to combine canvassing support for Prince Ferdinand's candidature with preparing the ground for the candidature of a Hungarian nobleman, Count Ladislaus Hunyadi, who also fancied the throne of Bulgaria. Waldapfel was about to pull off a major financial swindle in Bulgaria when the authorities realized in the nick of time what was happening, and he had to beat a hasty retreat across the Danube to Romania.

He had talked Metropolitan Kliment, the fanatical Russophil churchman who became Bulgaria's Prime Minister for four days after the *coup* against Prince Alexander of Battenberg, into organizing a rigged lottery. Metropolitan Kliment was President of Bulgaria's Red Cross and Waldapfel organized a country-wide lottery as a Red Cross benefit. The cleric and the grain merchant stood to gain a huge amount of money until the scheme was discovered. During all that time, Waldapfel sent back glowing reports to Vienna and depicted the mood in Bulgaria as enthusiastically pro-Ferdinand. It was not until he wrote to Ferdinand from Bucharest, offering a 'reconciliation with Russia' in exchange for a large sum of money, that Ferdinand's suspicions were aroused. Waldapfel's further letters and requests for funds were left unanswered.

In the autumn of the following year, 1887, when Ferdinand was already installed on the Bulgarian throne, Waldapfel and Count Zichy showed themselves under their true colours. Waldapfel returned to Sofia, tried to extort money from the Prince, was thrown out of Bulgaria, and then threatened to publish 'disclosures' about how Ferdinand had become Prince of Bulgaria under the title *The Purchased Throne*. He tried to start court proceedings against the Prince in Budapest, but the court ruled that there were no grounds for prosecution. A few days later Count Zichy called on Princess Clémentine in Vienna late in the evening and terrified the old lady with detailed accounts of what would happen to her beloved Ferdinand if Waldapfel's demands for money were not satisfied. He told her that the matter was urgent and that she had no time to inform her son in Sofia. Princess

Clémentine paid out the 10,000 francs he asked for, and the Count promised that that would be the end of the matter. Nevertheless, a few days later the newspapers published a story about the settlement. The Press accounts implied that Prince Ferdinand had paid hush-money, inevitably suggesting that he had something to fear from Waldapfel's 'disclosures'.

Another ostensible supporter of Prince Ferdinand's candidature also proved distinctly suspect. That was the Archduke Johann Salvator, a gifted romantic and erratic member of the Habsburg clan, whose ambition and thirst for adventure were frustrated by the rigidity of the Viennnese Court and its patriarch, the Emperor Francis Joseph. He was a friend of Alexander of Battenberg, whom he admired as the victor of the Serbo-Bulgarian war, and offered to fight as a volunteer alongside the Bulgarians if Russia invaded their country. He contacted the Bulgarian delegates and would have liked to have been elected to the throne of Bulgaria. But as a member of the House of Habsburg, his way was barred by the Treaty of Berlin which excluded as ineligible all members of any reigning European dynasty. The young Archduke nevertheless took passionate interest in the Bulgarian question and tried to help 'the poor Bulgarians' by finding a ruler for them.

For this reason he became involved in Prince Ferdinand's candidature, though he cared little for the Prince. It was his close friend and confidant Major von der Laaba who arranged the first meeting between Ferdinand and the Bulgarian delegates at the Vienna Opera. Johann Salvator's deep involvement with the Bulgarian problem angered the Emperor, who insisted on discipline and forbade members of the Imperial house any kind of independent political activity. As a result, the Archduke, who for years had been the *bête noire* of the Viennese Court, severed all connections with the Emperor, renounced his title and his position, and assumed the name of Johann Orth, a commoner. Following the suicide of his cousin and friend Crown Prince Rudolf of Austria, at Mayerling, Johann Orth left Austria, bought a merchant ship which he captained and which was wrecked on the rocks off Cape Horn. His disappearance and presumed drowning naturally set off a host of wild rumours linking his death with the tragedy at Mayerling.

Before his final sea voyage, Johann Orth called on Prince Ferdinand in Sofia, and according to the latter, begged to be accepted as an officer in the Bulgarian army. Ferdinand said that he had turned him down out of respect for the feelings of the Emperor Francis Joseph.

If Prince Ferdinand used such doubtful champions to support his candidature, he saw them merely as possibly useful tools, without seriously relying on them. From the moment he decided to make his bid for the Sofia throne, he was nobody's dupe or man of straw.

Europe found this hard to believe. Even Bismarck, quite out of character, indulged in lurid fantasies that Ferdinand had been put up by an unholy alliance of interests which included the Vatican, the 'Austrian Jesuit party' and those working for the restoration of the House of Orléans in France. The candidature of the Prince, Bismarck wrote, was not a Coburg inspired undertaking, but a 'maternal, Orléanistic one'. In this, Bismarck and Tsar Alexander III were in agreement, for the Russian Emperor and leading Panslavists, such as Pobedonostseff, saw Ferdinand as an anti-Orthodox agent of the Pope.

Though less sensational in its appraisal of Prince Ferdinand's candidature than Bismarck, *The Spectator* of London also saw it in a conspiratorial light. It was not conceivable, said the journal, that a man like the Prince would offer himself as a candidate without some assurances of success:

> The Prince selected is not the kind of man to put himself forward without strong reason to believe that he will be elected. He is not one of the hungry Princes.
>
> Head of the Catholic branch of the Coburgs, very wealthy, a Prince of a reigning house in Germany, and a great magnate in Hungary, he would not resign a position of such dignity and ease to engage in an unwarranted pursuit of an uncertain and thorny sovereignty in a far-away corner of Europe.[13]

The writer of the leading article concluded: 'We cannot help thinking that the election of Prince Ferdinand of Saxe-Coburg has been arranged by Europe, and that the hesitations in recognizing him which are recorded from day to day form part of a solemn comedy.'

Europe's newspapers rang the changes on the presumed conspiratorial background to Ferdinand's candidature. Only a few people found it possible to accept the truth: that Prince Ferdinand's motives and drive were personal, based on his mother's ambition and will to power for the child of her middle age.

CHAPTER 7

Bismarck's Rebuff

The Bulgarian Crisis of 1886-7 can be seen as a dummy run for 1914. For the first time Europe began to fear the implications of a European war made all the more dangerous by the rising giants of the arms industry and the blind forces of economic and national imperialism. Count Kálnoky expressed these anxious forebodings in a speech at the Delegations in Budapest on 13 November 1886, when dealing with the Bulgarian Crisis: 'At a time when in Europe it is possible, in a few days and with a speed hitherto unknown, to put into the field five million soldiers fully prepared for battle, the weight of responsibility resting on a minister and a state is immense if one of his actions were to result in setting in motion such monstrous war-masses.'[1]

Ferdinand was dismayed when the full implications of his position dawned upon him in the early months of 1887. The vacant Bulgarian throne, viewed from the drawing-rooms of Vienna, had seemed to promise the fulfilment of his dynastic longings. He had felt that once Prince of Bulgaria, a way, though tricky and difficult, lay ahead to restoring the Bulgarian kingdom with himself as King. The ancient glamour of the Bulgaria of the Middle Ages had invested the practical task that lay ahead with the romantic glow that Ferdinand so frequently sought and found in grand opera. That Prince Ferdinand should have chosen to make his first step towards a throne at an operatic performance in Vienna was fortuitous, and aptly symbolic.

Despite his initial self-confidence and the illusions he had about the task that lay ahead with the romantic glow that Ferdinand so frequently naivety. Even during his first meetings with the Bulgarian delegates, Ferdinand had avoided giving them a straight answer to their one vital question: was he prepared to go to Bulgaria *without* the unanimous approval of the European powers? The Bulgarians, acting on the instructions of the Regent Stefan Stamboloff, had pressed their point by telling the Prince that everything depended on whether he was prepared

to come to the throne without Russian support, even in opposition to
Russia's wishes. The Prince's reply was non-committal. The Bulgarians
were even more puzzled: a commitment was central to the whole issue.
Their disappointment increased when the Prince said that he would
have to make several conditions before he would accept becoming the
official candidate for the Bulgarian throne. He refused to say what the
conditions were.

Stamboloff did not like this at all. To him, as the leader of a country
fighting for its survival under the very real menace of a Russian
invasion, such cryptic subtleties were repellent and suspect. The
delegates left Vienna. They had agreed with Ferdinand that they would
continue to tour the European capitals and try to obtain the support of
the Powers for his candidature. He would agree to come to Bulgaria if
the Powers agreed. He would also do his best to obtain Russia's
agreement. They would keep in touch by correspondence and meet at a
neutral *rendezvous* once the delegates had completed their tour.

This was not promising. The rash of speculation about Prince
Ferdinand's role in the Bulgarian Crisis in political discussions and in the
European Press died down as quickly as it had appeared.

The Bulgarian delegation, after leaving Ferdinand in Vienna, travelled to Cologne to meet Alexander of Battenberg.

There was general agreement that the meeting could only mean one
thing: the likelihood of Prince Alexander's return to Bulgaria. The
spectre of Prince Alexander returning to Sofia at the head of his
victorious troops sent shudders down the spines of Europe's statesmen.
It must be the beginning of a general war. Tsar Alexander's hatred for
his cousin was so intense that only the long-feared military attack
against Bulgaria was conceivable as Russia's reaction to Sandro's
return. The other European Powers, with the exception of Germany,
were bound to stand in the way of what would amount to the Russian
take-over of the Balkan peninsula.

The news of the meeting between Prince Alexander and the Bulgarian delegation at the end of December 1886, appalled the Tsar. There
and then he decided to write to Kaiser William of Germany and ask him
to do everything in his power to prevent Prince Alexander's return. The
intensity of his feelings was such that he did not trust himself to write to
his Imperial relative in Germany without first asking for Bismarck's
approval.

The Tsar did not know that the Bulgarians had indeed asked their
former Prince to return to Bulgaria and that he had refused. But it was
not an outright refusal. It could be summed up in the phrase: 'I cannot
return now – but later, perhaps.' The Prince explained that if the
Bulgarian Regency could keep the country calm until the expected

death of Germany's Kaiser William I, his heir, Crown Prince Frederick, would almost certainly part ways with his Chancellor Bismarck. The latter had been a main obstacle to the projected marriage between the Crown Prince's daughter, Princess Victoria of Prussia, and Prince Alexander.

Prince Alexander hoped that in the event of Bismarck's retirement, Germany's attitude to Bulgaria would change and make it possible for him to return to the country as the son-in-law of the German Kaiser and the husband of Queen Victoria's granddaughter. As a plan for the future, it was perhaps a shade too optimistic, but not totally impossible. Queen Victoria herself went on believing, well into 1887, that Sandro would one day return to Bulgaria in very different circumstances, but not yet and not as an adventurer. She wrote to him to say that the Bulgarians would never find or choose another Prince. But the Tsar of Russia's hatred of Prince Alexander was such that his return would have brought the risk of war. Bismarck placated the Tsar and promised, in the Russo-German Treaty signed in June 1887, the so-called Reinsurance Treaty, that Germany would 'not under any circumstances give her consent to the restoration of the Prince of Battenberg'.

But as far as the Bulgarian Regents were concerned, Prince Alexander's plans involved an indeterminate period of waiting. That was just what they could not do. As the months passed since the forced abdication of Alexander of Battenberg and the break of diplomatic relations with Russia, the unsolved question of the throne grew more and more menacing. The provisional, temporary nature of the government of Bulgaria at that moment and the ever present fear of a Russian occupation were demoralizing the nation. This state of affairs was aggravated by the country's bad finances. Bulgaria found it almost impossible to obtain credit from abroad, chiefly as a result of pressure by Russia and France on the international money market. The Regency was obliged to increase taxes and bankruptcies were becoming frequent.

Russia tried to exploit the uneasy stagnation in Bulgaria. At the beginning of March 1887, the military garrisons in Silistra and Rustchuk, two of the main Bulgarian towns on the Danube, rose against the Regency. The mutinies had been organized by Russia's Ambassador in Bucharest, Mikhail Hitrovo, with the help of former Bulgarian officers who had been involved in the kidnapping of Prince Alexander of Battenberg and had fled from the country after Stefan Stamboloff's counter-*coup*. As *émigrés* in St Petersburg, Odessa, Bucharest and Constantinople, they had lived on money supplied by the Russians.

Mikhail Hitrovo, their paymaster, was a prototype of many Soviet diplomats of today. An Ambassador by name only, he was using his position to organize subversion in Bulgaria and to promote the fall of the Regency. His plan, approved by the Tsar, was to set up a government in Sofia composed of Russophils and a Russian Minister of War. By nature a conspirator, a libertine who fancied himself as a poet of sorts, he might easily have been a typical Russian revolutionary of the Bakunin or Nechayeff sort. But chance, or his insatiable financial needs, made him deploy his talents as a conspiratorial revolutionary in the service of Tsar Alexander III, Europe's supreme autocrat.

His preparations for the military uprisings in Bulgaria were characterized by contempt for the Bulgarian Regents, an easy arrogance (so that he hardly bothered to keep his plans secret) and large helpings for himself and the *émigré* Bulgarians from the fund of one million roubles which the Russian Foreign Office had provided for subversion in Bulgaria.

The nature of Hitrovo's activities in Bucharest was so evident that Austria's Military Attaché reported to Vienna in tones of shocked indignation that the Russian Ambassador had organized the uprisings with 'almost shameless' lack of secrecy. He had not undertaken 'even the most elementary security precautions' and had allowed 'uncyphered telegrams of the most compromising kind, messages, money orders and requests for payment to move openly on the Romanian telegraph service'.[2] The Bulgarian *émigrés* were at the same time sending letters to correspondents in Bulgaria. Those from one of the officers who had kidnapped Prince Alexander spoke with gloomy bombast of the 'terrible bloody drama' to take place soon in Bulgaria and of the 'torrents of innocent Bulgarian blood' which would flow.

Stefan Stamboloff and the other Regents were in any case well aware that a Russian-backed *coup* was being prepared. The Russians were still working under the influence of the 'Kaulbars myth' and expected the population of the Principality to rise as one against their government and declare for Russia. All that was needed was a local uprising, as a signal for a general revolution. That did not worry Stamboloff, who was well aware of his countrymen's feelings about Russia after all that had passed. He was also sure of the loyalty of the majority of military garrisons. But he was afraid that should the uprisings in the two towns on the Danube lead to any kind of situation which could be made to look like a civil war, then Russia would almost certainly have an excuse to intervene. And that would mean the end of the Principality.

The military uprisings were easily put down due to advance knowledge of the plot and the loyalty of the local population and of the troops. Stamboloff dealt harshly with the nine ringleaders, most of whom were officers. They were court-martialled and sentenced to death by a firing-squad. The sentences were carried out despite a Russian claim that six of the sentenced men were of Russian nationality.

On hearing of the executions Tsar Alexander, already upset by the failure of the mutinies, nearly ordered the invasion of Bulgaria. He offered thirty million francs from his private purse towards the costs of the operation when his ministers told him of Russia's financial difficulties. It was Giers who finally managed to calm down the Tsar.

The successful quelling of the mutinies was greeted in the majority of European countries as yet another Russian fiasco. But the Russian Press and some of the leading French newspapers acting under Russian influence, denounced the suppression of the mutinies and the execution of the ringleaders as 'the new Bulgarian atrocities' and depicted Stamboloff and the other Regents as bloodthirsty tyrants.

Despite the defeat of the Russian-inspired attempt to overthrow the Regency, Stamboloff was convinced that the general mood of the country was reaching a critical stage and that the only way out of the demoralizing uncertainty of the present lay in finding a new prince. A new and disturbing development had taken place in the early months of 1887 as a result of the prevailing mood of national frustration. All over Bulgaria there had arisen 'patriotic unions' which agitated for the return of Alexander of Battenberg. The Prince who had brought victory to Bulgaria against the Serbs was seen as the saviour who would lead the country out of its difficulties.

It was a tricky situation. Stamboloff knew that Alexander of Battenberg's return was probably impossible, certainly politically hopeless at that time, and likely to plunge the country into even greater danger and difficulty in view of Russia's attitude. On the other hand, he did not openly dare to set himself against the popular demand for the return of the former Prince. The trouble was that Prince Alexander's written refusals to appeal for his return had not, so far, been couched in sufficiently categorical terms to discourage his supporters. In fact, Prince Alexander was still equivocating and trying to gain time in the hope of future developments which might make his return possible.

At the end of March 1887, Konstantin Stoiloff, the Bulgarian Minister of Justice and a member of the three-man delegation which had been approached by Prince Ferdinand in Vienna the previous winter, was sent out of Bulgaria by Stamboloff. Stoiloff had a two-fold confidential mission: to try to get Alexander of Battenberg to renounce, without ambiguity, any intention of returning to Bulgaria, and to resume contact with Prince Ferdinand, from whom nothing had been heard for a long time. Stoiloff saw Ferdinand in Vienna and asked him point blank whether or not he was prepared to be elected Prince of Bulgaria by the Grand Sobranie. This amounted to an ultimatum.

Ferdinand's perplexity was growing every day. While the prospect of becoming a sovereign ruler tempted him as strongly as ever, if not more so now that it was within his grasp, the dangers that would certainly threaten him if he went to Bulgaria became increasingly real to him. The military uprisings in Bulgaria had greatly disturbed him. From the outside, Bulgaria seemed full of danger and turmoil. In April, the house of a pro-Battenberg officer in Sofia was dynamited with an 'infernal machine' by Russophil plotters.

On receiving Stoiloff's ultimatum, Ferdinand wrote to his uncle Duke Ernest II, the head of the Coburg family, asking him to get in touch with Bismarck and to find out from him whether, in view of the 'dangers at present', he considered that Ferdinand should accept the Bulgarian offer and whether the Tsar would accept Ferdinand as Prince of Bulgaria. The Prince was already aware that the Tsar did not want him in Bulgaria. But he was hoping that somehow Bismarck might influence Russia in his favour. Ferdinand must have known that this was wishful thinking on his part.

Meanwhile, the negotiations between the Prince and Konstantin Stoiloff broke down. The Bulgarian envoy had again forcefully pointed out to Ferdinand that Bulgaria needed a prince immediately, one who would be prepared to go to Bulgaria even against Russian wishes. Stoiloff repeated that there was no lack of candidates who would go to Bulgaria with Russia's blessing. Prince Ferdinand argued that the Bulgarians should wait until he had managed to get the approval of Russia and the other Powers by patient and persistent diplomacy. The Bulgarian insisted that there was no time for this: the situation in Bulgaria was critical and the need to fill the throne was urgent.

Negotiations only resumed as a result of the intervention of the Archduke Johann Salvator. Prince Ferdinand agreed to see Stoiloff again on condition that the Bulgarian Regency should officially request his candidature for the throne of Bulgaria. Accordingly, on 28 April 1887, the Bulgarian Regents sent the Prince a telegram in which they formally offered him the Crown of Bulgaria. All that was now needed was for Ferdinand to accept and for Bulgaria's Grand Sobranie to vote on his election.

And yet, only a few days after the offer from the Regents, Prince Ferdinand informed a thunderstruck Stoiloff that he had decided to withdraw his candidature. Of all unlikely reasons for turning down something he himself had so clearly desired right from the beginning, the Prince pleaded illness. The Bulgarians could not then know that Ferdinand's *volte-face* was due to his having received Bismarck's answer from his Uncle Ernest. The German Chancellor had written to the Duke of Coburg:

When the question of the Prince of Coburg's candidature for the

Bulgarian throne first arose in December last year, the Vienna cabinet adopted a discouraging attitude and the Russian government one of harsh disapproval and hostility. There is neither any indication nor any likelihood that the views of these two major powers, which are most directly concerned in the Bulgarian question, have changed since then. I know of no reason why this should have happened.

In these circumstances I would advise you not to consent to an acceptance by Prince Ferdinand of the offered candidature. This undertaking, begun against the advice of Austria and against the will of Russia would, in my opinion, have no prospects. I fear that it would only further complicate the Bulgarian tangle and would give our enemies in Russia new means of exerting an anti-German influence on Tsar Alexander.'[3]

Bismarck was so determined that his role in the Bulgarian Crisis should not be misunderstood by Russia, that before sending the letter, he showed it to the Russian Ambassador to Germany, Count Shuvaloff.

Bismarck's resounding 'no' shattered Ferdinand, and for several weeks reduced him to something like nervous prostration. His tendency towards neurasthenia had increased as a result of the acute state of indecision in which he had lived for months, wavering between his intelligent awareness of the dangers of the Bulgarian venture and his ambition, spurred by vanity and romanticism, for the throne.

His anxiety was aggravated by an attack, of all things, of German measles. It took four weeks before Ferdinand found it possible to write a reply to Duke Ernest. The Prince wrote: 'I am not at all well and the Bulgarian worries have done much to harm my convalescence.'[4]

Prince Ferdinand's dilemma was to become much more acute later that summer.

CHAPTER 8

The Hesitant Suitor

—◦❦◦—

In Bulgaria, tension rose further in the early summer of 1887. Widespread agitation for the return of Alexander of Battenberg and demands for the convening of the often-postponed session of the Grand Sobranie convinced Stamboloff that the provisional rule of the Regency could not continue much longer. It had become imperative to find a prince. Yet there was not a single acceptable candidate on the horizon. Now even Prince Ferdinand, who had put himself forward the previous winter, had withdrawn his candidature. Nevertheless, Stamboloff could see that Prince Ferdinand coveted the throne, despite his fears and hesitations.

Stefan Stamboloff realized that his only hope lay in overcoming the Prince's hesitations and presenting him with a *fait accompli*. The Government decided to summon the Grand Sobranie on 3 July in Tirnovo, the medieval capital of the Bulgarian Tsars, and to elect Ferdinand of Saxe-Coburg-Gotha as Prince of Bulgaria. The signatory powers of the Treaty of Berlin were alarmed and protested against the proposed meeting on the grounds that they had not yet unanimously approved the person to be put forward as candidate for the throne. The Bulgarian Government answered untruthfully that the Grand Sobranie had been summoned due to the internal situation in Bulgaria and that no election would take place. Not only Prince Ferdinand, but the whole of Europe, were to be presented with the *fait accompli*.

In order to ensure a trouble-free, unanimous election of Prince Ferdinand by the Grand Sobranie it was essential to confront the assembly with a quite unequivocal and final refusal to return to Bulgaria from Prince Alexander of Battenberg. The former Prince's supporters had to give up their lingering illusory hopes that Prince Alexander's return was still a possibility.

Four days before the Grand Sobranie opened, the Bulgarian Government at last obtained from Prince Alexander a refusal whose wording could leave no doubts in the minds of even the most optimistic of the ex-

Prince's supporters. Alexander wrote: 'It would be pointless for me to accept the election, as I have no intention of going to Bulgaria. Therefore, as the present state of affairs cannot continue any longer, the best course of action for the Bulgarian people would be to elect a prince who is prepared to go to Bulgaria.'[1]

The attention of Europe was focused on Tirnovo. The four-hundred-odd delegates of the Grand Sobranie met in a hall which, when the assembly was not in session, was frequently used for shows by touring magicians and other performers and which one English traveller described as resembling 'the public hall of some small English provincial town'.[2] At a secret session, the Regent Stefan Stamboloff read out Prince Alexander's final refusal and in a powerful, effective speech spoke of the need for a prince and of Prince Ferdinand's hankering for the throne of Bulgaria. The following day, the President of the Grand Sobranie proposed Ferdinand's name for election. The deputies rose from their seats and cheered loud and long. Prince Ferdinand was unanimously proclaimed ruling Prince of Bulgaria on 7 July 1887. The deputies scrambled over their benches to look at a photograph of Ferdinand which Stoiloff had brought from Austria.

At that moment Ferdinand was with his mother at her palace of Ebenthal near Vienna. When he was brought the telegram announcing his election, he was out-of-doors, butterfly net in hand. The telegram struck a high, ceremonious note which resounded in Ferdinand's imagination:

> The members of the Grand National Sobranie, with absolute faith in your competence and in the benevolent interests shown by you to the Bulgarian cause, have today, in the public session of the Sobranie, warmly and unanimously acclaimed you as their elected Prince. In sending you on this occasion my respectful congratulations, I express the warm hope of the members of the Sobranie and of the entire Bulgarian people that you will arrive as soon as possible in our midst, to take up the government of the nation which thanks you for devoting your noble and precious life to the progress, liberty and greatness of Bulgaria.[3]

The telegram was signed by Toncheff, the President of the Sobranie. Ferdinand did not hide his elation. Count Kálnoky wrote to the Emperor Francis Joseph that 'Prince Ferdinand seemed quite delighted by his election'. Prince Reuss, the German Ambassador in Vienna, reported to Bismarck that Ferdinand had called on him: 'I let the Prince speak and saw that he is incredibly keen to become Prince of Bulgaria. This is the more inexplicable the more he sees the difficulties which face him.'[4]

The following weeks were a period of great anxiety. The Prince's appetite for the throne had grown in intensity after the election, as had his fears. His hesitancy was reflected in his telegram to the Grand Sobranie, in which he thanked it for his election:

> I am ready to bear witness for my gratitude to the Bulgarian nation; in devoting my life to it, I shall rely on your zeal, your capability and on your devotion to help me achieve its prosperity: from the moment my election has been approved by the Sublime Porte and recognized by the Powers I shall respond to the call of the Bulgarian nation by coming into its midst.[5]

The Prince's reply was seen as weak-willed, not only in Bulgaria, but in all Europe. It amounted to an acceptance – yet it was still conditional. And the condition was Russia's approval of Ferdinand's election, which would allow the other European powers to recognize him as Bulgaria's ruler. Ferdinand had no reason to believe that Russia would change her mind. In that case, the Bulgarians asked, why was he accepting the throne on the one condition he knew would not be fulfilled at the time? Yet it was clear to Stamboloff that Prince Ferdinand was hooked – it was up to him to land him. Even the language and tone of Ferdinand's message of thanks to the Bulgarian nation was that of a ruler addressing his subjects and showed that he already saw himself on the Bulgarian throne.

Immediately after his election, the Prince went into action to try to obtain the support of the European Powers. He met with little success. Count Kálnoky advised the Austrian Emperor not to grant the Prince the audience which he had requested the day after his election. A meeting between the Prince and the Emperor, said Kálnoky, 'would give rise to misleading interpretations'.[6] Ferdinand then called on the German Ambassador in Vienna to complain 'that he found it painful that the Imperial government [of Germany] had shown him so little sympathy'.[7]

Bismarck scrawled his marginal comment on this phrase from his Ambassador's report: 'Why should it? What do we care about Bulgaria? The Prince and the Bulgarians do not matter to Germany; it is Russia that matters.'[8]

Much of what puzzled the Bulgarians and other diplomats in Prince Ferdinand's attitude was to be explained by his diminishing, but still existing, belief that he personally was well regarded by the Tsar. His delusions in this respect might have been dispelled had he seen the Tsar's written comment on his Foreign Minister Giers's letter announcing the election by the Grand Sobranie: 'What a disgusting business!' Giers told the German Ambassador in St Petersburg that the election of Ferdinand was 'a slap in Russia's face'.[9] Ferdinand, however, sent a telegram to the Tsar in which he tried to obtain Russia's recognition of the election. He received the same answer as before: though there were no objections to his person, Russia did not recognize the legality of the Bulgarian Regency and Sobranie. Ferdinand tried to keep his latest approach to the Tsar a secret from the Bulgarians. But when they learned of it, they resented the fact that he apparently still had not understood that he had to choose between Russia's goodwill and the Bulgarian throne.

At Windsor, Queen Victoria was very annoyed by the election of Ferdinand. She was still determined that 'dear Sandro' should return. On learning of the election from the newspapers, she sent Lord Salisbury this telegram: 'Trust it will be made clear that we have no hand in Prince Ferdinand C.'s election. The Standard says Prince Alexander's refusal is forever. That is quite false. His refusal is till Europe will support him, and till he would be independent.'[10]

Ferdinand's election brought renewed fears of a European war. Count Kálnoky told one of his ambassadors that a Russian military action against Bulgaria would be tantamount to a European war. As the complexities of the great Bulgarian crisis increased there arose the unvoiced hope of a war which would at least clarify the situation in Europe. Austria's mistrust of Russia was sufficiently strong for there to be a military lobby which advocated the launching of a 'preventive war' against Russia, an idea with which even the Emperor Francis Joseph sympathized, so as to forestall the expected Russian attack.

The situation was so tense that none of the Powers actually took any action following the election: they merely observed each other, each waiting for one of the others to take the initiative. Bismarck remarked: 'The Eastern Question is a game of patience. He who has most time, carries the day!'

The position of the major European Powers on the Bulgarian Question was threatening, yet intractable. Russia was not prepared to accept at any price Ferdinand's election as Prince of Bulgaria. Germany, and that meant Bismarck, was all for keeping Russia happy. In the so-called secret Reinsurance Treaty which Russia and Germany signed a month before Ferdinand's election, Bismarck pledged that Germany would recognize Russia's historically acquired rights in the Balkan peninsula and especially the legitimacy of her preponderant and decisive influence in Bulgaria and Eastern Rumelia. It was in a special secret protocol to that Treaty that Bismarck promised never to consent to Prince Alexander of Battenberg's restoration. Turkey, formally Bulgaria's suzerain power, was too weak for action of any sort. On the one hand the Sultan could do nothing to help Bulgaria, for fear of

Russia; on the other, he could not act against Bulgaria for fear of Britain
and Austria. Austria, despite the fact that she had not backed Prince
Ferdinand's candidature, was privately not displeased at seeing a
possible increase of her influence in the Balkans with him on the
Bulgarian throne. But publicly Austria had to appear to share the views
of her ally Germany and to avoid any appearance of supporting the
Prince.

The situation was particularly unsuited for a person of Ferdinand's
political temperament. Russia's rigid position made it impossible for
him to bring into play his own peculiar talents for diplomacy, finesse
and intrigue. The political situation was not merely intractable, it was
also potentially dangerous. However, it was not so much a general war
that Ferdinand feared as a result of his going to Bulgaria, but the danger
to himself from future Russian-organized subversion. There had, after
all, been attempts to assassinate Prince Alexander of Battenberg. The
news from Bulgaria spoke of 'infernal machines', mutinies and executions. Every time his indecision veered to a particularly pessimistic
mood, his intelligence told him that it was mad to exchange his
agreeable mode of life for one of certain personal danger.

Nevertheless, Bulgaria's Regent, Stamboloff, was more determined
than ever to get the Prince to Bulgaria. On 15 July 1887, a large
deputation of the Sobranie, headed by President Toncheff, arrived at
Ebenthal to present Prince Ferdinand with the official act of election
and to ask him to leave for Bulgaria without delay. Stamboloff had read
the Prince's character shrewdly. Ferdinand immediately responded to
the ceremonial aspect of the occasion, to the idea, which he easily
romanticized and which flattered his vanity, of the envoys of a 'distant'
land travelling to *him* to offer him a crown. The Prince and his mother
stage-managed the occasion as the Prince's first State ceremony. The
Bulgarian delegates' train was met at the railway station by a file of
open ducal coaches, their lanterns topped with small golden crowns and
the coachmen wearing their parade livery of black coats and gold
frogging.

On arriving at the palace, the delegates were led into a carefully
posed scene. Princess Clémentine was seated at an antique writing table,
with one of her ladies-in-waiting. Beside her stood the Prince in
evening dress, decorated with the Coburg star. President Toncheff read
out, in French, the text of the Grand Sobranie's resolution.

Prince Ferdinand replied in a speech full of festive solemnity and fine,
orotund phrases. But the Bulgarians present instantly realized that the
fine words amounted to only one thing; Ferdinand was again refusing to
come without Russia's recognition of his election: 'If I were free to
follow the impulse of my heart, I should hasten to go amongst you, to

place myself at the head of the Bulgarian nation and take in hand the reins of government.'[11] At this first 'if' the Bulgarians looked at one another. The Prince went on:

> But the Prince-Elect of Bulgaria must respect treaties. This respect will form the strength of his rule and will assure the greatness and prosperity of the Bulgarian nation. I hope we shall succeed in justifying the confidence of the Sublime Porte, and reconquering, after some lapse of time, the goodwill of Russia, to whom Bulgaria is indebted for her political emancipation, and to whom she consequently owes a debt of gratitude. I hope also that we may be able to obtain the approval of all the other Great Powers. Trust in me, and believe in my devotion to your country, of which I hope to provide the proof when I consider the fitting moment to have arrived.[11]

After this, Ferdinand's final words only irritated the delegates, some of them grizzled veterans of the Bulgarian fight for independence. They listened to the twenty-six year-old Prince, as he solemnly urged them in French: 'Show courage, prudence and patriotic unity! May God bless Bulgaria and send her a brilliant future!' Their most enthusiastic comment about Prince Ferdinand after that meeting was '*Il est très diplomate*'. A disappointed Major Popoff, one of the delegates, told a group of Bulgarian officers after his return: 'The Prince of Coburg may well be a very charming, distinguished gentleman, but he would be no good as Prince of Bulgaria, he has no right understanding of Bulgaria's position and in any case he isn't a real soldier. He will probably not come and that would be best.'[12]

The Bulgarians were also riled by Ferdinand's reference to Russia, clearly intended for the Tsar's eyes. To them it seemed a servile and pointless gesture and, worse, suggested that the Prince still had not understood that Russia's opposition was absolutely insuperable. If he did not know that Russia would not change her mind, the Bulgarians argued, then he ought to have known. Very simply, he ought either to have refused the Bulgarian offer of the throne, or, having accepted it, to have proceeded forthwith to Tirnovo to be sworn in as Prince of Bulgaria. Right up to the end, Ferdinand tried to get round the stark choice that faced him. One of his more convoluted efforts consisted in suggesting to the British and German ambassadors in Vienna that they should induce the Sultan of Turkey to send him to Bulgaria as Regent. There he would dissolve the Sobranie, which the Russians regarded as illegal, reconvene a newly-elected Sobranie acceptable to Russia and get himself re-elected as Prince of Bulgaria!

Prince Ferdinand's refusal to come to Bulgaria deeply disappointed

Stamboloff. Knowing of the Prince's ambitions for the throne, he had felt that the *fait accompli* of the election would have tipped the scales. When asked by the correspondent of the London *Times* about the disappointment that his speech had caused in Bulgaria, the Prince replied: 'I am quite prepared to hear that my answer to the deputation has caused dissatisfaction in Bulgaria; but this dissatisfaction will have arisen because strange hopes were raised without any warrant from me. From the first I told M. Stoiloff and others that I would not pose as a revolutionary pretender.' Ferdinand then told *The Times* about his 'absolute respect for treaties'.[13] He stressed the fib he was to repeat throughout his life: 'I did not seek the Bulgarian crown; it was offered me with the assurance that I could do much good in the country. The mission was a noble one which tempted me, and I accepted it, promising to devote my life to its fulfilment; but this was on the clearly expressed condition that I should go to Bulgaria invested with authority which could not be challenged.' The Prince ended the interview with what amounted to a promise to Europe: 'What Europe may take for certain is that I shall not let myself be enticed into any course which would widen the estrangement between Russia and Bulgaria and add to the confusion of parties in the latter country.' Three weeks later Ferdinand went to Bulgaria.

The failure of the Bulgarian deputation had not discouraged Stamboloff. He instinctively felt that Prince Ferdinand's hesitations were genuine and that what was needed was the right push, at the right moment, to force a decision. The internal situation in the country was still critical and Prince Ferdinand's vacillations only made it worse. Stamboloff decided to have one more go. He instructed Nachovich, the Bulgarian Foreign Minister, to travel to Austria on a confidential mission to the Prince. Nachovich's instructions were categoric, either to bring back Prince Ferdinand, or a renouncement, in writing, of the throne. He was to tell the Prince that Bulgaria could not wait. If Ferdinand could not or would not take the Crown as offered, Bulgaria must look for somebody else who would. With true insight into the Ferdinand's mentality, Stamboloff told Nachovich to present him with a new Bulgarian general's full dress uniform, complete with white fur cap, surmounted by a white plume, a foot high.

Stamboloff had judged rightly. In his talks with Prince Ferdinand, Nachovich spoke bluntly, alternating threats with persuasion. The Prince realized that the moment to choose had come. There would probably never arise another chance of obtaining a throne in Europe. Princess Clémentine, who was by his side, was all for daring. She had never forgotten that her father had lost the throne of France in 1848 through what she considered was lack of nerve. 'Fortune Favours the

Brave', she repeatedly told her son, as she pointed out to him that taking the risk without delay was the surest way of winning immediate and genuine popularity with the Bulgarian nation.

By this time Prince Ferdinand was the laughing-stock of Europe. Daily there were reports that he had left for Bulgaria – only to be followed by sarcastic denials. When, with great inner misgivings, he at last decided to risk the adventure, the flight before ridicule was one of the major factors which helped him to make up his mind.

Ferdinand and his mother prepared for his journey to Bulgaria in haste and secrecy. Inevitably, there were leaks in the newspapers which added zest to the 'will-he-won't-he?' speculation in the European Press. One newspaper reported that a stationery shop in Vienna had visiting cards printed for the Prince's coachman saying, 'Revitsky, coachman to H.R.H. Prince Ferdinand of Bulgaria'. A china shop was reported to have received an order for a dinner service, all the pieces to bear the monogram 'F' with a crown. Another rumour said that a Viennese tailor was making a Bulgarian uniform for Ferdinand – with the resulting vain search by reporters for that tailor.

At the same time, with less publicity, Princess Clémentine was busy assembling a court for her son. With the help of her nephew, the Comte de Paris, she secured the services of two French Orléanist noblemen, Comte de Grenaud and Comte de Bourboulon. The Prince had already engaged the services of a young Bulgarian student in Vienna, Dimitri Stancioff, who acted as his Political Secretary and began to teach him Bulgarian. Ferdinand, with his gift for languages, was making considerable progress in learning the language, though he was never to lose his strong foreign accent. Others who were to go to Bulgaria with the Prince were his former tutor, Dr Fleischmann, now his private adviser, and Dr Neisser, his personal physician. As his Press attaché, and his 'adviser on court matters', the Prince decided to take with him the same Major von der Laaba who had approached the Bulgarian delegates at the Vienna Opera on the Prince's behalf the previous winter.

While Prince Ferdinand and his mother were busy preparing for his departure, Russia's Foreign Minister Giers wrote to his ambassador in Berlin that Russia was counting on Germany's support and cooperation in case of a 'precipitate action by the Prince of Coburg'.[14] The Prince would 'risk grave difficulties if he were to occupy the throne of Bulgaria' and, added Giers, 'we could never accept Ferdinand of Bulgaria'. The letter was shown to the German Foreign Office by the Russian Ambassador. Bismarck wrote: 'I have never doubted that a Catholic, a Hungarian and a Coburg would each by itself be unacceptable to Russia, let alone Prince Ferdinand who carries the three Russian Cerberus heads on his shoulder.'[15]

CHAPTER 9

A Secret Journey

On 9 August 1887, Ferdinand left Austria for Bulgaria. On the same day it was announced that Ferdinand's resignation of his commission in the Austro-Hungarian army had been accepted. For the Emperor Francis Joseph had insisted that the Prince should sever his official connections with Austria-Hungary before going to Bulgaria, to avoid giving the impression that his 'Bulgarian adventure' was in any way supported by Vienna.

Ferdinand had intended to keep his depature a secret. He had reasons to fear the Austrian authorities as well as agents from Russia. Austria might well have decided that by arresting the Prince, or preventing his departure to Bulgaria by some other means, she would give Europe both proof and alibi that Vienna was not responsible for the actions of Ferdinand and the Bulgarian Regents.

At four o'clock on the morning of 9 August, before sunrise, Prince Ferdinand had attended a special Mass at Ebenthal and immediately afterwards, wrapped in a long yellow travelling coat and wearing a brown felt hat, boarded the second-class carriage of the *Orientexpresszug* from Marchegg to Orsova, the last port on the Hungarian side of the Danube. The relief of the clandestine dawn departure after eight months of indecision must have elated him as the train steamed southeast through the farmlands of Hungary and the opulent fertility of the Banat. However beneath his elation Ferdinand's natural pessimism nagged on. He became convinced that his departure was being observed by Austrian police agents (and, for all he knew, by agents from Russia and Germany) and grew increasingly anxious that a sudden arrest by the Austrian police might nip his great adventure before it had really begun. Fear of arrest eventually drove the Prince to lock himself in the swaying W.C. for much of the long, hot journey.

On the day of his departure Princess Clémentine forwarded a note from Ferdinand addressed to the ambassadors of the major European

Powers in Vienna, in which he gave his reasons for going to Bulgaria:
'The task which I have set myself is noble and lofty, even holy, because I
want to devote all my future life to the cause of a noble nation; ·the
Almighty will sustain me so that I should not stumble on the road but
walk with firm steps towards my goal.'[1] He asked the Powers for their
recognition which he would await in Bulgaria.

In London, *Punch* published its own version of Ferdinand's note,
entitled 'Why he Went':

Having discovered on inquiry that the palace required repapering
and was sadly out of repair, with both gas and water rates seven
quarters in arrear, while it appeared that both the throne and crown
would have to be hired and possibly only a lame omnibus horse
available for our use at the coronation procession, and taking in
regard the fact that no guarantee was forthcoming that our allowance
from the Civil List would touch anything like £150 a-year, we at first
reluctantly decided, spite its undeniably flattering nature, to
decline the offer so spontaneously made to us. And we conveyed as
much to the delegates who received the news crestfallen, and were
about to depart in sulky silence when a telegram arrived from Sofia of
such an encouraging and startling description, that it seemed, to us at
least, to put the question in an entirely fresh and original light, and in
one that we felt might make us waver in our determination.

It simply announced the fact that the government, never doubting
of our acceptance of the crown, had already taken the bull by the
horn, and ordered *at a local Ready-Made Clothing Establishment a complete
brand-new Uniform* for us to wear the moment we set our foot on
Bulgarian soil. 'Buttons and all?' we asked. 'Buttons and all!' was the
reply. This gracious and patriotic and quite unexpected act profoundly touched us. Indeed, it decided us; and when it was further
intimated to us that *the bill would not be sent into us* but go to increase the
deficit in the forthcoming Budget, we did not hesitate, but accepted
the full responsibilities of the situation, and informed the Deputation
that, spite the hostile attitude of Europe, we would go to Sofia, and at
least 'try it on'.[2]

Ferdinand arrived at Orsova the following day. Waiting for him
there were Nachovich, the Bulgarian Foreign Minister, Stancioff and
Major von der Laaba.

They had left Vienna two days before the Prince. Other members of
his entourage had also gone to Orsova on different trains with the
luggage, but the secret had got out. While the advance party in Orsova
was preparing for the embarkation of the Prince and his companions on

the steamer *Orient*, chartered by the Bulgarian Government (the same ship on which the Prince, as a boy, had gone on a cruise to Constantinople with his father), Major von der Laaba turned up and reported that he had heard that the Danube had been heavily mined by the Russians. Soon other alarming reports reached the party, the mildest of which was that torpedo boats were waiting in a hidden bay along the Danube ready to seize the Prince. Laaba urged Ferdinand to postpone his departure. But now the Prince was all for daring. Moreover, the captain of the *Orient* assured Stancioff that no mines had been laid in the Danube.

Ferdinand and his entourage spent the night in their cabins, as the steamer was to leave Orsova at 4.30 the following morning. Whether he slept well or not, is not known. But he certainly would not have had a good night's sleep – and indeed might have gone back there and then to the rural joys of Ebenthal, heedless of ridicule – if he had been able to read the cyphered telegram the authorities in St Petersburg had just sent to Mikhail Hitrovo, Russia's ambassador in Bucharest and the Tsar's arch-plotter against Bulgaria:

> The Imperial Government has decided to consider Prince Coburg as an usurper who stands outside all the laws. Accordingly, all actions directed personally against Coburg so as to bring about his removal from Bulgaria cannot be considered punishable or subject to jurisdiction. While informing you of the above decision of the Imperial Government, I beg you to give your support to trustworthy persons who are prepared to take an active part in the removal of Prince Coburg from Bulgaria.[3]

As J.D. Bourchier, the correspondent of *The Times* in the Balkans wrote later about Ferdinand's arrival: 'He had embarked upon what seemed an almost hopeless adventure; he was confronted with the hostility of a power which knew no scruple in the prosecution of its designs.'[4]

The *Orient* left Orsova as planned and, after navigating the Iron Gates, passed the first Bulgarian village on the steep right bank of the Danube. The villagers, mainly fishermen, stood shouting their greetings and the steamer raised the Bulgarian tricolour of white, green and red. Ferdinand stood on the narrow deck wearing for the first time in public his Bulgarian uniform, its tall white plume bent back by the steamer's progress. He was also wearing the red ribbon of the Bulgarian Order of St Alexander which Alexander of Battenberg had given to him at the coronation of the Tsar Alexander III four years earlier.

It was an exceptionally hot day. Just after noon the *Orient* was met by the Bulgarian yacht carrying Stefan Stamboloff and his two co-Regents, the Prime Minister Stoiloff and members of his Cabinet. It was the same yacht on which Sandro had been taken to Russia. Stamboloff exulted as Ferdinand received them on board the *Orient*. Shaking hands with the Prince, he knew that he had at last landed his fish – appropriately enough, on the Danube. And what a fish: six-foot-tall Ferdinand, with his hat, plus feather, loomed some two feet above the intense Bulgarian patriot, the stocky son of a Tirnovo inn-keeper, with his thick, black eyebrows and domed, powerful forehead. Stamboloff later told an English journalist friend: 'No words can picture my delight at the arrival of the Prince. It had been a perpetual nightmare and terror to me that Bulgaria might lose her independence under my Regency, and that my name would be handed down to posterity as a reproach.'⁵ He added that after Ferdinand had been sworn in as Prince of Bulgaria, he 'spent three days with my friends celebrating deliverance. They were three of the happiest days of my life.'

The contrast between the two young men (Stamboloff was thirty-two at the time, and Ferdinand's senior by only six years) was striking in all respects. The ambitious, intelligent dandy with the beautiful hands, the affected decadence, and the nasal drawl, who loved Wagner and butterflies, and who would startle and upset more conventional people by remarks such as, 'If I ever feel tired or depressed I have only to look at a bunch of violets to become myself again,'⁶ must have appeared even less comprehensible to a man of Stamboloff's limited social experience.

As far as the Prince was concerned, the intense, smouldering man standing beside him was equally outside his experience of people. Stamboloff's elementary education at a Bulgarian school in his native Tirnovo had been a far cry from Ferdinand's botanical and historical studies in Austria. It had ended when he was fourteen and the school was closed by the Turks. His father, an inn-keeper, apprenticed him to a tailor, but Stamboloff left and managed to get a scholarship to the university in Odessa. At first he studied for the priesthood, but was almost inevitably drawn to join the Russian nihilists – well over half the students belonged to the movement. After a raid by the secret police they were rounded up, but Stamboloff as a Bulgarian and a Turkish subject, was given twenty-four hours to leave Russia. He went to Bucharest and made contact with the headquarters of the Bulgarian revolutionaries who were planning a national uprising against the Turks. The Central Committee of the Bulgarian Revolutionary Party in Bucharest sent him to Bulgaria where, disguised as a book peddler, he organized underground revolutionary committees. He managed an unsuccessful uprising at Stara Zagora, which was to coincide with an attempt to set fire to Constantinople by Bulgarian fifth columnists.

Stamboloff escaped to Bucharest while the Turks sentenced him to

death. Although his portrait and description were in the hands of every
Turkish post, he again crossed the Danube. It was February 1876 and the
ice-bound Danube was breaking up. He had to hop, swim and scramble
from ice-floe to ice-floe, as they drifted about a foot under the icy
water. Disguised as a Turkish gardener, Stamboloff, then aged twenty-
one, took part in the 1876 uprisings against the Turks which resulted in
the 'Bulgarian Atrocities'. Later he served with the Bulgarian irregulars
in the Russo-Turkish war and after the liberation became president of
the Sobranie. It was largely due to his energy – and brusqueness – that
the 1885 union between north and south Bulgaria came about. As Prince
Alexander of Battenberg was hesitating whether to recognize the
union, Stamboloff said to him: 'The union is made – two roads lie before
Your Highness – the one to Philippopolis and as much farther as God
may lead; the other to the Danube and Darmstadt. I advise you to take
the crown the Bulgarian nation offers you.'[7]

Prince Ferdinand was to find out before very long that there was not
an atom of the courtier in Stamboloff. Not only was he flint hard but
also capable of the most grinding sarcasm, irrespective of whom he was
addressing. Almost single-handed he had braved the fury and might of
the Tsar of Russia, and by a combination of courage, pig-headedness and
shrewdness, defeated Russia's plots, suppressed the mutinies, and now,
despite the anathemas from St Petersburg, had brought a new ruler to
Bulgaria.

His successful stand against Russia had already brought him admiration and fame in Europe. As Ferdinand's Prime Minister, his continued
defiance of Russia's powerful and insidious efforts to engulf Bulgaria
led one American publicist to describe him in 1914 as 'one of the half
dozen greatest European statesmen of the last half of the nineteenth
century'.[8] The *Cambridge Modern History* was to say of him in 1910 that as
Ferinand's

> great Minister ... Stefan Stamboloff defied Russia and won the
> admiration of Great Britain as 'the Bulgarian Bismarck'. Alike in his
> methods and in his fall, the son of the Tirnovo inn-keeper resembled
> the German Chancellor. During his long tenure of the premiership,
> he was absolute master of Bulgaria; for the Prince was at first much in
> the position of our George I, ignorant of the language and the customs
> of his subjects, and Stamboloff was for some years indispensable to
> him.[9]

The venomous conflict that was to develop between Prince Ferdinand
and Stamboloff lay in the future. Right now, as the steamer chugged
heavily downstream past the Bulgarian shore of the Danube all was

cordiality on board. The grandson of the King of France and the inn-keeper's son had each got what he wanted. If Stamboloff very soon realized from even the little that he had seen of Ferdinand that they would not get on well together, it did not matter overmuch: Bulgaria needed a Prince as a condition of her survival. Ferdinand, the new-comer, was to realize very quickly that whatever his personal feelings about Stamboloff, his guidance and help were, for the time being, vital.

The *Orient* visited the main Bulgarian ports on the Danube. At Vidin, Ferdinand first set foot on Bulgarian soil, reviewed the assembled troops, posed for his first official photograph in Bulgarian uniform and issued a manifesto to his new subjects. At successive ports, the Prince was greeted by local dignitaries and cheering crowds. It was a res-trained welcome: the Bulgarians are not a particularly expansive people and naturally could not see the newcomer as the embodiment of the Bulgarian nation. He was not ruler by divine right or dynastic succes-sion; the contract between the foreign Prince and his subjects was one dictated by personal ambition on his part and on theirs by political convenience. The lack of overwhelming enthusiasm did not mean that Prince Ferdinand was unwelcome. There was general rejoicing that the throne had been filled, and much curiosity about the new Prince.

Ferdinand left the steamer at Svishtov. There he made his official entry into Bulgaria and was received with a symbolic offering of bread and salt, flying flags, decorated streets and crowds carrying bunches of roses and marigolds. It was 13 August, normally a day on which the deeply superstitious Prince would avoid doing anything important; but he got round the difficulty by reckoning the day by the old-style Julian calendar, then still officially used in the Eastern Orthodox countries, which meant that he made his entry into his new country on the harmless 1 August.

From Svishtov, that same day, Ferdinand and his party travelled south in open carriages with a cavalry escort. Covered in fine, white dust kicked up by the horses on the baking road, they arrived in the evening at Tirnovo. Tirnovo, the capital of the medieval Bulgarian kingdom, was built on an amphitheatre of steep bluffs through which winds, in hairpin bends, the river Yantra. The following morning Prince Ferdin-and was to be sworn in as Prince of Bulgaria.

All those present at Ferdinand's investiture on the stage of the public hall in Tirnovo, where the Grand Sobranie held its meetings, were impressed by the young Prince's solemn and imposing bearing. After he had taken the oath, Stoiloff read out Prince Ferdinand's proclamation. When the text reached the outside world a few hours later, the cat was right amidst the European pigeons. Beginning with 'We, Ferdinand I, by the Grace of God and the Will of the Nation, Prince of Bulgaria', the proclamation spoke about 'mounting the throne of the glorious Bulgarian Tsars'. He thanked the Regents for their 'wise and successful conduct of affairs, whereby they were able to defend our country's independence and liberty in the most critical times.' The text ended with the words: 'Long live free and independent Bulgaria!'[10] When Stoiloff finished, Ferdinand sprang up and loudly and resonantly repeated the words in Bulgarian. The effect was electrifying and amidst cheering, Ferdinand was seized and carried shoulder-high to his carriage by the deputies.

Europe's politicians were angry and worried. What did the Prince mean by 'the Grace of God', 'mounting the throne of the Tsars' and, worst of all, by an 'independent Bulgaria'? Had Ferdinand's ostensibly secret, and correspondingly highly publicized, journey to Bulgaria been a comedy? Or did it in fact represent a flagrant breach of the Treaty of Berlin? Was it a 'unilateral declaration of independence,' headed by *Tsar* Ferdinand? Would it mean war in Europe?

In Vienna Count Kálnoky wrote to one of his ambassadors that 'it is extremely regrettable that the inexperienced and weak-willed Prince Ferdinand, in his proclamation at the swearing-in ceremony, has spoken in tones dictated by megalomania. It must cause offence in Constantinople by as much as it has helped Russia.'[11] If Kálnoky saw Ferdinand as weak-willed, it was because he only knew him as the drawing-room effeminate of Vienna, whose prolonged throes of indecision about the offered throne had made Europe laugh. But now, his die cast, Ferdinand was full of confidence and bravado. He could joke about the insecurity of his position: 'I am quite happy, I enjoy myself like the flea in the bear's ear, a place nobody dares to scratch.'[12]

Bismarck, who had already instructed Germany's diplomatic representative in Sofia not to recognize Ferdinand and to regard him 'purely and simply as a Hungarian officer travelling privately',[13] and to treat him as such, ordered that the flag on the German Consulate-General in Sofia be lowered, after he read of the Prince's proclamation. He also prepared to recall Germany's Consul-General. The German Chancellor was determined to keep the Tsar of Russia sweet.

Ferdinand quickly learned of the unfavourable European reaction to his proclamation and how it had been interpreted. Immediately he tried to explain that the Bulgarian word *nezavisima,* as used in the final phrase of his proclamation ('Long live free and independent Bulgaria!') did not mean 'independent in the context of the law of nations', but merely 'free in the exercise of its rights' or 'able, on it own, to conduct its affairs'.[14] This hair-splitting was unconvincing; the translation of the word *nezavisima* into any European language is 'not dependent'.

The swearing-in was followed by a festive tour of Bulgaria in open carriages which lasted several days and culminated in Ferdinand's arrival in Sofia. The journey took him across the Balkan range into the Valley of Roses, and then on to Philippopolis, the city founded by Philip of Macedon, the father of Alexander the Great. Ferdinand's enchantment with the natural beauties of his new country was matched by his discomfort. Flaming August sat inexorably on the open carriages as they shook and rattled from stone to pot-hole and the dust settled like fine flour on their occupants. Encased in his new uniform, the Prince drove through towns and villages, through cheering but mainly curious crowds, and under triumphal arches, at times improvised from the town gallows and wreathed in flowers. There were military parades, speeches and banquets. The last were the greatest trial for Ferdinand who, even at that time, had made a name for himself as a fine gourmet. After his arrival in Sofia, he wrote to Crown Prince Rudolf of Austria about the food in Bulgaria: it roused in him 'feelings of dread and horror'.

These were more or less private agonies. What really astonished those people who had known Ferdinand in Vienna and were now members of his suite, was the speed and ease with which he assumed the monarchical role. Count von Burian, Austria's astute diplomatic representative in Bulgaria, wrote in a despatch that all those who had carefully observed the Prince in the first few days since his arrival considered that he had

> vigorously seized the reins of government and has not allowed, even for one moment, that there should arise any doubt about his determination to occupy to the full the position which has been given to him by the will of the people and to invest his dignity with an unassailable authority.
>
> His attendants note with amazement how the timidity of the moment when the Prince stepped on Bulgarian soil has been disappearing hourly, and how the awareness that he is the ruler has penetrated him and given his appearance a dignified, if somewhat rough, firmness.[15]

Von Burian shrewdly compared Prince Ferdinand with his predecessor: 'Prince Ferdinand's character is in sharp contrast with that of Prince Alexander. While he was charmingly kind and affable, the new Prince surprised the Bulgarians with his proud reserve, his taciturnity, his sharp criticisms of all the arrangements during his journey and his insistence on the exact observance of a strict etiquette.'

Even before his arrival, Prince Ferdinand had decided that he had to impose upon his new subjects. He thought that Prince Alexander's easy ways were among the reasons for his downfall. In 1904, at Marienbad, Ferdinand told Sir Frederick Ponsonby, King Edward VII's equerry: 'When I ascended the throne of Bulgaria, I determined that if there was any killing to be done, I would be on the side of the killers and not of the killed.'[16]

Hyperbole came easily to the Prince. But it is certainly true that this twenty-six-year-old, whose life till then had provided no hint of such firmness and will-power, was able to overawe the battle-scarred veterans who now surrounded him. Much of what was effeminate in Ferdinand's character pertained to the tougher kind of woman.

The monarchical role came easily to Ferdinand, it suited him. The pride in his French royal ancestors which he had learned at his mother's knee blazed brightly in his consciousness of his Bourbon ancestry, and most of all, in his constant awareness of the genealogical and biological link which connected him to the Sun King, Louis XIV, the embodiment and apotheosis of the monarchic idea. His mother often said, with all the signs of maternal pride, that none of the living descendants of Louis XIV bore such a strong facial resemblance to the Great Monarch as Ferdinand. The elaborate court ceremonial, the fêtes and the elegance which Prince Ferdinand later instituted in peasant Bulgaria were not, as some contemporaries believed, based on the petty ceremonial of Germany princely courts. They were an expression of Prince Ferdinand's – and his mother's – feelings for the *Grand Siècle*.

Before Ferdinand made his entry into the capital, the rumour went round that he was planning to arrive in Sofia on 18 August, the day of the Emperor of Austria's birthday, when the offices of the European diplomatic representatives would be beflagged in honour of Francis Joseph. The Prince would then have easily been able to claim the honours on his own account and as a sign of his recognition by the European Powers. It was the first of the many stories about his craftiness which eventually were to earn him his alliterative, vulpine nickname.

In fact he entered Sofia four days after the Emperor's birthday. Just outside Sofia a cavalry escort awaited him. Ferdinand got out of his carriage and in a tumbledown roadside cottage changed into full dress Bulgarian cavalry uniform and mounted a carefully chosen, docile horse. At the head of a long procession of mounted staff officers and carriages carrying members of the government, he rode into his capital to the sound of cheering, brass bands and a gun salute of one hundred and one salvoes.

However consciously regal and majestic Prince Ferdinand's bearing was on *terra firma*, he was at a considerable disadvantage in the saddle. A junior member of the British diplomatic agency in Sofia, Robert Graves, witnessed Ferdinand's arrival:

All were curious to see what this young man was like who had dared to accept this thorny crown, without the approval of the Suzerain Abdul Hamid or the Russian Tsar who claimed so preponderant a voice in the destinies of Bulgaria.

I was present when he rode into Sofia, and heard some of the unfavourable comparisons drawn by the crowd between him and his handsome and soldier-like predecessor. Tall, but awkwardly built and already too stout at six-and-twenty, his seat on horseback was deplorable, in spite of his having nominally served in an Austrian Cavalry regiment, and it was remarked that a groom walked near his bridle rein in case his well-broken charger gave any trouble when the band struck up or the people cheered.[17]

It was not until the motor car had established itself that Ferdinand was able to avoid the agonies of the saddle. His later passion for his large stable of motor cars probably owed something to a feeling of relief.

As had been expected, none of the diplomatic agencies of the major European Powers put out flags along the procession route. Nor did their representatives take any part in the festivities. Ferdinand was not to receive official recognition as Prince of Bulgaria by the outside world for seven years. Though he perfectly well understood that this was a European diplomatic fact of life, which would last for as long as Russia maintained that he was an illegal usurper, he nonetheless, right from the beginning, saw it as a personal insult.

The menace of Russia and the hatred of Tsar Alexander III were symbolized by the empty, shuttered Russian legation building as described by Anna Stancioff: 'from the British legation you could see the outlines of a finely built residence, standing in a shady garden, and you would note its forbidding and sinister aspect recalling that of a forsaken prison; closed doors and shutters completed the illusion.'[18]

While Russia, as represented by Hitrovo in Bucharest, was spending a fortune plotting the assassination or removal of Ferdinand, the diplomatic agents of the other powers in Sofia were in a tricky position. Unlike Russia, they were allowed by their governments to deal with the Bulgarian Government, which they recognized as existing *de facto*. Yet, at the same time, they had to ignore officially the Head of Government, Prince Ferdinand. Mindful of Bismarck's instruction to Germany's representatives in Sofia to regard the Prince purely and simply as a Hungarian officer travelling privately and to treat him as such, the recently appointed German Consul-General Aichberger, happened to pass the Prince in a street in Sofia. The Prince, as keen on walking as he hated riding, was exploring the streets of his capital. The German, confused by this sudden encounter and about the correct attitude required of him by the Wilhelmstrasse, neglected to salute Ferdinand. To prevent a repetition of the painful incident, Bismark instructed Aichberger to greet the Prince as one would 'greet any other *étranger de distinction* known to one by sight. He is not only a pretender, but an Austro-Hungarian of distinction.'[19] This, at any rate, was a notch higher than a mere 'Hungarian officer travelling privately'. Prince Ferdinand gave as good as he got and responded to the diplomat's formal coolness towards him with a frigid reserve.

Bismarck's firm resolve not to offend Russian sensibilities by an act which could be seen in St Petersburg as implying a recognition of Prince Ferdinand did not of course apply to the other Powers. Austria-Hungary was pleased, deep down, to have what she considered as being 'our man' in Bulgaria. Count Kálnoky instructed his representative in Sofia, Count von Burian, how to deal with the Prince. His letter is a smooth example of Austrian diplomatic equivocation:

> We most pressingly urged the Prince not to go to Bulgaria just now. But we now wish that the undertaking should succeed, since its failure would have far more dangerous consequences.
>
> Your Excellency should stay away from receptions, festivities, etc., of an official nature and should avoid anything which could be considered as an official recognition. But towards the Prince, a member of a great princely family closely related to the all-highest Imperial family, you should render all due respect, on a personal basis, as it were.
>
> Should he wish to speak to you in private, you may agree, on the definite understanding of the unofficial nature of the proceeding. The Prince is highly cultivated and capable, but he is inexperienced, he lacks manly decision in his appearance and an understanding of Bulgarian manners. He will soon find it necessary to seek the advice of objective people. Be careful, but if you can be of use to the Prince, do so.[20]

Kálnoky never forgot his Viennese impression of Ferdinand and would have been quite taken aback if he had seen the Prince in his new regal role. Count Kálnoky's instructions were nicely calculated to woo Ferdinand by means of minor kindnesses without allowing Russia or Germany to accuse Vienna of contravening treaties.

The British and Italian Diplomatic Agents in Sofia, as well as those of the neighbouring Christian states in the Balkans, soon established similar unofficial contacts with the Prince. Once they had made the first approach, Ferdinand willingly granted them private audiences. The young Prince's self-possession impressed his visitors. He tailored his role to his visitor's background, which he had researched before the meeting, and to his presumed character. The aim was to impress or charm, or both. It worked well – except on one occasion described by the young English diplomat Robert Graves:

In these interviews it was noticed that the Prince was inclined to play the part and assume the character with which he thought to impress his interlocutor. An amusing instance of this versatility was when he gave audiences at very short intervals to my Chief O'Conor in his capacity as British representative, to Chirol, special correspondent of a great London daily [Valentine Chirol of the *Pall Mall Gazette*], and to a young Conservative Member of Parliament who' was paying O'Conor a visit in the course of a pleasure tour of the Continent.

For the diplomatist, the Prince adopted a correct and serious demeanour, expressive of his sense of the very grave responsibilities of his position, and his determination to do nothing to endanger the peace of Europe. When the journalist was ushered in, he found the Prince standing in a Napoleonic attitude before the window, with one hand thrust into the breast of his tunic, and gazing fixedly in the direction of Mount Vitosha. Turning suddenly, he addressed Chirol with the words – *'Voyez-vous cette montagne? C'est la clef de la Macédoine, et c'est moi qui tient cette clef!'* [Do you see that mountain? It is the key to Macedonia and it is I who hold the key!], tapping himself on the chest as he spoke, with the air of a bold and adventurous spirit who meant to make history and incidentally provide the Press with plenty of sensational copy.

He probably knew quite well that Vitosha was a position of no strategic importance whatever, but no doubt he thought to give the Press-man the impression that he was the coming figure in Balkan politics. To the gentleman at large, travelling only for his pleasure, he gave a friendly welcome, as one young man of the world to another. 'Sit down, have a cigar? Yes, and a drink, a whisky and soda, eh? Well, it's awfully good of you to come and see me in this God-forsaken place and bring me a breath of the great world outside' – or words to that effect, without any reference to politics and affairs of State. I suppose that it had not occurred to him that his three interviewers would meet at dinner and exchange their experiences, greatly amused by the Prince's histrionic talents, but naturally somewhat sceptical of his sincerity in any of the characters which he had assumed.'[21]

In her admirable memoirs, Queen Marie of Romania wrote perceptively about Ferdinand's histrionic gift:

> Bulgaria's monarch [this was written about a later period in his life] was a great actor. Il *aimait s'écouter* and saw himself in the parts it in turn pleased him to interpret, be it that of a wily, ceremonious politician, the easily offended ruler whose every susceptibility must be respected, or that of the debonair, polite, sarcastic *homme du monde*, super-refined, all smiles and amiability, or even that of the sombre, almost tragic, tyrant of a mysterious country always in ebullition. His talk would be then of danger, plague, treason and sudden death; his voice would become dramatic, his accents thrilling, and he managed to evoke sinister pictures full of dark possibilities. But never for a moment during these recitations would he quite lose that expression of half-amused irony, in fact he had almost a wink in that small, sly, all-seeing eye of his, meant for those clever enough to share with him the fun he was having by thus incorporating these different exciting personalities.[22]

There is no doubt that Ferdinand took to ruling as a duck takes to water: he *enjoyed it,* he felt that he was in his element. He had been brought up to this by his mother, and her ambitions, in becoming his own, coincided with his phantasies about himself as monarch. Like Ludwig II of Bavaria he was now in a position to act out his phantasies in real life; but unlike poor, mad Ludwig, his phantasies at that time in no way dominated his sense of the political realities which surrounded him and his keen awareness of the dangers of his position, which during 1887 and 1888 became increasingly threatening.

He heard the growl of the Russian bear from the mouth of one of his subjects on the day of his arrival in Sofia. At the *Te Deum* service in the cathedral, Prince Ferdinand sat on his throne as the Metropolitan Kliment, the leading Russophil in the Bulgarian·Church, publicly admonished him that it was his duty to restore relations between Bulgaria and 'our liberator Russia and her great Monarch'.

In a sense, Bulgaria in 1887 was the proscenium of the main stage of Europe and the characters and action on the proscenium caused great anxiety on the main stage. The footlights trained on the happenings in Sofia also caught the gleam and glitter of the armies of Europe massed behind. The occasional clank of weapons could be heard distinctly. The curtain was already up. The Austrians and some of Germany's leading military men were urging Bismarck to agree to a preventive war against Russia. They were to urge it increasingly during the winter of 1887-8. Four days before Ferdinand entered Sofia, Russia's Ambassador in Berlin asked the Germans how they would view Russian military action against Bulgaria. The long-feared general European war – possibly a world war – seemed at hand.

Russia's frustrations about Bulgaria grew even more acute as the Tsar and his ministers, while wanting to intervene militarily, were afraid of the consequences, and of the bad impression it would create if giant Russia were to attack the small nation of 'Orthodox Christian Slav brothers' it had liberated from Turkish rule only ten years before.

The supreme irony of Russia's attitude became apparent when Ferdinand was being sworn in at Tirnovo. Russia put pressure on Sultan Abdul Hamid of Turkey, the man who had been defeated by Alexander II in 1877-8, to launch a military attack against Bulgaria. The Sultan was horribly embarrassed. The more Russia tried to press and threaten him, the more the British, Austrian and Italian ambassadors in Constantinople warned him against any 'inconsidered undertaking'. To appease the Russians, who scared him most of all, he sent a note to Prince Ferdinand telling him that the Sublime Porte and the Powers saw his undertaking in Bulgaria as illegal and contrary to the treaties, and would he please leave the country. The note, handed to a member of the Prince's suite on the day of his arrival in Sofia, was not even signed. The Bulgarians immediately realized that there was therefore no need to answer it. But just to make sure that he would get no reply, the Sultan verbally informed Prince Ferdinand via his Foreign Minister that nothing would happen and that he need not answer the note.

With no immediate prospect of getting rid of Ferdinand by military or diplomatic means, Tsar Alexander was pinning his hopes on Hitrovo's 'cold war' subversion directed from Bucharest. The groundwork for numerous plots against Ferdinand was being laid during his first weeks in Bulgaria, though the majority of them were not to reach to full flower until months or even years later. Hitrovo's brief declaring the Prince a 'usurper outside the laws', and all actions against him as exempt from punishment, was supplemented by a budget of millions of roubles.

One of the first assassination attempts was being prepared as the Prince was settling down in Sofia. The plotters were two Bulgarian officers, Bendereff and Grueff, who had carried out the coup against Prince Alexander, and who, after Stamboloff's counter-coup had fled to Russia. They got in touch with a worker who dealt with explosives, a certain Franz Maktich. He agreed to blow Ferdinand up with a landmine for 6,000 French francs. The money was provided by the Russians. A test explosion took place near Odessa and its effectiveness gave full satisfaction to the two émigré officers and other observers who were sheltering at some considerable distance. Maktich and his explosives travelling via Constantinople and Varna, and arrived in Sofia. But he was immediately arrested. Bulgarian agents in Constantinople had become suspicious about Maktich, had warned the sub-prefect of Varna who, in turn, contacted Maktich and gained his confidence by leading him to believe that he too was an anti-Ferdinand conspirator. The sub-prefect was thus able to warn the authorities in Sofia about the details of the conspiracy before Maktich arrived. It was a lame ending to the first of many attempts to extirpate that 'thorn in our flesh', as Giers later described Ferdinand to Herbert von Bismarck, the great Chancellor's son.

From Vienna Prince Ferdinand's mother had watched his journey to Bulgaria, the swearing-in and the arrival in Sofia with a mixture of pride and fear. Anxiously, she scanned Europe's newspapers and questioned the many diplomats and statesmen she knew. The newspapers were a source of great sadness: for when Ferdinand was mentioned, the intelligent old lady could not avoid seeing the sarcasm and mockery that so frequently went with her son's name.

Ferdinand's name was so well known to the public after he was proclaimed Prince of Bulgaria that the London *Punch* of September 1887 carried a brief item on him without even having to explain with its customary heavy pointers designed to help the reader to understand the joke. It was merely headed 'Learning the Language' and was written in phrase-bookese:

'Have you perceived the Triumphal Arch at the entry of the City?'
'No, I have not perceived the Triumphal Arch at the entry of the City, but I have noticed the cold shoulder of the Generals.'
'This must be the congratulatory Round Robin of the Officers.'
'Yes, it is the congratulatory Round Robin of the Officers, but here also is a placard proclaiming me a Usurper.'
'Has the Snub arrived from the Porte?'
'Yes, the Snub has arrived from the Porte, and with it the Ultimatum from the Czar.'
'In any emergency would you depend upon the omnibus horse provided for you by the War Department?'
'No, in any emergency I would not depend upon the omnibus horse provided for me by the War Department, but on the list of trains proceeding to the frontier, as furnished in the local *Bradshaw*.[23]

The moment Ferdinand was proclaimed Prince of Bulgaria, Princess Clémentine hurried off on a pilgrimage to Lourdes to consecrate the golden crown she had promised to the Virgin Mary. When news of this reached the Tsar of Russia, he was furious: it was one more proof that the 'usurper' was a dagger pointed by Roman Catholicism at the heart of Orthodox Slavdom.

CHAPTER 10

Settling In

—◦❦❦◦—

At the beginning of his reign Prince Ferdinand was much in the position of George I of England. He was only just mastering the language of his subjects, and was ignorant of the passionate intricacies of party politics and of Bulgarian customs. Sensibly, he got his priorities right and arranged to continue his Bulgarian lessons a few days after his arrival. The tutor he chose was Dobri Gancheff, a lecturer in history at the Sofia Military Academy. From the beginning, Gancheff was fascinated by the curious personality of his princely pupil. He held Ferdinand under sharp observation for some thirty years and his memoirs, published long after their author's death, are shrewd, indiscreet and often bitter, but always patently honest.

Dobri Gancheff presented himself at the palace for the first lesson, wearing a dress coat which he had managed, after much searching, to borrow from a friend in the Bulgarian Foreign Ministry; there were not many people who owned dress coats in the Bulgarian capital at that time. Prince Ferdinand received him in his study and almost immediately complained about the palace, which he said was uncomfortable, tasteless and badly planned, 'a house fit for an ordinary Viennese *rentier*, not a palace'.[1] The building was originally the residence or *konak* of the *pacha* of Sofia, the Sultan's representative in Bulgaria. During the seven troubled years Prince Alexander had spent there, it was considerably improved and had gained a modern 'French Renaissance' façade. But the standards of comfort and luxury of the warrior Sandro and of the aesthete Ferdinand were poles apart: what Prince Alexander considered a pleasing residence in his last years in Sofia was barely habitable for the newcomer. In a short time Ferdinand was to transform the palace, according to no less an authority than Princess Pauline Metternich, into 'the most refined and exquisitely kept in Europe'.[2]

When Ferdinand finished complaining about his residence, his tutor pointed out that the building had been much smaller and more uncom-

fortable when Prince Alexander had first arrived. Ferdinand's reply
took Gancheff aback: 'Do you know, Mr Gancheff, that the moment I
entered the palace I noticed Prince Alexander's smell?' The Prince went
on about Sandro's smell and said he had met him four years before at the
coronation of Tsar Alexander III, where he had seen him over a period
of three or four days. He had not seen him since that occasion, but 'the
moment I entered his bedroom and his study I noticed the smell of his
body!' Gancheff wrote:

> I looked at him with amazement. I had heard it said that a
> Chinaman can notice the smell of a European in a closed room. But
> that one German prince should be especially able to detect the smell
> of another one, amazed me. I tried to believe it, not because Prince
> Ferdinand tried to assure me that it was true with all the appearance
> of sincerity, but because I was looking at his huge nose. A veritable
> chimney. It particularly reminded me of a chimney when he picked it.
> Wide, long and voluminous, it was often left out in the cold. He
> poked about inside it with the calm and patience of a chimney sweep.
> Why should I not admit to myself that the enormous intake of air of
> which this gigantic nose was capable might not contain odours which
> would remain undetected by other, ordinary noses?

The tutor soon became aware that there was an unpleasant smell in
the Prince's study. It emanated from Ferdinand's pet pug-dog Bubi,
which lay at his feet: 'old and fat, it could hardly walk. Its bulging eyes
were wet and full of sleep. A revolting animal which from time to time
filled the room with its stink.'
Prince Ferdinand loved the dog: 'How he would praise it, and with
what animation he would talk about the intelligence of his "Bubi"!' At
one point Gancheff tried to score a point by praising the spaniels –
'those small and lively dogs' – which Prince Alexander used to breed in
Sofia. Ferdinand snapped back and told him that he knew the breed and
that Queen Victoria was devoted to spaniels: 'She's got dozens of them.
They are as nasty and ill-natured as she is. She is an exceptionally ill-
natured woman, she doesn't like anybody.'[3]
In his references to Prince Alexander, the new Prince betrayed his
feelings towards his predecessor, and his fear of a Battenberg Restoration, which were to last until Sandro's death six years later. Although
his remarks about Prince Alexander's bodily smell seemed to be purely
spiteful, his remark that Queen Victoria was incapable of affection is
quite revealing. Ferdinand knew perfectly well of her fondness of
Sandro – feelings she did not have towards Prince Ferdinand.
Ferdinand astonished his language tutor by the speed with which he

managed to learn Bulgarian. He refused to study grammar and simply picked up the language by conversing with Gancheff. He had a remarkable memory and was an excellent mimic. It was the former gift, wrote Gancheff, that had made it possible for him to master five languages as a child. 'He spoke in French with his mother and with diplomats; in German to his brother and to the servants; he swore in Hungarian, and boasted in English and Italian.'[4] As a mimic, Ferdinand could be very funny. He made his guests laugh by imitating his ministers and even more successfully with his imitation of Grigoryi, the Metropolitan Bishop of Rustchuk, a wise and venerable cleric for whom Prince Ferdinand had a high and genuine regard. It was his best party piece, exceptionally lacking in malice, and he knew why: the Metropolitan had a nose as big and noticeable as his own.

Ferdinand's difficulties at the beginning were enormous. Four months after his arrival he admitted this to Count von Burian who reported to Vienna: 'His Highness owned that he cannot yet get fully to grips with the internal political situation. Despite careful observation he has not succeeded in finding his bearings in the maze of party politics. His experiences so far have depressed him.'[5] Ferdinand added that the task before him was 'Herculean'. Learning the language would at least make it possible to get closer to the politicans and avoid embarrassing pitfalls, such as the one he had experienced only a month after his arrival. Prince Ferdinand was in the palace when a crowd, or rather a mob, of about three thousand surged up to the building and called for him to appear. He stepped on to the balcony and received a long ovation. One of the crowd's speakers called for the condemnation of those involved in the kidnapping of Prince Alexander. Ferdinand replied in a firm voice in Bulgarian: 'Be devoted to me; be patriots; thank you for your sentiments. Long live Bulgaria!'[6]

What he had not known was that the mob, most of it drunk, had reeled to the palace after throwing bricks and stones and smashing in all the windows of the house and the newspaper office of Petko Karaveloff, a former Prime Minister and Co-Regent, whose ambiguous attitude at the time of the coup against Prince Alexander had left him open to accusations of extreme Russophilism. Whatever Prince Ferdinand's real feelings about the political demonstration, he was mortified when he realized that, through ignorance, he had seemingly endorsed the actions of a drunken street mob.

One of Ferdinand's first tasks was to form a new government. None of the political leaders who tried could form a ministry. It became clear that only Stamboloff had sufficient weight and authority to bring it off. But for several reasons Stamboloff wanted to stand aside: he wanted to rest after the turmoils and dangers he had confronted since the coup against Prince Alexander. He also considered that, having been Regent with practically unlimited power, it would be awkward for both himself and for Prince Ferdinand to have him as a Prime Minister. Lastly, the little he had seen of the Prince had convinced him that they would not get on well together. He did not care to start another fight.

The Prince, however, knew full well that Stamboloff was essential to him, he insisted and Stamboloff, in the end, gave way when Ferdinand threatened to set up a military *régime*. The Prince's determination to have Stamboloff by his side was only expedient. In fact, he could not abide him. He soon learned to hate and even fear Stamboloff's sarcasms and quite uncourtierly ways. When Prince Ferdinand appeared at an official reception wearing for the first time the ceremonial robe he had designed for the Bulgarian military order 'For Valour', Stamboloff laughed at him. The robe was of blue velvet trimmed with silver brocade, and the train was carried by four of the best-looking young cadets from the Military Academy. Ferdinand looked at him with cold fury. Stamboloff stopped laughing and said: 'I am not going with you if you wear that thing! People will just laugh at us!' This took place in full public view. The Prince muttered something to which Stamboloff replied: 'There are far more important things to be done! Highness, it would be far better if you thought about getting yourself a more reliable personal bodyguard!'[7]

However galling the realization that he could not afford to do without the services of Stamboloff, the Prince had achieved his first success as ruler by inducing him to form a Cabinet. The European Powers, minus of course Russia, welcomed the new government headed by Stamboloff as Prime Minister. In addition, Stamboloff also took over the Ministry of Internal Affairs. To Western Europe it was a guarantee that Stamboloff's West-orientated policy would continue. He was to remain Prime Minister for nearly seven years, in fact, until Prince Ferdinand had built his own personal power base and could afford to do without the sarcastic statesman-bohemian by his side, the one-time revolutionary and nihilist who had turned kingmaker out of patriotism.

Whatever his feelings about the Prince, Stamboloff realized that Ferdinand's continued presence in Bulgaria was absolutely essential. As Count von Burian put it: 'All the alarm and fears of the recent crisis would be as child's play compared to the dangers which could arise if Prince Ferdinand were forced by internal or external considerations to vacate the position he has just filled.'[8] Despite his temperamental inability to flatter or toady to the Prince, he was deeply concerned about his security. Much to Stamboloff's exasperation, Prince Ferdinand insisted on going for long walks in the streets of Sofia, accompanied by an orderly and the chief of his bodyguard. Occasionally, seemingly ordinary strangers would come up to him to express their happiness and gratitude for his presence in Bulgaria. At one street corner a peasant woman kept an apple stall at which the Prince would sometimes stop to buy an apple. A small crowd would form around the stall and Ferdinand would ask them questions about their work, their families and their political views. A German diplomat who noticed this expostulated with Stamboloff about the poor security. Stamboloff laughed and told him not to worry. 'That apple woman and all those who cluster round the Prince are employed by me. He is safer in their midst than among his soldiers.'[9]

The Prince's walks in the town took place almost every day. One day, outside the building of the War Ministry, he ran into one of the closest political supporters of the former Prime Minister Karaveloff, the same whose windows had been smashed in by the Sofia mob. Instead of greeting the Prince, he pointedly ignored him by standing and looking through him. Ferdinand moved off pale with fury. The chief of his bodyguard, a giant of man with huge moustaches, acting on his own initiative, knocked down the offender. Passers-by ran up to see what was happening, there were shouts and much swearing. By the time a policeman reached the scene, the offender had picked himself up and run off. The Prince calmly walked back to the palace, clearly pleased at the way the insult had been avenged.

That evening the Prince had a lesson with his Bulgarian tutor.

His first words were to ask me what was being said about the scandal. I told him what I had heard and how people had reacted to this street brawl. I condemned Baï Khristo's [the chief bodyguard] action.

'What? You are condemning my devoted servant! Should I be insulted in the street, before so many people, I the ruler of this country, and should my servants not dare to protect me?'

I did not speak because the Prince was in a very excited state. In any case, he was partly right, as far as the consequences of the scandal were concerned. Since that day no-one dared to walk past him without greeting him. Those who did not want to do this, took off into a side street the moment they noticed him in the distance.[10]

Prince Ferdinand's corps of personal bodyguards was composed of twelve tall, good-looking young men. Baï Khristo, who was in charge, was fierce and impressive in appearance though essentially mild and good-natured. The most remarkable thing about him was his moustaches. They looked exceedingly long and curly. He had achieved the majestic effect by parting, trimming and cutting his long beard so that it

formed a drooping, then curving extension to the moustaches. He and
the men under him wore a special uniform of Albanian-Turkish
appearance: loose, ample scarlet drawers, embroidered scarlet tunic, a
wide, many-coloured silk cummerbund from the top of which stuck out
the bone handle of a yataghan. They had been Prince Alexander's corps
of bodyguards and Ferdinand was so pleased with their gorgeous
appearance that he took them on – despite their failure to protect Prince
Alexander on the night he was kidnapped.

During Ferdinand's first years in Bulgaria, Baï Khristo accompanied
his master when he travelled round Bulgaria. He would sit next to the
coach driver and as they passed through villages, most peasants cheered
him, quite unable to imagine that the thin-faced, long-nosed young man
sitting behind the broad shoulders of the splendidly dressed and
moustached man was their country's new ruler. The peasants would
crowd round the commander of the bodyguard and admiringly stroke
his long moustaches. The Prince was delighted. Baï Khristo's days of
glory ended sadly when he was past his prime. One morning he was busy
in front of his looking-glass, dyeing and curling the moustaches, when
one of his children upset the spirit-lamp on which he heated the curling-
irons, spilling the fuel and setting fire to the curtains. By the time he had
beaten out the flames his moustaches and beard were a charred mess.
Nature was unable to replace what the flames had destroyed and
without the moustaches he lost his splendour. He was no longer able to
grace the grand staircase of the palace at Court balls and receptions.
Pensioned off, he lingered on for two or three years complaining about
the ingratitude of princes, then died.

The Prince's long walks through the streets of Sofia were not only an
exercise in public relations. He was bored. While in the rest of Europe
the political and military crisis resulting from his decision to go to
Bulgaria deepened, he was mostly conscious that all the excitement was
elsewhere and that he was in a Balkan backwater. True, he had had no
illusions about what sort of a place he was going to when he made his
decision. But the dusty, somnolent reality of a Balkan summer in a dull
town had its effect.

What weighed most was the lack of discreet and easy sexual outlets,
no elegant borderland between prostitution and easy virtue to which he
had become accustomed in his teens in Vienna and Paris. There were no
midinettes in Sofia. The Prince was bisexual throughout his life, but up
to early middle age, his homosexual tendencies were overshadowed by
his desire for women. In Vienna his homosexual leanings were only
surmised from such outward signs as his extreme fastidiousness about
clothes, his jewels, and, above all, his rings.

He saw his enforced chastity as a direct result of the international climate. His non-recognition by the European Powers prevented him from setting up an elegant, cosmopolitan court to spice and leaven the provincial simplicities of Bulgaria. The European Powers were represented by skeleton diplomatic missions, mostly unaccompanied by their womenfolk. In any case, the diplomats were under orders to avoid the palace.

For the moment the fleshpots of Paris and Vienna, of Karlsbad and Marienbad were all out of bounds. He could not leave Bulgaria with the unsettled international situation and the equally uncertain outlook in Bulgaria. He wanted to travel abroad, and told everybody of this desire, but realized that he had to resign himself to the realities of the situation. As it was he himself, his own person, who was the cause of Europe being on the apparent brink of a general war, anything might happen to him. He would be no safer abroad, possibly less so than in Bulgaria, from a Russian, or Russian-hired, assassin. Once in Vienna, might not the Austrians decide, for conceivable diplomatic and political reasons, to prevent his return to Bulgaria? And what if the unsettled situation in his country should lead to the Bulgarian frontier being closed against him on his return? He knew perfectly well that with the amount of Russian gold deployed against him all over Europe, the only sensible course was to stay put.

Princess Clémentine saw how her son was fretting when she came to Sofia in the late autumn, and tried to do something about it. She invited several of the Bulgarian ministers and their wives to spend a fortnight with Ferdinand as her guests in the Rila mountains, at the famous medieval Rila monastery in its beautiful valley. All those invited thanked her but declined.

Unwittingly, the old lady had shocked them and offended against the still prevailing patriarchal puritanism of Bulgarians. It was quite unthinkable that husbands should spend such a length of time with their wives in the presence of a young bachelor. Stamboloff had to explain the refusal to Ferdinand. For the Prince, the outlook was bleak.

Among the couples Princess Clémentine had invited were Colonel Racho Petroff, the Chief of Staff; and his young wife, a pert, buxom and attractive brunette to whom Prince Ferdinand had begun paying court shortly after his arrival in Bulgaria. It was when he realized that, in the absence of salons and social life as he had known it – nearly everyone in Sofia was in bed and asleep by ten – there would be no chance for him to have the kind of smooth, discreet affair to which he had been used, that the Prince had suggested his mother should organize the fortnight in the mountains.

Madame Petroff was the real inspirer of the Prince's prolonged walks in the streets of Sofia. Whichever way he went with his bodyguard and orderly, Prince Ferdinand would always pass the house of Bulgaria's Chief of Staff. Madame Petroff would at that moment happen to open a ground-floor window, the Prince would stop and they would talk for a moment. It must have been excruciating for the Prince, with a string of affairs to his credit in Vienna over the past ten years, to be standing in the street, looking up at his lady in the window, like any love-lorn village tenor in an operetta.

The Prince was highly sexed. There was no holding him in his pursuit of attractive women in his youth and the drive was as strong in later middle age when the homosexual in him more or less took over. When we speak of his affairs we do not mean love-affairs; there is no evidence of deep romantic or sentimental attachments, no love letters and no broken heart (on his side, at any rate). Romance loomed large in Ferdinand's life but not allied to the sexual urge. A strong sense of history, the sense of his personal royal destiny, grand opera and the occult: it was these that absorbed the romantic in Ferdinand and stimulated his phantasy. The one person he really loved was his mother, just as her love was centred in him.

According to an anonymous, though well-informed attack on Ferdinand published in London in 1916, when Bulgaria was Germany's war ally, it was Princess Clémentine who had early on exposed to her son the 'weaker side of feminine character'[11] with the result that by the time he was sixteen years old 'he was more cynical about the sex than many a *roué* of sixty'.

> He formed a style of conversation for feminine company in which a brilliant form of double-meaning predominated. He wielded this weapon so skilfully that a pure woman, even an understanding one, had no defence against it. The other kind were dazzled by the proficiency of this mere youth in innuendo of the vilest kind, wrapped up so skilfully that even the most alert mind hesitated over its ambiguities.
>
> He shocked, but he also captivated; and he was firm in never himself becoming a captive. He soon earned the reputation he sought; he was credited with being as fickle as he was successful in love affairs.[12]

The dominant note in the above description of Ferdinand is one of outrage at the cold-hearted, princely seducer. That is only to be expected from a piece of wartime propaganda. Yet, moral indignation aside, Ferdinand's way with women and the fascination he had for them is echoed in a book, this time very favourable to Ferdinand, by a French journalist, published in Paris in 1910:

It is not surprising that with his sensitive charm the Prince has so often attracted more than one susceptible heart. But what is more, he can address himself to women's imagination, to the point of agitating it with his virtuosity. Although all that which is in him of sensitivity, subtlety and feminine diversity might find itself competing against these same qualities in women, he nevertheless seeks them out, loves femininity and decodes and interprets it like the connoisseur he is, he enjoys it and at the same time he mistrusts it.[13]

Throughout his life, his admirers were women rather than men.

Although Madame Petroff was not the only woman who took his fancy, it was the attentions he paid to her that caused the most gossip in the small capital; for while wooing the wife, Prince Ferdinand was also wooing her husband, Colonel Racho Petroff, the Bulgarian Army's Chief of Staff. But in the husband's case, the Prince's motives were quite different. Almost on arrival in Bulgaria he tried to secure the friendship and loyalty of the senior officers. It was the best way to secure his position as the ruler of a country in which disaffected army officers, only a year earlier, had kidnapped the reigning prince. The Chief of Staff was an obvious man to be won over: he had been Prince Alexander's Chief of Staff during the 1885 war against Serbia and early in 1887 had put down the Russian-fomented military mutinies in the Danube garrisons and had confirmed the death sentences on the ringleaders. Like Stamboloff, he had done his higher schooling in Russia, and like Stamboloff he was clearly not a Russophil, the most important consideration in judging a person's loyalty at a moment when the Tsar of Russia was personally involved in plans to destroy the Prince.

While the Chief of Staff was the prime target of Ferdinand's attentions, the Prince was also wooing Major Popoff, a young officer who had distinguished himself during the war with Serbia and who was one of the most popular officers in the army. The Major, who was a member of the Bulgarian delegation which went to Ebenthal to present the Prince with the act of election, never forgot the shock when he was shown to the Prince's room, to see him reclining on a couch, holding a Malmaison carnation which he sniffed throughout the meeting, pointing out the exquisite formation of the petals.

The Prince showered decorations and presents, mainly rings and watches, on those officers whose loyalty he wished to secure. Nevertheless, his way of setting about securing a person's friendship and devotion by seducing his wife was, to say the least, odd. According to the anonymous author of the British wartime book against Ferdinand, he would try to worm out the secrets of his most powerful subjects by means of a love affair with the man's wife, or sister.

This did not alter the fact that Ferdinand found Madame Petroff's attractions irresistible during his first months in Bulgaria. The Prince's frequent promenades past his Chief of Staff's house had already set tongues wagging until things nearly came to a head. One evening Ferdinand was at a ball given at the Military Club in Sofia. The dancers could see the Prince talking to Madame Petroff alone in a small drawing room giving on to the ballroom. At one point the drawing room door shut, leading to ribald speculation among the dancers. Colonel Petroff's brother found the Chief of Staff playing in the card room and told him what was going on. He got up without saying a word, went to the door of the drawing room, threw it open and walked in. Ignoring Prince Ferdinand, he told his wife: 'Get up! We are leaving.'[14] Afterwards, the Prince's manner towards both Petroffs became markedly cool.

For a time there were continual slights from the Prince and on one occasion a public snub which caused the exasperated Chief of Staff to exclaim loudly afterwards: 'What I'd like to know is who is supposed to be a servant of the State here? Me? Or my wife?'[15] But soon Ferdinand showed signs that he had 'forgiven' Colonel Petroff, who became one of his principal weapons against Stamboloff. In this respect, Petroff was more fortunate that other public men whose wives had attracted the Prince. Jealous husbands, or the husbands of women who had rejected Ferdinand's advances with too much determination, subsequently found their careers taking a downturn.

Ferdinand's reputation as the princely Lothario of the Balkans reached new heights on his twenty-seventh birthday in February, 1888, his first birthday as sovereign of Bulgaria. Princess Clémentine organized a *tableau vivant* as a birthday surprise in the palace at Sofia. She had gathered some of the ladies her son admired most and for days they rehearsed under her direction. On the birthday a reception was held at which were present for the first time the diplomatic representatives of the countries which had recognized Ferdinand as *de facto* Prince of Bulgaria.

A stage had been set up in the grand ballroom. The curtain rose to reveal in the centre, at the front of the limelit stage, Princess Clémentine sitting on a *fauteuil* and covered from head to foot in white tulle, embroidered with fleurs-de-lis and dotted with diamonds. She was leaning slightly against a marble column, on which stood a bust of Ferdinand.

On the right of the stage were grouped three ladies in red, white and green dresses, the Bulgarian tricolour. One of the three beauties was Madame Petroff. On the left stood two ladies representing the colours of the House of Saxe-Coburg-Gotha. An angel in dazzling white stood by Ferdinand's bust, holding a laurel wreath above his head. It was the ravishingly beautiful Madame Belcheff, a talented poetess and the Prince's latest flame. Soon afterwards she was appointed lady-in-waiting to Princess Clémentine. The central figure was Comte Amédée de Foras, the new Marshal of the Court, a sixty-year-old impoverished French nobleman from Savoy, dressed in a magnificent Byzantine robe, with an imperial diadem on his head. He represented the medieval Bulgarian Empire and its tsars. He was pointing at the bust of Ferdinand: the past showing the way to the present. By him stood one of the Prince's aides-de-camp, with martial air and dressed in a sky-blue uniform: he represented the victorious Bulgarian army. At Princess Clémentine's feet sat a group of young men and girls dressed in Bulgarian national dress from all parts of the country. Beginning softly, and growing louder, the actors sang the new national anthem and when it ended to wild applause, the Prince, visibly moved, went forward, knelt at his mother's feet and kissed her hand.

The Princess knew her son. A spectacle such as that was bound to flatter his mind and senses: the allegorical link between a grand, romantic past and himself; the implied promise of monarchical greatness in the future; the similarity to the *tableaux* and ballets of Versailles, staged to flatter the Sun King, the ancestor whose imagined physical likeness to Ferdinand seemed both to the Prince and to his mother a gage of future greatness. And to stage this, the fond mother had had the wit to invite the ladies of Ferdinand's choice!

The *tableau* or 'The Apotheosis', as it was soon called, not only scandalized Sofia, but, incredibly, the rest of Europe. Those of the Prince's Bulgarian subjects who had been present at the palace were shocked, or pretended to be shocked, to see a respectable allegory on Bulgaria's history staged as a display of those beautiful women who had caught their new Prince's fancy, all adoringly clustered round his effigy. But it was the political implications of the amateur dramatics in Sofia that caused an outcry in Europe when a French magazine published a picture of 'The Apotheosis.' Besides numerous sarcastic and mocking articles in the French and Russian Press – France and Russia were growing closer and closer that year, prior to concluding their alliance – more serious questions were being asked. Did the prophetic finger pointed at Ferdinand's effigy by the Comte de Foras, dressed as a medieval Bulgarian tsar, mean that the Prince was planning to proclaim himself Tsar of Bulgaria? And that would naturally entail the unilateral declaration of Bulgarian independence. Would that be the straw to break the Russian camel's back, leading to the invasion of Bulgaria and general European war? With Russia's ominous troop movements on her western border and the Austrian generals calling for preventive war against Russia. Prince Ferdinand's birthday treat seemed full of menace.

Fear and speculation in Europe that Prince Ferdinand was about to proclaim an independent Kingdom of Bulgaria and himself Tsar of Bulgaria continued for many years, gaining in intensity on the eve of annual Bulgarian State anniversaries. But Ferdinand, however tempted, waited over twenty years – until 1908 – to become Tsar of an independent Bulgaria in conjunction with Austria's annexation of Bosnia and Hercegovina, the step that led directly to Sarajevo and the great war which Europe had expected and feared for so many years.

CHAPTER 11

The Thorn in Russia's Flesh

Prince Ferdinand's determination to secure the loyalty of Bulgaria's army officers and to build up the army was entirely realistic and practical. Whatever his private phantasies and fancies about himself, they were not military ones. Even when, twenty-five years later, Bulgaria's troops seemed on the point of capturing Constantinople, it was not martial zeal that fired Ferdinand but the historic and aesthetic considerations of leading the last Crusade and occupying the throne of Byzantium. Unlike his cousin Kaiser William II, the war-lord image held no great appeal for Ferdinand. And yet, as a diplomat, he appreciated from the very beginning that diplomatic policy had to be backed by military power held in reserve and he regarded the build-up of the Bulgarian army as a priority from the point of view of the statesman.

Always glad to provide journalists with usable quotes and that valuable newspaper commodity, 'new *clichés*', Ferdinand some years later encapsulated his views about military power in a conversation with a French journalist in the magnificent garden of one of his palaces: '*Oui....Mais pour avoir des fleurs....il faut avoir des canons*'. [Yes....But in order to have flowers...one must have cannon].[1]

Ferdinand's energy in building up the Bulgarian army was spectacularly successful. Within five years of his arrival the army had trebled in size and came to be regarded by foreign military experts as the best trained and equipped in the Balkan Peninsula. In a letter to Crown Prince Rudolf, written only three weeks after he entered Sofia, he made the broadest possible hint this side of a direct request, that Austria should supply the Bulgarian army with badly needed arms and ammunition. The letter is worth quoting in part as a good example of his characteristic mode of writing (the few explanations required are supplied below; omitted passages are indicated):

Since that night when I left you with a heavy heart in order to get
ready to pull the Bulgarian cart out of the Russo-Prussian...[in the
German original the Prince used *six* dots, presumably for *Scheiss*] in
which it had got stuck, I believe I have refuted various serious
accusations made against me; I have endeavoured, outwardly, to
appear as neutral as possible. But internally I have striven to give
fullest emphasis to the Bulgarian-patriotic point of view, in which
despite the unutterable heat, colossal exertions, and dreadful, horrible food, I believe I have more or less succeeded!

As far as things here are concerned... Consul-General von Burian
has, it would seem, provided his chief at the Ballplatz with such
minute and thorough reports about things here, that to write to you
about them would only bore you. By the way, I have seen the
gentleman: he impressed me as very gifted and clever....As far as the
situation inside the country is concerned, I am well satisfied: my
ministry is strong and popular, it identifies itself with the national
idea and is aware of the need to defend the integrity of the frontiers. I
have the love of the people, and the army stands loyally by my side; in
all the garrisons I visited (also in Philippopolis) the enthusiasm was
genuine and unaffected. In Sofia, my faithful Popoff guarantees the
loyalty of the troops and the inviolability of my person: in brief, I feel
secure (while, nonetheless, being extremely careful and constantly
mindful of Russia's money) and from this standpoint, I face the future
with calm.

As far as *'les Affaires Etrangères'* are concerned, the obstinacy of
Russia and the........of Chancellor Bismarck cause me some fairly
anxious moments. Still, they do not worry me unduly. I surround my
beloved mother-in-law Turkey with all imaginable signs of love, and
meanwhile I will also pay the Rumelian tribute and so try to satisfy the
bondholders up to a point. In that I see protection for myself and for
my programme for the future: the 'Balkan Federation'.

Should I be attacked despite this and should my territory be
violated, then I am prepared to fight together with my people and my
army, to win or to go under. Even more! It only requires a wink from
me for all the clans of Macedonia to rise as one man and to fight
alongside me for their own freedom and for their beloved neighbour
Bulgaria and perhaps to be victorious...

There is no more peaceable being than I am and that is just why,
should anyone lay hands on what is in my eyes the sacred and just
cause of my land and people, my vengeance (as that of the weaker)
would be incalculable!

Unfortunately I am short of weapons and ammunition. If really
necessary we could mobilize 130,000 men, but about 80,000 of them

would not even be partly armed. Who can give me arms at this moment? My success, the creation of a stable, peaceful Bulgaria, is the key to solving the Eastern Question and, I dare say it to you, of the greatest value to you.

When, filled with dark forebodings, I first set foot in the palace here on 22 August, there was a knock at my door and in came Major Dobner with a letter in his hand. There were a few lines from Kálnoky accompanying a letter written in the All-Highest handwriting of His Majesty the Emperor. This letter filled me with comfort and strength. It arrived at a tragic moment. I was so anxious to observe His Majesty's desire for secrecy, as expressed by Kálnoky, that I did not answer Kálnoky. I therefore beg you with all my heart to lay at your imperial father's feet my deepest gratitude with the assurance that his sanctified words shall never leave me!...

This letter is being brought to you by my faithful Hofrath Fleischmann, who is returning to the bosom of his family for a time. I beg you to destroy this letter after you have read it. I end by asking you to think of the lonely stranger from time to time, who ever is and shall remain

Your faithful cousin,
Ferdinand.[2]

Ferdinand's letter to the Austrian Crown Prince is not only of interest as an example of his oddities; it provides a measure of Ferdinand's early ambitions. By stating that his future programme was to bring about the federation of the Balkans, Prince Ferdinand, though only twenty-six and only just arrived, must have been aware that he was laying himself open to the charge of being a Utopian or a braggart – or both. At the time only incorrigible idealists could imagine the nations of the Balkans, rooted in their national antagonisms, as getting together and forming a corporate Balkan state. Yet it was not pure braggadocio nor Utopianism that lay behind his words. They reflected his nascent belief that his destiny might be to stand at the head of the Balkan sovereigns and to lead them in the last crusade which would end Ottoman rule in Europe and restore the cross on the dome of the church mosque of St Sophia in Constantinople. Twenty-five years later, his belief seemed to be on the point of becoming reality.

Ferdinand's secret meeting with Crown Prince Rudolf on the eve of his departure to Bulgaria was the last time that he saw him alive. The deaths at Mayerling in January 1889 happened at a time when Ferdinand still felt that he could not leave Bulgaria. (His brother Philip, whose sister-in-law was Prince Rudolf's wife, was staying at Mayerling on the night of the double suicide.) Rudolf and Ferdinand had seen much of each other in their youth and had a common interest in ornithology and shooting. The Crown Prince had been an ardent and enthusiastic admirer of Alexander of Battenberg and bitterly resented and criticized Kálnoky's cautiousness vis-à-vis Russia over the Bulgarian crisis. He had not approved of Ferdinand's original candidature for the Bulgarian throne but, like his father, was on the whole quite pleased when Ferdinand became Prince of Bulgaria. The latter had a genuine liking for Rudolf. In 1931, over forty years after Mayerling, Ferdinand spoke of his friendship with him. Rudolf, he said, was a 'remarkable, captivating and original man... one of the most attractive people I have ever known'.[3] As a friend he had been entirely trustworthy but he had been 'the victim of his love and of his preposterous upbringing'. The majority of crown princes were tired out by waiting when they ascended the throne, 'especially when the reigning monarch is intent on celebrating a record jubilee'. This had happened to Rudolf: 'He was too thirsty for life to play a secondary role. His personality had a fine edge which exercised an extraordinary charm on all women – most of all on Mary Vetsera. She was the most charming little creature with greyish-green eyes and the body of a Venus. Her bent was as pagan as his – they were both reincarnations of a famour pair of lovers from the past.'

Princess Clémentine had joined Ferdinand in Bulgaria in the late autumn of 1887. She travelled by train from Vienna to the Serbo-Bulgarian frontier where she was met by all the members of the Bulgarian Cabinet. The last stage of the journey to Sofia had to be done by carriage, as the final link in what became the Paris – Constantinople railway line was not yet complete. The seventy-year-old Princess was accompanied by her newly appointed lady-in-waiting, Comtesse Anna de Grenaud, a young French girl, whose father, Comte de Grenaud was Ferdinand's Marshal of the Court. They were shaken and jolted in their low carriages which, as Anna de Grenaud described them, were 'badly varnished, the seats covered with bright-hued stuffs and drawn by four horses placed in single row as those of a Roman chariot; gay with glittering metal ornaments, blue beads, amulets and bells, the sturdy little animals made a most picturesque sight in this primitive mountain scenery'.[4]

Halfway between the frontier and Sofia, the carriages passed the heights of Slivnitsa, where two years before the small Bulgarian army had defeated the invading Serbs. There Prince Ferdinand stood to greet his mother: 'For the fond mother who had played such an important part in fostering her son's future, it was a great and almost sacred moment when she recognized in the tall figure awaiting her on the barren hill the ruler of Bulgaria.' The young lady-in-waiting recorded her first impression of the Prince:

> His features bore the unmistakeable stamp of his race, and one could not fail to be impressed by the dignity of his deportment.... I could study the Prince at leisure after that hurried meeting on the road to Sofia, when he had seemed to emerge from a dream of romance and legend, his brave undertaking clouded by uncertainty. He looked very imposing, in spite of his youth, and the expression of his eyes, 'bleu de France', changed with unexpected swiftness – humorous, smiling or darkly ominous as suited the occasion.
>
> In those early days fair, wavy hair framed his strong, pronounced features, and a small pointed beard, trimmed in the way of the Valois princes, was very characteristic: so were his expressive tightenings of the jaw that struck one as a sign of contempt when he grew impatient or annoyed. His dignity, alertness and lightning power of scrutiny seemed to intimidate rather than to attract. The Prince took a certain pleasure in this fact, realizing his power over his audience and often stating that he would rather be feared than loved![5]

Ferdinand's choice of the battle-heights of Slivnitsa, the scene of his predecessor's famous military victory, as the place to receive his mother would have been criticized as both tactless and presumptuous by the many Bulgarian officers who supported Alexander of Battenberg and still hoped for his return – but for one thing. A few days earlier, on the second anniversary of the Battle of Slivnitsa, Ferdinand shrewdly and chivalrously sent a generously worded telegram of congratulations to Prince Alexander. He received this reply: 'I sincerely thank Your Highness for Your sentiments: I have no doubt that the army which I created and led to victory will always support Your Highness in Your endeavours for a happy and flourishing Bulgaria. Alexander'.[6]

Prince Alexander's reply, when it was published, did much to break the ice and dispel the army's suspiciousness towards its new commander. Stamboloff called it 'Prince Alexander's second abdication'. Princess Clémentine's presence in Bulgaria (where she was to spend several months of each year until her death in 1907) greatly helped to consolidate her son's position. Her venerable manner and appearance, her willpower, intelligence and energy, no less than the fact that she was the daughter of a king of France and the mother of their sovereign, created a deep impression in Sofia where her arrival was treated as a state visit.

Austria's Burian wrote to his chief in Vienna, soon after her arrival, that her presence was very helpful to the Prince's position: 'She has grasped the importance of winning many friends through civility and charity.'⁷ Her huge fortune was always at hand to help her son and the country to an extent well beyond the usual meaning of 'charitable works': for the completion of the last sections of the railway line, which in 1888 linked Bulgaria to the rest of Europe's rail network, she advanced the sum of four million French francs.

Princess Clémentine visited her son just as the conflict brewing between Russia and Austria-Hungary seemed to be on the point of exploding into war. At a meeting of the Delegations in Vienna on 5 November 1887, Count Kálnoky stated that while Austria-Hungary could not 'today' recognize Prince Ferdinand as the legal occupant of the throne of Bulgaria, Vienna nevertheless recognized the Bulgarian Government as existing *de facto*. This was seen as an official statement of support for Ferdinand and unleashed a storm of anti-Austrian, as well as anti-German, feeling in the Russian Press. In Vienna war jitters reached fever pitch as news and reports of massive Russian troop movements on Austria's eastern frontier reached the capital. The war parties on both sides pressed to be allowed to strike first. Crown Prince Rudolf had been in the forefront of those Austrians who urged that they must not lose that moment to strike, while they still had the military advantage. Germany's military men pressed Bismarck to agree to a preventive war against Russia. The Chancellor would not listen to them.

Anti-German agitation and propaganda by Russia's Panslav lobby was at its height when Tsar Alexander III visited Berlin on his way home from Denmark on 18 November 1887, and had talks with the German Kaiser and Bismarck. The meeting between the Tsar and Bismarck had a calming effect since each side was able to convince itself of the other's desire for peace. The meeting also gave rise to a scandal directly involving Prince Ferdinand.

In Copenhagen, where the Tsar, his wife Dagmar and their children had been staying with her family, Alexander III was presented with copies of letters which had apparently passed between Prince Ferdinand and the Countess of Flanders, the mother of the future King Albert of the Belgians. The correspondence, as the Tsar realized to his fury, seemed to prove that Bismarck was secretly supporting Prince Ferdinand. It meant that, despite all his protestations the German Chancellor was the blackest of double-dealers and deeply committed to an anti-Russian policy, hand in glove with Vienna. Although no originals of the letters were available, the Tsar, always the touchiest of men, easily allowed himself to be persuaded of Bismarck's duplicity and arrived in Berlin in a sulky rage. During a private audience, Alexander accused Bismarck of pretending to approve of Russia's policy towards Bulgaria, while secretly encouraging and actively supporting anti-Russian feelings there. The Chancellor 'in a loud voice and with strong emphasis' declared that documents ascribing such views to himself must be forgeries. Although Bismarck managed to convince the Tsar, the story leaked out in the Press and was used to the full to whip up anti-German feeling in France and Russia over Berlin's duplicity. Subsequent enquiries showed that the copied letters were forgeries prepared by the French secret service with the aim of inflaming the Tsar's suspicion towards Bismarck's policy and furthering the Franco-Russian alliance. The affair had been organized by Foucault de Mondian, a French secret agent, with the assistance of the Russian Press agent in France, Monsieur Katakazi. Although official relations between Russia and Germany remained good, the scandal caused bad blood, leaving Alexander III with one more chip on his shoulder.

Before it was realized that the forgeries were of French origin, Bismarck suspected that Ferdinand himself might be the forger: possibly with the aim of making the Tsar believe that he was a German *protégé*. As a result, numerous attacks against Ferdinand and even his mother appeared in both the official and independent German Press. Bismarck also wrote to the German Ambassador in Vienna, Prince Reuss, who was mentioned in the forgeries as championing Prince Ferdinand, and to the latter's uncle Duke Ernest of Coburg, to ask for their opinion.

Prince Reuss asked Ferdinand by letter to disown the correspondence, but even before receiving his answer, assured Bismarck that he did not believe that Ferdinand could be behind such obvious forgeries: 'I consider him far too bright to have dared to put about such a serious forgery; although he is very young, he has busied himself in political intrigue long enough not to do anything so imprudent.'[8] Prince Reuss added that although he was not familiar with Ferdinand's style of writing, his alleged letters to the Countess of Flanders did contain echoes of his manner of speaking, his 'mawkish' turn of 'emphatic phrases' with which 'he tries to awaken his audience's sympathies towards himself'. In his formal denial to Prince Reuss, Ferdinand protested against the 'calumnious' attacks in the German Press against 'my saintly mother' and himself.[9]

Prince Ferdinand was firmly convinced that all the Press attacks against him were directly inspired by Bismarck. His touchy and mistrustful nature found it hard to distinguish between political disagreement and personal dislike. Ever since Bismarck had opposed his going to Bulgaria, the Prince did not doubt that the German Chancellor was a personal enemy.

In his disclaimer to his uncle Duke Ernest of Coburg, the Prince wrote that he believed the whole forgery business – '*diese Schweinerei*' – to be the work of Hitrovo in Bucharest, 'my frightful adversary in Bulgarian affairs...a *canaille* who would frighten the devil himself!'[10]

The letter is full of pathos, written at a point in life 'full of cares and bitterness of all kinds'. Yet, amidst all the apparent self-pity, Ferdinand bristled with self-confidence and an almost smug self-satisfaction quite startling for a young man in his difficult and dangerous position:

> The nation loves me, supports me and understands my practical, mercantile nature, the intelligentsia fears me, likes my shrewdness, is ever on its guard from my eye; the army is most co-operative, though it partly wavers between fear of my severity and the memory of my predecessor. The machine of government functions very well and so does the court even though, for reasons of economic prudence, I have to be satisfied with the crumbs left behind by the Prince of Battenberg until the troubled atmosphere has cleared somewhat.

A medal in the Coburg colours, commemorating Ferdinand's installation as Prince of Bulgaria, accompanied the letter, which contained the following hymn of praise to the House of Coburg. The medal, wrote Ferdinand, was,

> new proof of the intellectual power of the Coburgs, of their undaunted dynastic spirit of enterprise, of their superior spirit of philanthropy which is active in nearly all parts of the world! From Lisbon to Petersburg, from Scotland to Adrianople there extend our material or spiritual, part positive, part negative, spheres of influence and power!
> It is a duty for all that is best in Europe to support me and the principle for which I stand and to save it from ruin! May God grant that some day I should be able to appear at Coburg with 'a great following' to pay due homage to the doyen of the Coburg dynasty....
> I embrace you in old affection and constancy,
> Your faithful nephew
> Ferdinand.[11]

From Ferdinand's point of view the worst consequence of the forgeries was the numerous personal Press attacks to which the scandal gave rise. They infuriated and exasperated him. 'The Prince...not unnaturally reacted to the unpleasant paragraphs in the European Press, whilst his poor mother took them even more to heart as personal insults.'[12] Anna de Grenaud recalled that 'the exasperated Sovereign looked round him for the supposed perpetrators of offensive articles, and his subordinates had to control their nerves and sensitiveness in order to preserve peace and restore their master's confidence'.[13] Later the old lady wept when, for the first time, she read a newspaper article praising her son's achievements.

The shadow of war in Europe grew darker still during December 1887. But neither Russia nor Austria-Hungary dared strike first for fear of Germany and Bismarck's system of treaties with both countries. According to Bismarck's system, if Russia attacked Austria, Germany would support the Austrians. If, on the other hand, Austria attacked Russia, Germany would remain neutral. However deeply the Tsar felt the blow to his prestige in Bulgaria, Russia could not afford to take on the might of the German Empire.

On 6 February 1888, Bismarck made his last great speech in the Reichstag. For the first time he spoke of the imminent possibility that Germany would have to, fight on two fronts against Russia and France. He set forth the case for a war over the Balkans and demonstrated its futility in words which prophetically summed up the causes and effect of the First World War. 'Bulgaria, that little country between the Danube and the Balkans, is far from being an object of adequate importance for which to plunge Europe, from Moscow to the Pyrenees, and from the North Sea to Palermo, into a war whose issue no man can foresee. At the end of the conflict we should scarcely know why we had fought.' The official report of the speech has the comment 'laughter' after the last sentence.

The speech, for which all Europe had been anxiously waiting, brought the great Bulgarian Crisis past its peak. The danger of a great war had been very real and the passions that it had aroused had been intense. But at the time the crisis seemed to have a tame ending. As a sop to Russian pride, Bismarck persuaded the Sultan against the wishes of Austria-Hungary, Italy and Britain, to send a second note to Sofia in which Turkey proclaimed the illegality of Ferdinand's status. Ferdinand showed the telegram to Stamboloff and asked him what the reply should be. Stamboloff told him to ignore it.

Gradually the international situation congealed. The Bulgarian problem was put on the shelf, unsolved. This did not harm Bulgaria's progress. Despite the dubious international status of its government, the country developed spectacularly during the next few years in comparison with its Balkan neighbours. The person who suffered most harm was Ferdinand himself. He was not to be granted official recognition by the European powers for seven more years. The slights and humiliations, sometimes real, often imagined, which the Prince had to endure soured and embittered him. His wounded self-esteem dwelt obsessively on questions of protocol and precedence and goaded his ambition.

Tsar Alexander's obsession with Ferdinand – 'the thorn in our Flesh' – became no less hard to bear as the Prince became more firmly established in Bulgaria. So, having failed to obtain satisfaction in Bulgaria by diplomatic means and dragging Europe to the brink of war in the process, the Tsar now concentrated on removing Ferdinand by stealth. That is to say 'by stealth' in theory – for Russia's numerous clandestine operations and plots against Ferdinand invariably failed, each time gaining wide publicity. It seems astonishing that with all the power and agents at his disposal the Tsar should have failed to get Ferdinand blown up or kidnapped. It is almost as if the series of fiascos which marked the successive Russian-organized conspiracies was a reflection of Alexander's split personality over the Bulgarian Question. While one part of him was consumed with pathological hatred of Ferdinand, another part of him felt distinctly uncomfortable about plotting the downfall of another sovereign. His grandfather, Nicholas I, had argued that terrorism and subversion were indivisible. If you fostered it abroad, it could boomerang home. The Tsar's own intense fear of assassination, after his father's death at the hand of terrorists, seriously impaired the courage of his convictions about Bulgaria. And how would it look if he *did* succeed in killing Prince Ferdinand and Europe blamed him for sponsoring an act whose very mention in Russia was enough to land a man in Siberia for the rest of his life?

The Tsar's illogicality was supplemented by his inability to disabuse himself of the entrenched, obstinate belief that the great majority of Bulgarians were still devoted to Russia and ready to rise against their own rulers if given a lead. The 'Kaulbars myth' died hard. As plot after plot ended in failure, Russian plans grew more grandiose and less practical.

The absurdity of this can be seen in the secret correspondence between Hitrovo in Bucharest, Nelidoff, Russia's Ambassador in Constantinople and the Russian Foreign Ministry concerning a plot to instigate an uprising in Bulgaria in January 1888. Captain Nabokoff, the same Russian agent who twice previously had been caught by the Bulgarian authorities, was to lead an armed troop into Bulgaria, thus triggering a revolution that would destroy Prince Ferdinand and Stefan Stamboloff. The twice unlucky captain was in Constantinople, and Vilamoff, a diplomatic official, was sent from St Petersburg before the planned raid for a final discussion with him about 'the kind of government he proposes to establish in the part of Bulgaria that he will occupy until the arrival of reinforcements from Odessa'.[14] The contrast between these plans for an invasion on the grand scale and what actually happened is a measure of Russia's self-delusion.

Nabokoff's troop consisted of thirty Montenegrins he had recruited from the slums of Constantinople and ten Bulgarian *emigrés*, one of them a priest. They embarked on a Greek tramp-steamer, the *Georgios,* landed at night at the Bulgarian – Turkish Black Sea frontier and marched north towards the Bulgarian port of Burgas, the scene of Nabokoff's previous fiascos.

On the march, the Captain and his men requisitioned horses and weapons from villages, which did nothing to endear them to the people who were supposed to join them in the uprising. Even more, their presence in Bulgaria was no longer a secret and the Prefect of Burgas was alerted by telegraph. That funtionary immediately ordered the soldiers from the local garrison to march against Nabokoff. The invaders were surrounded and after a short battle six or seven of them were killed, six captured and the rest, including Nabokoff, ran away. A hue and cry was raised and Nabokoff was tracked to a wood by a party of peasants. He begged them to be allowed to stand trial but the peasants said that they did not intend to give him up to the Russian vice-consul once again, and shot him down. The Russians had intended to link Nabokoff's expedition with an attempt to shoot Prince Ferdinand with dynamite cartridges. This scheme came to nothing because the Russian Novikoff, a merchant recruited and well paid by Hitrovo to kill the Prince, got cold feet, pleaded that Ferdinand was too well protected and asked for more money. No more was heard of him after the Russians told him that he would only get money if he produced the goods.

The Bulgarian Press made great capital of the fact that Nabokoff was a Russian officer and claimed that he was the son of the then Russian Minister of Justice. The Russian Press flatly denied this. But the Bulgarians, determined not to let the matter rest there, had the good, if grisly idea to exhume the luckless Captain (it was winter and the body deep-frozen). He was dressed in his uniform with all his decorations, propped up leaning against a tree-trunk, and photographed. The resulting *nature morte* was sent to the Russian newspapers and to all foreign diplomats.

One cannot escape the conclusion that much of the ill-luck that dogged Nabokoff's successive expeditions to Bulgaria was a result of his cavalier and peculiar conception of security. Aside from the fact that people on clandestine missions in enemy territory do not usually wear their country's uniform nor advertise their presence by requisitioning arms and transport from the local inhabitants, Nabokoff, to the Bulgarians' delight, carried documents and letters proving the connivance of Russia. Among them was a letter concerning the recruitment of Montenegrin mercenaries addressed to the arch Panslavist Count Ignatieff, by then A.D.C. to the Tsar, and another from Hitrovo.

With Nabokoff, Russian faith in the 'Kaulbars myth' finally died. His was to be the last attempt to try to get rid of Ferdinand and the Government by instigating a Bulgarian uprising. Later conspiracies concentrated on engineering a palace coup and on straightforward assassination.

Gancheff, Prince Ferdinand's Bulgarian tutor, was waiting to give him his daily lesson, when Stamboloff, looking grave and worried, rushed in to see the Prince. He spent half-an-hour with Ferdinand and then they came smiling to the door. The Prince was in a particularly good mood. Stamboloff had given a detailed account of the defeat of the invaders and of Nabokoff's death. Ferdinand repeated the story to Gancheff, sparing no details and 'with that air of enjoyment with which one imparts the most delightful news'.[15] The following evening a reception was held in the palace during which the Prince expressed his delight. Later he personally decorated some of the soldiers and peasants who had destroyed Nabokoff's troop.

The glow of satisfaction lasted until the celebration of the Eastern Orthodox New Year a fortnight later. In his address to a gathering of Bulgarian army officers, a buoyant Ferdinand declared that the army felt strong enough to face anything that the future might bring. He himself had become a Bulgarian in his thoughts and feelings: 'With an army such as the Bulgarian, one can dare anything; the glorious past is a guarantee of future success. If in the coming year I should be compelled to draw my sword, the Bulgarian army, led by its Prince, will show the world that the Bulgarians know how to die for the honour of their flag and for the protection of their fatherland.'

The role of the fire-breathing war-lord sat as uneasily on Prince Ferdinand as he sat on a horse. But he was well aware that that was the kind of thing his soldiers liked to hear. It was one way of edging into the blaze of martial glory his predecessor had left behind.

CHAPTER 12

'This Impure Spring'

—◦⋙⋘◦—

Although Prince Ferdinand was in the eye of the storm that threatened Europe in the winter of 1887-8, he himself felt exiled and remote from it all. The diplomatic activity in the capitals of the Powers reached him as if muffled by the deep blanket of snow covering the Balkans. The feeling of remoteness was exacerbated by his mother's deafness: the only way he could converse with her, his only confidante, was by shouting into her ear-trumpet. His non-recognition by the Powers turned his unofficial meetings with the diplomatic representatives of those countries which accepted his *de facto* position in Sofia – Britain, Austria-Hungary and Italy – into more or less furtive audiences.

He chafed at the social simplicity of Sofia, the lack of sexual opportunities and perhaps most frustrating of all, the fact that real power was in the hands of his Prime Minister Stefan Stamboloff. The latter's sarcastic high-handedness became the more galling as Prince Ferdinand increasingly and unwillingly realized that for the time being he was indispensable. The Austrian Envoy in Sofia, Burian, reported to Vienna:

> The Prince has recently thrown himself entirely into the arms of
> Mr Stamboloff. The stiff, unbending character of the Prime Minister
> became abhorrent to the Prince quite some time ago. On one occasion
> he told me himself: *'Nous sommes là, deux despotes, l'un en face de l'autre.'*
> Had he followed his own autocratic leanings he would have got rid of
> the 'kingmaker' long ago. But His Highness considers that he cannot
> do without Mr Stamboloff as long as his own position has not been
> regularized. He also considers that he cannot – as at one time it
> seemed that he would – carry on a continuous struggle with the
> Prime Minister about the limits of the sovereign's prerogative. His
> Highness therefore decided to put a good face on it and to let Mr
> Stamboloff govern and rule according to his own highly radical

conception of a constitutional ruler – but with the private reserva-
tion to change all this in the future.'[1]

Meanwhile Ferdinand did not mope. At the end of January 1888 he
went on an extensive journey through Bulgaria. His seventy-one-year-
old mother accompanied him despite the intense cold, the snow and ice,
and the abominable roads. It was Stamboloff who had suggested the
journey in his determination to strengthen Ferdinand's position at home.
For the Prime Minister, the continued occupancy of the throne was the
next best thing to a guarantee of Russian non-intervention. The trip was
the first of several that the Prince and his mother undertook that year.
Though the people of the towns and villages through which they passed
had no real affection for Ferdinand, there was no active ill-will: the
general feeling was one of indifference towards the Prince as a person,
but with the awareness that he symbolized the country's self-determi-
nation. The Prime Minister also wanted to see the Prince's position
strengthened for his own reasons: he was personally responsible for
bringing Ferdinand to Bulgaria. Stamboloff saw to it that the Prince was
greeted with as much pomp and enthusiasm as citizens and peasants
could summon. A lot was pure *façade*. According to a German journalist,
gypsies and other vagrants were hired to swell the welcoming cheers.

After the winter trip, once the snows had melted and the mud dried,
the Prince and his mother set off on another journey. They were
accompanied by Stamboloff, their French court officials, the Prince's
Bulgarian tutor, other Bulgarian officials and the bodyguards, fourteen
carriages in all.

In those days, long before Prince Ferdinand had built and personally
directed the furnishing of his numerous country residences, monasteries
and cloisters offered the most convenient and agreeable places for such a
large party to stay in. Apart from the Rila Monastery, which he
frequently visited, Ferdinand and his mother liked to stay at a nun's
cloister near the town of Kalofer, on the southern slopes of the Balkan
mountains. In these surroundings the Prince relaxed. He went on long
walks and found some compensation for the dullness of his capital in the
flora and fauna of the Balkan mountains, then a treasure house for the
natural scientist. Stamboloff and Ferdinand's suite did not share his
enthusiasm for these long walks and stayed behind playing cards in the
cells the nuns had vacated. The aged and infirm Princess stayed behind
too, feeling bored. An inevitable hazard for those accompanying the
Prince were the long, shouted conversations with the deaf lady which
she was reluctant to end.

Dobri Gancheff, the tutor, was once caught in this way and recorded
a rare word of criticism by the Princess for her son. The tutor had been

reading Victor Hugo's *Les Misérables* and, trying to find a topic of conversation, told the Princess that Hugo had written some very flattering things about her father King Louis Philippe. 'Don't you consider that our Prince has inherited some of his qualities?' he added. 'Yes, he is very like his grandfather. Only, he seems more excitable. He gets easily annoyed, but it soon passes. Actually, his grandfather was like that. How my father managed to control himself! How I wish that my son had this quality to a higher degree!'[2]

Ferdinand's enthusiasm for the natural wealth he found on his mountain walks was deep and genuine. He set in motion an extensive programme to replant mountain slopes which had been recklessly stripped of trees by the Turks. He dug up specimens of the rare flowers he found and sent them to his botanical gardens in Sofia, which were to become the standard reference for the flora of the Balkan range and the Rhodope mountains.

His passion for ornithology and zoology soon came to be known and he was presented with numerous live eagles, hawks and falcons by the towns and villages through which he passed. News of his generous rewards spread, with the result that occasionally a hopeful peasant would present him with a chicken. Monsters, such as a cockerel that had grown a pair of horns, were eagerly brought to him as well as wolf cubs, foxes and snakes. Within two years of his arrival his aviaries contained all known examples of bird life in Bulgaria.

Ferdinand's ornithological interest lasted all through his life: several bird-sellers' establishments along the Paris *quais* carried notices 'By Appointment, Purveyor of Birds to H.R.H. the Prince of Bulgaria'. But his love of the bird kingdom did not include owls: as birds of ill-omen he shot them down at every opportunity. On occasions he expressed his love of birds rather oddly. Once he shot down a magnificent soaring Balkan eagle which later, stuffed, its huge wings spread out, loomed in a palace hall.

The stay in the nuns' convent at Kalofer gave rise to an incident which, despite the beautiful surroundings, served to remind the Prince of the threat from Russia. He and his mother had arranged for Mass to be celebrated by a Catholic priest in the cell occupied by Ferdinand. This was seized on by Metropolitan Kliment, the Russophil cleric who, on the day of the Prince's arrival in Sofia, had reminded him of his 'duty' to Russia. Kliment and some of the higher clergy denounced the celebration of a Catholic Mass in an Orthodox convent as 'the crime of Kalofer'. The hostility shown by the higher Orthodox clergy towards Ferdinand was actively encouraged by Russia and equally strongly resisted by Stamboloff. As a result of Kliment's hostile and even provocative attitude to the Prince, Stamboloff compelled him to leave

Sofia and return to his proper see, Tirnovo. The Russians, on the other hand, sent him a gift of 50,000 roubles to strengthen his opposition to Ferdinand.

When in May 1888 the Prince and Stamboloff attended the Easter service in Tirnovo at the Church of the Forty Holy Martyrs, where the medieval tsars of Bulgaria had been crowned, Kliment refused to greet them or to leave his residence during their stay in the city.

The splendid Easter service in Tirnovo provided the right setting for Prince Ferdinand and Stamboloff to put aside their mutual antipathy in a harmonious display of patriotism. At the end of the religious service Stamboloff addressed Ferdinand: 'This is the first time in five hundred years that a Bulgarian ruler has celebrated Easter in our midst and in the church of our Tsars. May God, the defender of the right and the truth, uphold our Sovereign and help him to lead Bulgaria along the right road!'

Visibly moved, Ferdinand replied:

I have taken an oath to lead Bulgaria to the goal indicated by history. This day I renew that oath, and with all my heart and soul I reaffirm my resolve to maintain my bounden duty to the people of Bulgaria. In this building I have renounced everything and have become a Bulgarian; in this same building I declare to you that the Bulgarian ideal has become my ideal. The independence of Bulgaria; that is the sacred aim to which I have devoted my life. Follow your Sovereign, and with God's help Bulgaria will become great and happy and its independence will be assured.[3]

The higher clergy's opposition to Prince Ferdinand came to a climax in January 1889 when the Holy Synod was convoked in Sofia. This body consisted properly of five metropolitan bishops – but only the three Russophils among them, led by Kliment, arrived in Sofia. They refused to pay their respects to the Prince on the grounds that he had infringed the canons of the Bulgarian Church. One of their chief complaints was that he had arranged for memorial services to be held in the cathedral in Sofia on the occasion of the death of the two 'heretical' German Emperors, William I and Frederick III. Stamboloff knew that the clerical trio's provocative behaviour in Sofia was a rallying point for Russophil agitation. When his agents reported that the bishops were planning to pronounce an Anathema against Prince Ferdinand during High Mass in Sofia Cathedral, Stamboloff told them to leave Sofia and return to their bishoprics. If they refused to leave within three days of their own free will, he would find himself under the 'grievous necessity' of expelling them by force.

The bishops could not believe that this was more than a threat, or that any minister would dare to use violence against the heads of the Church. They did not really know Stamboloff: at three o'clock in the morning the recalcitrant priests were woken up by gendarmes who escorted them out of Sofia in three barouches to their respective bishoprics.

In the outcry that followed, Stamboloff was even blamed by his friends. They said that he had given his enemies a powerful argument for enlisting the sympathies of Orthodox fanaticism to denounce the persecution of the Bulgarian Church by the government of a Catholic prince. A group of twenty of the most prominent Russophils addressed a petition to the Bulgarian Exarch in Constantinople, the head of the autonomous Bulgarian Church. 'Your Beatitude, – in order to dry up this impure spring [Ferdinand], which threatens to corrupt utterly all that is holy, pure and elevated in Bulgaria, and which is sapping the foundations of all grace in this country, it is necessary first of all to cut short the nourishment which it receives from the original foes of our race and faith.'[4]

Stamboloff struck back at once and arrested all the signatories. He was acting entirely on his own. An English journalist friend described Stamboloff's feelings:

> He often told me that whatever important step he had taken, relying upon his own judgment alone, had almost invariably turned out to be the right one; and when he had allowed himself to be influenced by the reasoning of others, he had been led into errors.
>
> So far had this belief in his luck gone that, as he progressed in his career, he became more and more confident in himself, and impatient of advice, till towards the close, he would scarcely brook the expression of contrary opinion, even from Prince Ferdinand. It was partly this superstitious trust in his own star which led to his fall.[5]

The swift action by Ferdinand's Prime Minister had the effect of curbing the provocative stand of the Russophil Church leaders, with the exception of the stubborn Kliment. Two years later the bishops, again with the exception of Kliment, made their peace with Stamboloff and for the first time called on Ferdinand.

Ferdinand's determination to succeed and Stamboloff's intransigence soon began to bear fruit. A little over a year after the Prince came to Bulgaria, Emperor Francis Joseph expressed astonishment that Ferdinand had maintained himself. He told Bismarck's son: 'I did not believe that the Coburg episode could have lasted even this long. I am by no means displeased: at least now there is peace and order in Bulgaria, which is all I could desire.'[6]

The growing signs of stability in Bulgaria encouraged financial confidence. In 1890 Bulgaria concluded trade agreements with Britain, France, Switzerland, Austria and Germany. Harbours and railway lines were under construction. The most spectacular results could be seen in Sofia. Visitors to Sofia who had seen it in the past were amazed to find that almost all signs of the old Turkish provincial town had disappeared. Large public gardens were laid out, long boulevards had taken over from the mud and rubble of the old town, new ornate bridges spanned the river and large public buildings and monuments had sprung up. Most of this was accomplished on the basis of a loan for Sofia contracted in London. In 1888, only two years after Ferdinand's arrival, the Bulgarian State loan for that year was oversubscribed six-fold.

A determining factor was the completion of the Bulgarian section of the Paris to Constantinople railway line. Prince Ferdinand, who declared the line open at an official ceremony in August 1888, considered the new railroad to be a concrete symbol of his own mission in Bulgaria, as the link between the East and West of Europe, between Western and Eastern Christianity, between Rome and Byzantium. The train, soon to be known as the Orient Express, also put Western Europe, its fleshpots, its culture and the opportunities for direct diplomacy within easy reach.

In the autumn of the following year, 1889, he felt secure enough to board the train and leave Bulgaria for Vienna and Paris. Shortly before this, his first trip outside Bulgaria, Ferdinand had celebrated the second anniversary of his accession. Europe experienced a renewed attack of diplomatic jitters and the Russian army was put on the alert as rumours circulated that Ferdinand was planning to proclaim Bulgaria's independence and himself king on that occasion. Strong pressure was put on the Prince and Stamboloff to dissuade them from activating 'the powder keg of Europe'. In the event, nothing happened. Instead of an explosion, there was a gala dinner at the palace for 130 guests. The culminating point of the twelve-course dinner was a spectacular, and ironically titled, iced *Bombe Bulgare*.

When Ferdinand appeared on the palace balcony that evening, there were shouts of 'Long Live the King!' from the crowd. However, Ferdinand's excellent mood did not last. The gala dinner was followed by a 'Venetian evening' in the lavishly illuminated palace gardens. Somehow several gatecrashers, including some beggars, had managed to get in. Ferdinand was furious when one of these bedraggled gatecrashers stepped out from behind a bush and drunkenly called out to one of the footmen: 'Mr General, sir, bring me a glass of champagne!' Totally outraged, the Prince retired at once to his apartments and the following morning the palace officials quailed before the onslaught of his anger and sarcasm. His fury was not mainly due to the bad security arrangements which the gatecrashers had shown up. It was the artist and perfectionist in him that resented having his grand setting for the evening spoiled and himself made to appear ridiculous.

Despite his *incognito* as Count Murany, Ferdinand's steps during his one-month journey in Western Europe were dogged by reporters. There was much speculation about the political reasons for the trip. He was discreet and assured newspapermen that his journey was completely apolitical and that he had no intention of seeking recognition by roundabout means. He pointed out that the very fact that he had been able to embark on his journey without any preparations showed how much the situation had improved in Bulgaria. The Prince's discretion about politics also extended to the fleshpots of Vienna and Paris: not a breath of scandal reached the newspapers, probably due to extreme caution rather than abstemiousness. In later years he saw no need for such wariness and on one occasion kept three of the most attractive chorus girls of the Vienna Opera in a suite of the leading hotel in Karlsbad.

In Vienna the Prince saw Count Kálnoky. The Austrian Foreign Minister found Ferdinand much matured and improved. The Prince was firmly convinced at that time that his best chance of obtaining official recognition from the Powers lay in being the 'good boy' of European politics, while Bulgaria at the same time increased in prosperity and strength. Even before his meeting with Kálnoky, the Austrian Foreign Minister had instructed his Ambassador in Constantinople to suggest delicately to the Sultan that it would be better for Turkey to recognize Prince Ferdinand than to run the risk of the consequences of an eventual unilateral declaration of Bulgarian independence. He wrote:

> It must be wounding to Bulgarian national feeling that Bulgaria, whose correct behaviour in Europe is widely acknowledged, should still be treated as an outlaw. Its illegal status acts as a perceptible check to the aspirations of the industrious Bulgarian people who were able to assert their political and economic independence with remarkable calm and moderation. Recently Bulgaria has undeniably become a pillar of peace and order in the Balkan peninsula – what will happen there, should Bulgaria abandon this prudent policy?[7]

The Sultan, who would have been only too pleased to recognize Ferdinand, carefully sounded out the Russian Ambassador. He reacted with such a steaming display of indignation and threats, that the Sultan at once let the whole matter drop. Lord Salisbury, when approached by Kálnoky about the possibility of recognizing Ferdinand, replied that the risk of war with Russia was too great.

Despite Europe's *de facto* recognition of Ferdinand as ruler of Bulgaria, he suffered deeply from having no officially recognized status. It meant that he was unable to frequent the monarchs of Europe as Prince of Bulgaria; it also barred his way to kingship. The humiliations of the years ahead and the wounds to his self-esteem and pride embittered him and honed his readiness to take offence to hypersensitivity. It was a torment to him that having got that far, he, with all his pride in his family and royal ancestry, his self esteem, his monarchical obsession, his inkling of a predestined great role in history, should not be able to mix with the monarchs of Europe as an equal – especially when he thought himself to be far ahead of them in intellect and talents.

The slights to which he was subjected stung deep. Europe's rulers and diplomats realized that the easiest and cheapest way to soothe sulking Russia and appear to be faithful to the Treaty of Berlin was to snub Ferdinand. When Germany's Kaiser William I died in 1888, Bismarck returned the official Bulgarian telegram of condolence with the comment that he was 'not in a position to accept such documents'.[8]

Although Prince Ferdinand knew perfectly well that he would not be recognized as long as the Tsar persisted in his hostility, he was determined to use all available opportunities and even to create situations which allowed him to appear as the actual sovereign of Bulgaria. At times the outcome was absurd. When Duke Ernest II, the head of the House of Coburg, died in the summer of 1893, Ferdinand immediately left for Germany to attend the funeral in Coburg. It was to be a major gathering of Europe's royalty. Kaiser William II was to be there as well as numerous representatives of ruling houses.

Four days before the funeral, the German Kaiser's new Imperial Chancellor, von Caprivi, advised his master not to attend since Prince Ferdinand would use the occasion to engineer an encounter with the Kaiser and many of those present would treat him as the sovereign of Bulgaria. For political reasons this would be quite undesirable.

Angrily the Kaiser replied that he was not going to be hindered from performing his royal and family duties because of the appearance in Germany of 'this conceited buffoon'.[9] He would personally see to it that Ferdinand was treated correctly and would explain the true position to the Tsar. Whereupon he sent a telegram to the new Duke of Coburg, Queen Victoria's second son Alfred Duke of Edinburgh: 'After consulting with my people from the government, I suggest plain clothes for Ferdinand and not Bulgarian uniform. Am very thankful for your right ideas in this matter. William.' The new Duke disagreed: 'Ferdinand not appearing in uniform would prevent his taking part in the procession... it would be best to let the uniform be worn and take no notice of it.'

The Kaiser went on insisting. The vestimentary problem added yet another headache to the Coburg court already overburdened with preparations for the great funeral. On the morning of the funeral day, a telegram reached Berlin: 'Prince Ferdinand will appear in civilian dress or not at all.'[10] Ferdinand kept to his room until the last moment and then joined the mourners in full Bulgarian military regalia. Kaiser William and he shook hands but not a word was spoken. The former glared as Ferdinand gravely sat down opposite him for the funeral meal.

The absurdity of such incidents is patent. Nevertheless, the minute interest paid to State ceremonial, precedence, protocol, uniforms and decorations by King Edward VII (who attended the Coburg funeral as Prince of Wales), Kaiser William II, Prince Ferdinand, and most of their contemporaries, was not as foolish an obsession as might be supposed. If, after all, relations between two of Europe's major Powers, Germany and Russia, could become dangerously strained and be influenced by the clothes worn by a young prince, then it was reasonable to take the matter seriously.

Prince Ferdinand's first journey to Western Europe was undertaken for a variety of reasons. The call of the bright lights of Western Europe was not the least of them. He also used his absence from Bulgaria to show Europe that the political situation in Bulgaria was calm and his throne secure.

That was good public relations. Ferdinand was very consciously putting on a front, knowing perfectly well that he was at all times exposed to death at the hands of a Russian-backed assassin. His enemies at that time and for years to come used his perfectly reasonable precautions against assassination (by comparison with those taken by Tsar Alexander III, they were lax) to create a caricature of a trembling hermit sovereign who only felt safe in his allegedly 'steel-walled' smoking-room in his palace in Sofia. His increasingly frequent trips abroad and in Bulgaria, and the numerous public occasions which he attended, his Wagnerian pilgrimages to Bayreuth, his sojourns in the spas and capitals of Europe, gave the lie to the caricature.

During his first years in Bulgaria he wore a light-weight chain-mail vest under his uniform on public occasions and gave out misleading details about his travel plans. His ministers grew used to being given wrong information about the time and place of his arrivals and departures. On his return from his first foreign trip in November 1889, a group of Cabinet ministers travelled north to wait for his arrival by steamer on the Danube, following his telegraphic cancellation of the originally scheduled Orient Express route, only to find that Ferdinand had laid a false scent and arrived the following day in Sofia by rail.

On that occasion Ferdinand's fears were quite justified. A few weeks after his return the Bulgarian authorities uncovered the biggest

Russian-backed conspiracy for a *coup d'état* by disaffected Bulgarian officers with the object of arresting Prince Ferdinand, Stamboloff and the other members of the Bulgarian Government. It was the conspirators' intention to have Ferdinand judged and sentenced to death as a usurper by a special court.

The uncovering of the 'Panitza Conspiracy', so named after its Bulgarian organizer Major Panitza, was preceded by a farcical curtain-raiser which had nothing to do with the plans of the plotters. By coincidence, the day before Prince Ferdinand's departure for his first foreign trip, Sofia saw the arrival of the first Russians of distinction since diplomatic relations were broken. They were Prince Dolgorukoff and his wife. At first it seemed that the couple were merely travelling privately through Bulgaria. They called on Stamboloff and the other ministers; this was seen as mere courtesy.

Stamboloff took notice of the fact that the visitors got in touch with Bulgarian officers, including Major Panitza, and began agitating against Prince Ferdinand. Stamboloff was still prepared to treat the Russian visitors as harmless eccentrics until Prince Dolgorukoff made arrangements for holding a Requiem Mass in the cathedral for Tsar Alexander II, 'in expiation of the insult to the memory of the late Tsar' by Bulgaria. This was too much. The Prime Minister gave orders cancelling the Mass as an overt political demonstration. Undaunted, the Russian visitor arranged for the Mass to be held the following Sunday and sent out printed invitations. At that Stamboloff ordered him to leave the country.

The German Consul General in Sofia, who was responsible for Russian subjects in Bulgaria, had great trouble in persuading Prince Dolgorukoff to leave of his own free will. A forcible deportation could have had serious international consequences. Stamboloff's newspaper mocked Bulgarian Russophil politicians who had flocked to the Russian visitor, believing him to be the Tsar's viceroy, and compared them to the people who swarmed round Gogol's 'Government Inspector'.

There was no evidence that this farce had official Russian backing; the Russian Prince, an ardent chauvinist, was acting on his own. The much more serious 'Panitza Conspiracy', whose roots stretched back to 1887, was set up with the full knowledge and approval of the Tsar by the indefatigable Hitrovo in Bucharest.

Major Panitza was a Bulgarian from Macedonia, a turbulent, fire-eating young soldier, fine-looking and with an attractive personality, according to Lord Hardinge of Penshurst who knew him. He had fought with great bravery during the Serbo-Bulgarian war at the head of a volunteer Macedonian brigade which he had organized, and had been greatly liked by Prince Alexander of Battenberg. His total commitment to bringing about the unification of Macedonia and Bulgaria had turned him into a popular hero in both. Even after Prince Ferdinand's arrival, he still hoped for Prince Alexander's return. Stamboloff liked him and did not take him too seriously until reports began to reach him about Panitza's wilder tirades against Ferdinand in Sofia's cafés. For Panitza, such behaviour was not unusual, but now behind the hot-headed, tap-room demagogue there stood his solid achievement in the war and his continuing popularity. Stamboloff had underestimated Panitza and his utter dedication to the union of Macedonia with Bulgaria. The Macedonian firebrand was exasperated at what he considered to be Stamboloff's over-cautious, hesitant attitude to the Macedonian Question.

Panitza was by then one of the leaders of the Macedonian under-ground movement for union with Bulgaria. He soon came to share their conviction that their goal could only be achieved with the help of Russia. The rest followed logically: in order to obtain Russian help, it was necessary to satisfy the Tsar's desire to get rid of Ferdinand. Acting in almost total ignorance of the reality of European power politics, Panitza established contact with Hitrovo in the autumn of 1887, some weeks after Ferdinand had become Prince of Bulgaria.

Panitza proposed to remove Prince Ferdinand on several conditions. Among the most important were: that Russia should deliver weapons and ammunition for an uprising in Macedonia; and that there should be no Russian objections if Prince Alexander of Battenberg were to be one of the candidates for the throne vacated by Prince Ferdinand. The Russians turned down Panitza and instead backed Captain Nabokoff's third and fatal expedition into Bulgaria. After that fiasco, Hitrovo resumed negotiations with Panitza and it was decided to give him full backing. On 20 September 1889, Hitrovo told Panitza that the Russian Government wanted the *coup d'état* to take place as soon as possible. That summer Panitza had formed a Revolutionary Military Committee over which he presided and which included the Commandant of the Sofia Garrison, Colonel Kissoff, and the Prefect of Police. Major Panitza's prestige was such that the greater part of the garrison was in the plot and nearly three-quarters of the officers in the army knew about it. It was not until January 1890 that the full gravity of the plot was revealed and Stamboloff realized how disastrously he had underestimated Panitza's threatening café outbursts.

The *coup d'état* was to take place during the night of 1 February 1890, while the members of the Government, some two hundred officers, and many other officials were at a Court ball in the palace. The officer in charge of the palace guard was one of the conspirators. It was an ideal setting for a *coup d'état*, with all the eggs in one basket.

On 31 January, the day before the ball, Hitrovo, in Bucharest, received a cypher telegram from Panitza. The telegram read: 'Prince of Coburg, ministry and police authorities are in our hands. Please request Imperial Government to appoint imperial commissioner as soon as possible and arrange his departure for Belgrade. Any delay would seriously endanger the business in hand.'[11] Major Panitza had sent this premature telegram in order to ensure that the coup should coincide with the arrival in Sofia of an official representative of the Tsar. Despite the Major's insistence on this point, the Russians hesitated for fear of compromising themselves before the eyes of Europe. What Panitza did not know when he sent the telegram was that Stamboloff and the Prince by then knew all about the plot.

It had been betrayed to Stamboloff by Colonel Kissoff, the Commandant of the Sofia Garrison, four days before the Court ball was due to take place. He told Stamboloff that Panitza, when in his cups a few days earlier, had proposed to Kissoff that he should hand over the command of the capital. In return he had offered Kissoff the position of commander-in-chief. It was quite clear to the Prime Minister that Kissoff had in fact known of the plot for a long time (he was one of the original conspirators) and was trying to put his last minute betrayal of the conspiracy in a better light.

Immediately Stamboloff set his agents on the track and within three days had a nearly complete picture of the conspiracy. The extent of disaffection in the army left him thunderstruck. Many of the details were obtained from Panitza's servant, who had been used as a confidential messenger by the plotters. The scale and timing of the plot meant that he had to move very quickly and as secretly as possible. The day before the court ball he summoned the Council of Ministers. This in fact was a meeting between himself and the only two ministers he felt he could trust. They deliberated until three in the morning of the day of the Court ball. For various practical reasons – but perhaps mainly due to a sense of grim humour – Stamboloff decided to have Panitza arrested at his house at night by *his* betrayer Colonel Kissoff and the Prefect of Police (who also defected from the conspirators once he learned of the former's defection) accompanied by ten soldiers and six gendarmes. But as he had no confidence in the two men, he ordered five police commissaries whom he trusted to follow the first party with fifty men. They were to see that the first party executed its mission. If not, they were to arrest the first arresting party together with Panitza.

Panitza was arrested as planned and in his house were found masses of documents and letters showing that the artillery, the cavalry and nearly half the infantry were in the plot. So many officers were involved that Stamboloff dared not arrest more of the ringleaders until loyal officers could arrive from the provinces to take the place of the disaffected ones.

The Court ball took place as planned. It was the most sumptuous since Prince Ferdinand's arrival in Bulgaria and a testing time for the two hundred officers among the guests. They were all aware that Panitza had been arrested that morning. More than half of them – some 130 according to a contemporary estimate – were Panitza's friends and accomplices.

The officers, wrote an English guest, 'were walking about the saloons, under the angry eye of the Prince, and the cold scathing scorn of Stamboloff, like men in a dream. They fully expected to be arrested *en masse* in the Ball-room, and it was a relief to everybody when the evening came to a close.'[12] The officers' anxiety was made the more oppressive by the splendour and glitter around them. Many of them had never seen such luxury as drawing rooms banked with flowers in the middle of winter; these had come from Vienna hot-houses on the Orient Express, while the favours for the cotillon had been sent from Paris. As Prince Ferdinand moved through the rooms with his mother on his arm, his face a set mask of suppressed fury, he indicated each conspirator with a glance to Princess Clémentine. The Prince and Stamboloff had loaded revolvers in their pockets.

The next forty-eight hours were a time of intense anxiety for them both. They were waiting for loyal officers to arrive from the provinces. Even after their arrival, very few arrests were made in comparison with the extent of the conspiracy. Mass arrests would have been too embarrassing by demonstrating to the world the extent to which the disaffection had spread. Stamboloff's main catch was the wine merchant Kolobkoff, a former Russian officer and a Russian subject, who had acted as the communications link between the conspirators and Hitrovo. At his house were found numerous documents which proved beyond any doubt Russia's guiding role in the conspiracy.

Count Kálnoky congratulated the Prince and Stamboloff for foiling the conspiracy. He advised the latter to use all necessary severity but to avoid anything that might be seen as personal revenge. The advice was unnecessary – Stamboloff and the Prince had already resisted the temptation to carry out wholesale arrests.

The trial of Panitza, the Russian Kolobkoff and eleven others took place in Sofia in May. It was followed with great interest by the rest of Europe, and Sofia swarmed with foreign correspondents. The role of revolutionary martyr came easily to Panitza who, with one eye to the gallery, declared that he took all the blame on himself. After a fortnight Panitza was sentenced to death and the others received prison sentences of varying length. In Bulgaria, the death sentence on Panitza was greeted with disbelief; his popularity and almost legendary exploits seemed to confer on him a kind of immunity. Several members of the military court which sentenced him were his friends and the court recommended that the death sentence be commuted to fifteen years' imprisonment at the Prince's discretion. No one in Sofia believed that Panitza would be executed and he himself, together with most officers, was convinced that he would be saved by a popular uprising or Russia's intervention.

The Prince, who had left Sofia when the trial began, wanted to commute the sentence, believing that the execution of Panitza would lead to unrest. Stamboloff, on the other hand, was adamant – an act of clemency by the Prince would only be seen as an act of weakness dictated by fear. When the sentence was confirmed by the highest military tribunal on 27 June, Ferdinand was aboard a Danube steamer on his way to Austria. Stamboloff managed to join him and after long and heated discussion, the Prince signed the death sentence and continued his journey. The following day Panitza was brought to the summer camp of the Sofia garrison in a heavily guarded carriage. The entire garrison, consisting of two infantry regiments was lined up as Panitza was tied to a willow tree.

It was Stamboloff's own setting. He was determined to drive home his personal message: 'I will sacrifice anyone or anything, without exception, for Bulgaria and its independence.' The tension in the ranks was almost unbearable; several soldiers swayed and fainted as the firing squad lined up. Stamboloff had ordered the firing squad to be selected from a regiment of Panitza's fellow Macedonians. The officer in charge was also a Macedonian. In Stamboloff's mind there was no borderline between a sense of grim humour and poetic justice. They complemented each other. Panitza, pale after five months in prison, died according to the romantic convention which had governed his life. Before the bullets hit him, he cried out in a loud voice: 'Long live Macedonia and Bulgaria!'

CHAPTER 13

Courtships

—◦❧❦◦—

On the morning after the execution, a paper notice was found pinned to the trunk of the stunted willow against which Panitza was shot. It read: 'Here Stamboloff and Prince Ferdinand will be shot.' The notice was removed and a few days later a black banner appeared on the tree with a similar threat. The tree was then cut down.

Among Macedonians, the execution of Panitza resulted in a surge of blind hatred directed against the Prince and Stamboloff. The Prime Minister in particular came to be seen by militant Macedonians as the Antichrist, to be held responsible for the continuing enslavement of the Christians of Macedonia by the Turks. Almost immediately plans were made to assassinate Ferdinand, since attempts to get rid of him by means of a revolution or a *coup d'état* had so often failed. Eventually a group of Macedonian extremists changed their minds and decided that they should murder Stamboloff, as they would then both be rid of him and of Ferdinand, who would be frightened into abdication. In any case, the Prince would be left without his main support. Such at least was the apparent political rationale of the extremists. But they did not need one, being in the grip of a far more powerful urge, the obsessive requirement of the Macedonian vendetta: the need to avenge the death of Panitza. Even the fact that during that year Stamboloff, through adroit diplomacy, managed to get the Sultan to approve the appointment of three Bulgarian bishops in Macedonia (a significant step in the struggle for unity with Macedonia) did not deter Panitza's would-be avengers.

Through his agents and informants, the Prime Minister knew that several killers had crossed the Bulgarian border and were waiting for an opportunity. He became even harder and his irritability betrayed his inner tension.

In Bucharest, Hitrovo was indignant when he learnt about Panitza's death. Russia's arch-plotter was busily discussing ways of blowing up Ferdinand with a new kind of dynamite bomb recently invented in Paris by a Russian 'pyrotechnician', one Fyodoroff. All the same, he found time to send a telegram to the Russian Foreign Minister in which he bitterly condemned 'this pointless atrocity committed by the self-styled Bulgarian Prince and his ministers'.[1]

While the uncovering of the plot and the execution earned Stamboloff the undying hatred of a number of determined and desperate people, it also undeniably strengthened Prince Ferdinand's and his own authority in the country. Even Bismarck, who had been 'dropped' by Kaiser William II earlier that year, for the first time found a good word for Bulgaria and its ruler:

> From what one can see among the Balkan states, it seems to me that the Bulgarians have in them the quality needed to build and maintain a state. They are also an efficient, hard-working and economical nation which believes in gradual and prudent progress. The Bulgarians are proud, they multiply and they defend themselves. I like them much better than their neighbours, the Serbs.
>
> Prince Ferdinand, is without doubt more able than is suggested by his reputation in the humorous newspapers. He is also abler than the majority of other sovereigns. Unfortunately, he is surrounded by too many questionable people – but what can he do, he can't hang them all. But he is forced, of necessity, to string up blackguards like Major Panitza.[2]

From Bismarck this was praise indeed.

There was also public praise from Vienna. In a major speech on foreign affairs, Count Kálnoky said that it was 'satisfying to see that Bulgaria perseveres in its wise policy of political reserve, does not jeopardize its steady development by indulging in dangerous adventures and by raising dangerous problems, and is determined to maintain good relations with its neighbours, especially with the Porte'.[3]

While the rest of Europe continued to be impressed by Bulgaria's solid progress, Stefan Stamboloff realized that all the hard-won gains could be lost in a second. He lived in daily fear of the Prince's assassination. His own popularity was beginning to wane and his tough measures were gaining him more and more enemies. Most important of all, he had lost considerable support among the army officers, who were the one body of people that could guarantee calm and order. If Ferdinand were killed, the officers would be freed from their oath of allegiance. Anarchy would almost certainly result if the officers and the men under them went their own ways to back the political faction or party of their choice. There was only one answer: the Prince had to get married and found a dynasty. The Prime Minister's nightmare was to see the Prince killed before he had managed to produce an heir. He reasonably thought that the motive for killing Ferdinand would disappear once there was an infant crown prince: the murder party would realize that his death would lead to a Regency.

The British Prime Minister, Lord Salisbury, was of the same opinion. He wrote to Queen Victoria:

> The Bulgarian subjects of Prince Ferdinand are not confident in the stability of his rule; and he runs the risk of assassination in consequence of the general unrest and doubt which his uncertain irregular position is causing. Any notice from Your Majesty, though of course it cannot convey legal recognition under the Treaty of Berlin, yet will powerfully strengthen the Prince's position among his subjects.
>
> The thing most to be desired is that he should marry and leave an heir; for then the motive for his assassination would to an extent disappear. But of that there seems little hope.[4]

When Stamboloff confided his ideas of marriage to Princess Clémentine, she was quite clear about the difficulties of finding a suitable and willing bride from a royal house. But, in fact, Stamboloff's plan answered her dearest wish and greatest ambition: to see her son's dynasty established in Bulgaria, a dynasty which would rekindle the Bourbon flame that died in 1848 in Paris with her father's abdication and ignominious flight to England.

As for Ferdinand, he made no objections. He agreed that it was the best thing for him to do and steeled himself to face new humiliations which would go hand-in-hand with those he suffered from not being recognized. Where was a suitable and willing object of his wooing to be found?

Ferdinand was twenty-nine in 1890. He was fine looking, many thought handsome, he was very rich and his family connections were numerous and splendid. He was however, the unrecognized ruler of a Balkan state which had just woken up from a five-hundred-year sleep, and he was the object of the intense personal and political hatred of the Tsar of Russia, a hatred exacerbated by the latter's unsuccessful attempts to have him murdered.

Were a member of any of the reigning houses of Europe to agree to marry him, that reigning house would then find itself automatically burdened with Russia's enmity and all the ensuing diplomatic, political and military difficulties and complications. Prince Alexander of Battenberg, now at last happily married to a beautiful and talented actress, had had many a bitter experience when he and Princess Victoria of Prussia tried to marry. He had to suffer the formidable combined enmity of the Tsar and Bismarck.

Apart from this major obstacle, there was the very real and natural fear of assassination – a wife does not feel reassured on being told that the assassins only want to get her husband. If all that wasn't enough, there was also a religious problem. The Bulgarian Constitution stipulated (Article Thirty-Eight) that the heir apparent had to be christened and brought up in the Eastern Orthodox religion. It was an obvious stumbling block to obtaining a wife from a Catholic family.

Dreading the task before him, in the summer of 1891 Prince Ferdinand set out to find a wife, urged on by his mother and his Prime Minister. Princess Clémentine had, earlier that year, had a long shouting match with the Grand Duke of Tuscany (she was getting more and more deaf) about arranging a marriage between his eldest daughter, Luisa, and Ferdinand. The impoverished Grand Duke was all for it; his wife, who hated the Coburgs, was against. Nevertheless, arrangements were made for Luisa and Ferdinand to meet in the Castle of Alcsuth in June.

Ferdinand had been nearly four years in Bulgaria. He had greatly changed for the better in the opinion of those who had known him in the past. There was little left outwardly of his earlier affectations. Ferdinand went through the motions of wooing Luisa of Tuscany. His stilted manner on this occasion, a slapdash imitation of his own earlier *persona,* and his lack of enthusiasm for the task in hand are apparent even in Luisa's ghosted memoirs published twenty years later:

> Ferdinand was most elaborately attired in a light grey suit with an *ultra chic* Panama hat. He constantly waved his well manicured hands, and displayed the costly rings which glittered on his fingers. He attitudinized like a Narcissus, and kept posing until he thought doubtless I was sufficiently impressed by his fine figure, his rings, and last, but not least, his smart yellow boots; he then suggested a walk in the castle gardens.[5]

Ferdinand cut her some red and white roses and told her that the flowers and their leaves represented the Bulgarian tricolour. According to Luisa, the following dialogue took place:

> 'Would you like to see Bulgaria, Cousin Luisa?'
> 'Oh yes, if it isn't too uncivilized.'
> 'Is that all you can find to say?' he cried in an excited tone. 'Then *I* will speak. I have known you long enough to appreciate your good qualities, I admire you – I feel lonely.'
> 'Well, get married,' I said lightly.
> 'I have thought of it but I have met with no success,' replied

Ferdinand; 'and that is a good thing, for now I know that you alone
are the woman I can love.'

'Well,' I said with mock earnestness, 'let me assure you at once that
I do not and could not love you, and should not be happy as your wife.'

'Oh, Luisa,' he pleaded, 'I would do everything for you.'

'It would be of no use,' I answered.

'But I love you so dearly,' he persisted.

I lost patience with him, 'Cousin,' I said, 'do realize once and for all
that I can never love you.'

'*C'est la première fois qu'une femme me dit cela,*' he exclaimed. 'Be wise,
Luisa; think of all that it lies in my power to give you.'

'I quite realize your worldly advantages, but you would never be
able to give me real happiness. Listen Ferdinand,' I continued
seriously. 'I'm sure you only want to marry me because I am an
Austrian Archduchess; the word Archduchess stands for love in your
vocabulary, and you have promised to your ministers to return to
Bulgaria betrothed to one.

Well – *I* shall not marry you.'

At that Luisa, who throughout her memoirs got all the best lines,
turned and left him 'looking the picture of despair'. She added: 'Even
now I can see Ferdinand, faced with explanations to his ministers,
standing in that sunny garden among the roses, wringing his large white
hands and exclaiming: "*Oh, Mon Dieu! Oh, Mon Dieu!*"'

Luisa later married the Crown Prince of Saxony. She did not get on
with him and his family, was threatened with incarceration in a lunatic
asylum, ran away from the Court at Dresden, was compromised with
her children's tutor, had a nervous breakdown, a scandalous divorce and
married an Italian singer.

The extract from her memoirs has been quoted, despite her unrelia-
bility as a witness, because it unconsciously seems to reflect Ferdinand's
half-heartedness on that occasion. He could have done far better had he
really wanted to. He was probably only going through the motions of
courting Luisa, to please his mother who had arranged the meeting.
Luisa may have sensed his total lack of ardour, which would help to
explain the above caricature as a case of delayed pique. Her memoirs
were written in 1911, when Ferdinand as Tsar of Bulgaria was one of the
most admired men in Europe. On another occasion Luisa had spoken of
Ferdinand in his youth as 'handsome, rich and not unamusing'.

Ferdinand's meeting with Luisa took place after an incident in Sofia
earlier that year which caused Stamboloff to press the Prince harder
than ever to get married. The founding of a dynasty became the Prime
Minister's *idee fixe* after he narrowly avoided assassination on 27 March

1891. Instead of hitting Stamboloff, the assassin's bullet killed his close friend Belcheff, the Finance Minister, with whom he was walking at dusk in a Sofia street. When the fatal shots were fired, the two friends were discussing, of all things, the merits of *The Vicar of Wakefield*. The assassins ran off and then Stamboloff heard two more shots and an exultant cry of 'Stamboloff is killed!' He reacted to this double shock – the death of his close friend and the attempt on his life – with sombre fury. Though the murderers were not caught, he ordered mass arrests of all suspects: 'There was a fierce determination, a terrible concentration of purpose, a doggedness of resolve that, come what might, by fair means or foul, the guilty should be detected and punished',[6] wrote *The Times* correspondent in Sofia, James Bourchier. The jails were filled with suspects, cases of maltreatment and police beatings were almost becoming the rule. By the end of the year, almost all of Stamboloff's enemies had fled to Russia, Turkey or Serbia.

The assassination had been carried out by Macedonian extremists with Russian connivance: two of the organizers, arrested by the Romanian police when trying to reach Odessa, were freed after Russian diplomatic pressure on Romania, got to Odessa and were given pensions by the Russian Foreign Ministry. This was done quietly but the Russians felt uncomfortable enough in the face of European public opinion to transfer that indefatigable 'diplomat' Hitrovo from Bucharest to Lisbon.

Stamboloff, who was never likely to forget the profound shock of that evening, nevertheless commissioned an oil painting to commemorate the assassination. The picture was to hang in the drawing room of his modest house for the rest of his life. The artist had done his best: a very black canvas with four light blots: the pale faces of Stamboloff and Belcheff and two reddish-yellow revolver flashes.

Ferdinand returned to Bulgaria from his 1891 summer trip to Western Europe empty-handed, with no bride in the offing and had to face Stamboloff's increasingly exasperating urgings. A note of desperation can be detected in a letter he wrote from his palace near Varna, on the Black Sea, to his 'dearest aunt', the Duchess of Coburg, about a prospective bride whose name is not mentioned. But it can be inferred from the family relationships mentioned in the letter that he had his eye on one of Queen Victoria's granddaughters, the children of Alfred Duke of Edinburgh who had married Marie, the only sister of Tsar Alexander III. The girls were still young, the eldest was sixteen, the youngest seven:

... granddaughter of the Queen of England, granddaughter of the Tsar-liberator and cousin of the German Kaiser! *Que voudrait on de plus*. That would be a terrible blow for the Russophil party in this country – it would be forced to be loyal to the granddaughter of Alexander II! I see from the Coburg newspapers that the respective parents are already at Coburg. May God give them wisdom, for I am thoroughly sick of this marriage question and long for a result! I do not fear the father: he would agree out of hatred for Russia. But as for the mother? Will she have the good sense to defy her pig-headed and odious brother? I shall remain here in my beautiful Miramare until 15 September...[7]

He went on to discuss the financial aspects and 'guarantees' which he could offer if the marriage took place. The fact that he actually put this daydream down on paper (it is inconceivable that the realist in Ferdinand for one moment believed that Queen Victoria would allow one of her schoolgirl granddaughters to become engaged, let alone marry, a man so many years her senior and, on top of that, with the reputation of a *viveur*) is a measure of his vexation.

The marriage question, non-recognition and the threats of assassination and Russian subversion were the dark side of the picture. But Bulgaria's 'economic miracle' continued to be the admiration of Europe, while Ferdinand scored some notable successes. His travels were not only devoted to finding a bride. In July 1891, much to the anger of the Tsar of Russia, he managed to be received (of course, not as Prince of Bulgaria but as Prince of Saxe-Coburg-Gotha) by Emperor Francis Joseph at Gastein. That year he concluded a major contract with Krupp, the German arms manufacturers, and Ferdinand stayed with the head of the firm at the fabulous Villa Hügel in Essen. Ferdinand was delighted when he was received with full royal honours. Throughout he maintained close relations with leading European financiers and industrialists.

The following year, 1892, began with another terrorist act. The Bulgarian diplomatic agent in Constantinople, Dr Vulkovich, was stabbed in the back while returning to his house in broad daylight in the Turkish capital. The Carnival was in full swing and the assassin's mask attracted no attention. As he stabbed the Bulgarian diplomat, he shouted, 'This is to avenge my wife's honour!' – the idea being to lay a false trail for the authorities. The victim died the next day. Dr Vulkovich, a gentle and very able man, had done much to maintain friendly relations between Bulgaria and Turkey and was on excellent terms with Western European diplomats. As such, he was seen as a serious obstacle to the aims of Russian diplomacy in the Balkans. The assassin and another terrorist were given false papers with the assistance of the Russian Ambassador, Nelidoff, were smuggled aboard a Russian ship, and taken back to Odessa from whence they had come.

The murder caused a great outcry not only in Bulgaria but in all
Europe. The European Press was loud in its condemnation of Russia.
The embarrassed Nelidoff wrote to his Foreign Minister Giers to
suggest that the assassins be arrested and sent to Siberia. Tsar Alexander
thought this was too near and wrote in the margin of the letter: 'It seems
to me better to send them both to Vladivostok.' Hitrovo, who had been
sent to Lisbon after the Belcheff murder, was also too embarrassing to
have around in Europe now: Giers sent him even further east than
Vladivostok – to Tokyo.

The Constantinople murder, so close on Belcheff's, had a devastating
effect on Stamboloff.

> Those who had known Stamboloff for years could not fail to see
> that the balance of his mind was affected by this tragic occurrence.
> There was still the same courage and confidence, the same
> clearness of brain, the same caustic humour, the same pleasant
> *bonhomie,* vivacity and brilliancy of repartee; but to speak to him on
> that one subject, and you found him an altered man....[8]

So wrote James Bourchier in *The Times* obituary on Stamboloff three
years later. He could have added that, after the Vulkovich assassination,
the Prime Minister's resolve to see Ferdinand produce an heir became
obsessive.

Determined, and oppressed by Stamboloff's injunctions, Prince
Ferdinand set out at the end of the spring of 1892 on a prolonged journey
through Europe. His most important destination was London, and then
Balmoral; Queen Victoria's invitation had seemed full of promise.
Ferdinand and his mother arrived in London on 30 May. The Prime
Minister and Lady Salisbury called on him at Claridge's the following
morning. Lord Salisbury, who was not only Prime Minister but Foreign
Secretary as well, came a second time the next day and in the evening
the Prince went to a reception at the Foreign Office given by Lady
Salisbury. It was after these meetings that the Prime Minister told the
Queen of the favourable impression he had received and advised her to
strengthen his position by giving Ferdinand some mark of encourage-
ment. In addition, Lord Salisbury pointed out the importance of
Ferdinand maintaining his position:

> Lord Salisbury thought it probable Your Majesty would wish to
> show some civility to Prince Ferdinand, both on account of the
> relationship, and because Lord Salisbury had often heard Your
> Majesty speak in affectionate terms of Princess Clémentine.

But it was also most advantageous for public reasons that Your Majesty should show some mark of interest in Prince Ferdinand. His position is very peculiar. It is of the greatest importance that he should not be murdered or driven from Bulgaria; and that is strongly felt, not only by England, but also by Austria and Italy, and in some measure by Germany.

But though these Powers are very anxious to sustain him, they are unable to recognize him; because the recognition of the Sultan must be given *in the first instance,* and the Sultan is too much afraid of Russia to give it.[9]

Before going to Balmoral, Ferdinand accompanied his mother to France, where she was going to spend a few days with her brother, the Duc d'Aumale at Chantilly. When the latter saw Ferdinand, whom he had not seen for years, he exclaimed: *'Ferdinand, c'est toi?... Eh bien! Je suis comme l'Europe... je ne te reconnais pas!* [Ferdinand, is that you?... Well, there we are! I am like Europe... I don't recognize you!]'[10]

On 6 June, Ferdinand arrived at Balmoral. The Queen wrote in her diary that she found him 'grown older, since five years of an anxious life, and I think improved'. The next morning he joined her where she sat on the terrace with the dispatch boxes under a green-lined parasol:

Balmoral, 7th June. – Ferdinand came out to see me, and sat some little time talking of his difficulties, trials and dangers (he cannot now go about without an escort, since the two murders, of one of his Ministers, and of his Minister at Constantinople, Dr Vulkovich, both instigated by the Russians; and the murderers, though convicted, are not given up by them but are still at large). He says his position is very difficult and anomalous. He is the Sovereign and yet not acknowledged as such, the Powers, who were parties to the Treaty of Berlin not having done so. He does not expect or mind it, but what is of all importance is his marrying.

He is quite sensible and impartial, and devoted to his country, for whose good only he wished to work. After I went in, I saw a servant of Ferdinand's, a Bulgarian, who was with Sandro, and remained faithful to the last on that dreadful night. He is an excellent, good-looking young man, who is still devoted to Sandro, and told Beatrice [the Queen's youngest daughter, married to Prince Henry of Battenberg] a great deal that was interesting about all that terrible time.[11]

All in all, Ferdinand made a very favourable impression on the Queen, as she told Lord Salisbury later. It appears that he touched a tender cord when he referred to the fact that he was born in the same year that the Prince Consort died; he managed to do it without making the obvious gaffe of implying that the loss to the House of Coburg had been made good by his own arrival.

Before he was due to leave Balmoral, the Court Circular announced that, at the request of the Queen, Ferdinand was to extend his visit for one day longer. He was taken on a drive round Glen Beg by the Queen and the Princesses Louise and Beatrice. It was all very flattering and agreeable but, as to the matter which was uppermost in his mind, the Queen gave him to understand that there was no chance of his making an English royal marriage. Russia would have seen it as throwing down the gauntlet; Tsar Alexander might have picked it up.

A rather dejected Prince Ferdinand travelled back to London with a Queen's Equerry in attendance for the rest of his stay in England. The following day restored his morale. While at Balmoral he had accepted an invitation from the Lord Mayor of London for luncheon at the Mansion House. The day began with the Prince of Wales and his brother, the Duke of Edinburgh, calling at his hotel.

At the Mansion House he was gratified when the Lord Mayor proposed a toast to him as Prince of Bulgaria – it was recognition of a sort. The Lord Mayor went on to say that while he could not but refer to the Prince's relationship to the Queen, there were stronger claims than birth: 'we are not unmindful that for a period of five years his Royal Highness has discharged efficiently and well the government of his country'. He had discharged his duty 'in the interest of peace and with a single-minded purpose: for the prosperity of his country.' Answering in fluent English, Ferdinand spoke of his 'most respectful veneration' for Queen Victoria 'to whom I am bound by ties of close family relationship'. He spoke of his efforts to ensure the developments of Bulgaria as well as 'the tranquillity of the Balkan Peninsula'. A great crowd outside the Mansion House cheered him when he left. In the evening he dined at Marlborough House with the Prince and the Princess of Wales and joined his mother in Paris next day.

In a letter to Queen Victoria, Princess Clémentine said that Ferdinand had returned from England 'very happy' and thanked her for her kindness to her son and 'the affection for him of which you gave proof by your help and advice to ensure that inner happiness which he so much needs'.[12]

Ferdinand next tried his luck with Germany. But he was rebuffed by both Kaiser William II and Chancellor Caprivi. Ferdinand had asked the Austrians to see if Caprivi would receive him in Berlin. The German answer to Vienna read: 'The Imperial Government feels no necessity to adopt a position about a marriage of the Prince.' It went on to ask the

Austrians to advise the Prince not to request a meeting with Caprivi and thus spare him the 'distress of a refusal'.[13] The German minister in St Petersburg was instructed to leak the fact that Ferdinand had been turned down.

All the doors on which he knocked remained closed for fear of Russia and Tsar Alexander's obsession. Finally the Prince turned to the fountainhead of diplomatic sagacity and asked to be received by the ex-Chancellor of Germany. They met in Munich. When he asked Bismarck, now seventy-seven, what he should do, he received an old man's advice which, despite its apt metaphors, did nothing to help Ferdinand find a way out of his predicament:

> Be circumspect and avoid doing anything in your policy which could ignite the spark that will soon turn into a great conflagration. Play dead! You have shown the world that you can swim; but do not try to swim against the current. Let yourself be carried along slowly and stay on the surface as you have done up to now. Time is your greatest ally – the force of habit; avoid doing anything which might irritate your enemies. If you do not provoke them, they cannot act against you and in time the world will become used to seeing you on the throne of Bulgaria.[14]

Respect towards the veteran statesman prevented Ferdinand from pointing out that his enemy the Tsar certainly *could* and *did* act against him with or without any provocation. But then Bismarck had not spent the past five years under the constant threat of assassination.

While the Prince was still abroad the trial of the suspected assassins of Belcheff took place in Sofia. The trial, conducted with the still fresh memory of the second and more recent murder of Dr Vulkovich, was conducted with great severity. Stamboloff wanted to break the will of any future conspirators and crush them. Although the actual assassins were never found, four men were sentenced to death for complicity. On receiving a petition for pardon from the four, Stamboloff wrote in the margin of the document: 'Traitors to their country deserve no mercy.' The death sentences were carried out at the end of July 1892.

During the trial the Bulgarian Government published the text of numerous secret telegrams and letters which had passed between the Russian Legation in Bucharest and St Petersburg over the previous ten years. It was the most damaging evidence of Russia's guiding role in the downfall of Prince Alexander and the subsequent conspiracies against the 'outlaw' and 'usurper' Ferdinand. This windfall had come about after Jacobson, a clerk at the Russian Legation in Romania, defected to London with documents and transcripts of Russian despatches. He got in touch with the Bulgarian authorities and sold them the material. As could have been expected, the Russian foreign ministry officially denied the authenticity of the documents. Inexplicably, it instituted legal proceedings *in absentia* against Jacobson for *theft* of documentary material.

Prince Ferdinand returned to Bulgaria a fortnight after the death sentences on the four condemened men had been carried out. Shortly after his return there took place two events which marked Bulgarian successes in diplomacy and economics. Stamboloff was invited and received in audience by the Sultan in Constantinople. It was a successful meeting at which the Sultan expressed his admiration for Stamboloff's administration of Bulgaria and expressed the hope that the Bulgarian people would 'continue to show its love for Prince Ferdinand'. He also promised to recognize Ferdinand the moment conditions were favourable. All Europe took note of the meeting which appeared a first step towards recognition. Russia was mortally offended and reacted with a furious protest note to Turkey. Bulgaria's economic successes were highlighted when the Prince opened the first international trade fair in Philippopolis. Ferdinand began to feel that his days as the 'pariah of Europe' (his own phrase) were numbered.

He and his mother were also beginning to become reconciled to the fact that he would not be able to make the kind of splendid marriage they had both envisaged at first. Both had been determined on a rich marriage into a reigning family, despite some feelers in the direction of former ruling houses. Stamboloff had been urging this less ambitious course, only to see Ferdinand's pride bristle. For some time Princess Clémentine had been in touch with Duke Robert of Bourbon-Parma, who had lost the duchy in 1860 and whose eldest daughter, Marie-Louise, seemed to offer a possible way out of Ferdinand's marital predicament. The Duke, however, refused to give his consent unless there was a change in Article Thirty-Eight of the Bulgarian Constitution stipulating that the heir to the throne should be baptized in the Orthodox Church. Marie-Louise's father insisted as a *sine qua non* that any issue of the marriage should be brought up in the Catholic faith.

This put Stamboloff in a dreadful quandary. The pressing necessity for the marriage was counter-balanced by the great danger to himself of altering the Constitution. He was well aware that he would be risking his position if he were to carry through such an unpopular measure. To his enemies he was already 'the tyrant'. By altering the constitutional provisions for the religion of the heir to the Bulgarian throne, he would also become 'the heretic'.

After long and anxious reflection, the Prime Minister decided to take upon himself the whole odium of the measure. It was only due to his great personal authority, demonic energy and impassioned speeches that he managed to persuade his own supporters and then get the change approved by the National Assembly. With great self-devotion, Stamboloff insisted that it was he who wished the change and that the Prince was in fact opposed to it.

Prince Ferdinand was only too ready to concur with Stamboloff in this whitewashing of himself, as he realized that the measure was being regarded unfavourably at home and with concern abroad. He told foreign diplomats that it was 'a means for Russian agitation', 'a danger to the throne' and that 'Stamboloff's cure is worse than the illness'.[15] He assured one diplomat that no wedding plans existed. By this time relations between the Prince and Stamboloff had deteriorated to complete mutual antipathy. They were already unable to converse calmly and without evident signs of nervous irritation. Their only link was the *raison d'état*.

The Sobranie approved the change in Article Thirty-Eight on 19 December 1892. Quite in contradiction to the disapproval he had expressed about the measure and notwithstanding the continuing negotiations with the Duke of Parma, Prince Ferdinand lost no time in trying to use the constitutional change – he seemed to regard it as a kind of hunting permit for Catholic brides – as a means of improving on the Parma marriage. On 20 January the following year he travelled to Munich, hoping to obtain the hand of one of two Bavarian princesses, Clara or Sophie. Count Eulenburg, the Prussian Envoy in Munich, telegraphed Baron Marschall von Bieberstein, the German Foreign Secretary, informing him of Ferdinand's arrival and intentions. What were his instructions? The Foreign Secretary consulted Kaiser William and Eulenburg received his answer within a few hours: 'A union between a Bavarian princess and the Prince of Bulgaria would be undesirable for the foreign policy of the German Reich.'[16]

Obediently, the Bavarian Prince Regent informed all branches of his family that he would not consent to any union with Prince Ferdinand (actually, the Prince Regent would have personally welcomed such a marriage). The Kaiser's veto was yet another humiliation which Ferdinand had to swallow. He immediately left Munich and made an appointment to visit Krupp, so as to save face by making business the ostensible reason for his trip to Germany. At the end of January, Ferdinand arrived in Vienna and was received by Emperor Francis Joseph and Count Kálnoky. At that meeting the final details regarding Ferdinand's marriage to Princess Marie-Louise were discussed. The engagement was celebrated a fortnight later at a family gathering at the Castle of Schwartzau, Duke Robert of Bourbon-Parma's seat in Austria.

In her diary, Queen Victoria expressed her pleasure at the news, 'as Ferdinand has been wanting to marry so long and Bulgaria wishes it so ardently'.[17] Princess Clémentine who was present at the engagement celebration, wrote to thank the Queen for her letter of congratulations. Ferdinand's mother was as clear-sighted, and perhaps less sentimental, than Queen Victoria: 'Ferdinand is very happy and so am I. My future daughter is unhappily not very pretty, it is the only thing which is lacking, since she is charming, good, very witty, *intelligent* and *very* likeable.'[18]

The Sultan of Turkey sent a telegram to congratulate Prince Ferdinand and described the engagement as 'a valuable pledge for the consolidation of Bulgaria'.

In Russia, where the earlier news of the change in the Bulgarian Constitution had already provoked paroxysms of rage, the announcement of the betrothal had a devastating effect: 'One cannot understand what on earth is happening in Livadia', wrote Princess Radziwill in a letter some weeks later after the marriage:

> Everybody is ill, starting with the Tsar, one of his aides-de-camp has died, it was decided not to receive an embassy which was to bring to the Emperor of Russia the Sultan's greetings, *and the Russian Government has forbidden the Sultan's Government to receive Prince Ferdinand of Bulgaria.* A veritable system of ill-humour exists there, one which Stamboloff will allow to calm down in time; then he will resume marching forward, something he has not done too badly so far. This Catholic marriage will not let the Orthodox sleep in peace and they give proof of lack of skill by allowing it to be seen so plainly.'[19]

By contrast, the Austrians were delighted with the betrothal, which they had helped to bring about. Emperor Francis Joseph praised Ferdinand's 'intelligence, tact and courage' to such an extent that Count Goluchowski, later the Austrian Foreign Minister, told a German diplomatic colleague that 'sooner or later Constantinople will fall to the Bulgarians' and that it 'could not fall into better hands than those of the now firmly established Coburg dynasty...which maintains its Catholic character'.[20] Princess Clémentine wrote to her lady-in-waiting that the Austrian Emperor gave 'a family dinner, unspoilt by restraints or stiffness'[21] in honour of Ferdinand and his future father-in-law.

Through her paternal grandmother, Marie-Louise was a lineal descendant of King Charles X, the last of the senior Bourbons to sit on the French throne. Ferdinand was the grandson of King Louis Philippe, whose July Monarchy in 1830 replaced that of Charles X. Would not the marriage between these two and the new dynasty they would found heal the breach that had existed between the two branches of the family, the Bourbon and the Bourbon-Orléans, since 1830?

However significant these considerations were to Princess Clémentine, they meant nothing or very little to the Bulgarians, although there was much turning of pages in the Almanac de Gotha in Sofia when the engagement was announced. It was the fact that the Prince had found a bride that mattered and that caused great rejoicing, possibly the first display of genuine popular enthusiasm since Ferdinand had arrived in Bulgaria. Stamboloff, who was getting ready for the elections for the next Grand Sobranie, which had to ratify the change in the Constitution approved by the ordinary Sobranie, exclaimed: 'This news has saved me the entire election campaign!' A national collection for a present for Marie-Louise quickly raised 300,000 francs. Two-thirds of the sum was spent on a tiara in the shape of a fleur-de-lis (to mark her French royal descent), made of rubies, emeralds and diamonds (the Bulgarian national colours). The remaining sum, at Marie-Louise's later request, was used to build a maternity hospital. In addition, the city of Sofia presented her with a silver dinner service for sixty people. There were two basic reasons for the popular enthusiasm. In the first place, there was a heightened sense of national identity at the prospect of a Bulgarian ruling dynasty being re-established after five centuries of foreign rule. Second, the event found a strong echo in the Bulgarian peasant's profound respect for patriarchal morality.

There is no evidence that Ferdinand had met, or even seen, Marie-Louise before the engagement party at the Castle of Schwartzau. It was to be, uncompromisingly, a marriage of convenience, a blind date with wedlock as its certain outcome. There was no attempt to give the occasion a varnish of sentiment. Such an anachronistic procedure in an age still bathed by the afterglow of nineteenth-century Romanticism did not worry the protagonists unduly. Indeed, Ferdinand's own kind of romantic fancy found greater satisfaction in the awareness that Louis XIV, the ancester he tried to emulate, had also experienced a 'blind marriage' with Marie-Thérèse of Austria. Marie-Louise, whatever her feelings for Ferdinand later on, was to retain a feeling of pride at Ferdinand's apparent facial resemblance to the *Roi Soleil.* Unlike Louis, Prince Ferdinand was fancy free: there were no partings, no tears, no regrets and no Marie Mancini.

Princess Marie-Louise was twenty-three, nine years younger than Ferdinand, and the eldest of her twice-married father's nine children (her half-sister Zita, the future and last Empress of Austria, was born just before Marie-Louise's betrothal). She was no beauty, nor strikingly ugly: Princess Clémentine had got it about right by describing her as 'unhappily not very pretty'. Her narrow, long face with its long nose and small ears that stuck out was redeemed by 'beautiful eyes, the colour of aquamarine, large and transparently clear behind their thick dark lashes',[22] a well delineated, sensitive and humorous mouth, and a clever expression. She was said to resemble her unfortunate great-great-uncle Louis XVI in his youth. In build she was slight, with small hands and feet. She was nearly always dressed in dark clothes, considering that light colours only suited larger women.

Her mother, Maria-Pia of Bourbon-Naples, died when she was twelve and her upbringing in Biarritz and Switzerland had been in the hands of a capable English governess, Miss Fanny Fraser. She was fluent in five languages: on receiving a letter from her, Queen Victoria wrote that she was touched and was impressed by Marie-Louise's 'beautiful English'. She had received a conventional education for a girl of her class and time, though her talents as a painter and musician – she played the guitar and piano – were judged to be well above the average. She read voraciously and knew a lot of Dante and Leopardi by heart.

According to those who knew her, she was intelligent, kindly, good-natured, unaffected, and witty without malice. There is no doubt that she was sincerely religious. Though patient, she was no mouse. She had a strong will, at times obstinacy, and according to her Bulgarian tutor, the same Gancheff who taught Ferdinand, she 'was armed with that terrible female weapon: passive combativeness'.[23]

The contrast between Ferdinand and Marie-Louise was not of the kind that could resolve itself into harmony. Despite his great respect for her ancestry, the straightforward character of the Princess soon jarred on his nerves. When the engagement was announced, people reacted with malicious glee, as Princess Radziwill wrote in a letter: 'The future Princess of Bulgaria must be exceedingly ugly, but in Vienna, where Ferdinand is known through and through, people agree he is getting just what he deserves.'[24]

Before the wedding Prince Ferdinand and Stamboloff were received in Vienna by the Austrian Emperor and Kálnoky, an event which so mortified Russia that when the Russian Foreign Minister Giers passed through Vienna a few days later, the Emperor and Kálnoky called on him. The honour was meant to soothe the Tsar.

Prince Ferdinand had invited Stamboloff to the wedding, which took place at the Duke of Parma's Italian seat, the Villa delle Pianore, surrounded by beautiful gardens and overlooking the sea. The fact that the Prince and his Prime Minister dared to leave Bulgaria together caused considerable astonishment and was taken as a sign that the Russian-backed conspiracies were running out of steam.

Princess Marie-Louise, in flowing white, with her veil held by the fleur-de-lis tiara, looked slight and fragile next to the Prince looming over her in full uniform. Stamboloff was deeply disappointed on meeting her. In his mind's eye he had visualized Marie-Louise as the eventual Queen of Bulgaria, a vision of opulent and majestic femininity. Later, when the antagonism between the Prince and his minister deteriorated to open hostility, he told his friends that the Prince had no eye for a beautiful woman and couldn't choose a decent-looking wife – apparently quite forgetting that it was he who had pressed Ferdinand so hard and long to get married. Marie-Louise, for her part, was upset by the appearance of Stamboloff who, as it happened, was at that time suffering from an outbreak of neck boils. She said later: 'From the day that I first met him, I was repelled. Those suspicious-looking boils on his neck.... Goodness, how. disgusting!'[25]

The majority of the wedding guests were her relatives and Pope Leo XIII gave a special blessing through the Archbishop of Lucca. At the wedding banquet, Stamboloff made a speech in which he expressed Bulgaria's joy that for the first time in five centuries of foreign oppression a princess had mounted the throne of Bulgaria. Addressing himself to the Duke of Parma, he said: 'Bulgaria is grateful to you for having confided your daughter to her Prince. Bulgaria will honour her and guard her like a treasure.'[26] It was at the banquet that a flushed Ferdinand marked the climax of his own speech with the shout: 'in my veins too flows the blood of St Louis!'

From Spezia, the newlyweds embarked on the steam yacht *Amphitrite* for a honeymoon cruise round the Mediterranean. They were accompanied by a small suite which included Colonel Petroff, the Bulgarian Chief of Staff, whose wife had been the object of Ferdinand's attentions after his arrival in Sofia. Prince Ferdinand had intended to cruise as far as Constantinople, after the Sultan had expressed his desire to receive the couple. But the plan was dropped by both sides following the Tsar's furious reaction and threatened recall of the Russian ambassador from Turkey.

In the middle of May, Ferdinand and Marie-Louise were present in Tirnovo for the session of the Grand Sobranie, which unanimously ratified the change in the Bulgarian Constitution. After a tour of Bulgaria, during which they were rapturously received in towns and villages, they arrived by train in Sofia on 11 June to a reception of such pomp and glittering display as had never been seen in Bulgaria; at least not since the days of the medieval tsars. It was Ferdinand's own *mise-en-scène* – not the sort of thing he left to others. The procession route from the railway station to the palace was intersected by triumphal arches and lined by rows of tall, flower-covered pillars connected by chains of flowers and greenery. Prince Ferdinand and his bride travelled in a huge gilt state coach in Louis XIV-style, ordered from Vienna and drawn by

six magnificent horses in gilt harness, their heads topped by tall ostrich
feathers.

It was just the sort of thing that Stamboloff despised as pretentious
ostentation quite unsuited to a young peasant state. But on this occasion,
Ferdinand was spared his Prime Minister's morose sarcasms. The Prince
had just informed him that Marie-Louise was pregnant, in the second
month since the wedding. From that moment the Prince assumed
secondary importance in Stamboloff's thoughts; they were centred on
the hoped-for male heir.

When news of the Princess's as yet undetectable pregnancy filtered
out, there were those who professed themselves scandalized that the
Prince should announce the fact quite so early. None of this mattered
when on 30 January, nine months after the wedding, the inhabitants of
Sofia woke to a 101-gun salute announcing the birth of a son.

CHAPTER 14

Severed Hands

—◦❦❦◦—

The birth of Prince Boris of Tirnovo, the first heir to the Bulgarian throne in five centuries, was received with immense joy throughout Bulgaria. Princess Clémentine was in seventh heaven as she showed her grandson to the crowds from the palace balcony. In Prince Boris she not only saw the first-born of her favourite child and the beginning of a new dynasty: in her eyes, Boris, the direct descendant of Louis Philippe and Charles X of France, was an earnest of the rebirth of Bourbon glory.

On receiving Queen Victoria's message of congratulations, Prince Ferdinand summoned the British Envoy in Sofia, Henry Dering, to thank him and tell him that Prince Boris was 'a fine boy and possessed many of the Bourbon qualities in good-shaped hands and feet and other characteristics'.[1] The baby was looked after by Miss Inman, an English nanny selected by Queen Victoria and Princess Beatrice. Ferdinand told Dering that Miss Inman was a 'perfect treasure and had taken charge entirely of the baby, prepared to defend him against any and all dangers to which the poor child might be exposed in this country'.

It was a difficult birth and Princess Marie-Louise's convalescence lasted several months. It was said that her condition was in part due to nervous shock, the result of Stamboloff's insistence on his constitutional right as Prime Minister to be present at the delivery.

The Duke and Duchess of Parma came to Sofia for the christening which was performed with great pomp in the palace by Monsignor Menini, the Papal nuncio and Catholic Archbishop of Sofia and Philip-popolis.

The birth of an heir and the consequent founding of a Bulgarian dynasty greatly strengthened Prince Ferdinand's position both at home and abroad. The new confidence he felt was boosted by the death in Austria some two months before of Alexander of Battenberg, at the age of thirty-five. He died on the anniversary of the 1885 victory over Serbia. Ferdinand had always felt uneasy about Alexander's possible return to Bulgaria. The danger was not so much from Alexander, who had settled for a life of happy domesticity as Count Hartenau, but from disaffected Bulgarians who might use Battenberg as a rallying point to attack Prince Ferdinand.

Prince Ferdinand had always taken care to behave impeccably towards his predecessor. On his death, he made arrangements for a splendid State funeral in Sofia. The body, dressed in Alexander's Austrian general's uniform, was put into its coffin in Austria and then on a funeral train to Sofia. On Stamboloff's orders, a group of Bulgarian officers boarded the train at the Bulgarian frontier, secretly forced the lock of the coffin, stripped the Austrian uniform and dressed the body in a Bulgarian general's uniform. No one at the funeral was any the wiser; The coffin remained unlocked but shut. Stamboloff did not feel it right that his countrymen should give a State funeral to an Austrian general! Prince Ferdinand built a mausoleum in the centre of Sofia as a final resting place for Prince Alexander. 'Ferdinand seems to have been most kind and to have done everything he could',[2] wrote Queen Victoria in her journal.

Ferdinand's new confidence made him more resentful than ever at the irregularity of his international standing. Official recognition by the signatories of the Treaty of Berlin would not only strengthen him; it would stamp the mark of political legitimacy on his new dynasty.

The obstacle to recognition was, as ever, Russia. Ferdinand decided that he could no longer tolerate his dubious position. If in order to obtain recognition he had to conciliate Russia, then conciliate her he would. But in that direction stood another obstacle in the form of his powerful Prime Minister. Stamboloff was implacably opposed to anything that could be seen as weakness towards Russia. He told Ferdinand:

What do you need recognition for? You are recognized by the Bulgarian people, more than that you do not need. The other grapes are sour, let them hang. The day will come when Russia's friendship will, of itself, fall into our lap. We should not go as petitioners, for then we would have to pay a high price for the goods; even if the price were not too high for you, it is too high for me and too high for Bulgaria. If history were to say of you that you had a successful reign against Russia's will, then that would be a great achievement – far greater than if it was said: the Prince recognized the error of his ways and set out on the road to Canossa.[3]

Stamboloff could not then know that Tsar Alexander III was to die shortly and to be succeeded by the far milder Nicholas II. His entire political life had been a battle against the obstinate hatred of Tsar

Alexander; it was impossible for him to have any illusions and he rightly feared the terrible conditions which the Tsar would exact, conditions which he feared would mean the end of Bulgarian independence. In this, Stamboloff was as inflexible as the Tsar. Prince Ferdinand accordingly decided to remove Stamboloff from power, a decision that came easily since he had already taken it years earlier but postponed it until he felt sufficiently strong. There had been a recent precedent – Ferdinand was going to drop his pilot, just as the German Kaiser dropped Bismarck in 1890.

In March he privately told Richard von Mach, the Sofia correspondent of the *Kölnische Zeitung*, what to expect:

> How is it that we all change? In so short a time, too! Stamboloff is no longer the jolly, confident, untamed, popular tribune of the past. He worries and he broods. I noticed this on our travels. In the past the question that everybody asked – and that was almost insulting for me, but I swallowed it, as so much else besides – was: 'Where is Stefan? Long live Stefan!' And Stefan Stamboloff would get out of the carriage, beaming, good humoured and cry to the crowd: 'There is the Prince!' Now faces are downcast and only those in uniform cheer. His officials are scoundrels, his prefects are cattle-thieves who long ago ought to have been hanged or chained to the galleys. How often have I told the Minister: 'You are destroying your own handiwork.' It doesn't help. I have the impression that Stamboloff will soon be out of office.[4]

In planning Stamboloff's political downfall, Prince Ferdinand was not relying solely on his own strengthened position. He was fully aware that Stamboloff and his party, the National Liberals, were in a more and more isolated position. Stamboloff's timely, severe and necessary dictatorial measures following the conspiracies and assassinations had continued for too long and left an accumulation of hate and resentment. Stamboloff's party was now opposed by all the other political parties. The opposition had coined and was successfully exploiting a slogan which further widened the breach between the Prince and the Prime Minister: 'Protect the Prince from Stamboloff's excesses and violence!' In addition to his other reasons for wanting to rid himself of Stamboloff, there was Ferdinand's fear that he and his reign would perish alongside the Prime Minister in an eventual outbreak of popular violence against Stamboloff's excesses.

With such arguments the Prince visited Vienna to prepare the Austrian Government for Stamboloff's downfall. He told Kálnoky that he had to part company with the Prime Minister because popular

dissatisfaction with his regime had reached boiling point. Kálnoky
urged him not to drop Stamboloff. He knew the latter's position at home
and abroad was so strong that his dismissal would have serious consequences for the Prince. Ferdinand was less candid with the Austrian
Emperor. When Francis Joseph asked him during a private audience
about the state of his relations with Stamboloff, Ferdinand forced
himself to reply that they were excellent.

The Prime Minister's downfall came about more quickly than anyone
expected. It came as a result of an intrigue aimed against Stamboloff's
private moral reputation, mounted by members of the opposition
parties. It was skilfully exploited by Ferdinand. The Prime Minister had
already handed in his resignation on several occasions in the past,
confident that it would not be accepted. This time the Prince accepted
it.

The lever used to topple Stamboloff rested on the far from happy
marriage of the then Minister of War, Colonel Mikhail Savoff. Some of
the opposition leaders managed to persuade the insanely jealous Savoff
that he had been cuckolded by Stamboloff. Mme Savoff's extra-marital
activities were notorious, but there had at no time been anything
between her and the Prime Minister. Undeterred by this, the opposition's newspapers launched a campaign in which Stamboloff's 'immoral
life' was luridly and minutely described as well as condemned on a note
of high moral indignation. Driven nearly out of his mind by the daily
Press stories, the husband challenged Stamboloff to a duel.

Stamboloff let it be known that he could not give him satisfaction at
that time since he was representing Prince Ferdinand during the latter's
absence abroad. At the same time, the seconds appointed by the two
men agreed that there were no grounds for a duel. The upshot of the
complex intrigue was that Savoff resigned and that Colonel Racho
Petroff, the Prince's own candidate, was appointed Minister of War.
Stamboloff committed a very great error in accepting Petroff as a
member of his Cabinet. He was entirely Ferdinand's man and through
him the Prince had secured the full backing of the army, the decisive
factor in the coming trial of strength. The attentions that Ferdinand had
paid to Colonel Petroff, and to his wife, soon after his arrival in Bulgaria
some seven years earlier were now to bear fruit.

Emboldened by the presence of Colonel Petroff in the cabinet and as
chief of the army, the opposition Press renewed its attacks against
Stamboloff. It accused him of cowardice in not accepting Savoff's
challenge to a duel. Goaded beyond endurance, Stamboloff fought back.
He published in his own newspaper the text of a letter which Savoff had
written to the Prince at the height of the duel affair. Stamboloff's
intention was to show that Savoff was suffering from persecution

mania: in his letter Savoff had begged the Prince to protect his life from Stamboloff who, he said, wanted to kill him. It was certainly an odd plea from a man who had recently challenged Stamboloff to a duel.

That was the moment Ferdinand had been waiting for. He sent a telegram to his private secretary in which he condemned the publication of Savoff's letter by the Prime Minister as the 'vile deed of a churl'. The text of the telegram found its way into the opposition newspapers. At that, Stamboloff wrote a letter to the Prince in Vienna protesting against the words used, listing all his griefs of seven years and tendering his resignation.

When Ferdinand returned to Sofia on 28 May 1894, he was welcomed at the station by all his Ministers with the exception of Stamboloff. The Prince felt that his absence was ominous and, with Kálnoky's warnings still fresh in his mind, turned to his new Minister of War and with words that betrayed his anxiety said: 'I am laying the fate of Bulgaria and of the crown into the hands of my brave army, whose minister you are; I do not want a single drop of Bulgarian blood spilt.'[5] Later Ferdinand joked about the Government crisis, 'brought about by Mme Savoff's dirty drawers'.

The following day Stamboloff saw Prince Ferdinand at the palace – his last day as Prime Minister. It was not a moment of triumph for the Prince. Stamboloff made him feel increasingly uneasy. The Prince reproached him for the 'rude' letter he had written. Why did he threaten him? Stamboloff had written to advise the Prince not to play with fire by vexing Ministers who had an almost 'unlimited command of power', as sooner or later it would cost him his throne. Why, asked Ferdinand, had he not been at the railway station to receive him with the other Ministers? Stamboloff replied: 'Circumstances might well bring Your Royal Highness and myself together once more. I did not want to expose myself to the kind of public encounter at the station which would have made any further contact between us impossible.' Towards the end of their three-hour talk, Stamboloff warned the Prince not to allow any persecution of his party. Should that happen, he would seek revenge by publishing the text of the last letter he had written to the Prince. The Prince exclaimed: 'Are you persecuting me?' Stamboloff replied that anybody could become a danger to the Prince except himself: 'Was it not I who made you Prince of Bulgaria? And in consequence I have borne the responsibility for your mistakes.'[6]

The news of Stamboloff's resignation quickly spread all over Bulgaria. Hundreds of telegrams from his supporters reached the palace, begging the Prince to reconsider. In Sofia there were serious riots when supporters staged a mass meeting and were attacked by detachments of soldiers and cavalry acting under the orders of Racho Petroff, who was just then promoted to general by the Prince. He also ordered divisional commanders in the provinces to take over from the prefects, most of them appointed by Stamboloff, from fear of a general rising by Stamboloff's supporters.

On 1 July a new Government was formed under Konstantin Stoiloff as Prime Minister. The Prince did not like him, and in fact distrusted him as one of the men who intimately knew the full background to his original candidature for the Bulgarian throne (Stoiloff was one of the three Bulgarian delegates whom Ferdinand first approached in Vienna in December 1886).

Yet, in him Ferdinand had found a man who could skilfully find his way in the maze of Bulgarian party politics, who, while not being an extreme Russophil, would not oppose, as had Stamboloff, the Prince's efforts to woo Russia. Most important of all, he would give Ferdinand a free hand in foreign policy. That is what the Prince wanted most. He could now proceed, unharassed, to engineer his recognition by Europe. Once again he was hoping that the family links he held with the Russian court would ease the rigidities of the political situation. Ferdinand always gave his greatest attention to the personal element in any diplomatic concern and nearly always ascribed personal motives to any political action. His greatest problem however, recognition by Russia, was not to be solved in this way, for Ferdinand was trying to fight something just as personal and subjective: Tsar Alexander's hatred of him.

Within days of the formation of the Stoiloff ministry, Ferdinand's seventy-seven-year-old mother went to Russia to plead for recognition. Meanwhile, her son, in a series of interviews with Russian, French and even Austrian newspaper correspondents, was sending signals to St Petersburg. He hinted at his admiration for Russia and conveyed the impression that he had acted as the second liberator of Bulgaria by dismissing the Russophobe Stamboloff. While Russia maintained a stony silence, Western newspapers mocked Ferdinand for these 'love serenades' under the balcony of his recent would-be assassins.

As Austria grew steadily more unhappy about the muted pro-Russian noises made by Ferdinand and the new Bulgarian Government, the Prince tried to calm Vienna's fears with flat denials. Characteristically, he used the very same arguments Stamboloff had repeatedly urged on him when trying to convince Ferdinand that a 'sell-out' to Russia was too high a price to pay for recognition; a formal recognition which would not even benefit him. Ferdinand told Burian, the Austrian Envoy, and journalists: 'I am not interested in the recognition question. I know that my strength lies in non-recognition. Of course, when I am abroad I sometimes have to swallow some rather bitter pills due to my peculiar position, but it has always been clear to me that both I and the country in the meantime are better off as we are.'[7] It was and remained one of his favourite ploys: to pre-empt an objection to a proposed course of action by first producing the anticipated counter-argument as his own point of view. Burian found this very frustrating and wrote to Kálnoky that it was hopeless to argue with Ferdinand about the question of recognition: 'All one's arguments remain ineffective, since His Highness is frequently in complete agreement with them and asserts that he does not even think about recognition, that recognition would be degrading as it would expressly mark him as a vassal, etc.'[8] Even if this ploy failed it always left Ferdinand's critics convinced of his clear-sightedness and lack of illusions.

During a short period immediately after Stamboloff's final resignation, Prince Ferdinand, whatever his personal feelings, tried to maintain reasonably good relations with his former mentor. He addressed a formal Rescript to Stamboloff which, in the most glowing terms, thanked him for his long and faithful service, his loyalty and patriotism. The former Prime Minister had for seven years, 'under my supervision', been 'extraordinarily successful in defending the crown and maintaining the honour and independence of Bulgaria'. The document could not have been expressed more flatteringly and ended with the Prince's assurances of his 'princely goodwill, endless gratitude and friendly feelings'.[9]

Although the words 'under my supervision' must have stuck in Stamboloff's throat, Ferdinand's generous phrases had a mollifying effect. Stamboloff did not know that Ferdinand wrote the Rescript only after strong and repeated urgings by Kálnoky, Burian and Stamboloff's friends. They succeeded in persuading him that for form's sake he had to acknowledge Stamboloff's great services, irrespective of how much he hated him.

Ferdinand's aide-de-camp who took the hard-wrung letter to Stamboloff's little house, informed him that His Highness would prefer that no letter of acknowledgement should be sent, but that Stamboloff should come himself to the palace to see him. Stamboloff, accordingly, went to the palace on 11 June and stayed two hours talking with the Prince. During that time a crowd was gathering outside the palace. Though both of them could see this happening, neither alluded to it.

They parted in a very friendly manner. When Stamboloff approached the palace gates, the crowd outside began booing and shouting, 'Down with Stamboloff! Down with the tyrant!' Though Ferdinand's private secretary urged him to leave by a back door, Stamboloff coolly walked out, accompanied by his manservant. The crowd, mostly youths and street urchins, jeered, jostled and spat on him. One man leapt out with a knife, but disappeared when the servant covered him with his revolver.

The incident added venom to the furious attacks against the Prince and the Stoiloff Government which Stamboloff launched in his newspaper *Svoboda* (Freedom) in response to the former's pro-Russian public statements. The newspaper, written with vigorous, racy sarcasm, was edited by Stamboloff's close friend Petkoff, the ex-Mayor of Sofia. *Svoboda*'s daily attacks very often drew blood – they certainly both alarmed and wounded Ferdinand. The newspaper war that developed between Stamboloff's newspaper and the Government Press day by day widened the rift between the Prince and the ex-Premier. The more level-headed of Stamboloff's friends, particularly the foreign ones, advised him to moderate what had turned into a hate campaign. But Stamboloff was by then wholly in the grip of personal and political passion. Ferdinand was accused of preparing to sacrifice the independence of Bulgaria for the sake of a nod of recognition by Russia. The Government, which was busily purging thousands of officials appointed by Stamboloff throughout Bulgaria, cowered under the withering attacks of *Svoboda*.

The hatred between the two men, both still in their thirties (Ferdinand was thirty-three, Stamboloff thirty-nine), distressed yet fascinated neutral observers who knew them both. Their strong wills and the violence of their feelings envenomed and infected their partisans to a pitch of intensity unusual even for the passion-ridden political atmosphere of the Balkans. Burian wrote to Kálnoky: 'One can no longer expect the Prince to behave sensibly as far as Stamboloff is concerned. He hates and fears him, has never understood how to manage him and would readily lend a hand to destroy him.'[10]

When friends visited Stamboloff's house one evening, he pointed at Ferdinand's portrait on the wall of his study and said: 'You see there, still hanging, the portrait of the man I was foolish enough to bring to Bulgaria. Here,' he added, striking his forehead with his fist, 'here is the place where my assassins should strike when they come to kill me! Here is the stupid brain that was capable of such foolishness!' One day at the Union Club in Sofia, where foreign diplomats, journalists and politicians met, he said: 'The Prince is a zero, and everything he has ever done is nothing but a row of zeroes – unfortunately I was the figure one in front.'[11]

On one occasion Stamboloff told Burian how the Prince had arrived unannounced during a Cabinet meeting and had stayed for two hours. 'His appearance and his remarks made such an impression on the Ministers, that after his departure they said to each other: "But he is mad!" I said to them: "Would Prince Ferdinand have agreed to become our sovereign in 1887 if he was quite normal?"'[12]

Following the mobbing of Stamboloff outside the palace, Prince Ferdinand ordered police sentinels to guard the ex-Premier's house round the clock. They were there, ostensibly, to protect him from further violence. But on 9 August 1894, the sentries told him that they had been ordered not to allow anybody to enter or leave the house between 9 p.m. and 9 a.m. He immediately wrote to Ferdinand to complain, and concluded: 'If I have been guilty of any crime, arrest and try me: but do not put my wife, my mother, my family, and my friends under general arrest in my own house.'[13] Ferdinand did not reply. When the news got round, Stamboloff's friends and the foreign diplomatic representatives called at his house in the daytime. Henry Dering, the British Envoy, spoke to Prince Ferdinand on the subject. With affected carelessness, Ferdinand replied, 'Ah! I dare say they are worrying him a little on account of the manner in which he attacks them in his paper; that is all.'[14]

On this being repeated to Stamboloff, he went into a towering passion. He pointed out that without the support and encouragement of the Prince, the Government neither would nor could have taken the police measures against him. It was at that very moment that the correspondent of the *Frankfurter Zeitung*, newly-arrived in Sofia, called on him. Stamboloff granted him an interview on the spot: the resulting despatch, reprinted all over Europe, created a nine days' sensation everywhere. Ferdinand saw it as an attempt to pillory him before the whole world, an unpardonable sin. The ex-Premier's friends deplored his action. His friend Beaman wrote:

Stamboloff, by this outburst, committed what was worse than a crime – a mistake. There can be no real excuse made for it. It may be urged that he was smarting under great provocation, as he doubtless was, but how much worthier and more dignified it would have been to show himself superior to such petty revenge by silence.

He has often admitted since, that he said what he should never have allowed to pass his lips concerning the Prince, and that it was wrong and utterly unworthy of him, but having once entered the lists, with the dangerous plough handle of the European Press, he could not turn back.[15]

Beaman concluded by scrambling his martial metaphors even more: 'The buttons were off now; it was no longer a fencing match, but a duel to the death.'

The trouble was that Stamboloff attacked the Prince personally, holding him up to contempt and ridicule. It was not the act of a statesman. The one mitigating factor was his physical condition: the intense mental strain which he had undergone since the assassination of his two friends and colleagues had been aggravated by tuberculosis and diabetes.

He told the journalist that the Prince had only one policy: to be recognized by Russia – 'It is his *idée fixe*, almost a kind of malady.' Further on, Stamboloff said:

> The Prince is undoubtedly a clever man, but he wastes his cleverness on petty matters. He is nervous and excitable; he reads everything that is written about him, perhaps some fifty newspapers a day, and tears one into pieces if it contains disparaging remarks.
>
> I have often told him, 'Do not read so many papers, but study public affairs. Get a French or an English colonel to teach you the elements of military knowledge so that you may be able to understand your War Minister....' But he thinks of nothing but his Court, his uniforms, etc. Even with regard to his recognition, his great object is to be able to travel abroad as a reigning Prince, to show himself in his Bulgarian uniform, and to be received at a railway station by a General. Of course now he can do as he likes; but he must not think that he will be allowed to sacrifice Bulgaria for such a consideration.[16]

The sting of the interview lay in its occasional devastating truth:

> No, the Prince will not gain anything by this kind of humiliating *hermaphrodite* policy [author's italics]. He is simply gambling away the little popularity which he still enjoys in Bulgaria, and which he owes to me. For, after all, if I am not popular today, it is because I have worked for the Prince and exposed myself like a father for his child. I took the responsibility for measures, some of them even of a dangerous character, in order to shield him, and so that his popularity should not suffer.

Stamboloff's allusion to Prince Ferdinand's bisexuality was perhaps unintentional, although some gossip had reached him and he must have wondered about the ring-bedizened hands and the blond, blue-eyed orderlies. Intended or not, it was, as far as Ferdinand was concerned, a direct hit.

The ex-Premier also complained about the 'ignoble campaign' that was being waged against him by the Government and the fact that he was a virtual prisoner in his house. He said that he believed the authorities were trying to drive him out of Bulgaria. 'But I don't dream of going away. I would rather be hanged in Bulgaria than live in Russia, Austria, or elsewhere.'[17]

Three weeks later Stamboloff was summoned to court and charged with defamation of the Prince's character. His counsel pleaded that there was no Bulgarian law by which his client could be held responsible for what a foreign journalist published in a foreign newspaper. Although it was impossible to bring the interview within the pale of Bulgarian law, the judge found that an offence had been committed and demanded a huge bail. It was to be paid in gold before Stamboloff could leave the building, except to go to prison.

To the consternation of the judge, who was wholly in the Government's pocket, Stamboloff managed to collect the sum from his friends in the courtroom. Anticipating what might happen they had come loaded with gold cash. When Stamboloff and his counsel left the court building they found a hired mob of about two hundred and fifty ruffians. They had been told that Stamboloff would be leaving in custody on his way to jail. When they hesitated, a policeman shouted, 'What are you waiting for?' and set the example by throwing the first stone. The two men managed to get to their carriage and away under a hail of brickbats.

This incident was merely the first of a series of harassments by the Government, usually on a legalistic pretext. In the autumn a Commission was set up by the Sobranie to inquire into the acts of Stamboloff's Ministry for evidence of anti-constitutional measures, peculation and abuse of office. Persecution ranged from the petty to the farcical. When the former Minister applied for a new shooting licence and filled the application form using red ink (it was well known that he always used red ink, even in his correspondence), the form was returned with the request that he should reapply, using black or blue ink and a warning that if he should send another red application, he would be fined!

Stoiloff's Government overreached itself when, on a legal pretext, about a dozen notorious prostitutes were brought to a court to accuse Stamboloff of rape or seduction, some claiming that they were under the age of consent. In the court, wrote the correspondent of the London *Standard,* 'these wretched creatures were joking with the public, and relating how they had been fetched by the police out of the brothels to perjure themselves'.[18] Stamboloff for once refused to rise to the bait and the case, was quietly dropped.

Despite their absurdity, the whores' depositions were an effective smear. It was soon generally believed that Stamboloff had dishonoured seventy virgins. The stories gained credence, due to the earlier campaign, which linked his name with that of Mme Savoff. The slogan 'Down with the fornicator!' took its place alongside 'Down with the Tyrant!' at subsequent anti-Stamboloff demonstrations.

Prince Ferdinand was not directly responsible for the hounding of his former mentor. The persecution was sanctioned by the Government and the driving force behind it was Dr Nachovich, the Foreign Minister, a secretive, dogged and ambitious intriguer who had privately detested Stamboloff since their student days together. The Government, smarting under the daily lashing by Stamboloff's newspaper, was trying to silence him. Prince Ferdinand stood on the sideline – later it would look as if he had been consciously establishing an alibi. When Grekoff, a friend of Stamboloff and one of the three Bulgarian delegates who first met Ferdinand in Vienna, went to the palace and told Ferdinand about the illegality of the Government's proceedings, the Prince exclaimed: 'What! Stamboloff complaining of illegality after his seven years' rule!' Grekoff pointed out that as the new Government had made law and order its main platform, the illegality of its proceedings was producing a very bad impression. The Prince listened politely nevertheless, Grekoff found out later that his name had been struck off the palace invitation list.

The Government's unsuccessful attempts to silence Stamboloff by imprisoning him on legalistic pretexts culminated outrageously at the beginning of January 1895. A warrant was issued for Stamboloff's arrest for the murder of his friend, the Minister Belcheff, in 1891. News of the warrant's existence became public. After strong remonstrances to the Government by the newly-arrived British diplomatic agent Sir Arthur Nicolson (later Lord Carnock, and father of Sir Harold Nicolson) and his Austrian colleague, Count von Burian, the proceedings were dropped. The diplomats convinced Stoiloff that he was risking a political scandal which would lead to the condemnation of his Government by the rest of Europe.

Sir Arthur Nicolson made great friends with Stamboloff. The latter, as Sir Harold wrote in his biography of his father, was just the sort of man Sir Arthur admired and liked; he was impressed by his 'impersonal generosity'. The two would once a week dine openly together at the Union Club, much to the annoyance of Prince Ferdinand who 'devoted two hours to abusing Stamboloff' during an audience with Sir Arthur.

The feeling that Stamboloff was doomed gained strength among his friends and admirers in the first half of 1895. The most preposterous aspect of the attempt to charge him with Belcheff's murder was the fact that Belcheff's actual Macedonian killers were free and roaming the streets of Sofia as a result of an amnesty which followed Stamboloff's fall from power. At the end of March, Stamboloff told the German newspaper correspondent Richard von Mach that these men, together with other Macedonians, were planning to kill him. Three of the men took lodgings in a villa overlooking his house. Whenever Stamboloff left his house in daytime, he was followed by two or three of the Macedonians. As the authorities took no action, Stamboloff's friends took it in turns to accompany him in the streets.

A month later Stamboloff handed several of his foreign journalist friends sealed envelopes with the instruction to open them in case of his sudden death, and to publish the contents. He told Richard von Mach: 'The conspiracy is ripe, my murder is imminent'.[19] The envelopes contained a text headed 'The Plan for my Murder'.[20] The people named in the text were his subsequent assassins and their backers.

Towards the end of May, Stamboloff at last complied with the repeated entreaties of his friends and demanded his passport from the authorities in order to take a cure for diabetes in Karlsbad. His application was refused on the grounds that he was about to be impeached.

Urged on by an increasingly apprehensive Sir Arthur Nicolson, Stamboloff wrote to Prince Ferdinand on 23 June to ask for permission to go abroad. In the letter Stamboloff expressed regret about the *Frankfurter Zeitung* interview, explaining that he had been goaded beyond endurance by the illegal persecution against him, and by the Prince's failure to put an end to it. He gave the names of the Macedonian killers who were after him, their addresses and occupations. The letter ended by asking Prince Ferdinand, as guardian of the law of the land, to afford him that protection which was the right of each one of his subjects. By that time Ferdinand himself was in Karlsbad. Stamboloff received no reply.

The Government's refusal to allow Stamboloff to go abroad after his first application, in May, had angered Ferdinand. He informed the Prime Minister, Stoiloff, that he disapproved and that he, Stoiloff, was 'entirely responsible'. But when Stamboloff applied for the second time Ferdinand had his own reasons for keeping him in Bulgaria. Stamboloff had threatened to disrupt the Prince's latest and crucial negotiations with Russia by alerting Austria and other Western European Powers about Ferdinand's planned switch to a pro-Russian policy.

The danger threatening Stamboloff from his Macedonian enemies became clear to everybody in Bulgaria in the early summer. A series of anti-Turkish uprisings in Macedonia, tacitly supported by Stoiloff's Government, provoked Stamboloff to angry attacks in his newspaper. It had been a basic principle of his foreign policy to keep on the best possible terms with Turkey and to avoid stirring up trouble in Macedonia. The Macedonian extremists accused him of treason and the killers in Sofia were openly boasting of the coming revenge. On 13 July, a pro-Government Sofia newspaper declared that Stamboloff and his newspaper's editor deserved to have the 'flesh torn from their bones'.

It happened, almost literally, two days later.

At 7.50 p.m., while it was still light, Stamboloff and Petkoff left the
Union Club where they had been talking to Nicolson and Mach, and
hired a waiting cab to drive to Stamboloff's house only some five
hundred yards away in the same street. Stamboloff's servant climbed on
to the box. About half-way to the house, a man stepped out of a side
street and fired a revolver shot. The driver reined in, the cab stopped as
Stamboloff shouted to his companion, 'We are lost' and jumped out.
Petkoff tried to follow but just as he jumped, the cab started moving.
Petkoff could not steady himself (he had lost an arm during the Russo-
Turkish war) and fell forward. When he looked up he saw Stamboloff,
who had managed to run some twenty paces back towards the club,
lying on the ground surrounded by three men who were hacking at him
with Turkish cutlasses. The two policemen who were in the street
before the shot had vanished.

At that moment, the servant, who had managed to jump off the box of
the rapidly moving cab, rushed up, firing his revolver. The three
attackers ran away, pursued by the servant – Lady Nicolson saw one of
them running past her window, cutlass in hand.

By the time several club members, alerted by the shots, had rushed
out, the street was empty except for Stamboloff and Petkoff. It was an
appalling sight. Stamboloff, a gory mess, sat on the ground with his
bleeding arms in his lap. He had received twenty-three deep cuts:
twelve on the head and the rest on his hands and forearms which he had
put up to shield his head. His right eye hung out of its socket and three
sliced-off fingers lay on the ground. Petkoff stood behind him. Stamboloff was taken to his house. A surgeon amputated both hands at the
wrist. Three days later Stamboloff died while drunken gangs of
Macedonians openly enjoyed the sweets of revenge in the pot-houses of
Sofia: Panitza, they shouted, could now rest in peace.

The murder shook Europe. Mme Stamboloff received hundreds of
telegrams, including two from Queen Victoria and one from the
Austrian Emperor. The Queen instructed Nicolson personally to place a
wreath upon the coffin, and to attend the funeral as her representative.

Stamboloff's German friend Richard von Mach recorded the scene at
the dead man's house before the funeral:

> It is an ugly custom to dress up a corpse as if for a ball. The yellowy-
> white face stands out in harsh and discordant contrast to the black
> clothes. For this special journey, which no one undertakes twice, only
> special clothing is fitting. A winding sheet is the correct attire for the
> wanderer's last journey. Stamboloff's corpse is clothed in a dress-
> coat; the wounds on the head are visible, narrow reddish lines on the

temple, above the right eye, above the nose, thin as the back of a knife-blade and yet deadly. The expression of the face is calm and peaceful. The sleeves of the dress-coat cover the stumps of the arms whose white bandages can be seen. An icon rests between the arms.

The feet are in patent leather pumps, wrapped in a strip of white tulle. On a table beside the corpse is a glass bowl; it contains the lacerated, deformed hands which once guided the destiny of Bulgaria; like discarded gloves they float in alcohol; sunrays play tremulously over these ghastly relics. The room smells of iodoform and flowers. The coffin, tables and chairs are covered with wreaths bearing inscriptions which commemorate the dead man as a great patriot, a brave statesman and as the founder of Bulgaria's independence.[21]

One tribute was conspicuous by its absence. Prince Ferdinand, who was in Karlsbad, had sent a telegram to Mme Stamboloff the moment he learned of the attack. The day Stamboloff died he instructed his adjutant to visit the widow with a wreath on his behalf. The widow refused to receive either. She pointed to the hands in the glass bowl and said: 'These are the hands which placed the crown on *his* head!'

The funeral was a shambles. The cortège was repeatedly attacked by gangs of Stamboloff's enemies. The first attack was at the place where Stamboloff had been cut down. The cortège halted for a short address by Petkoff, when men armed with sticks tried to charge the hearse. A white box flew over the crowd, someone shouted 'Dynamite!' and the panic became pandemonium when mounted police charged in from two side streets with drawn swords. When some order was restored and the procession moved on between two lines of mounted police, it was found that the cathedral bell-ropes had been cut. On reaching the cemetery, the mourners saw a small crowd already there, ostensibly to attend a Requiem Mass held by the graves of Panitza and the four men executed for Belcheff's murder.

The burial service was constantly interrupted by the demonstrators who shouted insults at the coffin. It was only the arrival of a detachment of cavalry which made it possible to complete the burial. The moment the mourners withdrew, the demonstrators surrounded the fresh grave, tore up the wreaths and danced a *horo,* the Bulgarian *carmagnole.* One eyewitness saw them 'defiling the grave in a most shameless manner'. That evening cavalrymen dispersed a gang of youths who tried to disinter the corpse in order to hang it from a gallows.

One of the mourners, Sir Arthur Nicolson, saw red early in the day, when he witnessed the disgraceful *mêlée* at the spot where Stamboloff was butchered. His son wrote: 'Nicolson lost his temper. Escaping down a side-street, he proceeded at once and on foot to the house of M. Stoiloff. He found some difficulty in gaining admittance. The door was eventually half-opened by the Prime Minister himself, who held a revolver in his hand. Nicolson, for a space of twenty minutes, was able to tell M. Stoiloff exactly what he thought.'[22] Ten days later Nicolson left Sofia for England, on his way to take up a new appointment in Morocco. In the following year he came face to face with Prince Ferdinand and his wife at a garden party in Buckingham Palace. The Prince failed to recognize Nicolson. 'The Princess stopped for a moment, placed her hand upon her husband's arm, and said, *"Tiens, voici Sir Nicholson."* *"Notre chemin,"* replied Prince Ferdinand, turning in the opposite direction, *"est par ici.'*[23]

Stoiloff had not gone to his predecessor's funeral, at Ferdinand's request. In a long telegram to Stoiloff from Karlsbad, the Prince expressed indignation and genuine shock at 'the news of this cowardly attack on M. Stamboloff and the death of the man who has played such an eminent role in the annals of our history'. Ferdinand's shock stemmed not so much from the assassination as from the accusations which were being made against him from all sides.

The Prince clearly saw himself as the injured party; it was *he* who was being victimized, not least by the widow's 'improper' refusal to accept his wreath:

> I considered it my duty to render to the eminent deceased those honours which his services have merited: a national funeral.
>
> Yet, [he complained] in view of my pious and loyal proceedings, the improper behaviour of a family – whose terrible anguish I both understand and respect; the outrageous insults flung at me and my counsellors by the followers of the deceased, the shameful slanders whose [word missing] I shall not stoop so low as to challenge, the unprecedented attacks to which you and I are exposed in Europe through the malice of some and the blindness of others, all these force me to advise you not to take part in the obsequies of the ex-Prime Minister.
>
> I foresee that this decision, which I have taken regretfully, will give our enemies a pretext for new insults, but I believe that this decision, which circumstances force on us, is the only one worthy of the honour of the sovereign and his ministers before the nation which has placed its trust in them.
>
> Fully, and more than ever in accord with my faithful counsellors whose worth I appreciate, proud to bear together with them the heavy burden of suspicions and iniquities, drawing strength from the rightness of a liberal and enlightened policy, I wait with composure

for the storm to blow itself out, being certain that my government will do its full duty, will discover and punish in an exemplary manner the assassins of the late Stamboloff.[24]

The morning after Stamboloff died, his newspaper *Svoboda* accused Prince Ferdinand: 'Who killed Stamboloff? Whosoever struck the actual blow, the moral murderers are the Prince and his Government who refused to let him leave Sofia, and so gave an opportunity to their assassins.'[25] *The Times* despatch from its Sofia correspondent, without naming the Prince, stated that 'a heavy responsibility rests with those who refused Stamboloff permission to leave the country, and who, detaining him here like a prisoner, neglected the measures necessary to ensure his safety'.[26] James Bourchier, *The Times* correspondent, had had a long conversation with Stamboloff a few hours before the attack.

Six years later Ferdinand told Sir George Buchanan, the British Minister in Sofia, that '*feu Lord Salisbury m'a toujours traité en assassin de Stamboloff!*' Buchanan protested feebly and went on to tell Ferdinand that Lord Salisbury, after meeting the Prince in London during Queen Victoria's Diamond Jubilee in 1897, had remarked 'Now *there* is a man.' Buchanan did not repeat to the Prince the rest of the phrase: ' – but I would not like to be his Prime Minister'.[27]

Prince Ferdinand did not quite avoid the storm which, as he wrote to Stoiloff, would 'blow itself out' while he remained in Karlsbad. Princess Radziwill's daughter who was there wrote to her mother:

Prince Ferdinand is here; in fact he is my neighbour as he inhabits the villa next to my hotel. At the beginning of his stay one saw him frequently but, since this drama he avoids society in the company of two gentlemen and a detective who follows him everywhere. Public opinion is against him and it seems that yesterday at the mineral springs he heard two people, who did not appear to know who he was, talk about him. They described him as an assassin and a cowardly blackguard who always left his country whenever something horrible was about to happen.[28]

A few days later she wrote: 'The Princess of Bulgaria arrived yesterday to see her husband. They say she wants him to abdicate; he is insulted in the street and I believe that he is horribly afraid to return to his country!'

In the sealed letter which Stamboloff gave to Mach, together with instructions for it to be opened in the event of his sudden death, he wrote, after the details about the planned assassination: 'I do not know if the Prince knows about all this; but it would not be all that surprising if he did.'[29]

All the circumstances surrounding the assassination are not clear to this day. The accusations against Prince Ferdinand and his Government seemed natural to his contemporaries; they were based on the fact that the most determined opponent of better relations between Bulgaria and Russia happened to disappear from the scene at precisely the moment Ferdinand had chosen to court Russia. The most damaging evidence was the refusal to allow Stamboloff to go abroad and away from his enemies. But in the general indignation the details got blurred. Ferdinand had been furious with Stoiloff for not letting Stamboloff travel when he *first* applied for a passport at the end of May. When he reapplied a month later, Ferdinand himself did not want him to go abroad, but for purely political reasons: Stamboloff was threatening to sabotage plans for sending a Bulgarian delegation to St Petersburg. Princess Clémentine explained this to a Hungarian magnate in a conversation which appeared in a Budapest newspaper:

> Prince Ferdinand went to Karlsbad as usual and Panitza's people used his absence for the murder. Stamboloff could not be given permission to go abroad until the return of the Bulgarian delegation from Russia.
>
> Once abroad, Stamboloff would have taken steps which would have hindered the task of the Bulgarian delegation. It is not desirable that one man, however great a patriot and statesman, should contravene a country's policy, a policy whose outcome will determine that country's position in the European order.

As usual, the sharp old Princess made good political sense. But it did not satisfy the accusing voice of the German, Mach: 'Why, in that case, were security precautions not doubled to prevent a murder about which even the sparrows on the town roofs were chattering?'[30]

Here the brunt of the responsibility had to be borne by Stoiloff and his ministerial colleagues. There was no suggestion that Stoiloff, a timid and over-scrupulous man who, though he disapproved of Stamboloff's radicalism and bohemian ways, had in any way planned or intended the murder to happen. He was well-meaning but had little authority over civil servants and the police. The only way to personal popularity that he could see was by supporting and encouraging the more extreme Macedonian irredentists whose ranks happened to contain Stamboloff's most determined and bloodthirsty opponents. He was certainly not the man to court unpopularity and incur the perilous enmity of the wild men of Macedonia by forcibly expelling from Sofia, and from Bulgaria, the men who were openly threatening to kill Stamboloff. Such action would have seemed particularly suicidal to him just before the assassination, when a series of anti-Turkish revolts had broken out in Macedonia.

There is not a single bit of evidence to suggest that Ferdinand instigated or connived at the murder. One of the strongest defence arguments is based on his temperament and character: his almost morbid loathing of blood and wounds (closely linked to his phobia about infection, the source of numerous anecdotes); his hatred of violence and violent solutions to political problems; his extreme reluctance to sign death sentences (a reluctance which only succumbed to Stamboloff's pressure); his disapproval of Stamboloff's strongarm methods and the corresponding nemesis which he foresaw and feared. The Prince was far too intelligent and canny not to have foreseen the resulting harm to himself and to Bulgaria in the eyes of the European public. Even if he had been tempted to have Stamboloff killed, he would have realized that any gain would have been heavily outweighed by the losses. These losses he incurred in any case while waiting in Karlsbad for 'the storm to blow itself out'.

The killing itself had all the characteristics of a personal vendetta. The bloody shambles wrought by the hacking cutlasses bore the marks of the medieval savagery of the Macedonian mountains, not of the age of dynamite and the 'infernal machine'. There was no sweetness in modern, sudden revenge. Richard von Mach, who at the time of the murder held Prince Ferdinand 'morally responsible', wrote many years later, in 1931: 'Some have thought Ferdinand responsible; but it is a mistake – the Macedonian *vendetta* required no outside assistance to take its course.'[31]

Much to Ferdinand's distress the authorities failed to find all the assassins. The three who were caught and judged in the following year did not receive the 'exemplary punishment' for which the Prince had asked. Two of the defendants received three-year prison sentences for 'committing and helping to commit' the murder with extenuating circumstances: the brother of one of the two Macedonians had died after being tortured by the police during Stamboloff's 'reign of terror' which followed the assassination of Belcheff in 1891. The third accused was found not guilty and set free. The European Press called the trial a farce. A characteristic touch was the disappearance during the proceedings of a revolver, a vital piece of evidence. Even these mild sentences outraged the Macedonian extremists who had expected to be acquitted for the 'patriotic deed'.

Naoum Tufekchieff, the one who had avenged his tortured brother's death, was himself assassinated shortly after his release from prison. It was not until 1901 that another of the killers was caught and eventually condemned to death. The sentence was afterwards commuted to fifteen years' imprisonment, which, perhaps amazingly, he survived. The mildness of the sentences caused much comment and there was a widespread belief that prior to Stamboloff's murder the assassins had been promised leniency by some members of the Stoiloff Government. But, more than anything, it would seem that judicial severity was tempered by fears of the Macedonian vendetta and the recent memory of its horror.

For Prince Ferdinand, the death of Stamboloff and the ensuing public outcry had a silver lining – apart from the obvious fact that his most violent critic was now silent. Beyond the clamour and indignation in the Press, people were astonished that the much mocked, effeminate young Coburg had got the better of Stamboloff, seen as the tough, demonic veteran of so many battles. Those who knew Ferdinand better than the general public and had been prophesying his downfall ever since he went to Bulgaria, were even more surprised. How had the affected young man with the manner of a 'vieille cocotte', managed it?

There were those who believed that he was doomed, nevertheless. According to one German diplomat: 'Eventually it will be the same old game again and the two millstones, the self-esteem of the Bulgarians and the arrogance of the Russians, will grind Ferdinand as they ground Alexander [of Battenberg].'[32]

Yet, at the same time, Ferdinand was being credited with a new persona, one which was soon to eclipse the vaudeville prince. He was beginning to emerge as a political factor in Europe who would have to be reckoned with. The almost Jacobean horror of the carnage in Sofia, the reputation for diplomatic finesse and intrigue which the Prince had already acquired, his apparent mastery of the art of establishing a political alibi, his effeminacy and love of the arts and sciences, even his bejewelled person, were investing him with a sinister fascination and decadent glamour which had overtones of both Machiavelli and Nietzsche. His character seemed made to order for the *fin de siècle*, with just the right elements of decadence and overtones of the superman. Ferdinand was delighted. A very partisan French journalist wrote that 'I know that in political matters Ferdinand is not displeased to be considered as a contender inbred with Machiavelli's teachings; in fact it would seem that he readily affects Machiavellism.'[33]

He would certainly have enjoyed the following passage in the memoirs of the Russian diplomat Neklyudoff:

If Ferdinand had lived in the very middle of the quattrocento as *podesta* either of Ferrara or Mantua, he would have vacillated between the Pope, the King of France, the Roman Emperor and the *Serenissima*; he would have pillaged orphanages and erected beautiful buildings;

he would have caused his enemies to be stabbed at night in the streets, or he would have poisoned them at his feasts; he would have surrounded himself with scholars and artists, and luxurious palaces, with brocaded halberdiers covered in gold lace.[34]

At this point Ferdinand's face would have darkened; the passage continues: 'He would certainly have possessed that fine and true artistic taste which he now only pretends to have... [he was born] four centuries too late.'

CHAPTER 15

Anathema and Recognition

—◦✦✧✦◦—

By midsummer 1895, Prince Ferdinand had benefited from the deaths of three people in less than two years. The death of Prince Alexander of Battenberg had removed the fear of a rival. That of Stamboloff had silenced a hated, turbulent and powerful internal critic. But it was the death of Tsar Alexander III in November 1894 that eliminated his most dangerous and powerful enemy and the greatest obstacle to his ambitions. Things began to look up almost immediately. To Ferdinand's enormous surprise and delight, his telegram of condolence to St Petersburg was answered by the new Tsar Nicholas II. The Tsar's reply read: 'I thank you with affection for the words which you have sent to me in the name of the Bulgarian people. Tsar Nicholas.' Stoiloff also received a telegram of thanks from Giers. These were the first civilities from Russia in nearly ten years, and Bulgaria's Russophils and the majority of the population saw it as the melting of the ice.

Ferdinand might well have believed that destiny was on his side. Tsar Alexander's death could not have been timed more neatly. The Prince had accepted Stamboloff's resignation five months earlier and could not therefore be accused of dropping him in order to exploit the Tsar's death. Also, if Stamboloff had still been Prime Minister, he would have fought far more effectively against a reconciliation with Russia. Stamboloff had refused to believe that the death of Alexander III would have any effect on Russia's designs against Bulgaria. His views had set rigidly in the mould imposed by his long and bitter battle against Alexander's single-minded malevolence.

Yet another death, shortly after that of the Tsar, improved even more Ferdinand's chances for a reconciliation with Russia. In January 1895, Russia's Foreign Minister Giers succumbed to a long illness and was replaced by Prince Lobanoff, the personal friend of Princess Clémentine and Ferdinand who as Russia's Ambassador in Vienna in 1887 had tacitly encouraged the Prince's candidature for the Bulgarian throne. He had always been a critic of the Panslavists and considered that the break in relations with Bulgaria had been the fault of 'overzealous and incompetent Russian officials in Bulgaria'.[1]

The first official step towards a reconciliation was taken by the Sobranie. It decided to send a seven-man delegation to Russia, led by the Russophil Metropolitan Kliment, to lay a golden wreath at the grave of Alexander III. (It was because of that delegation, and Ferdinand's fears of Stamboloff's disruptive tactics, that the latter was not allowed to leave Bulgaria.) In July, the Bulgarian delegates were received by Nicholas II, Lobanoff and Konstantin Pobedonostseff, the Procurator of the Holy Synod, who told them that Russia wanted to see Bulgaria with a government 'whose soul, together with the nation, is united in the Orthodox faith'. Lobanoff spoke in more concrete terms. Reconciliation and, beyond that, recognition of Prince Ferdinand could be had, at a price: the abrogation of Article Thirty-Eight of the Bulgarian Constitution (as amended by Stamboloff to allow Ferdinand's heirs to be Roman Catholics) and the conversion of the baby Prince Boris to the Orthodox faith.

This was not news to Prince Ferdinand. In December 1894, a month after the death of Tsar Alexander, the Prince had just heard that Russia's price for reconciliation was a change of religion for Prince Boris. It seemed too high a price at the time. He tried to change Russia's mind. In May 1895, he left Bulgaria on the pretext of going to shoot capercailzie and secretly travelled to London to ask the Prince of Wales to act as go-between with Nicholas II. Ferdinand was also in touch with Gabriel Hanotaux, the French Foreign Minister. At a secret meeting in a fifth-floor flat on the Boulevard St Germain, the Prince asked Hanotaux to put his case to the Tsar. In the margin of a diplomatic report on these meetings, the Kaiser wrote: 'Whenever H.R.H. [the Prince of Wales] has a hand in the game, a new intrigue is brewing against us.'[2] William II was right up to a point: any rapprochement between Russia and Bulgaria would constitute a diplomatic setback for the Triple Alliance of Germany, Austria-Hungary and Italy and a gain for the Dual Alliance of Russia and France.

While these were the big issues on the scale of Europe, Russia's conditions presented Prince Ferdinand with appalling personal and political problems. Politically, inside Bulgaria, enormous pressure was rapidly building up for reconciliation. The mood of the country, with the exception of Stamboloff's demoralized supporters, was for ending the 'unnatural' break with Russia. Bulgaria's politicians could not understand why the Prince hesitated about his son's change of religion.

The situation was not without personal danger for Ferdinand. When Metropolitan Kliment's delegation returned from St Petersburg, one Sofia newspaper commented:

> It is now quite clear that His Royal Highness the Prince is the obstacle in the way to a solution; there remains nothing else for us but to ask him, in all sincerity, to leave the country, so that we can do our duty and escape demoralisation and destruction. For this reason we again urge our ruling politicians to enlighten the Prince about the true state of things and then to ask him to bid us farewell, and not to wait until he should be assassinated like Stamboloff since, were this to happen, no greater misfortune could befall Bulgaria.[3]

The Prime Minister Stoiloff urged the Prince and Princess almost daily during the later part of the summer of 1895 to agree to Boris's conversion. He was quite unable to understand Ferdinand's reluctance and once said: 'No Bulgarian would understand the Prince's great doubts about the change of religion. Religion here is understood quite differently, almost entirely from a national viewpoint and dogmatic considerations are simply not understood.'[4] Stoiloff himself was out of his depth: he earnestly assured the Prince that there was nothing to prevent the infant Prince from receiving a strict Catholic upbringing after his conversion to Orthodoxy.

Against the pressure from his subjects and Ferdinand's own overwhelming desire for recognition as Bulgaria's sovereign, stood ranged his mother, his wife, his Catholic relations, the Catholic clergy and the frail but formidable Pope Leo XIII. Princess Marie-Louise's former lady-in-waiting, herself a Catholic, wrote:

> The two Princesses were already troubled...by the negotiations with Russia, the price of which was to be a change of religion for Prince Boris. Princess Clémentine, very firm in her Catholic faith, tinged with Jansenism, offered a cold, dignified opposition to the project in question; while Princess Marie-Louise brought all her youth and passion, and her fanaticism as God-daughter of Pius IX, and daughter of the most Catholic Duke Robert of Parma, to the defence of her cause.[5]

During one quarrel with her husband, Princess Marie-Louise, who was pregnant, declared that she would rather leave the country than allow such an 'atrocity' to take place. Her father, an ardent campaigner for the restoration of the Church-State, bitterly opposed the proposed conversion. He had both moral and legal rights on his side: he had allowed the marriage between Ferdinand and his daughter to take place only on condition that their children should be brought up in the Catholic Church. The marriage contract contained a clause to this effect and the two families, Coburg and Parma, had engaged themselves as guarantors of this clause *vis-à-vis* the Pope.

The reports reaching him from Sofia also deeply angered the Emperor Francis Joseph. Personally, he was angered as a Catholic, and as a man who had helped to bring about the marriage. Politically, Prince Boris's conversion and the *rapprochement* between Russia and Bulgaria would signify a strategic defeat for Austria. The Emperor had believed that Bulgaria was firmly on Austria's side in the Balkans. Now the dreaded spectre of a Russian military advance into Constantinople with Bulgarian help again rose before him. He spoke of Ferdinand's 'arrogance and vanity' which had 'brought forth such evil fruit', and said that 'Prince Ferdinand's lies could cost him his throne'.[6]

Once again Ferdinand was tortured by doubt. By opposing his son's change of religion he not only risked losing all that he had achieved in Bulgaria, but beyond that, the opportunity to consolidate these achievements by obtaining Europe's recognition. His own religious ideas were by no means the main obstacle. He would probably have readily taken the decision had it depended on religious considerations alone. This is clear from a despatch written by Burian in 1893:

> From what the Prince has frequently told me in private I can say that he renders the Orthodox confession not merely an outward, formal respect, but rather that he regards it with the fullest sympathy, due to his historical views and the fact that it forms an integral part of his most daring ambitions. I believe that I would not be going too far if I were to say that His Highness would not experience a very severe collision with his own conscience if he joined the Orthodox Church; apart from all this, His Highness considers that the Papal Curia has frequently offended him. . . .[7]

Burian's despatch is evidence that Ferdinand's dream of putting on the Byzantine Imperial diadem in Constantinople, a dream that was to become almost overpowering twenty years later, was already taking shape. An essential part of the vision was of himself as the healer of the breach that had divided Eastern and Western Christianity for nine centuries.

Throughout the summer and autumn of 1895 he vainly bombarded with letters the Pope, the Duke of Parma and the Catholic members of his family. He only succeeded with his mother. She overcame her religious scruples at a Coburg family meeting. Alone she spoke up for her son and said that she had come to the conclusion that the security and well-being of Bulgaria weighed more heavily than personal considerations. The great effort this must have cost the old Princess, famous for her ultramontanism, was seen less charitably by Princess Radziwill, who wrote in a letter: 'She [Princess Clémentine] invested part of her large fortune in Bulgaria to help her son win the hearts of his subjects, and she is too much Louis Philippe's own daughter not to avoid anything which might make her lose any of her money.'[8]

At the beginning of September Prince Ferdinand secretly sent Dimitri Stancioff, at that time the Bulgarian diplomatic Agent in Bucharest, to Rome to appeal to the Pope. It was an impossible assignment: to ask a Pope of the calibre of Leo XIII to condone the apostasy of a Catholic prince! Stancioff also visited the Duke of Parma, who, inevitably, said he would abide by the decision of the Holy See.

Princess Marie-Louise, whose pregnancy was well advanced, fought bitterly against her husband. She remained inflexible even after she received a petition from the members of the Cabinet who, on behalf of the Bulgarian people, asked her not to oppose the conversion of her son, an action of major importance to her country of adoption. Her tutor Gancheff said that she was using all her strength to prevent Boris's imposed apostasy. He was impressed by her 'intractable tenacity' and her use of 'that terrible feminine weapon: passive combativeness'.[9] With pride she told Gancheff that as a young girl she had once drunk a whole bottle of ink alone in her room after an unjust reprimand from her governess.

If Marie-Louise's intransigence doubtlessly stemmed from her religious convictions, her passionate opposition to Ferdinand was equally a result of her successive disillusionments in their private life. She learned of his bachelor affairs quite soon after the wedding and on occasion had to outface the deliberately provocative behaviour of some of her former mistresses. Any illusions she might have entertained about Ferdinand turning over a new leaf as a married man, disappeared as she heard of his continuing adventures during his frequent absences from Bulgaria. Once married, the Prince became, however illogical it might seem, less discreet than as a bachelor. In the summer of 1896 Princess Radziwill's daughter wrote to her from Karlsbad:

> Prince Ferdinand is amusing himself here with a *cocotte* quite openly and heaps flowers and jewellery on her. It appears that he even made her come to Sofia as a companion to read to his wife, but she found out what was going on, and it is more this than the baptism of the son that caused their estrangement.... Stories about this Prince are going round Karlsbad; they are our great diversion.[10]

The Princess was acutely conscious of her lack of physical attractions. The fact that the Prince found her sexually unattractive yet saw to it that she bore him children in rapid succession to secure his dynasty, cannot have been comforting. For the Princess his heterosexual activities were no doubt humiliation enough; but just how much did she know or guess about the other side of the coin? Gancheff wrote in his posthumous diary about the year after the wedding:

In 1894 he [Ferdinand] took into his service Lieutenant M., a youngster with blond, wavy hair, well-built and with a firm, soldierly stride. I knew him from Military School where he had been a pupil of mine: an uncouth character, there was something primitive in his nature. The Prince had seen him in some provincial regiment, liked him and arranged for him to appointed as a palace orderly. The young man only lasted a few months in his honorary duties. He became unbearable and was dismissed. He had quarrelled with Lieutenant S., another of Ferdinand's favourites, had called him a 'tart' and walked out of the palace.

Before returning to his regiment in the provinces, he tried to see Stamboloff to tell him something. At that time the 'tyrant' had fallen and was bitterly at war with Ferdinand. Stamboloff did not receive him, fearing that he had been sent to spy on him. Lieutenant M. asked one of Stamboloff's friends to tell the former Prime Minister that Ferdinand had attacked his honour with an indecent proposal. The circumstances... were as follows: Ferdinand is in his bathroom and sends for M. The orderly, as is his duty, knocks and opens the door. Before him, naked as the day, sits Ferdinand on a cane-seated chair, grinning at the orderly and inviting him to get undressed. The Macedonian slams the door shut and walks away.[11]

Some seven or eight years later Gancheff met the former orderly, 'this tempter of Ferdinand's,' and asked him if the story was true. M. pointed at his two small children: 'You see them? May they not live if I am not telling the truth.'[12]

The notorious newspaper interview during which Stamboloff attacked Ferdinand's 'hermaphrodite policy' took place at about the same time as the bathroom incident. Conceivably, Stamboloff's allusion to Ferdinand's bisexuality was prompted by the young orderly's report. This would explain the extreme violence of the Prince's reaction to the interview.

Ferdinand was still torn between increasing pressure from his

Bulgarian subjects and the determined opposition to his son's change of faith from the Parma family and the Pope, when the Sobranie opened on 31 October 1895. In his speech from the throne, Ferdinand played for time. Patience and perseverance, he said, were necessary to bring about improved relations with Russia. About the conversion of Boris, he would 'as far as is possible make efforts to realize the wish of the Bulgarian nation'.[13] The delegates cheered. But later, in the Sobranie's reply to the speech from the throne, the Prince was again asked to consent. On 11 November, the Prince promised to further the nation's wish 'when the extraordinary obstacles can be removed'.[14]

Just then Princess Marie-Louise was delivered, after an easy birth, of a son who was styled Prince Cyril of Preslav, the ninth-century capital of Bulgaria's greatest ruler, Tsar Simeon the Great. The birth of his second son placed Ferdinand in a new dilemma: to have him baptized in the Orthodox Church would only further enrage the Catholics, without solving the political problem of his first-born's religion; yet, how much conviction would his only days-old promise about the conversion of Boris to Orthodoxy carry if this new member of the ruling dynasty of Bulgaria was not baptized according to the religion of the country?

Very quietly and privately the newborn prince received a Catholic baptism with Ferdinand's French relations, the Duc d'Aumale and the Duchesse de Chartres, as godparents. Princess Marie-Louise was only momentarily appeased. If Ferdinand had hoped that the christening would lessen Catholic opposition to Boris's apostasy, he was soon disappointed. It merely resulted in increased Bulgarian pressure for his conversion to Orthodoxy. The Government presented him with an ultimatum: that by the end of January 1896, the end of the current sitting of the Sobranie, he was to make an 'unequivocal, public declaration' of his intentions, otherwise the Government would resign. Princess Marie-Louise was full of foreboding and wrote to a friend: 'I think there is nothing which makes one so sad as the end of a year. One always asks oneself with anguish what the future will be and in spite of all, each year brings its ever increasing burden of sorrow and bitterness.'[15]

On 27 January Prince Ferdinand arrived at the Vatican for one last attempt to win over Leo XIII. Though he was travelling *incognito* he was accompanied by a suite of twenty and wore all his orders for the audience with the Pope. The Prince was shown into a small drawing room, where Leo received him standing, with a severe expression. In an unsteady voice Ferdinand asked for permission for his two-year-old son to enter the schismatic Orthodox Church. Leo looked at him steadily and said: 'You wish that I should sanction your son's death, the death of his soul? It would be spiritual murder.'[16]

The Prince then explained the reason necessitating his son's change of religion, the fact that the internal stability of Bulgaria depended on it. The Pope interrupted: 'Prince, it is your own fault that things have reached this stage. If you had acted as a good Catholic a year ago and had answered in the negative, when you were asked if your son would go over to the Bulgarian Church, the difficulties would not have grown quite so big. At the time you did not speak with the firmness of a Catholic!'

Leo went on: 'When the Duke of Parma came here and told me of his daughter's proposed engagement to you, I foresaw the difficulties. He gave me his word of honour and on your behalf, yours, that the children of this union would be brought up in the Catholic Church. It was only then that I agreed to the marriage.'[17] At one point Leo's voice became strident and he shouted: 'Abdicate, Prince! Abdicate!'[18] At the end of the audience Ferdinand begged the Pope to spare him the disgrace of excommunication. 'If you deliver your son Boris into schism, you are excommunicate *ipso facto*.'[19] Leo refused to give Ferdinand his blessing. The Prince departed angry, upset and disappointed. The audience had lasted thirty-five minutes.

Deeply depressed, the Prince left Rome and arrived in Sofia on 1 February, 1896. At the time, he was genuinely upset. The threatened anathema was bound to affect his peculiar religiosity, a compound of Catholicism, superstition, a fascination with the occult and his sense of history. In his perplexity he was considering abdication, as the Pope had advised him, or setting up a military dictatorship which would allow him to remain on the throne without having to drive his son into schism. The Prime Minister Stoiloff managed to persuade him to stay on the throne – and to follow the desire of the majority of Bulgarians.

On 3 February, three days after the Government's ultimatum had expired, Prince Ferdinand issued a proclamation announcing that Prince Boris would enter the Bulgarian Orthodox Church in nine days' time. The proclamation was also a bitter, hardly veiled reproach to the Pope: 'As I failed to find a judicious understanding of Bulgaria's needs in those quarters where I had expected it, I have resolved, faithful to the oath that I swore to my beloved people, and on my own initiative, to remove all obstacles and to offer on the altar of our Motherland this heavy and inestimable sacrifice.'[20]

The Prince had cast the die, just as when he finally decided to go to Bulgaria in 1887; to escape the intolerable tension of indecision. As on that occasion, his choice bent in the direction of his monarchic ambition. And, just as then, his ambitions and the wishes of the nation coincided.

Three days later Tsar Nicholas congratulated Ferdinand by telegram for his 'patriotic decision' and informed him that he was sending his representative to Sofia. He would act as proxy for the Tsar, who accepted to be the two-year-old Boris's godfather. The same day Princess Marie-Louise left Sofia for the south of France, accompanied by Prince Cyril. On the way she spent two days in Vienna with Princess Clémentine at the Coburg palace. In a letter to her mother from Vienna, Princess Radziwill's daughter wrote that Marie-Louise's health was 'greatly shaken by all her recent emotions. Her parting from little Boris was horrible, they had to tear the child from her arms and the poor woman was in a faint for two hours.'[21] She was afraid that Ferdinand would arrive to take her back by force and, according to her sister-in-law, Louise of Coburg, 'she insisted upon remaining near Princess Clémentine, who had a camp bed put in a little room adjoining her own'.[22] Ferdinand's mother appeared 'equally tortured'.[23]

Once arrived in Beaulieu, on the French Riviera, 'the enchantment of the sun, Nature and flowers brought a little relief to painful thoughts, but letters, telegrams and news of the forsaken child, unconscious of the part he was being made to play, all combined to crucify the unhappy mother, who seemed more fragile and ethereal than ever'.[24]

Prince Boris entered the Orthodox Church during a two-hour ceremony in the Cathedral of Sofia which the correspondent of The Times found 'laboriously grand'. After three-quarters of an hour of church music – 'good of its kind, though monotonous and severe' – Prince Ferdinand arrived and sat down on one of two thrones set up near the altar. Later 'the Ministers left their places and went to the church door, whence they returned escorting Prince Boris borne in the arms of his gouvernante, who after divesting him of his broad white hat and pelisse, placed him on the throne seat nearest to the altar, where he sat in perfect composure, wearing half a dozen orders over his little white frock'.[25]

The ceremony was not a baptism, but a confirmation into the new Church (re-baptism was not required, since the Orthodox Church recognizes Catholic baptism). After the Imperial godfather by proxy, General Kutuzoff, had answered the ritual questions, 'the infant Prince was borne off to the vicinity of the altar where encircled by Bishops, he received unction at the hands of the Exarch'. The chrism was holy oil from the Kremlin which Tsar Nicholas had sent in a jewelled casket. The press of bearded bishops, the chanting, the clouds of incense and his anointed head were too much for Prince Boris: 'the little man was weeping when, in about ten minutes, he was brought back a convert, but he soon found consolation in the ministrations of his gouvernante, with whom he shortly left amid the thunder of a salute from the batteries'.

That evening there were fireworks and illuminations as an enormous crowd gathered outside the palace in 'demonstration of gratitude' which Ferdinand acknowledged in a speech from the balcony. 'It is impossible,' wrote *The Times* correspondent, 'to overstate the popular satisfaction and enthusiasm awakened by the conversion.'[26]

Within the next five days the official recognition of Ferdinand as Prince of Bulgaria came from all the Powers which had signed the Berlin Treaty nearly eighteen years previously. Bulgaria's irregular position in Europe had been put right and Ferdinand's throne secured. But apart from Ferdinand's sense of satisfaction there was another, equally strong sentiment – resentment. He felt keenly that he had been misunderstood and humiliated by those who should have been his friends and supporters: the Pope, the Western Powers and their Press, who had stupidly and maliciously attacked him and failed to see the importance of what he was trying to do. He even considered that Queen Victoria's telegram of condolence to Stamboloff's widow had been an arrow aimed at himself. He went so far as to 'rationalize' Prince Boris's apostasy as a 'revenge' against those European Powers which had failed to support *him*, a descendant of one of the greatest houses of Europe. The strength of his feelings was discernible in the extraordinary speech that he made to the Sobranie after he had taken his decision about Prince Boris:

> What I have done was imposed on me by my duty towards my beloved people who, a decade ago, trustingly put their fate in my hands. The sacrifice I have made to the Fatherland is so great, so cruel, so terribly harrowing that history has no equal to it. For Bulgaria's happiness and prosperity I have pledged my own son and by so doing loosened the bands of my family and torn the ties which bound me to the West.
>
> In return I do not ask my beloved people for noisy ovations or for hypocritical homage, but merely for their respect and confidence in me.[27]

He specifically asked for an end to personal attacks against himself in the Bulgarian Press. He trusted that there would no longer exist in the country a 'worthless press, which only serves the basest interests of intriguers' and an 'unprincipled opposition which dishonours the person of the sovereign and the honour of Bulgaria with its insults. I am fully confident that those words in the constitution which speak of the sanctity and inviolability of the sovereign will no longer be an empty phrase and that all Bulgarians will feel united in the motto: "One God, one Ruler, one Fatherland".'

He ended exaltedly with a sentence that combined his sense of grand opera and history, and that was to be reprinted all over Europe: 'The

West has pronounced its anathema on me, the dawn of the East shines its rays on my dynasty and brightens our future!'[28]

Pope Leo carried out his threat and declared Ferdinand anathema in the form of the so-called 'greater excommunication'. This nevertheless fell short of the Vatican's greatest sanction, the publication of a Bull of Excommunication. The Papal punch was pulled for fear that Ferdinand himself would be driven into the arms of Orthodoxy. As it was, the Prince was formally denied the sacrament of communion and the confessional. He was however able to attend Mass, which he did regularly in the palace chapel. Prince Boris's conversion was celebrated with thanksgiving services in all the principal churches of Russia.

CHAPTER 16

Cannon and
Flowers

—◦❧❦◦—

It had taken Prince Ferdinand nearly nine years to be recognized as a legitimate sovereign. When he set out secretly from Austria in 1887, hiding in the swaying, stifling WC of the train that took him to Bulgaria, few believed that he would last out a year. From that moment of recognition he was to hold the reins of power a further twenty-two years, despite the fact that Bulgaria enjoyed the most liberal constitution in the Balkans. His years of apprenticeship, many of them under Stamboloff's increasingly onerous tutelage, had taught him the intricacies of Bulgarian party politics. This knowledge allowed him to stay on top by stimulating and using the rivalries between Bulgaria's political factions. In foreign politics his tactics were the same: he tried to get the best for himself and Bulgaria by exploiting the rivalries of the Great Powers. His political see-saw never ceased moving, always in the context of the rivalry between Austria-Hungary and Russia. By the end of the first decade of the present century, his skill was becoming almost legendary.

His legitimization as Prince of Bulgaria was sealed by a triumphal tour of foreign capitals a few weeks after Prince Boris's conversion. On 26 March 1896, he arrived in Constantinople to be received by Sultan Abdul Hamid II, his nominal suzerain. Though Ferdinand quite enjoyed making fun of the tattered, tinsel splendour of his reception, he was very pleased with the Sultan's evident desire to welcome him in the grand manner. As his residence, he was given an Imperial palace, and all the furniture in his apartments bore his insignia. The Sultan, who received him several times, gave him the highest Turkish decoration and allowed

179

the Prince to add yet another uniform to his wardrobe by appointing him a Field-Marshal in the Turkish army.

The Prince stayed nearly three weeks. One evening he attended a reception held in his honour at the Russian Embassy. The Prince was amused: in that building some of the major Russian plots against Ferdinand had been hatched for years, including Captain Nabokoff's ill-fated final expedition to Bulgaria. His host the Ambassador, Nelidoff, had been at the centre of all the anti-Bulgarian conspiracies and assassinations.

It was probably during this prolonged sojourn in Constaninople that his 'dream of Byzantium' began to turn into a concrete desire to occupy the Byzantine throne. Phantasy and historical romanticism were undeniably among the prime movers. Yet, at the time, it would not have appeared as an *impossible* dream. In the eyes of most Europeans, the continent's Sick Man was not only bed-ridden and racked with disease: he was dying, the illness seemed ·terminal and the stink of decay stimulated the potential claimants to the inheritance. With the chief claimants, the major European Powers, locked in a stalemate over the loot to come, their ambitions curbed by fear of each other and of the cost of a great war, would it not be possible for Ferdinand, as leader of a league of the Balkan nations, to enter Constantinople at the head of a Christian army and replace the cross on St Sophia?

Prince Ferdinand saw all the principal sights. He asked the Sultan's permission to enter St Sophia alone 'so as to be able to admire the matchless edifice quite unhampered'. The Sultan complied but asked that an officer of his bodyguard should stand inside the church-mosque; but so as not to disturb the 'movements and meditations of the august visitor', he was to stand against the door.

Later, Ferdinand told of his experience:

> You may imagine my delight at finding myself alone under the marvellous dome, on the spot where the entry of the Turks, on 29 May, 1453, abruptly interrupted the Mass at the sublimest moment of the Elevation. . . . But let me tell you just why I begged Abdul Hamid for the favour of walking alone in Saint Sophia. I wanted to fix the position, from some clues I had, of a certain slab of porphyry which marks the place occupied by the Byzantine autocrats during religious services. And so, while the Sultan's officer, glued to his door, was watching me with an air of speechless stupefaction, I took my cane and pushed back one of the mats covering the floor. I thus disclosed the slab of porphyry on which the *Basileus* Justinian planted his feet, shod in the imperial purple. And I too, I too, set my feet on the slab of porphyry![1]

One may wonder how much of what Ferdinand was saying was due to the fact that, when he was telling this anecdote in 1908, his interlocutor was Maurice Paléologue, the French Minister in Sofia and thought by some to be collateral descendant of Constantine XI Palaeologus, the last Byzantine Emperor.

In Constantinople, the Prince saw a lot of Paul Cambon, the French Ambassador, to whom he showed much amiability – most of all when he advised him to dine at home before coming to the official dinner given by Ferdinand at his residence. Cambon had reason to be grateful; the Prince's dinner, prepared in the Sultan's kitchens, was 'detestable' as Cambon wrote to his mother. When Ferdinand left Constantinople he gave Cambon a picture of himself in knee-breeches, rings on all his fingers and a bracelet on one of his wrists. Cambon commented: '*C'est la passion du costume, de la représentation, de la pompe* [It is a passion for costume, for display, for ceremony].'[2]

Despite the Prince's numerous kindnesses to Cambon, the Frenchman was annoyed when Ferdinand told him that after leaving Turkey, he would only visit St Petersburg and Paris. 'Why is he telling us this nonsense? He has received an invitation from the German Emperor for 30 April and will go there.' How much better, wrote Cambon, if Ferdinand had said that he was visiting the six Major Powers whose recognition he had at last received.

Everybody would have thought that simple and straightforward. It was the same thing with the Pope. I would be ready to believe that he had promised him to bring Bulgaria into the Catholic Church. Instead he turns his son into an Orthodox Christian, and then further complicates this paternal apostasy with a trip to Rome in order to explain and try to obtain an impossible agreement. His taste for what is complex must have been of use to him during the past ten years, when he had to live in an ill-defined situation and, in order to get out of trouble, had to deepen the obscurities of the Bulgarian regime. But now a little more clarity and candour are probably needed.[3]

But Cambon was wrong in thinking that Ferdinand's cageyness about his tour was merely the product of an innate love of intrigue. The truth was that the Prince still wasn't sure about his plans. Was there any likelihood that Austria's anger at the conversion of Boris would abate? And if he did go to Vienna, would the Emperor receive him? The answer, though Ferdinand could not be sure, was a furious 'No'. Francis Joseph and his new Foreign Minister, Count Goluchowski, seemed to be taking over the roles which Alexander III and Giers had played opposite

Bulgaria. Just as the latter could not forgive the Bulgarians for 'betraying' the country by placing it under a Catholic ruler, so now the Austrians were enraged by the 'apostasy' of the Bulgarian dynasty from Catholicism to Orthodoxy.

Even before Prince Ferdinand had left Sofia on the first leg of his round trip, Goluchowski told the German Chancellor Hohenlohe that, as far as the possible visit of the Prince to Vienna was concerned, 'the Emperor has no desire to receive him'.[4] Goluchowski said that he was personally well aware of the political disadvantages of not receiving Prince Ferdinand, but that he could not persuade Francis Joseph.

The German Kaiser and his Chancellor were trying hard to calm down the Austrians. 'A great pity!' Kaiser William wrote alongside a despatch from his ambassador in Vienna which quoted Francis Joseph as saying: 'I will definitely not receive the Prince should he pass through Vienna. I will not receive him at all!'[5]

The German Chancellor also tried to steer the Austrians away from emotionality into the discipline of *Realpolitik,* by citing Ferdinand as an example of the latter:

> As far as Prince Ferdinand's reliability is concerned, precedent proves that he can be relied on to incline to the side which he believes will best serve his interests. If on the one hand Austria were to show herself as his adversary, he will consider himself bound to provide proofs of his links with Russia. If on the other hand Austria, instead of being guided by the politics of sentiment, were to act solely from the point of view of her own interests and did not handle Bulgaria any worse than the Russians do, then, according to the opinion I have formed so far about Prince Ferdinand, he will endeavour to secure the greatest freedom of action and independence by zig-zagging between Russia and Austria. In this endeavour he would be in full accord with the Bulgarian nation.[6]

In trying to make the Austrians accept the Prince's see-saw policy as the only rational and feasible one from his point of view, Hohenlohe leant backwards to excuse Prince Boris's conversion in Austrian eyes. It was, he said, to be condemned highly from a human viewpoint but 'politically he has merely made use of the right of religious freedom, which is a cornerstone of the Bulgarian Constitution'.[7]

William II was exasperated by Francis Joseph's continuing resentment against Prince Ferdinand. 'For nearly 20 years [sic] Austria has tried to get Russia to recognize the Prince! How could this come about in any other way? [by Boris's conversion] And now?! Is there any logic in all this?'[8]

Austrian attacks against the Prince reached fever-pitch following the murder in Sofia of a beautiful Hungarian singer, Anna Simon, by Captain Boicheff, one of the Prince's hand-picked and handsome young adjutants. The Austrian Press, whose efforts to pin Stamboloff's murder on the Prince had grown stale, seized on the *crime passionnel* and, regardless of evidence and the fact that Boicheff was hanged for the crime, accused Ferdinand of being the main culprit. Things got no better when the Bulgarian Prime Minister Stoiloff told a German newspaperman that the crime was of the kind that could happen anywhere. This was immediately interpreted in Austria as an allusion to the tragedy of Mayerling. In the ensuing diplomatic and Press furore, the Austrian diplomatic representative in Sofia went on indefinite leave.

From Constantinople, Prince Ferdinand went to St Petersburg where, wrote Princess Radziwill, he was received like the Prodigal Son. Next he went to Paris, where his mother stood among the crowd on the corner of the Avenue de Marigny as Ferdinand was driven to the Elysée Palace and received by President Félix Faure, who decorated him with the *grand cordon* of the Legion of Honour. It was probably the greatest moment in the life of the old Princess: her son was being honoured as a sovereign ruler in Paris, nearly half a century after her father, herself and her family had fled ignominiously from the city. In her eyes, Ferdinand's success was an earnest of her family's indefeasible right to a throne.

The Prince, whose incognito visits to Paris over the preceding decade had been hole-in-the-corner affairs, was delighted. On arriving at his residence, he stopped between the two officers of the cuirassiers who were his escort and purred, '*Ici, je suis bien à ma place* [I really feel I belong here].'⁹

The visit to Berlin was not quite so unclouded. He was offended that there was no guard of honour to greet him at the railway station. His reception by the Kaiser and the Chancellor – both gave gala dinners in his honour – was marred by William not giving him the Order of the Black Eagle, which he had expected. Relations between the Prince and the German Kaiser had been quite good up till then and William had a grudging admiration for Ferdinand's 'cleverness'. After the religious service for Prince Boris's conversion, Ferdinand had sent William a letter describing the ceremony, and said that he only felt sorry that he had no photograph of the ceremony to send to Berlin, as he had felt sure that William would have appreciated it with his sense of humour.

The excessive attention which Ferdinand paid to questions of protocol and ceremonial offered an easy target for ridicule. Yet in his case this preoccupation was more justifiable than in the cases of the equally punctilious but far more secure William II and Edward VII. For him, as he learned through the many humiliations of his long years as unrecognized Prince of Bulgaria, outward and visible marks of status were important precisely because they were a gauge of his political success or failure, a measure of his chances of survival. That, of course, was not all. Glitter, panache, glamour – these he could not resist, no more than he could resist *Aida* or *Parsifal*. Still, if ever there was a case of the pot calling the kettle black it was when Kaiser William once described Ferdinand as 'festooned with decorations like a Christmas tree'.[10]

Ferdinand returned to Sofia on 9 May, and four days later his wife returned to Bulgaria. Princess Clémentine had played a leading part in persuading her to rejoin Ferdinand for the sake of the infant princes. Meanwhile Ferdinand received a personal invitation to attend the coronation of Tsar Nicholas in Moscow later that month (the thought that he would not be invited had worried him since his recognition).

The coronation was for him a milestone by which he could judge the distance he had travelled in the thirteen years since he had attended the coronation of Alexander III. This time his regal bearing, the aura of scandal and glamour, his reputation for diplomatic *finesse* rendered him both impressive and interesting. To some of those present he seemed to eclipse Nicholas. Also, things always seemed to be *happening* when he was around: he was a heaven-sent gift for the gossip columnist. On his way to the coronation banquet, Ferdinand passed by the Papal nuncio, as impressive and dignified a figure in his robes as the Prince. Queen Victoria's granddaughter, Princess Victoria of Battenberg (later Marchioness of Milford Haven) wrote that the Catholic prelate who, 'being a true Italian, could forget his dignity when impulse moved him', marked his contempt for Ferdinand's apostasy by proxy and 'made the gesture of spitting at him. Prince Ferdinand, not to be beaten, spat back!'[11]

The Prince's gesture was quite spontaneous. He needed no prodding to show his resentment against 'the West', which meant Austria and the Vatican. There was probably less play-acting than was believed at the time in the exaggerated respect he showed for Slavdom. While in Russia he seemed *plus Slave que les Slaves*. A Russian newspaper seized on this and in a satirical *feuilleton* claimed that Ferdinand not only imitated the most pious Russians by taking off his headgear and crossing himself every time he passed a church, but that he showed similar piety on entering Russian theatres and concert halls.

In Sofia, Princess Marie-Louise had her tutor Gancheff read out a Bulgarian newspaper report of the *feuilleton,* much to the latter's embarrassment. He gave an account in his posthumous memoirs:

I read it to her and appeared indignant at the slander. 'You think that it is a lie?' said the Princess.

I looked at her, surprised. She hastened to assure me that this was no satire, but the naked truth. 'You do not know Ferdinand. There is no greater liar in all Bulgaria. Yes, yes, I am telling you the truth...'

Dumbfounded by these words, I remained silent and went on turning the pages of the newspaper in the hope of finding some other item, and changing the subject.... But, determined, she continued in the same vein: 'Stupid hypocrite!... Let him find others to lie to as he did to me....He lies to people, and he lies to God.'

Her eyes became humid and a small tear ran down her face. She stood up, silently inclined her head and gave me to understand that the lesson was over. On other occasions, she would let me know when I was to appear for the next lesson. This time she said nothing. She was trying to hide her distress from me.[12]

The Princess's scorn would have been even greater had she been present as her husband told members of the Russian Imperial family of his own Slav ancestry. This was indeed far-fetched – he went back some nine hundred years to trace Slav blood in his father's family. On his mother's side, he pointed to the Dark Ages when a Russian princess married a Capet! His deep and serious interest in atavism in all probability blinded him to the absurdity of what he was saying.

The coronation of Nicholas II was the first major State occasion of European importance which Ferdinand was able to attend as a sovereign ruler. As legitimate ruler, he no longer had to endure the snubs and humiliations of his twilight status, a painful battering under which his exasperated vanity and ambition had grown while resentment had become an instinct. That his *de jure* status as Prince of Bulgaria did not mean an end to personal humiliation was soon brought home to him when, at the Moscow coronation, he was placed next to the Khan of Khiva and the Emir of Bokhara. He was not to be allowed to forget that, according to the Treaty of Berlin, Bulgaria was still an 'autonomous and tributary principality under the suzerainty of the Sultan' and he the Sultan of Turkey's vassal. True, the vassal status was purely nominal, a fiction necessary for the maintenance of the Berlin Treaty. But it was the kind of fiction that, for Ferdinand, acquired an outrageous reality when translated into the language of diplomatic protocol: it lumped him, a descendant of Louis XIV, to the malicious delight of the Russian Court, together with the moth-eaten puppet rulers of two Central Asiatic states, which had only recently been absorbed into the Russian Empire.

His next task was clear: the abrogation of one of the main articles of the Treaty of Berlin. Bulgaria had to achieve *de jure* independence from Turkey, and become a kingdom with Ferdinand as King. Kingship had all along been Ferdinand's goal and the justification for his original decision to face the dangers of the princely throne. To become a kingdom, Bulgaria had to achieve independence from the Sultan. Here Ferdinand's monarchic ambition coincided with the wishes of his subjects: where he saw himself in the full enjoyment of royal attributes, the great mass of his peasant-democrat subjects saw total independence as a further step towards the realization of the Great Bulgaria of the Treaty of San Stefano, the brief promise of the restoration of former greatness abolished by the European Powers in Berlin. For different reasons his ambitions coincided with those of the Bulgarian people: like her ruler, the new Bulgaria was a *parvenue* in Europe and like him, her ambition drew nourishment from the consciousness of past greatness.

It was to take Ferdinand twelve years to proclaim Bulgaria's full independence and himself Tsar in 1908. For all his irascibility and quickness to take offence in relatively small things, he was able to take the long view on political matters and to wait patiently for the opportune moment to further his plans. War or violent political action were utterly repugnant to his temperament. His only resorted to them with great misgiving after he had exhaustively and patiently explored the ways of diplomacy and intrigue.

During these twelve years, Bulgaria's economic and social progress continued unabated, despite a chronic shortage of money and occasional bad harvests. Ferdinand became increasingly interested in economic development. His connections with Western industrialists and bankers were of prime importance in raising foreign loans and concluding commercial agreements. After a harvest failure in 1899 he voluntarily cut his Civil List by half. Public works continued to expand and Ferdinand officially opened the newly built Black Sea harbours of Varna and Burgas, which were linked by rail to Sofia and soon handled forty-three per cent of the total foreign trade of Bulgaria.

Communications – telegraph, telephones, roads and railways – were also expanding. Ferdinand's passion for trains, a passion that his son Boris inherited, dated from early boyhood. He constantly supervised the new plans, discussing technical details with the Companies in charge and giving valuable advice based on his knowledge of the country. But most of all he enjoyed climbing into the cab and driving. He was delighted to find that one of the perquisites of his position was the chance to realize a boyhood longing to drive a train. He joined the German union of railwaymen. On one occasion a German engine driver was disciplined for allowing Ferdinand, against safety regulations, to take the controls. When Ferdinand failed to get him reinstated, he gave him a more lucrative job as a driving instructor in Bulgaria.

Like father, like son: Tsar Boris became, if anything, an even more enthusiastic engine driver between the two world wars and often insisted on taking the controls of the Orient Express. That grand body, the *Compagnie Internationale des Wagons-Lits et des Grands Express Européens*, intervened and firmly asked the Tsar not to enter the cab. Drivers who allowed him in were threatened with dismissal. 'Little daunted, Boris would sit in his private carriage until the train crossed the border into Bulgaria. Then he would alight, already garbed in his overalls, and defy anyone to stop him from driving a train in his own kingdom.'[13]

Ferdinand's private train was by all accounts a cosy and elegant marvel, *'un vrai bijou d'intimité voyageuse'*, according to a French journalist. The drawing-room carriage had pale green velvet walls, the bed-rooms were lined with turquoise silk. The food in the dining-room, very likely the best on any train since the invention of the railway, was served in silver dishes marked with the royal arms of France, the fleurs-de-lis. Delighted to see the 'lilies of France blooming anew under the sun of the East', the French journalist enthused, Ferdinand had a *'véritable passion d'artiste'* for locomotives, which for him represented something at once 'monstrously powerful and subtle, mysterious and implacable'.[14] A less sympathetic English observer considered that Ferdinand in his 'sumptuous saloon-carriage, known in diplomatic circles as 'The Bulgarian Foreign Office on Wheels', presented a veritable apotheosis of ostentatious swagger'.[15]

Ferdinand's passion for trains was good newspaper copy. On one occasion he was explaining the finer points of engine driving to a foreign journalist, who, wishing to please, tactlessly remarked – it was a moment of political crisis in Bulgaria – that the accomplishment was a useful one which might one day save his life. Ferdinand growled: 'I am sorry I have no locomotive now to escape from such silly remarks.'[16]

He was an indefatigable traveller, liable to leave on long journeys abroad on the spur of the moment, much to the annoyance of his ministers. For Ferdinand, diplomacy meant personal diplomacy, the need to *speak* to foreign statesmen and diplomats. There was the added advantage that he did not have to commit himself in writing. Diplomacy, pleasure – be it the fleshpots, shooting game or Bayreuth – whatever the reasons for his travels, they were often a mere pretext to assuage a fundamental restlessness.

If he was not travelling abroad, he travelled inside Bulgaria. The number of his motor cars grew as the roads improved. He began with six limousines, the best of them a Mercedes, as well as an assortment of electric broughams; an impressive stable for the early days of the motor car. As the number of cars increased, so did that of his blue-eyed chauffeurs. 'Goodness, all these chauffeurs!' wrote Gancheff in his memoirs. 'Ever since motor cars made their appearance, our good Tsar was plucked out of our midst. He was captured by these chauffeurs, dropped all his former favourites and even his duties. Where is he? He has gone off somewhere in his motor car, with his chauffeur. Cabinet ministers look for him, affairs of state await him, and he is somewhere in the fields and woods.' He would simply drop everything in Sofia and disappear for a day or two in the mountains. There on some mountain top or other, he would 'push champagne bottles into the snow and eat and make merry with his favourite chauffeur'.[17]

Like his passion for trains, Ferdinand's fancy for chauffeurs lasted many years. Gancheff's memoirs relate how once in 1918, General Savoff, the Bulgarian War Minister, had to find Ferdinand to discuss a vitally important military matter. The Tsar could not be found. After a lot of questioning, a palace guard told Savoff that Ferdinand had gone off by car with two of his chauffeurs to visit the parents of one of them in his native village.

> The good Tsar had ordered provisions for the journey: roast piglet, several chickens, a brace of pheasants, cakes, sweets, wines and liqueurs.... The car was loaded with these delicious things, the Tsar sat in the driver's seat, next to him Mincho [the young chauffeur whose village they were going to visit] and a relief chauffeur in the back.... A few hours later they arrived in Mincho's village and the house where he was born. What then happened is similar to the naive, child-like phantasies of our folk tales: the good Tsar brings the meritorious son to his delighted parents, invites them to a feast of roast piglet and pheasants, calls on them to drink and gives them some money. When Mincho returned to Sofia, he swanked and told his friends about the high honour done to his parents by the Tsar.[18]

Ferdinand was fascinated by all means of transport, with the exception of horse and saddle. In 1910 he became the first crowned head ever to go up in an aeroplane. The following eyewitness account published in 1916 in London is straight First World War propaganda against an enemy and is certainly unfair, if not self-contradictory, in the final sentence:

> One of my most vivid recollections of him [Ferdinand] is of a struggle with his craven fear which took place in the sight of a very considerable crowd. It happened curiously enough at Brussels, where I saw him in 1910 [at the International Exhibition]. He was then, as always, most interested in aviation, and in a weak moment had engaged to make a flight with the Belgian pilot Delamines. Up to that time no king had ever ascended in an aeroplane, and Ferdinand was

probably impelled to make his rash engagement by his desire to be the first monarch to fly.

But when the time came for him to enter the machine, he was possessed by nothing but fear. One could only sympathise with him, so pitiable a spectacle was he in his terror. His face was livid, and his thin lips were ashen grey. His jaunty walk had completely gone, and he tottered to his seat as though he were going to the gallows.

With a supreme effort he gasped, 'I am too fat to fly, but let us fly nevertheless.' It did not sound jocular but pathetic. But he was in for it and was strapped to his seat. There was a cheer when the aeroplane rose, and the Tsar of Bulgaria, with eyes tightly shut, soared off. Two circuits of the aerodrome he made and then descended to earth more dead than alive. A flask was offered him as he dismounted, and with unaffected joy he drained it, and the colour came back to his cheeks. The reaction set in, and he was sprightly in his satisfaction at the feat he had accomplished. Nothing could have been more evident of his will to do bold things, and of the craven fear that held him back from his wish.[19]

The point here, surely, is that Ferdinand's 'craven fear', if such it was, failed to hold him back. That anyone should feel some nervousness at the prospect of a first flight in those days of unenclosed machines, all struts, wire and air, is understandable. Louis Blériot had only just crossed the Channel. During the summer of 1910 hardly a week went by without a fatal aeroplane crash. Three weeks before King Ferdinand's flight the Hon. Charles Stewart Rolls died when his machine crashed at Bournemouth. Shortly before his crash he had achieved his great feat of flying from Dover to Calais and back.

The years between recognition and the declaration of Bulgaria as an independent kingdom were not only a time of material advance for the country. It was also a period in which Ferdinand deliberately, busily and with great enjoyment, set about building, furnishing and decorating a *royal* setting for himself and his family. In a man so fond of grand opera, the style of Louis XIV and ceremonial, an excess of façade and stucco would not have been surprising. But a predilection for luxury and comfort, allied to a real artistic sense and a feeling for elegance, saved him from some of the banalities of the royal stereotype. The palaces, country houses, hunting lodges, gardens and parks whose plans and building he supervised were judged delightful even by his enemies. To a departing guest who was leaving Romania for Bulgaria, King Carol I said, 'You are leaving my woodland chalets for Sofia where you will find the splendour of the court of Versailles.'[20] If there was a hint of mockery in his tone, it was tinged with respect. The majority of

Ferdinand's guests who recorded their impressions expressed their admiration. Their impressions were probably made more vivid by the contrast between Ferdinand's Court and the peasant simplicities of life in the Balkans.

The palace in Sofia, as the main official residence, was greatly enlarged and rebuilt by Ferdinand and was intended to impress – but avoided bombast. Meriel Buchanan, the daughter of the British Minister in Sofia, wrote:

> Now and then ... there were private theatricals, fancy dress dances or parties at the Palace – the latter always set in tremendous pomp and luxury, perfect in every detail of service, food and order. Entering the Palace one was greeted by a company of Prince's bodyguards, who stood on every step of the wide staircase, gorgeous in their scarlet, silver-braided uniforms, with the grey astrakhan cap and the eagle's feather held in a jewelled clasp. Ushered into a white and gold room, one waited for the Prince's entry before going into the enormous dining-hall with its big horseshoe table covered with wonderful flowers. One ate off priceless china, gold and silver plates; the service was faultless, the food perfect; a concealed band played loud enough to cover any lull in the conversation, but never too loud to drown it. The glitter of decorations, the medley of uniforms; the Prince with royal dignity, which so many sovereigns entirely lacked; his keen, penetrating eyes; the guards in their brilliant scarlet and silver; little Prince Boris, with his dark, sad eyes, all these made a picture that was full of colour, a little unreal and fantastic, and gave one the feeling that one was on a stage, taking part in a musical comedy or a romance of Ruritania, that at any moment a bomb might go off, or the armies of some rival, neighbouring country break into the room with a clash of swords and a burst of music.'[21]

His own love of good food apart, Ferdinand saw it, to paraphrase Clausewitz, as a way of waging diplomacy by other means. The excellence of his fare became famous. He discussed the menus in minute detail with the palace chefs. The French Minister, Maurice Paléologue, wrote: 'He is as much a gourmet as he is a gourmand. Above all he loves intricate dishes, succulent, highly-seasoned food, sauces, salmis, aspic, ragoûts, marinated fish, gamy venison. When one of his favourite dishes is set before him, he sniffs at it and his huge Bourbon nose dilates with pleasure.'[22]

He was 'instantly aware of even the slightest error in the preparation of one of his favourite dishes, a *salmis,* a *ragoût* or a *Boeuf Stroganoff.*'[23]

Sometimes good food and diplomacy clashed. In Marienbad in 1904,

Ferdinand and King Edward VII dined together and, according to
Meriel Buchanan, the Prince 'never quite forgave our King for helping
himself so liberally to a dish of creamed mushrooms that hardly any
were left for himself, and, as creamed mushrooms were one of his
favourite delicacies, he considered this an outrageous injustice'.[24]
A menu card of an 1894 dinner at the palace in Sofia has survived:

Consommé froid
(*Zucco*)

Tartelettes à la Diplomate
(*Johannisberg 1868*)

Filet de Boeuf à la Bordelaise
(*Château Léoville 1875*)

Mousseline de foie gras en aspic
Suprêmes de dindonneaux à la crème
(*Clos Vougeot 1875*)

Sorbets de griottes au vin de Romancé
Bécassines rôties sur canapés
(*Dry Impérial*)

Salade

Haricots verts à l'Anglaise

Profiterolles au chocolat
(*Château-Yquem 1878*)

Bombe gaufrée à la pistache
Dessert
(*Muscat Rivesaltes*)[25]

Except on rare occasions, Ferdinand retired before midnight. Alone,
before going to bed, he played piano arrangements of favourite operas,
pieces from Gluck's *Orphée* or Wagner's *Parsifal:* unlike that other, the
greatest royal Wagnerite King Ludwig of Bavaria, Ferdinand could
actually play a musical instrument; in the palace in Sofia there was a
large music room with an organ and several pianos.
Like Wagner, Ferdinand's favourite colour was mauve or violet and
this colour dominated his study in Sofia, which was filled with flowers,

bibelots, family paintings, ornithological albums and trophies of the hunt. Even in exile, many years later, he had his drawing room in the Hotel Regina Palast in Munich decorated in mauve and white. Worshippers entering his chapel in Sofia dipped their fingers in a holy water stoop filled with violets. During the winter months the central heating in the chapel was kept up day and night to the temperature of a hothouse. Ferdinand insisted on the use of the most fragrant incense. The heat, the incense, the massed flowers, the burning candles were all a deliberate assault on the senses, no doubt resented by the more austere and fresh-air loving worshippers. A perhaps less decadent, though equally artificial, atmosphere assaulted visitors to his palaces immediately on arrival: Ferdinand had the entrance halls sprayed with pine essence.

Ferdinand's palaces and country houses reflected his many moods. His palace of Euxinograd on the Black Sea, some five miles from Varna, had no *fin de siècle* trappings. Built in the style of Louis XIII, it was magnificently situated on a promontory, allowing a view of the sea in nearly all directions. It dominated a wide sweep of terraces, gardens, plantations and vineyards down to the sea. In the summer, the inside was light and airy, the tall windows framed by cretonne curtains waving in the sea breeze. Innumerable swallows swooped and circled around. Ferdinand had ordered their thousands of nests along the cornices of the building to remain undisturbed, despite the advice of architects and builders.

Ferdinand had repaired a disused monastery perched on a cliff nearby. The monks' refectory, jutting out over the cliff, became a summer dining-room and gave guests the impression of floating in mid-air over the sea. Ferdinand had a ground-floor cell as his study, half-hidden by creepers and rhododendrons. The walls were inset with fragments of antique bas-reliefs. He delighted to show visitors his desk: when sitting at work he could pull aside a small yellow curtain to reveal a porthole in the back panel, giving on to the sea and the horizon.

He was justifiably proud of the gardens, the result of many years of terracing and landscape gardening under his direction with the assistance of a French architect. Thousands of cartloads of earth were transported from inland to make a series of terraces down to the sea. From Marseilles, Ferdinand ordered over fifty thousand trees. In the beginning the work was very difficult, due to the frequent ravages of streams swollen by torrential summer rains. It took the gardens and the park some ten years to become established. By then they were one of the enchantments of the Black Sea coast. A profusion of roses, rhododendrons and azaleas tumbled down to the water, which Ferdinand in later years described as 'a sea like black sapphire'. In exile he often spoke

Right: Prince Augustus of Saxe-Coburg, from a painting by Winterhalter. Below: Princess Clémentine d'Orleans, with her youngest son, Ferdinand, 1866

Prince Ferdinand (below) at the coronation of Tsar Alexander III of Russia, 1881 and (at right) in 1887

Alexander of Battenberg, Prince of Bulgaria

A contemporary woodcut, showing Prince Alexander's enforced abdication

ficial photograph, showing Ferdinand's
essive collection of decorations

Ferdinand, with one of his beloved dogs, before he
left for Bulgaria

Prince Ferdinand (4) on his arrival in Bulgaria, at Vidin, with Stancioff (1), Stoiloff (2), Stamboloff
(3) and Colonel Petroff (5)

1   2   3   4   5

Ferdinand with his Bulgarian
tutor, Dimitri Stancioff

Ferdinand being greeted by a
Bulgarian peasant woman

The Royal Palace in Sofia

Ferdinand and Princess
Clémentine at the monastery of
Trnovo

The Palace at Euxinograd

Ferdinand at Euxinograd, gazing over the Black Sea towards Constantinople

Ferdinand dressed in Montenegrin national costume

Shooting sea birds at Euxinograd

Ferdinand in the robes of a
Byzantine Emperor, from a
painting in Sofia Cathedral

Princess Marie-Louise in
neo-Byzantine dress

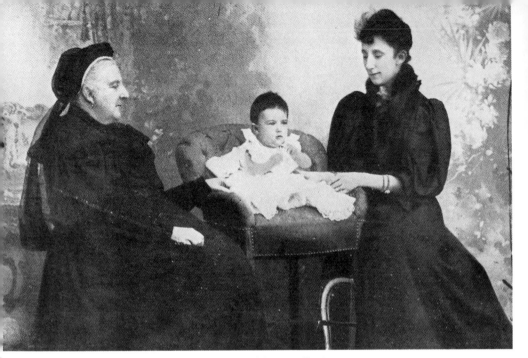

Princess Clémentine with Princess Marie-Louise and her son, Boris

A French cartoon of 1908 showing the Emperor Francis Joseph, Ferdinand, and the Sultan tearing up the map of Europe

Ferdinand and Princess
Eleonore of Reuss, his second
wife, at their wedding in
Coburg, in March 1908

The wedding group, including
many members of the Coburg
family

The Tsaritsa of Bulgaria

ove: The fashionable crowd
Marienbad. *From left to right:*
rdinand; George I of Greece;
ward VII; the Marquis de
veral; Sir William Harcourt,
Liberal statesman

Left: Princess Clémentine in the
uniform of her Bulgarian
regiment

Tsaritsa Eleonore with
Ferdinand's four children,
in 1908

inand's two sons, Boris and
l, in school uniform

One of the last large gatherings of sovereigns in Europe, at the funeral of Edward VII. *From left to right: Back row:* King Haakon VII of Norway, Tsar Ferdinand of Bulgaria, King Manuel of Portugal, Kaiser William II of Germany, King George I of Greece, King Albert of the Belgians. *Front row:* King Alphonso XIII of Spain, King George V, King Frederick VIII of Denmark

...ritsa Eleonore in the uniform of a Red Cross Nurse during the Balkan Wars, and (at right), Ferdinand and Boris near the front line during the First Balkan War

...garian troops entering a Serbian town during the Second Balkan War

Ferdinand following his troops during the First World War

Ferdinand and Kaiser William during the First World War

...inand at Aswan, Egypt, in 1927

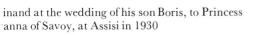

...inand at the wedding of his son Boris, to Princess ...anna of Savoy, at Assisi in 1930

Ferdinand in exile in Coburg

Ferdinand in old age

eloquently of Euxinograd, of the vintage when 'the grapes hung like miniature harvest moons' and the Japanese garden for which he had ordered thousands of Japanese butterfly chrysalids so 'that the flowers might not be lonely'.[26] When he talked in this vein, it was difficult to determine how much of it was aesthetic clowning, an echo of the *fin de siècle* poses of his younger years. Nevertheless, the depth and sincerity of his love of nature were genuine.

Ferdinand invariably pointed out to his French guests the wall supporting the main terrace, into which was set the main pediment of the French palace of St Cloud, which had been burnt by the German armies in 1870 and razed in 1891. Showing the French royal blazon, it had been transported stone by stone to Bulgaria on the Orient Express.

Despite the breathtaking beauties of Euxinograd, Ferdinand's favourite residence was at Vrana, only some twenty miles south-east of Sofia, in open country dominated by mountains. The large house, which he had built in the old Bulgarian style with jutting eaves, verandas and galleries, was set in a great park of woods and meadows by the River Isker. Vrana was begun by Ferdinand soon after the turn of the century on what had been uncultivated country, a rough area of land producing an abundance of tall nettles. Within a few years Ferdinand turned it into a horticulturalist's dream. He was fortunate in that his adoptive countrymen, with their love of the soil and plants, provided some of the best gardeners in Europe: many of the more ambitious gardens on the French Riviera are the result of the labours of green-fingered Bulgarians. At Vrana there were several *tours de force,* including a row of flower beds containing all the varieties of French roses, backed by all the French varieties of lilac, and a bed displaying all the flowers of Touraine. The hot-houses were stocked with rare plants from all over the world. One hot-house contained a specimen of every known Chinese flower, another represented all the flowers of North Africa. Ferdinand took particular pride in the water lily house, where floated the giant *Victoria regia,* with its tray-shaped leaves reaching six feet in diameter. The produce from the enormous kitchen gardens and vegetable greenhouses was not only intended for the table. Ferdinand, who no doubt would have made a good and enthusiastic judge at a horticultural show, encouraged his gardeners to improve the look of vegetables as well as their taste. He was pleased and flattered when Russia's Grand Duke Vladimir returned from a morning walk during his stay in Vrana with a splendid head of cabbage under his arm which, as he told Ferdinand, he had found irresistible and just had to cut and bring along.

Bison and antelope roamed free in the park. Ferdinand also kept three elephants whom he visited several times a week. 'I enjoy studying

their heads – they bear such a strong resemblance to my own,' he told
Paléologue.[27]

The interior of the house was furnished and decorated entirely
according to his instructions. He saw it as his most intimate residence, a
house for his family. By all accounts, he succeeded in giving it an air of
rustic sophistication, comfortable and elegant without oppressive
opulence. The main hall, with its coffered ceiling, was panelled in oak
and had a Dutch air with glints of copper and Delft ware. The main
drawing room was 'a soothing blend of colours: steel grey, light blue
and mauve.'[28] A long gallery with orange and lemon-coloured tapes-
tries – at that time still considered a daring clash of colours indoors –
was hung with a collection of original drawings from *Simplicissimus,*
most of them of Ferdinand with the accent on his nose. This gallery led
to the dining room which he considered the most successful room in the
house: white with blue peasant motifs and cherrywood panels. Ferdin-
and's bedroom was a model of *fin de siècle* decadence: an enormous yellow
silk canopy hung over his bed, which was made of carved wood and
covered with a sumptuous Breton chasuble; there was a profusion of
Japanese flowered silk and bouquets of dried flowers in vases. The walls
were hung with aquarelles of flowers painted by the Duchesse de
Chartres and, looking out of the windows, there were more flowers in
the window boxes.

For his botanical expeditions Ferdinand built several chalets in the
Rila mountains, the biggest at Sitnyakovo, accessible by an excellent,
though dangerous, road built by him. There he was at his happiest. The
floral wealth of the Rila mountains is still unequalled in Europe. In these
mountains he found the wild rhubarb of Rila, an endemic plant known
by the Romans as a healing herb, the Rila *matricaria,* the Bulgarian *geum,*
the golden-yellow *anagallis,* clove pinks and hundreds of other flowers,
some of them not to be found anywhere else in the world. The chalet
stood high up the mountain, surrounded by dark, ancient forests of fir
and pine. Wagner was the genius of the place: the chalet was filled with
paintings and prints of *Ring* subjects. Appropriately, outside there were
wolves and eagles. Inside all was warmth and luxury.

There were other hunting lodges, country houses, cottages which
Ferdinand built for himself all over the country. He was always on the
move. Each of his residences could, according to how he felt, enhance or
dispel his many moods. If tall forests, Wagner and mountain crags
failed, he could go south to his house near Philippopolis, where he had
installed magnificent aviaries, and to the nearby island in the River
Maritza, which he bought to rear pheasants, including the Versicolor.
When the river, the ancient Hebros, was in full flood he would tell his
guests that the yellow waters must have looked just the same when they

bore down Orpheus' head after he was torn to pieces by the Thracian Women.

Ferdinand built Vrana and the other places after the death of his wife on 31 January 1899. Marie-Louise, suffering from pneumonia, died twenty-four hours after giving birth to her fourth child, Nadejda. Many people saw her death at twenty-nine as the result of the emotional shock of the conversion of Prince Boris. It was said that she purposely neglected to take care of herself and that the cause of the pneumonia which killed her was her refusal to dress warmly during the particularly hard frosts that winter. Marie-Louise's Catholic relations held Ferdinand responsible for her death. It was an inevitable reaction, inspired by their lasting resentment over Boris's change of religion.

It is true that during the months before her death she was worn out by illness. She told a near friend that she was afraid that her end was approaching, while she herself was weary of life. The probable real cause of her depression was exhaustion by her successive pregnancies: she gave birth to four children in five years, too great an effort for her frail constitution.

When Marie-Louise returned to Bulgaria in May 1896 she seemed to have become reconciled to Boris's change of religion. Her third child, Eudoxia, was conceived in the early spring of the following year and in June she and Ferdinand went to London for Queen Victoria's Diamond Jubilee. In a letter to a woman friend, Marie-Louise described the jubilee celebrations in detail. There was no hint of melancholy; she seemed delighted and interested in everything. The Princess of Wales was 'marvellously beautiful, amiable and very elegant'. One evening, 'we had dinner with the Queen. At dessert, three Highlanders carrying their bagpipes came in and walked round the room playing national tunes. It was charming. Then came the presentation of the suites of the Princes, and of deputations of Indians, Africans, Australians and many others. A very curious sight.'[29]

The gala evening at Covent Garden made a deep impression on her: 'the whole of the auditorium was transformed into a bower of roses, and bunches of orchids hung from the Royal box. The splendour of the jewels was fantastic.' At Windsor, 'the Queen was very amiable and gave me a pretty brooch with her monogram.'[30]

In January the following year, she gave birth to Princess Eudoxia. Though weakened, she was again pregnant by spring. In July 1898 she and Prince Ferdinand took the four-year-old Prince Boris to St Petersburg at the invitation of Nicholas II, ostensibly so that he might see his godson. Prince Boris was accompanied by his tutor, the Bulgarian monk Vassili. His presence at the side of the boy excited a good deal of curiosity and interest in St Petersburg; a few years later the monk

Rasputin was to gain ascendancy in the Russian court through the influence he exercised over the Tsar's young son. The State visit was a greater success than could have been expected and Princess Marie-Louise won all hearts: 'her clear-sighted and quick intelligence shone in her conversation with statesmen, as her observant and caustic wit charmed and amused the humblest of those who conversed with her.'[31] Madame Stancioff, the wife of the Bulgarian Envoy in St Petersburg who wrote this, was also struck by Prince Ferdinand's uncharacteristic lack of self-assurance on that occasion:

> Prince Ferdinand, generally so sure of himself, and inclined to be arrogant rather than amiable, appeared to me timid at the Russian Court. The Emperor alone showed a little sympathy towards him, but there was a note of hostility in the crowd of Grand Dukes as they stood grouped together, tall and proud, against the gilded panelling of the reception rooms, scanning the newcomers with sarcastic glances.[32]

The visit to Russia exhausted the Princess. Her depression was not helped by an indiscretion Ferdinand made later that summer. While spending the rest of the summer at the palace by the Black Sea with his family, he asked a Mademoiselle Fuchs to join them as a guest. She was a slim and distinguished-looking beauty whom he had met in Karlsbad. Marie-Louise treated her coldly, an attitude which was imitated by Ferdinand's entourage. One day the entourage, mainly Bulgarian officers, were waiting for Ferdinand and Marie-Louise to appear before lunch, when Mademoiselle Fuchs entered the drawing room. The officers merely acknowledged her arrival with curt bows. No one approached her or addressed a word to her. Abashed and half in tears, she left and went to her room, which she did not leave for the rest of the day. Ferdinand was furious and punished the officers by posting them to provincial duties.

In reporting Marie-Louise's death the following winter, the Bulgarian newspapers all published affecting accounts of how she had called for Ferdinand and her children in her agony. Her parting words to Ferdinand were, 'I am dying, but I shall always be with you and I shall watch over Bulgaria, over you and the children from up there.'[33] To Prince Boris she was reported as saying: 'When it will be your turn to reign one day, try to be an exemplary ruler' and 'Be kind, always be kind.' Her Bulgarian tutor received these reports with scepticism and wrote:

> The accounts of the last minutes of Princess Marie-Louise and the

words which she apparently addressed to her husband and her children could only have been reported by Prince Ferdinand.... There was a theatrical element in the description of these tragic minutes and people were in two minds whether to believe them. All his life, whatever the occasion or circumstances, Prince Ferdinand liked to act and to put on a show. Why, therefore, should one not believe malicious tongues which claimed that even during these tragic days of his life Ferdinand remained true to his nature?[34]

Ferdinand made the most of his wife's funeral a week later. The buildings along the streets through which the funeral cortége passed were 'entirely covered in crape'. The coffin was taken from the chapel in the palace, where the Princess had lain in state, to the Roman Catholic Church of Sofia for the funeral service. The huge procession, headed by numerous military detachments and bands playing funeral marches, culminated with the impressive catafalque of black, gold, silver and bronze followed by the tall, bent and visibly harrowed, bareheaded figure of Ferdinand on foot. After the funeral service the coffin remained in the church until two o'clock the following morning. The church was then surrounded by hundreds of soldiers bearing burning torches. Just then, Ferdinand arrived, entered the church and prayed by the coffin.

Then, at dead of night, the coffin was borne by the light of hundreds of torches to the railway station. From there a special train, all covered in crape, took it to Philippopolis to its final resting place in an aisle of the Roman Catholic Church of St Louis, a church of which Marie-Louise had been particularly fond. The next morning's newspaper accounts of the funeral read like dramatic criticism: 'In the dark of the night and in deepest silence, this mournful procession with burning torches, silent as the night itself had a deeply moving, even mystic, aspect. It was an imposing, fairy-like spectacle....'[35]

CHAPTER 17

Macedonian Sickness

—•❧❦•—

The rest of the year, following Marie-Louise's death in January 1899, was a gloomy period for Ferdinand. Bulgaria's finances were in a bad way after disastrous harvests, his four motherless children were a problem, he was irritated by his eighty-two-year-old mother who had come to supervise their care and, on top of all that, he was suffering from a painful swollen knee. Three months after his wife's death he wrote from the Rila monastery to Dimitri Stancioff:

> I spent a dreaful night. With ice on my knee, I am incapable of any movement and had to postpone my departure.... I must have been in poor condition generally to get such a swollen knee. I am writing on the bed of Father Nikifor who died on it fifty days ago!
>
> My sons left yesterday morning; both of them hate the beloved Rila and longed to leave it – horrid little brats – especially Boris who only likes Sofia and *his* court; he is becoming very disagreeable and full of authority. [Prince Boris was only five.] The Rila in May is a dream. Nature incomparable! The monastery an evil-smelling sewer and in full monastic anarchy! I shot a superb capercailzie (cock) on the Tsarev Peak yesterday. My mother is worrying herself in Vienna with the idea of coming to Sofia as soon as possible; how tiring it will be for me! Things are going badly here; no government to speak of, a virulent anti-dynastic opposition; no money; my statesmen: X a mollusc, Y infamous, Z beneath contempt. Are we going towards an even darker future?[1]

Such doleful complaints were not unusual and his regular correspondents did not take them too seriously. But at this time the gloom was no affectation. He felt a deep unease about his future course of action and the prospect for his ambition to become king of a fully independent

Bulgaria. The political situation in Europe at the turn of the century was such as to frustrate his efforts in that direction and to cramp his diplomatic style.

The really inhibiting political factor was the unexpected secret agreement concluded by Austria and Russia in 1897, following a visit by Emperor Francis Joseph to St Petersburg, to maintain the *status quo* in the Balkans. The agreement, which freed Austria's hands to deal with bitter problems inside the Habsburg Empire and at the same time allowed Russia to devote her efforts to advance in the Far East, in effect put the Balkans on ice or, to use the expression of the Austrian Foreign Minister Goluchowski, 'under a glass cover'. This state of affairs was to last for a decade. The agreement relaxed the Balkan antagonism between Russia and Austria, one of the most disturbing factors in Europe since 1815, and delayed their inevitable clash.

For Ferdinand this agreement had the effect of a political straitjacket. By 1900 he was fully aware that the only chance of political advancement for himself and his small country was in using the antagonisms and jealousies between Vienna and St Petersburg. In 1910 he told Maurice Paléologue: 'When Austria and Russia walk together there is nothing I can do; I am paralysed.'[2] He was to achieve his greatest successes later by exploiting the rivalry between the two powers and by deftly avoiding a total commitment to either of them. Inevitably Ferdinand's continuous playing off of one side against the other led to alternate accusations of duplicity by the two empires. Their recriminations seem almost absurdly naive today, mostly displays of bad temper and ill-concealed pique. Even at the time the more realistic of Europe's politicians were dismayed by these 'sentimental politics'. France's Maurice Paléologue, though no apologist for Ferdinand, criticized those who accused Ferdinand of duplicity for his characteristic tactics: 'The fact is that he could not do anything else, since these two Powers never ceased quarrelling and then becoming reconciled. Had he remained completely faithful to one of them when they were quarrelling, what would have been his fate when they again became allies and accomplices?'[3]

The *status quo* imposed on the Balkans by the Russo-Austrian agreement not only hampered Ferdinand's initiatives but put him under new dangerous pressures. By trying to ignore the unease felt in the Balkans, Austria and Russia exacerbated it. The main source of trouble was Macedonia, the last large Christian-inhabited area of the moribund Ottoman Empire in Europe still under direct Turkish rule. With an area just over twice that of Belgium it contained a mixture of races and nationalities which inspired the French culinary term for a hotchpotch of ingredients – the macédoine. It was to be Ferdinand's main preoccupation and the cause of his and Bulgaria's triumphs and disasters for many years.

At the end of the last century, Bulgaria, Greece and Serbia all laid claims to Macedonia. Each, in the expectation of the future collapse of Turkish rule in Macedonia, sought to establish prime kinship with the land on the basis of vehement national propaganda putting forward conflicting ethnographic, religious, historical and phonetic claims. The historical claims were mutually destructive. There had in fact been no Macedonian state since the days of the kings of Macedon in the fourth century B.C. Since that time Macedonia had belonged successively to the Roman Empire, the Byzantine Empire, the medieval Bulgarian and Serbian Empires, and the Ottoman Empire.

Population statistics compiled towards the turn of the century tend to agree (with the exception of Greek statistics) that the majority of the Christian inhabitants of Macedonia were Slavs. The Bulgarians claimed that these Slavs were Bulgarians. Belgrade claimed they were Serbs. Neutral statisticians played safe and listed them as 'Macedonian Slavs'. But, in considering the Macedonian Question in so far as it affected Ferdinand and Bulgaria, it may suffice to quote from a work on Macedonia published by the Royal Institute of International Affairs in London in 1950: 'In regard to their own national feelings, all that can be safely said is that during the last eighty years many more Slav Macedonians seem to have considered themselves Bulgarian, or closely linked with Bulgaria, than have considered themselves Serbian, or closely linked with Serbia (or Yugoslavia).'[4]

The Treaty of San Stefano in March 1878 spurred the determination of the Bulgarians of Macedonia to free themselves from Turkish rule. The Treaty included Macedonia in an autonomous Bulgaria. The Treaty of Berlin which four months later put Macedonia back under Turkish rule, with a total disregard of the interests of those immediately concerned, had a traumatic effect both in Macedonia and Bulgaria. It was impossible for the latter to remain indifferent to the sufferings of the Bulgarians of Macedonia. Conditions in Macedonia deeply affected Bulgarian internal politics, especially after some 100,000 Macedonians immigrated into Bulgaria by the mid-1890s. About half of the inhabitants of Sofia were Macedonians. The Bulgarians of Macedonia were determined not to accept the decisions of the Congress of Berlin as final. By 1900 two Macedonian 'freedom organizations' had come into being. Macedonian refugees in Bulgaria founded a 'Supreme Committee', whose chief aim was to organize the liberation of Macedonia from the Turks and its annexation to Bulgaria.

This organization soon became closely linked with the Bulgarian Government and the Crown. Another organization of a more revolutionary nature was the Internal Macedonian Revolutionary Organization (IMRO) founded by two Macedonian Bulgarians inside Macedonia. Before long it had grown cells and branches throughout the country. In its objects, formation, methods and influence, IMRO resembled Sinn Fein. Its aims were to put pressure on the Bulgarian Government, to keep the Macedonian Question before the Powers generally, to have an armed force ready which, with or without outside help, would be able to overthrow Turkish rule and set the country free. The leaders could not agree completely about their aims, some wanted an autonomous Macedonia, others one united with Bulgaria.

Despite the differences and rivalries between the Macedonian revolutionaries, they exerted increasing pressure on Ferdinand and the Bulgarian Government to take military action over Macedonia. Ferdinand and his ministers had been steadily increasing the strength of the Bulgarian army. Essentially, however, Ferdinand had placed his hopes on a diplomatic solution of the Macedonian problem. His critics pointed out that the maintenance of an inactive army at enormous cost to the country was simply an expensive luxury. The Prince repeatedly tried to get the signatories of the Berlin Treaty to put pressure on Turkey to carry out reforms in Macedonia. The reforms had been promised to the province by Article Twenty-Three of the Treaty as a means of calming down the inhabitants' burning grudge at being again subjected to Turkish oppression. No reforms were even contemplated and the two Powers deputed by the Berlin Congress to carry them out—Russia and Austria-Hungary – neutralized each other's efforts in the Balkans. The *status quo* was maintained at the cost of the suffering peasants of Macedonia.

The French traveller and writer Victor Bérard, who visited Macedonia in 1899, wrote:

> One could compare Macedonia to a chess board of which some of the squares are sparsely inhabited by Turks striving to emigrate to Asia Minor, Christians yearning to return to Serbia, Bulgaria, Greece, all unsettled, irrespective of their nationality, by the raids of the Albanians, the provocations and thefts of the Turkish Prefects, the cruel conduct of the Turkish police and especially by that admirable instrument of depopulation known as the Turkish Army.[5]

In spring 1897, Prince Ferdinand saw Marschall, the German Foreign Minister, in Berlin and told him that he could not forever maintain peace in the Balkans if pressure was not put on Turkey to carry out the reforms promised by the Treaty. He himself had tried to give no encouragement to Macedonian irredentism, with the result that the

Bulgarian Press now went so far as to call him a 'Turkish lackey'. The Prince repeated similar arguments to Kaiser William, who brusquely told him to keep the peace or else he would have to face the Great Powers. On a later occasion the Prince said that the Macedonian Question had become 'a real emetic [*vomitif*] for the whole of Europe'.[6]

It is not surprising that the Macedonian problem made him feel sick. He was immobilized by the Powers, while the 'wild men' of Macedonia growled and snapped at him. The revolutionaries had no time for, or understanding of, the niceties of European power politics. For years they believed that Macedonia would be freed with Russian help. Panitza's plot against Ferdinand and· the assassination of Stamboloff were meant to remove the obstacles to obtaining Russia's help. The Macedonians were bitterly disappointed in their hope that Russia would at last act in Macedonia's favour after the 1896 reconciliation between Bulgaria and Russia. Immediately after the conversion of Prince Boris, Russia hastened to warn against a possible revival of agitation in Macedonia under the mistaken supposition that the reconciliation with Russia would cover any aspirations and machinations in that direction. Nothing would be allowed to disturb the *status quo*.

By the end of 1898 Ferdinand realized that there was no hope of Russian help. He urgently needed room to manoeuvre and to exploit the basic antagonisms between Russia and Austria-Hungary which just then had been so frustratingly papered over. Worst of all, Ferdinand's diplomacy had remained pro-Russian, ever since Emperor Francis Joseph's outrage over· the apostasy of Boris. In Ferdinand's eyes this amounted to a commitment to Russia. For him, commitment meant immobility, the negation of diplomacy and intrigue. A year later he managed to regain his freedom to act. In January 1899 the pro-Russian Bulgarian Government of Stoiloff resigned and was replaced by one led by the pro-Austrian Grekoff. As Ferdinand had expected, welcoming noises were immediately heard from Austria and in the autumn of that year he was received in Vienna by the Emperor Francis Joseph, with exceptional honours.

After Prince Ferdinand had re-established friendly relations with Austria in 1899, to Russia's predictable annoyance, there soon came signs that he was yet again preparing to put the helm hard over. Only six months after Ferdinand's visit to the Austrian Emperor, Lord Salisbury was saying in London that he had learnt of the Prince's wish to marry a Russian grand duchess. Bulgaria's pro-Austrian Government was soon replaced by a Russophil cabinet, followed by a series of official visits to Bulgaria by Russian grand dukes and ministers. By now, Ferdinand's personal power in Bulgaria was well established, allowing him control over party politics remarkable in a constitutional ruler.

His control of Bulgaria's party politics made it possible to change the ruling Cabinets in accordance with the requirements of foreign policy – in essence an alternation between pro-Austrian and pro-Russian Governments. There were to be no more Stamboloffs. This did not mean that he could manipulate the politicians at will, nor that he was allowed the role of autocrat. While he managed to establish himself as the fount of favours and final arbiter in political life by stirring up and using irreconcilable rivalries among the politicians, he also benefited from the Bulgarians' realization that they had to depend on him for his knowledge of the wider world of European politics. The Russian diplomat Neklyudoff, who knew Ferdinand well, wrote:

> Prince and subjects were agreed on other points than those of personal relations and sympathies. In politics, the Bulgarians considered Ferdinand an admirable tool for their national aspirations; his personal ambition, his intelligence, his great cunning, his parentage and connections, were all great natural assets for the Bulgarian cause.[7]

During the next ten years he steered a skilful and hazardous course amidst the many perils of the early years of the present century. His reputation as a consummate diplomatist during that period grew alongside his reputation for 'foxiness' or hypocrisy. The latter he would deny indignantly while at the same time complacently reading newspaper articles which described him as 'the new Machiavelli'. King Edward VII, according to his biographer Sir Sidney Lee, found Ferdinand 'so clever and witty... a most agreeable companion'[8] and 'l'homme le plus fin d'Europe'.[9] But on other occasions he 'detested his affected manner, biting tongue, love of intrigue... his ambitious cleverness'.[10]

But King Edward, who was so easily bored, was never bored by Ferdinand. Queen Marie of Romania, Edward's niece, provided this impression of Ferdinand in conversation:

> The French blood running in his veins made of him an incomparable causeur, his repartees were sparkling, his irony light, intangible and always to the point. Sharp-witted, all-observing, with a superfine sense of humour, he often indulged in the delicate luxury of laughing at himself, of making fun of his looks, his idiosyncrasies, his tastes, his likes and dislikes. All this furnished subjects for endless witty conversation and allowed him to use his sarcasm to his heart's content.... There may have been less comfortable sides to Uncle Ferdinand's nature, but a more pleasant, stimulating and erudite

companion, when he set out to charm his audience, cannot be imagined.[11]

The nadir in the relations between Edward VII and his cousin came at the time of Queen Victoria's death in January 1901. When the Prince heard of it he called at the British Legation in Sofia to announce his intention of attending the funeral. He wanted to be sure, however, that the precedence due to him as ruler of Bulgaria would be given. He said he did not want to be treated as he had been at the Queen's Diamond Jubilee, that is to say, as a cadet member of the House of Coburg. The reply from London cut him to the quick. He was told that this was not a fitting occasion to raise such a question and that no change could be made in the procedure already sanctioned. Prince Ferdinand took it as a personal slight by King Edward and thereupon cancelled the arrangements made for his journey, sent a deputation to represent him and spent the day of the funeral at Philippopolis where he celebrated Prince Boris's birthday with a military review and a gala luncheon to which the Russian Envoy in Sofia was specially invited. Edward was furious, possibly most of all at the marked attention to the Russian diplomat. By this time, Ferdinand had tipped the see-saw once more towards Russia.

Two years later, in 1903, Sir George Buchanan, who was about to leave London to take up his post as Britain's new Envoy in Sofia, begged King Edward to give a friendly message which he could pass on to his cousin Ferdinand. All the King said was: 'You may tell the Prince that I have not forgotten the fact that he is my cousin, but that, as long as he continues his present two-faced policy, he cannot count on my support.'[12] It was not an ideal message for an envoy about to take up a new post. He could hardly deliver it word for word, especially to a man as touchy as Ferdinand. Sir George coped, and glossed it over to the best of his ability.

The next year, 1904, Edward and Ferdinand met at Marienbad and a reconciliation took place. They enjoyed each other's company, though Edward was at the same time irritated by what he considered the 'unnecessary air of royal dignity' assumed by the Prince. It was August, and one morning King Edward was delighted to receive early news of a great Japanese naval victory over Russia in the war which had started earlier that year. He was almost as pleased by the Japanese success as by the fact that he had received the news before Ferdinand. Later in the day he 'chaffed the life out of Ferdinand of Bulgaria on the promenade, who knew nothing, though he always plumes himself upon being more rapidly informed than anyone else'.[13]

Try as he might, nothing came of Ferdinand's efforts to get the major Powers to carry out the promised reforms in Macedonia and honour the terms of the Berlin Treaty The Powers were the Establishment; in that sense, the Prince's efforts to get them to carry out the reforms that *they* had promised placed him in the paradoxical position of a political radical fighting against the *status quo*. Much of his bitterness against Austria and Russia, and his consequent resolve to *use* them as cynically as they were using him, stemmed from a genuine feeling of outrage at what he considered their shortsighted, unenlightened and illiberal attitude to the sufferings of the Macedonian Christians. Such feelings were bound up with his own resentment at the treatment he had received at their hands at different times, the sarcasms, the threats, the snubs and the plots. In 1906 he told Sir George Buchanan that 'he would never forget the manner in which he had been treated, after his recognition, by the Austrian court and government'.[14] In a fine burst of invective Ferdinand told Maurice Paléologue some years later:

In Vienna one breathes in an atmosphere of death and decrepitude. When the old Emperor Francis Joseph deigns to receive me at the Hofburg, he always appears to me surrounded by his tragic legend, his sinister ghosts....I don't know if you have ever visited the Imperial necropolis, the *Kaisergruft* [imperial vault], at the Capucin Church. It is airless, mouldy and decomposing. Well! The entire Austrian court is impregnated with this noisome smell... a smell which has spread from the court to all official circles.... I know of nothing more lugubrious than dining at the Emperor's table; there one only comes across archaic countenances, shrivelled intellects, trembling heads, worn-out bladders. It is an exact image of Austria-Hungary.[15]

Russia, he told Buchanan, had 'long realized that it had been a great mistake on her part ever to have called the Bulgarian Principality into existence, and she had persistently endeavoured to stunt its growth'. She consequently regarded the Bulgarian Macedonians with suspicion and would never tolerate 'anything in the shape of an autonomous régime in Macedonia'.[16]

Although Russia was at that time preoccupied with the Far East, this did not mean that Tsar Nicholas and his ministers had shifted their interest entirely to the plains of Manchuria. The old dream of Constantinople was still very much alive. Deep down Nicholas had a nagging anxiety that some day Ferdinand might manage to claim and take Constantinople from a defunct Turkey (this anxiety became a real fear after the Bulgarian victories against Turkey in 1912). In an account of a meeting in Wiesbaden in 1903 between the Kaiser William and Tsar Nicholas, Germany's Chancellor Bülow described how the two got on to the subject of Bulgaria and the latest rumours that Prince Ferdinand was about to proclaim himself king of an independent Bulgaria. Nicholas remarked: 'The Bulgarian has royal ideas.' William nodded, laughed and then went on to tease Nicholas by asking him if he knew how the kingdom of Bulgaria would look. The Tsar replied in the negative and the Kaiser said: 'Greater Bulgaria, including the whole of Macedonia and with its capital at Constantinople.' The result of this remark, wrote Bülow, was: '*Tableau!* The expression on his Russian Imperial Majesty's face spoke volumes!'[17]

On 2 August 1903, discontent in Macedonia culminated in a major Bulgarian anti-Turkish uprising. After initial successes the rebels were ruthlessly crushed by the Turkish army, which was aided by Greek irregulars. As a result some 10,000 houses were burnt down, 60,000 people were left homeless and 30,000 more refugees poured into Bulgaria.

This time Russia and Austria, acting as the 'mandatories' of Europe, recommended new reforms for Macedonia including an international gendarmerie for the territory. These and the subsequent appointment of an international commission to control Macedonian finance were well-meant but misdirected efforts. Under them Macedonia sank deeper and deeper into anarchy, while Ferdinand was under ever increasing pressure at home to declare war on Turkey.

The outbreak the following year of the Russo-Japanese war, the shattering victories of the Japanese navy and the ensuing social unrest and general strike in Russia, made it quite clear to Ferdinand that Russia, even if she had wanted to, was for the time in no position to help him and Bulgaria. Despite his deep suspicions about Austrian designs in the Balkans, Ferdinand again looked towards Vienna; with a corresponding change of Government in Sofia.

The year 1907, the twentieth anniversary of his arrival in Bulgaria, opened badly. In January, Prince Ferdinand was severely upset by a mass demonstration of university students in Sofia. It happened when he arrived to open the newly completed building of the National Theatre. As his carriage approached the square in front of the theatre, thousands of young people demonstrated their feelings with wave upon wave of sustained booing and whistling. The immediate object of the students' hatred was the Minister of Education, accused by the considerable number of socialists among the students, of subservience to the Prince. But Ferdinand also saw it as an attack upon himself. The Government ordered the closing of Sofia University, the dismissal of most professors and lecturers, the imprisonment of some students, while others, of military age, were called up. At the same time the Minister of Education, whose unpopularity had been the direct cause of the demonstration, was dismissed. The affair was to leave a considerable amount of resentment against Prince Ferdinand.

The following month Princess Clémentine died peacefully in Vienna, aged ninety. This remarkable woman had first fired her son's royal ambition and greatly helped him with her shrewd counsels, her determination and her money during the early dangerous years in Bulgaria. Her importance to Ferdinand was so well known that people immediately began to predict that without her advice he was bound to make political mistakes. A tough realist, she once startled Dr Daneff, the Prime Minister, by insisting that he should 'conduct the forthcoming elections in Bulgaria with a firm hand'. He had to shout down her silver ear-trumpet, 'I am afraid it is my belief that it is preferable for the people to express their choice freely', a suggestion to which the eighty-four-year-old Princess did not seem to take kindly.[18]

Although Ferdinand had often found her a burden in her old age, his sorrow was great. A clause in her will expressly forbidding an autopsy disappointed him; he was a firm believer in royal autopsies and maintained that they were of great historic and scientific interest. He also had to abandon his project of depositing her heart at the necropolis of the Orléans family at Dreux, near Chartres.

Princess Clémentine missed by one year seeing him crowned as king, the great ambition of her life. Soon after Ferdinand became Tsar of Bulgaria, he had a Latin inscription carved on her grave in Coburg. The inscription crisply captured the relationship between them: 'King's daughter, no queen herself, yet King's mother.'

The year of 1907 was one of tension for Ferdinand, dominated by the oppressive feeling of a gathering storm. There were evenings of intense anxiety when he ordered thirteen candles to be lighted in his bedroom in order to protect his night's sleep from baneful influences. It seemed that he was summoning the occult powers to fill the void left by his mother. The main cause of his anxiety was frustration at not finding an opening for a diplomatic initiative which would satisfy Bulgaria's aspirations over Macedonia and final national independence. He might have been cheered by outsiders' views on his position and achievements during his twenty years in Bulgaria. That year Maurice Paléologue, who had just taken up his post in Sofia, wrote:·

Bulgaria is preparing splendid celebrations to mark the twentieth anniversary of Prince Ferdinand's accession. The Bulgarian people are right to consider this event as a national holiday, for they owe their sovereign a great debt of gratitude.

If one measures the distance travelled by the principality since 1887, if one recalls the state of disorder and misery existing at the time

Prince Alexander of Battenberg had to abdicate, it is hard to realise the flourishing situation which Bulgaria now enjoys. In twenty years everything has been created: administration, police, finance, army, public education, railways, commerce, industry, etc., all the machinery of political, economic and social life. Exactly what part did Ferdinand play in this extraordinary transformation? First of all he saved his people from anarchy. That service along is sufficient to secure him a fine place in Bulgaria's history. Through his skill, his understanding of men, the influence of his manners as well as his complete lack of scruples, he has managed to dominate all the parties and maintain them in constitutional paths.

Secondly, he alone has conducted Bulgaria's foreign policy. He has been both the representative and guarantor of his country in the eyes of foreigners. Europe hardly knew the Bulgarians except through him and they have greatly benefited from coming to be known in this way. He never ceased negotiating during his perpetual travels. His government's diplomacy is entirely in his hands.

The Prince has exercised this personal double function for twenty years with remarkable consistency and intelligence. But that apart, one has to say that it was the qualities of the Bulgarian race, its energy, its sobriety, its tenacity, its patriotism, which achieved everything. As Head of State Prince Ferdinand has considerable deficiencies. He is a mediocre administrator. Day to day business bores him. He does not understand finance and he squanders money. He has no military instinct...[19]

The absence of the latter trait had its compensation:

The army believes that it is capable of playing a decisive role in the Eastern Question and is impatiently waiting to prove this. Very luckily, its supreme commander has no bellicose inclinations. A stranger to the military art, awkward at physical exercise, recognising that he is unfit to command the army, he will do everything to avoid war. At critical moments one can be sure that he will not take any action until he has exhausted the resources of diplomacy, at which he excels.[20]

As the twentieth anniversary of Ferdinand's accession drew near, the annual diplomatic speculation in Europe about an impending Bulgarian declaration of independence reached an unprecedented intensity. Diplomats were reporting to their foreign ministers that the Prince had finally decided to take the step, and, as contingency plans were being prepared on how best to absorb the blow against the *status quo* and preserve peace, Ferdinand and his Foreign Minister Stancioff were putting out feelers. The French Minister in Sofia was told by Stancioff that Ferdinand was worried about 'the necessity to change soon Bulgaria's international status'.[21] Later Ferdinand spoke to the French diplomat about his difficult situation, stressed the impatience of the Bulgarian people and the need to do something more than give counsels of patience. 'I am wearing myself out in the thankless role to which Europe has condemned me,'he said, with an appearance of 'discouragement and irresolution'.[22]

He had definitely contemplated having himself proclaimed king at Tirnovo, but with a growing sense of unease that this was not the favourable moment. About a fortnight before the planned date he was in Munich and received an invitation from the Austrian Emperor who was at his summer residence of Ischl. Both Francis Joseph and his Foreign Minister, Aehrenthal, warned him against undertaking any hasty actions. It appears that Ferdinand was almost glad to receive this extra bit of discouragement. It made it easier for him to put off taking a great risk at a moment he instinctively felt to be unfavourable. The morning after his meeting with the Emperor, an official communiqué published in Sofia qualified as 'a malicious invention' reports that he intended to proclaim the independence of Bulgaria. It went on to say:

> The Prince of Bulgaria has undertaken other duties towards the Bulgarian Nation and cannot busy himself with meaningless questions regarding formalities, titles and personal satisfaction. Bulgaria and her Prince are safeguarding the cause of progress and of humanity in the East and only pursue that noble ideal.[23]

The communiqué was accompanied by an announcement that Prince Ferdinand had been appointed honorary colonel of an Austrian regiment. The document bore the Prince's hall-mark in its condemnation of the very things of which he felt he could be accused. The royal title, he wanted the world to know, was nothing to him, mere vanity. It would have sounded more convincing if he had not coupled his condemnation of *meaningless questions of formality* with an announcement about his honorary colonelcy.

In a letter from Sofia to his chief Sir Edward Grey, the British Foreign Secretary, Buchanan reported the publication of the communiqué and the announcement about the Austrian colonelcy with the comment: 'The above facts speak for themselves, and there can be but little doubt that it is to the intervention of the Emperor of Austria that we owe the enunciation of these fine sentiments of disinterested patriotism on the part of His Royal Highness.'[24]

The danger to Europe had passed, Buchanan added, but only for the present; 'when the psychological moment arrives, we shall probably be surprised by a step, of which we shall have had no warning.' Ferdinand considered that the time, though not the exact moment, had come to have himself proclaimed king: 'the dream with which he has been possessed ever since he first put foot on Bulgarian soil.' Like his French colleague, Buchanan believed that Ferdinand would only use diplomatic means:

> A natural aversion for the profession of arms and an irresolution of character, which makes it always difficult for him to take a serious decision, dispose him to look to diplomacy rather than to the sword for the attainment of his ends. It is to his restraining influence that we owe the maintenance of peace in the past; but if Europe persistently thwarts his wishes, it is doubtful whether we shall be able to count for long on a continuance of his correct attitude.

The instinct which had made Ferdinand change his mind at the eleventh hour had been sound. In the following year, 1908, he was to achieve his aim in much more favourable cirumstances and with a dexterity which further enhanced his reputation for shrewdness and skill in using the rivalries between Russia and Austria.

Before that happened, Prince Ferdinand found time to settle a matter which had become increasingly urgent since his mother's death and which concerned his public as well as his private life. His four children, orphaned a second time after their grandmother's death, needed a new mother. And he himself needed a wife to represent him at public functions and preside over charitable work and hospitals. In September 1907, the Tsar's uncle, Grand Duke Vladimir Alexandrovich, and his wife arrived in Sofia for the solemn unveiling in the city's centre of an equestrian statue of Alexander II, the Grand Duke's father and Bulgaria's liberator. The forty-five foot high monument and statue, the work of the Italian sculptor Arnoldo Zocchi, carried the inscription 'To the Tsar Liberator. Erected by grateful Bulgaria.' During the festivities, which Ferdinand intended as a major display of Russophil sentiment and which were watched with jaundiced eyes by Austria, he told the Grand Duchess that he was looking for a wife.

He was matter-of-fact about it; he told her that he 'wanted a woman who would look after his four children and take an interest in the national charities. He did not want a wife who would expect affection or even get attention.'[25] Grand Duchess Marie Pavlovna had no illusions about what were described as Ferdinand's 'complex personality' and 'foibles'. She was also devoted to him and greatly admired his 'instinct for greatness'.[26] She realized straight away that she would be able to help him and after she left Bulgaria got in touch with her great friend and relative, the German Princess Eleonore von Reuss-Köstritz. In January 1908, Prince Ferdinand's engagement to Princess Eleonore was officially announced.

She was the daughter of the late Prince Henry IV of Reuss. Her uncle, also a prince of Reuss, had been one of three candidates whose names were submitted to the Grand Sobranie in Tirnovo for election to the throne of Bulgaria when Prince Alexander of Battenberg was chosen. A year older than Ferdinand, she was a plain, efficient, unselfish and kind woman of 'incorruptible integrity', who had distinguished herself in caring for wounded Russian soldiers during the Russo-Japanese War. She was in charge of a Red Cross train in Manchuria and was decorated at the front for her services. It was the general opinion that she had consented to marry Ferdinand from a spirit of self-sacrifice and because of the opportunities offered in Bulgaria for hospital and charitable work.

The marriage presented religious problems. Princess Eleonore was a Lutheran, Ferdinand an excommunicate Catholic, and the Bulgarian State religion Orthodox. There were two ceremonies, a Catholic one which was held at Coburg and a Protestant one at Gera, the capital of the principality of Reuss in Germany. In order to be able to have a proper Catholic marriage, Ferdinand made use of the intricacies of Roman canon law which allow the penalty of excommunication to be temporarily suspended for the accomplishment of certain important acts. The penitent is told: '*Absolvo te, cum reincidentia effecto secuto.*' After the Coburg marriage ceremony, the Papal censure against Ferdinand came into force again.

He had only received Rome's permission to marry a Protestant on the condition that he maintained a strictly passive attitude during the Lutheran wedding ceremony. When the pastor at Gera realized that the Prince would not pronounce the sacramental 'Yes', he at first refused to officiate. After long negotiations a compromise was found. Instead of asking them in turn, 'Wilt thou, Ferdinand' and 'Wilt thou, Eleonore', the pastor would ask collectively. 'Will you…', with the remaining words modified accordingly. To this joint question only she had to answer 'Yes', while he stood by silent. History does not relate whether the accommodating pastor had obtained his superior's permission. Either way, the marriage was celebrated in the presence of numerous representatives of Europe's ruling houses.

The wedding guests noticed that Prince Ferdinand 'did not show much enthusiasm during the festivities but was very affable to his hosts and interested in the long history of the house of Reuss'.[27] The Princess had no illusions and took things as they came. For Ferdinand, it was all a necessary chore. The day before the wedding he joked about her lack of youth and beauty to his confidants and showed them a necklace which he was about to give to her with the words, *'Ceci conviendra à son austère poitrine* [This will suit her austere bosom].'[28]

On their way back to Bulgaria, the newly-wed couple paid an official visit to King Carol I and Queen Carmen Sylva of Romania in Bucharest. There Eleonore must have lost even the tiniest shred of an illusion about her marriage – if she had any. Ferdinand was furious that they had been given a double bedroom in their apartment, protested and insisted that they be given separate quarters. Very soon after the marriage unverifiable anecdotes went the rounds. According to one of them, Ferdinand had asked his wife not to appear at the dinner table, except on official occasions, and to have her meals in her apartments. When one day he noticed the smell of food in a palace corridor and on asking was told that it was his wife's meal, he had replied: *'Désormais, quand la reine dinera dans son appartement, on lui servira des diners froids* [In future, if the Queen dines in her apartments, she is to be brought cold meals].'[29]

He took it into his head that she would bring him ill-luck and told his private secretary Monsieur de Chèvremont, *'Cette femme me porte la guigne!* [This woman brings me bad luck!]'[30] One evening he accompanied her to a charity concert. Maurice Paléologue, who stood near him as he entered the concert hall, noticed that his right hand, half hidden by a flap of his coat, was clenched to ward off the evil eye, with the index and little finger extended.

Despite all this, he was forced to acknowledge that his friend, the Grand Duchess Marie Pavlovna, had procured the kind of wife he had wanted. His four children took to her and grew to like her much sooner than might have been expected. It was as if they sensed that Eleonore was not the archetypal step-mother and there was no question of her usurping their father's affection.

She immersed herself in organizing hospital work with efficiency and genuine compassion. That in itself would have been enough to repel Ferdinand, with his phobia about hospitals, blood and infection. But he recognized the importance and necessity of having a consort who could deal with 'all these abominations'. There was also a bonus of which he was well aware: through her person and family relations with many of the crowned rulers of Europe, her tact and intelligence, she would be of considerable use to him in his diplomacy. In these respects she might have reminded him of his mother.

The frequent signs of superstitious unease, if not dread, which he betrayed at the time of his second marriage, were not so much due to his new wife, as to the assassination of King Carlos I of Portugal and his eldest son in Lisbon on 1 February of that year. The event made a vivid impression on Ferdinand, who was closely related to them on both the Coburg and Orléans sides. He had a healthy respect for the power of the political assassin, though he did not indulge in the elaborate security precautions with which his late enemy Tsar Alexander III had surrounded himself. Nor did he live in a permanent state of terror like his suzerain, Sultan Abdul Hamid, who banned any mention of regicide in the Turkish Press – with curious results. King and Queen of Serbia, assassinated in 1903, were said to have died of indigestion, while the death of Empress Elizabeth of Austria at the hands of an Italian anarchist was announced by a Turkish daily wi.h the headline 'Empress Elizabeth Dies in Geneva', followed by a second heading that the censor had missed: 'General Indignation in Europe'.

The moment Ferdinand heard of the Portuguese assassination, he lost no time in telling Prince Boris, by then fourteen, that both the King *and* his heir had been killed. Paléologue wrote at the time: 'It was to impress on his young mind that their interests were bound up with each other as far as the revolutionaries are concerned.'[31] It was part of the education of a future king.

Chapter 18

The Other Tsar

—◦❧❦◦—

Maurice Paléologue made himself agreeable to Prince Ferdinand almost from the day of his arrival in Sofia. Ferdinand was delighted when the French diplomat told him that he was very interested in him as the focus of historical hereditary strains. He described them as *rencontres d'hérédité* operating in him. Exceedingly pleased, Ferdinand replied:

> Now here is the kind of expression which I never get to hear. What do my Bulgarians care about the fact that some very varied atavisms are commingled in me? It is to the Bourbons I owe the pride of my race and my courage. But I do also owe a great deal to the Coburgs: my kind of intelligence and my political qualities. In that respect I believe I greatly resemble my great-uncle, King Leopold I of the Belgians. And if I have an ability to deal with eastern people, to understand them, to make them accept me, then I owe it to my Magyar ancestry, to the blood I inherited from my grandmother Princess Kohary.[1]

This complacent self-characterization was not lost on Paléologue, who realised that his own interest in history and knowledge of genealogy presented an ideal opportunity to get into the Prince's favour. One day early in February 1908, Paléologue received a message from Ferdinand thanking him for the present of a book about Louis XIV's relations with Madame de Maintenon. Ferdinand, said the messenger, would like to discuss the book with Paléologue as a friend and would be therefore pleased to receive him in his private apartments at the palace.

When the Frenchman got there he was taken to a small drawing room; at one time it had been Princess Marie-Louise's boudoir. He was asked to wait; the Prince would come presently. Paléologue sat down on the only sofa and found himself facing the only wall decoration in the room, a big picture clearly recently painted. When he examined it he knew that he had only been summoned in order to study it. During the ten minutes until the Prince appeared, he had nothing else to do.

That evening Paléologue wrote in his diary:

I quickly understood why he kept me waiting, why he made me spend several minutes of enforced solitude and contemplation in this out-of-the-way room. Here is a description of the picture. Painted in a rather naive manner with bright colours, it showed the Bosphorus, Constantinople, Saint Sophia, the Great Wall, the Golden Horn, the Asian shore. High above this panorama, in the glow of an apocalyptic sky, the painter had depicted the victorious gallop of a splendid horseman, Tsar Ferdinand!... No doubt about it, this crude painting was intended as the symbolic prelude to the interview to which I had been invited.[2]

When the Prince finally arrived he pretended that the diplomat had been taken to the wrong room: 'Why and how have you been shown to this unfurnished room which I never visit?... My orders have not been understood.... I had meant quite another drawing room, one I often like to hide in! I am so badly served!...My Bulgarian wolves are not made for court life!'[3]

Ferdinand then sat down and without a word about Madame de Maintenon, went on to complain about his difficult political position. Paléologue sensed the part he was expected to play:

I told him in a firm and friendly tone that his role was far from finished; that the Eastern Question would doubtless cause serious difficulties in Europe and that in the political crisis which was about to erupt Bulgaria would certainly be a factor of prime importance: 'Do not be discouraged. One day you may well become the arbiter of the Balkans.' At these words his face cleared and lit up. And without saying a word, with a brief look, he drew my attention to the symbolic panorama of Constantinople.[4]

By then Ferdinand clearly considered that he had made his point.

At once, the skilful actor changed masks. Smiling, he asked me playfully: 'And Madame de Maintenon?... In telling you my sorrows I nearly forgot to tell you how interested I was in the book you were so kind to offer me.... What an intriguer, what a hypocrite, what a vile woman!...'[5]

Ferdinand was often at his best and most amusing when discussing figures of the past, with a bitchy verve and enjoyment which made his interlocutors imagine he was gossiping about a contemporary. With his nasal voice, he talked incisively and with 'picturesque scorn' of Louis XIV's last wife, 'this reformed whore, this cold, desiccated ambitious woman who used to pour holy water into the wash-basins of the Montespan and the Fontanges'.[6] He made 'filthy jokes' about Madame de Maintenon in her seventies and her exhaustion by the Sun King's irrepressible sexual demands. With much relish he impersonated the Bishop of Chartres injunction to her to share the King's bed: '*Aimez le roi, madame, d'une très grande charité. Soyez-lui soumise comme faisait Sara, qui obéissait à Abraham!* [Love the King, Madam, with exceeding great charity. Submit to him as did Sarah, who obeyed Abraham].'[7]

It is not clear what precise purpose the Prince had in mind in staging this tortuous charade. He may have simply tried to demonstrate obliquely to one of the representatives of the major powers his awareness that it might be his destiny to play a prominent role in Europe.

Such a demonstration coincided with Ferdinand's realization at the beginning of 1908, that the *status quo* in the Balkans, imposed by the Austro-Russian agreement of 1897, was loosening, that the ice was beginning to melt. And this meant that the moment for the Prince to act was, mercifully, at hand. There were signs of disagreement between Vienna and St Petersburg and renewed suspicions about each other's motives in south-eastern Europe. A tone of renewed hostility was a direct result of the ambition and vanity of two men who had recently, disastrously, become the foreign ministers of Russia and Austria. By their actions they were to set Europe firmly on the course which led to the Great War. Ferdinand was to exploit their rivalry.

Alexander Izvolski became Russia's Minister of Foreign Affairs in 1906, at the age of fifty. Sir Harold Nicolson's portrait cannot be bettered:

> One's first impression was not favourable. He was obviously a vain man, and he strutted on little lacquered feet. His clothes, which came from Savile Row, were moulded tightly upon a plump but still gainly frame. He held himself rigidly with stiff shoulders. He wore a pearl pin, an eye glass, white spats, a white slip to his waistcoat. His face was well cared for, but pasty and fattening, with loose and surly lips. His hair and moustache were carefully parted; he had a way of turning his short Russian neck stiffly above his high white collar, glancing sideways, as so often with Russians, away from the person with whom he was shaking hands. His voice was at once cultured and rasping. He left behind him, as he passed onwards, a slight scent of *violette de parme*.[8]

From the moment that he was appointed Izvolski looked round for an opportunity to score a dramatic personal success, a dazzling international political gain for Russia, which would offset the humiliations of the war against Japan. A desperate snob, he itched to increase his social prestige and assure for himself the title of Count.

Izvolski was not destined to get a title. But his Austrian counterpart, Baron Lexa von Aehrenthal, started off with one when, at the age of fifty-four, he was appointed Minister of Foreign Affairs in the same year as Izvolski. Later he *did* become a Count. Aehrenthal, as Sir Harold Nicolson described him, was 'an unwieldy man, with heavy hapless jaws, a stubble head of hair, and sad turbot eyes'.[9] He was as vain as Izvolski. Unlike the Russian, who was nervous, timorous and exceedingly sensitive to public criticism, the Austrian was arrogant and impatient for action. He too wanted to restore the prestige of his country by some spectacular coup which would further his own position and at the same time would humiliate Izvolski.

The coup which Aehrenthal was planning involved the annexation by Austria of the Turkish provinces of Bosnia and Hercegovina, the two most north-westerly provinces of the Ottoman Empire. (Bosnia-Hercegovina now forms one of the federated republics within Yugoslavia.) At the Congress of Berlin in 1878, Austria had been given the right to occupy and administer the two provinces. Although the occupation was expected to be permanent, Austria-Hungary was constrained to sign a declaration that the sovereignty of the Sultan was not affected, and that the occupation should be considered 'provisional'.

The reason Aehrenthal wanted to convert Austria's thirty-year-old occupation of the provinces into a direct annexation was closely connected with increasing worries in Vienna about the growing restiveness of the South ('Yugo') Slavs inside the Habsburg monarchy. The South Slavs in the monarchy were receiving encouragement from their kinsmen in Serbia, the independent South Slav state. Serbia, in Vienna's eyes, came to be regarded as 'the Piedmont of the South Slavs', the magnet for the irredentist aspirations of the Slavs within the monarchy. The way to deal with the troublesome influence was to break Serbia, or at least to take her down a considerable number of pegs.

In Aehrenthal's view the annexation of Bosnia and Hercegovina would have that effect. It would end the Serb dream of adding the two provinces to the national state, a dream shared by the inhabitants of the provinces. It would also show the Slavs that their 'protectress' Russia, still licking the wounds of the war against Japan, was not strong enough to protect them. Beyond that, at a more remote moment, Aehrenthal planned 'to destroy the Great Serbian dreams of the future' by partitioning Serbia with Bulgaria.

While Aehrenthal was pondering on his master-stroke, Izvolski was elaborating plans for his own. The diplomatic success which would dazzle Russia and Europe, he decided, would be to get the Straits of the Dardanelles and Bosphorus open to Russian warships. The closure of the Straits, stipulated in several earlier treaties, was confirmed by the Treaty of Berlin.

Both men decided that the way to success lay through a double breach of the thirty-year-old Treaty of Berlin, an action 'deep-dyed with illegality'.[10] By July 1908 their separate plans were reaching maturity and Izvolski suggested to Aehrenthal that if Russia and Austria came to a preliminary agreement, they might approach the other signatories of the Treaty of Berlin with a good chance of getting them to consent to the proposed changes.

Though the Russian apparently made the overture, Aehrenthal had already given Prince Ferdinand a hint of the annexation to come in March. In his own account of their meeting, Aehrenthal wrote: 'In general I assured the Prince that he had the sympathy of Austria-Hungary and indicated that even if the politics of the *status quo* were to be abandoned, there would be no clash of interests between the monarchy and the principality.'[11] It was a preliminary nudge which Aehrenthal was to clarify later that year.

Prince Ferdinand did not need to have it spelt out and was quite aware of what was afoot. His antennae perceived the latent enmity between Izvolski and Aehrenthal months before it was to come out into the open and poison the political atmosphere of Europe. As far as he was concerned, it was the most promising situation that had faced him in years: renewed tension between the two powers which had constantly tried to use him for their own end. Even better, the fact that the hostility he could feel building up presented itself so palpably as personal antagonism, offered scope to a man who was secretly flattered when European newspapers called him 'the new Machiavelli'.

There was nothing remarkably subtle in the way Ferdinand set about egging on the Austrian against his Russian counterpart. In his account of that meeting, Aehrenthal noted that Prince Ferdinand expressed suspicion about Russia's politics and Izvolski in person, and smoothly went on to quote 'private information'[12] about Izvolski's personal dislike of Aehrenthal. Even such tiny stray seeds were to bear fruit in the Great War ahead.

Aehrenthal's hint became clearer in a letter he wrote to Ferdinand on 5 August: 'Your Royal Highness is aware – and in our talks I have always endeavoured to make it quite clear – that I have always advised Bulgaria to wage a policy of moderation and prudence, but that nothing could be further from my thoughts than to oppose an action which, in certain circumstances, could be dictated by Bulgaria's own interests.'[13] This was oblique even by the standards of the diplomatic language of the time. To Ferdinand the message was clear: were the *status quo* to be upset by the annexation of Bosnia and Hercegovina by Austria, Vienna would welcome it if Ferdinand also breached the Treaty of Berlin by proclaiming Bulgaria's· independence.

At that time the political situation was dominated by a new urgency. In Constantinople, in July 1908, the revolution of the Young Turks triumphed, and forced the Sultan to restore the Constitution. Liberal opinion in Europe was at first delighted by a revolution that seemed to foreshadow the reformation and liberalization of the corrupt and ailing Ottoman state. There were also other reactions. Ferdinand had hoped that Bulgaria would inevitably achieve her independence and the liberation of Macedonia as the inevitable result of the irreversible decay in Constantinople. Now the reforms apparently introduced and foreshadowed by the Young Turks threatened to deprive Bulgaria of any future opportunity to proclaim her independence and of a pretext for intervention in Macedonia. The intentions of Aehrenthal and Izvolski also appeared to be threatened if a rejuvenated Turkey were to set its house in order.

Events moved very quickly. On 12 September 1908, the new Turkish Government foolishly gave Bulgaria an opening by a deliberate act of arrogance which, although trivial, caused great indignation in Bulgaria and left no one in doubt about the unfriendly attitude of the Young Turks. The Turkish Foreign Minister deliberately failed to invite the Bulgarian Envoy in Constantinople to a dinner he gave for all the diplomatic representatives in Turkey. It was an insult which was intended to emphasize the Bulgarian Envoy's status as the representative of a vassal state: for many years reference to this inferior status had been conveniently forgotten on both sides. The Bulgarian Government seized on this, and after an official protest to the Turks, recalled its Envoy. A few days later the Bulgarian Government took over the running of a section of those southern Bulgarian railways which were owned by Turkey and declared that the use of that stretch of line by Turkish troops threatened the autonomy of Bulgaria. In both incidents, provocative actions of the Young Turks were ably exploited to prepare the setting for the declaration of independence which Ferdinand and the Government were contemplating. Britain's Envoy in Sofia, Buchanan, was one of the few diplomats not in the know to guess, correctly, not only that the Declaration of Independence was at last really on the cards but that it would probably proceed *pari passu* with the annexation of Bosnia and Hercegovina by Austria.

It was a shrewd guess, for on 16 September, the day Buchanan wrote about it to his chief Sir Edward Grey, Aehrenthal and Izvolski were meeting at the castle of Buchlau in Moravia. No definitive account has ever emerged about what the two men agreed and the exact terms of the bargain they reached there; their mutual recriminations afterwards about what each one had said, and thought that the other had accepted, poisoned European politics. Much has been said and written about the truly fateful meeting at Buchlau and it is beyond the scope of this book to examine the voluminous and mostly circumstantial evidence, or to enter into the controversy as to what was actually said there.

In broad outline it may be assumed that Izvolski agreed that Austria should annex Bosnia and Hercegovina without imposing any conditions except Austria's support over the freedom of the Dardanelles and Bosphorus for Russian warships. Aehrenthal, on the other hand, agreed to the opening of the Straits on condition that the other signatory Powers of the Berlin Treaty concurred. Izvolski also committed himself to Aehrenthal to an extent which allowed the latter eventually to threaten him with the publication of certain documents which would incriminate him.

What Izvolski had agreed at Buchlau had indeed made him vulnerable to blackmail. His subsequent venomous hatred of Aehrenthal who, as he was to insist to the point of hysteria, had tricked him ('*ce sale juif,*' as he said), was really due to his appalled realization that in trying to score a dazzling diplomatic success he had completely misread Russian opinion. The issue of the 'freedom of the Straits' had receded into the background over the years, while Slav sentiment counted for much. By agreeing to the unconditional annexation of the two provinces by Austria, he was in effect sanctioning a blow against the Slavs of Serbia in order to obtain the opening of the Straits, about which very few people in Russia cared. The one person who did was Nicolas II who originally approved of Izvolski's plan of getting the Straits open to Russian warships. Later he pretended that he knew nothing of these schemes when Stolypin, Russia's Prime Minister, threatened to resign.

By the time Aehrenthal and Izvolski had struck their secret equivocal bargain, Prince Ferdinand and the Bulgarian Government had decided, also in secret, on a speedy unilateral declaration of independence. A week after the meeting at Buchlau, Ferdinand and Eleonore were received in Budapest by Emperor Francis Joseph with exceptional marks of distinction and the honours due to a sovereign ('incredibly stupid'[14] was the Kaiser's marginal comment on a report of the reception). At the State banquet in the castle of Buda, the Austrian Emperor made a speech expressing his warmest wishes 'for the development of young Bulgaria, which thanks to the wisdom and foresight of Prince Ferdinand and the remarkable qualities of the

Bulgarian people, has made such extraordinary progress'.[15]

In Budapest Ferdinand saw Aehrenthal, who told him about the meeting with Izvolski. As in the case of Buchlau, there is no definitive record of what was said. It may nevertheless be assumed that Aehrenthal indicated to the Prince that Austria would annex Bosnia and Hercegovina and that this was his chance to declare Bulgaria's severance of her remaining ties with Turkey. Whether they agreed on the timing of this double breach of the Berlin Treaty is uncertain. They definitely came to an understanding on the interdependence of the two moves. Later both were to deny that there had been any collusion. Ferdinand's denials were vehement. At all costs he had to avoid giving the impression that he had in any way committed himself to Austria. His diplomatic see-saw, momentarily tipped to Vienna, had to be kept well-oiled to tip the other way at the right moment.

An extraordinary performance that he gave at the end of his stay in Budapest made many well informed diplomats doubt the overwhelming evidence that Ferdinand was on this occasion hand-in-hand with the Austrains. During an interview with Francis Joseph he pressed his claim to be given the Golden Fleece, probably the most coveted order in Europe and the premier order of chivalry in Austria and Spain.

The old Emperor told him that he could not possibly give him this most Catholic of orders since his quarrel with the Roman Catholic Church over the conversion of his son to Orthodoxy. Ferdinand left the room in what may not have been an altogether simulated rage, rejoined his attendants, and in full hearing of the servants and other visitors to the Buda castle, stalked along the corridors loudly reviling 'this Habsburg filth'.[16] A member of his suite said to him, 'Your Royal Highness, you can be heard!' Ferdinand just made an impatient gesture and went on consigning the Emperor to the devil. After his meeting with Aehrenthal, he paraded his fury with '*ce sale juif, digne ministre de cette maison d'Autriche!*'[17] (Unlike Izvolski, who also stressed Aehrenthal's Jewishness, Ferdinand was acting out of character – there was not a grain of anti-Semitism in him. Hostile and ignorant anti-Semitic journalists were often to deduce and denounce a Jewish ancestry from his huge Bourbon nose.)

He kept up the performance until he left Budapest. On leaving he was heard telling his private secretary: 'I was received like a mangy dog!'[18] In Budapest, he cut dead the Austrian envoy to Bulgaria, only to complain to him later, just before leaving, about the 'outrageous insult he had received in being refused the Golden Fleece'.[19] The acting worked. One British diplomat, who later refused to believe that any understanding had been reached between the Prince and Aehrenthal, described Ferdinand's departure from Budapest:

> He left in a state of blind fury with the Emperor and everything Austrian. So much so that when the old Emperor was standing on the steps of the palace and saluted the Prince on his departure, Ferdinand merely returned the salute in the most insolent and perfunctory manner, without even looking towards the Emperor, and drove off without attempting to conceal his rage.[20]

From Budapest he went to Vienna where he was joined by the Bulgarian Prime Minister Alexander Malinoff, who pressed Ferdinand to name a definite date for the proclamation. The Prince did not enlighten him in detail about the wider European issues involved, or about the nature of his discussions with Aehrenthal. He refused to name a date, told Malinoff to return to Bulgaria, and to await his telegraphic instructions. He was assailed by doubts. Was he not making a great mistake in appearing to commit himself to Austria's policy before the eyes of Europe? In his old age he explained that he had had qualms about proclaiming Bulgaria's independence first, and in doing so, giving Austria the pretext to join him in breaking the Berlin Treaty by annexing Bosnia and Hercegovina. He was, he said, reluctant to act as a smokescreen for '*les bêtises de l'Autriche*'.[21]

In Bulgaria, his fretting ministers sent him one telegram after another urging a decision. Finally on 3 October, Ferdinand, who had spent the past days shooting game in Hungary, boarded the Orient Express in secrecy for Bulgaria. The train was full and, just as he had done twenty-one years ago, he locked himself in the WC for much of the journey. His later account of the journey which he capped with the remark '*Voilà les dessous de la Royauté*' failed to amuse King Edward, who huffily exclaimed about his cousin: 'He is famous for using the coarsest language in the most undignified manner!'[22] In Rustchuk, on the Danube, Malinoff and the other ministers were waiting for Ferdinand. To their immense relief he told them that they would all travel to Tirnovo the following day, 5 October, to proclaim the independent kingdom of Bulgaria, with himself as Tsar at its head.

Princess Eleonore was already in Tirnovo when he arrived by special train the following morning. At the same time Paléologue in Sofia received a personal telegram from Ferdinand, postmarked 8 am: 'Today at 11 o'clock in the morning I shall proclaim the independence of Bulgaria. Long live the Bulgarian Tsar.'[23]

Ferdinand read out the proclamation in the Church of the Forty Martyrs, built by Tsar Ivan Assen II in 1230 to commemorate a victory over Byzantium, and received 'with pride and thanksgiving' the request of the President of the Sobranie and the Prime Minister that he should accept the title Tsar of the Bulgarians. The crown, made by a jeweller in Munich, had been ready for a month.

Tsar Nicholas II was furious when he heard that Ferdinand had styled himself Tsar, the 'act of a megalomaniac'.[24] Ferdinand was well aware of this and confided to a friend that he was 'placing himself on an equal plane with the Autocrat of all the Russias – who had so long held him at arm's length'.[25] Neither Nicholas's annoyance nor Ferdinand's apparent glee were justified by history or tradition. The title of Tsar (like the German Kaiser it comes from the Latin 'Caesar') was much more ancient in Bulgaria than in Russia; in the year 926 the Pope recognized the Bulgarian Tsar Simeon as Emperor. Since then, all the Bulgarian rulers were so styled and recognized until the Ottoman conquest in the fourteenth century. It was the only title that Ferdinand could assume without going against tradition. A week before the declaration of independence, the Bulgarian Cabinet had discussed the question of the title and unanimously decided on Tsar.

The diplomatic sensation created by the Bulgarian proclamation was heightened by the Austrian annexation of Bosnia and Hercegovina the following day. For Izvolski the blow fell when he reached London just after the annexation, and was told by the Foreign Secretary that Britain had no intention of agreeing to the opening of the Straits on Russia's terms. It was only then that the enormity of his blunder sank in. Political disgrace and ruin stared him in the face.

He had agreed that Austria should strike a blow against the 'Slav brothers' of Serbia. In return he had hoped to go home in triumph with the freedom of the Straits, about which Russian opinion now cared little. He realized that he probably would not even achieve that. From that moment he decided that his only chance of redeeming himself lay in vehement, bitter accusations against Aehrenthal's duplicity. He also had no choice but to maintain through thick and thin the lie that he had never consented in advance to the annexation, thus placing a weapon in his Austrian adversary's hands: Aehrenthal could now blackmail Izvolski by threatening to publish documents to prove that he was lying.

The Bosnian crisis kept Europe on tenterhooks for six months. War was averted – but it was only a postponement. The crisis played itself out in circumstances which were almost an exact parallel to 1914. Between them Aehrenthal and Izvolski cut the remaining strands of the 1897 agreement between Russia and Austria which for years had preserved a kind of balance in the Balkans.

Austria, backed by Germany, had scored a notable diplomatic victory. In essence, however, it was merely a display of diplomatic bravura. Aehrenthal had intended to solve the South Slav problem inside the Habsburg monarchy by cowing Serbia. Instead, by incorporating even more Slavs into the monarchy, he made the problem worse. The South Slavs in Bosnia and Hercegovina felt more than ever separated from their brothers in Serbia. Their resentment against Austria culminated at Sarajevo. Germany, knowing that Russia was in no position to go to war at the time, used the crisis to humiliate Russia by delivering what amounted to an ultimatum. A year after the annexation Russia began to reconstruct her armed forces on a large scale. She was resolved not to let down Serbia again and to restore her tarnished claim to be the 'protectress of the Slavs'. The crisis was the blueprint for the summer of 1914.

In the eyes of many contemporaries, the person who came out best was Ferdinand of Bulgaria. Had he not taken advantage of the unedifying rivalry between the foreign ministers of two major European powers, made the best use of their lies and bad faith, and good luck to him? Even Ferdinand's last-minute doubts about acting in tandem with Austria had been unnecessary: the illegality of the Bulgarian move, as far as breaching the Berlin Treaty was concerned, was overshadowed by the odium provoked by Austria. Instead of having acted – as he had feared – as a smoke-screen for Aehrenthal's ambitions, things looked the other way round in the eyes of Europe. Paul Cambon, the French Ambassador in London, wrote to Paléologue in the winter of 1908:

> M. von Aehrenthal's initiative was somewhat precipitate, he had not estimated the full repercussions of his action; all alone he has saddled himself, thanks to Prince Ferdinand's acumen, with the responsibility for having violated the Treaty of Berlin, and it is against him that popular opinion in Turkey, Serbia, Montenegro and, what is much more serious, in Russia, is directed.[26]

Lord Redesdale was at Balmoral when King Edward received the news of the annexation, and wrote years later: 'No one who was there can forget how terribly he was upset. Never did I see him so moved.... The King was indignant.... His forecast of the danger, which he communicated at the time to me, showed him to be possessed of the prevision which marks the statesman. Every word that he uttered that day has come true.'[27] For a time King Edward was convinced by Izvolski's hysterical accusations that Aehrenthal had committed an act of the blackest treachery.

The Kaiser's initial reaction was equally furious. Not only was he indignant that his Austrian allies had planned the action more or less behind his back, but he 'deeply deplored the manner' in which it took place. In the margin of the despatches announcing the annexation he wrote: 'The lying hypocrite Ferdinand and the worthy old Emperor appear together on the stage lit by Bengal lights as the spoliators of

Turkey!'[28] Like Tsar Nicholas he was concerned lest Ferdinand should now consider himself on the same plane of equality as the leading sovereigns of Europe. Kaiser William's reaction provides a classic vignette to illustrate just how wrong he could be. The annexation was, he wrote, a 'major triumph of Edward VII against us',[29] meaning that the Austrian move had ruined Germany's policy of friendship with Turkey and given Britain a chance to become pre-eminent in Constantinople. It may be assumed that even if he had been at Balmoral to see King Edward's annoyance with Austria's action, he would have felt that his royal English uncle was secretly relishing his 'triumph' over Germany.

Paléologue saw Ferdinand a few days after his proclamation as Tsar and found him very proud of what he had done. Meriel Buchanan, the daughter of the British Minister, described his triumphal entry into Sofia in a letter to a Bulgarian friend:

> We were on the balcony of the Ministry for Foreign Affairs and had a wonderful view. Of course I had been given careful instructions to keep well in the background and not let the King see me [foreign diplomats and their families had been instructed to avoid any action which implied recognition of Ferdinand as king], but I am afraid I was not quite careful enough, and really, I was glad that he did, because I wanted him to know that all my sympathies were with him and Bulgaria. I thought the procession really rather fine in its absolute simplicity. There was no band and there were no Court carriages, only just the King on horseback surrounded by the Guard and all the officers, and a great crowd of men running and cheering – and you know that I can never hear people cheering without feeling that I want to cry.
>
> While the King went to the Church service the Petroffs and I hurried off to the Square and managed to get into one of the houses there in order to see the review of the troops. The service at the cathedral lasted longer than had been expected, so by the time the King arrived and the review began it was six o'clock and nearly dark. But perhaps that made it all the more beautiful and impressive. The sun had just set, and Vitosh towered towered like a grim, menacing violet cloud against the golden sky. A faint haze of dust rose from under the soldiers' marching feet; in the rapidly falling shadows, one could just see the Queen's white dress, the King's tall, massive figure, something, a diamond perhaps, in one of his decorations, that shimmered brightly.
>
> One by one the houses round the square were illuminated; through the trees of the garden one could see the red flare of the torches

blazing in front of the theatre, somewhere a voice broke into the National Anthem, and presently they were all singing it, drowning the sound of the band, the soldiers' marching feet keeping time to the singing voices.[30]

The legitimate pride that Ferdinand took in what he had at last done was soon spoilt by the realization that in achieving his ambition he had also regressed to the position he had held from 1887 to 1896, as Bulgaria's unrecognized ruler. This time his equivocal position was to last only six months instead of nearly ten years. But until his recognition as Tsar Ferdinand I of Bulgaria, he again had no official intercourse with the representatives of the European Powers. During that time he became more than ever sensitive to anything in the nature of a personal slight.
An example of this touchiness was described in a letter which Princess Radziwill wrote from Berlin in January 1909:

> They have just organized an exhibition of international women's art here in Berlin. Bulgaria was among those asked to submit exhibits and the Prince's wife sent some of her embroideries on which they placed a card saying: 'Work executed by the Princess of Bulgaria'. Along came a Bulgarian envoy, a certain Monsieur Nikiforoff whom I had never seen before, who protested, making a terrible amount of noise and insisting that the card should read 'by the Queen of Bulgaria'.
> He was told that nothing could change since the Powers had not yet recognised the new title.... There was much wailing and gnashing of teeth, even an exchange of vulgar abuse, but the title of Princess remained, despite Nikiforoff's threats. What a silly business![31]

In November 1908, Ferdinand did not send his customary birthday greetings to King Edward and made a point of telling Buchanan that he had not done so on purpose. Edward was incensed, and expressed his feelings about his cousin to the Austrian Ambassador in London, Count von Mensdorff, in 'rather ungracious terms'.[32] The King also told Mensdorff that Ferdinand had threatened to return all his English orders and decorations if Britain did not soon recognize his new title. In reporting to Vienna, Mensdorff added: 'From what I know of him, that is one thing he certainly will not do.'[33] With signs of pleasure, Edward showed the Austrian Ambassador an anonymous article attacking Ferdinand which had just been published in the *National Review*. Its author was, in fact, Dr E.J. Dillon, the *Daily Telegraph*'s correspondent in Russia. It set out to demolish Ferdinand's extraordinary career, which 'seems to imply a Nietzschean Overman, and certainly a strong personality, who not only rough-hews his career, but carves it out to the last finishing touches, an understudy of Fate, who deliberately plans history and then leisurely makes it'. It claimed that Ferdinand in fact owed everything to his mother: 'If men had their counterpart in the vegetable kingdom, the King of Bulgaria would be the ivy, while his mother, Princess Clementine, would be represented by the oak.' Ferdinand's 'singularly successful life struggle' had been entirely due to his mother's support. She had singled him out as the one son,

> destined by nature to realize her dreams and reflect lustre on her family by winning, wearing and bequeathing a crown.

> She shaped his education congruously with the rôle of a ruler of men, as she herself understood it. No one can blame her for choosing as a model her own father, whose standard of statesmanship history describes as chicane, whose ideal of kingship is known to have been power without responsibility, and whose nearest approach to political principle is charitably termed finesse.[34]

It was a competent hatchet-job and certainly managed to upset Ferdinand. There were harmless sallies about Ferdinand's conversation which 'sparkles', with 'prettily turned compliments and beautifully combed and curled phrases... showered as from a horn of plenty' to which 'as spicy sauce he offers a fund of anecdotes which men often hesitate to tell each other over the walnuts and wine'. More ominously, the article repeatedly hinted at Ferdinand's bisexuality: 'He is hypersensitive, physically and psychically, and it is a form of sensitiveness which may be termed feminine. Indeed there is much of a woman's nature in Ferdinand.'

The author contrasted Ferdinand and Stamboloff at their first meeting, the former 'pale, smiling feebly', and the latter a 'thick-set man... raven-black beard and fiery eyes'. The meeting of the two was 'the ringing up of the curtain on a curious drama suggestive of that played by the spiders of the species Epeirides, of which the female devours the male after he has exercised his natural office'.

The metaphor of the female spider, with Ferdinand as the killer of the manly Stamboloff, was a nasty blow. Dr Dillon was less than fair in attributing all Ferdinand's successes to his mother's support. The diplomatic coup which culminated in his recognition as Tsar of Bulgaria was entirely his own doing, and took place two years after his mother's death.

Three days after the Bulgarian declaration of independence, the German diplomatic agent in Sofia wrote to Berlin to express his fears that in the changed circumstances there was bound to be renewed competition among the rival European Powers for Ferdinand's favour. Somewhat naively, he suggested that a 'new race for the goodwill of the new King'[35] could be avoided if the Powers could agree on unity of action. Fortunately for Ferdinand, no such unity existed, at least as far as the main contenders, Russia and Austria, were concerned. Izvolski and Aehrenthal had seen to that. Their mutual antagonism would soon – and literally – crown his ambitions. Ferdinand had started his coup by using Austria; he was to bring it to a successful conclusion by using Russia.

Russia's initial reaction to the Bulgarian move, apart from Nicholas's peevish objection to the title of Tsar, was mortification that the 'little Slav brother' had taken the big step under the aegis of Austria and not Russia. But soon, according to the German Minister in St Petersburg, there was a reawakening of 'Russian sentimentality' and 'complaints about Prince Ferdinand were replaced by self-indulgent declaration about this final act of the liberation of the Slavs by a magnanimous Russia'.[36] Sentiment apart, Izvolski was making frantic efforts to save his reputation. He, who a few months earlier had eagerly agreed to Austria dealing a blow against Serbia by annexing the two provinces, now posed as the champion of the Balkan Slavs. He was obsessed by the desire to score against Aehrenthal and to frustrate his attempts to draw Bulgaria into Austria's orbit. At the beginning of 1909, Russia finally decided to counter Aehrenthals latest overtures to Ferdinand by digging into her own pocket. She offered to pay the huge financial indemnity demanded by Turkey for the loss of Bulgaria. Both Bulgaria and Turkey were mobilizing their armies at the time and Izvolski tried to give the impression of a saviour appearing in the nick of time to save the Bulgarians from the Turks – despite the opinion of most European military experts that the Bulgarian army was well able to sweep the Turks back to Constantinople.

Aehrenthal was indignant at Izvolski's offer and sent dire warnings to Ferdinand about the danger of falling under Russian financial dependence. Ferdinand assured him that the financial arrangement would not affect Bulgaria's current policies. That year Bulgaria not only got Russia to pay compensation to Turkey; in December 1909, Ferdinand was able to raise a major loan from Austria for Bulgaria's finances. Predictably, this time it was Izvolski who was furious. Both men seemed unable to understand Ferdinand's determined refusal to commit himself to either of the two rivals. In its review of world affairs in the year 1909, *Schulthess*, the leading German political yearbook, stated:

> There is no doubt that Bulgaria can be proud of the fact that she, more than any other country in the year 1909, has achieved the greatest political progress. Without any sacrifices worth mentioning

she has obtained her independence and achieved the status of a
kingdom, has improved her finances and concluded a foreign loan. At
the same time she 'has obtained Austria's new friendship while
renewing the old one with Russia.[37]

These and other plaudits came at the end of the year. But at the
beginning of 1909, even after Russia's offer to pay compensation to
Turkey, there still remained the problem of Ferdinand's official
recognition as Tsar. When the chance came, he seized it. He was in
Vienna on 17 February when he learnt of the sudden death in Russia of
Grand Duke Vladimir, Tsar Nicholas's uncle, who was related to
Ferdinand through his wife, the Grand Duchess Marie. Ferdinand
immediately sent her a telegram expressing his desire to attend the
funeral in St Petersburg. He would, if necessary, arrive unofficially, as a
private mourner and not in uniform.

Ferdinand's intuition was functioning very precisely. He had foreseen
all that followed. On receiving his telegram the Grand Duchess
understood its political import despite her bereavement and asked
Izvolski for advice. He at once submitted the matter to Tsar Nicholas
and advised him to receive Ferdinand with the honours due to his new
royal rank. Tsar Nicholas agreed and, somewhat underestimating
Ferdinand's intelligence, said that this should be kept a secret from him.
Nicholas was a poor psychologist and considered that Ferdinand would
be overcome with delight if the royal honours arrived as a surprise.
That, Nicholas calculated, would make him feel like a happy child and
make him commit himself to Russia out of sheer gratitude.

Meanwhile Ferdinand had arranged for a uniform of the Russian
regiment of which he was honorary colonel to be ready for him by the
time he reached Russia. Before he boarded the train he told the
Romanian Minister in Vienna with a straight face, but with an air of
resignation: 'I am going to Petersburg although I am certain that they
will try and make up to me.'[38] For days afterwards the King of Romania
laughed in repeating the remark. It was quite characteristic of Ferdin-
and to try and give the appearance that he was on his way to perform a
tiresome duty while knowing very well that he was about to realize his
greatest ambition.

Izvolski next had the unpleasant task of explaining to the other
Powers that Russia had decided to treat Ferdinand as royalty. This
amounted to Russia acting single-handed against the principle that all
changes in the Berlin Congress Treaty should be approved by all the
signatory Powers.

Izvolski summoned the British Ambassador, Sir Arthur Nicholson,
with the French Ambassador and told them of Ferdinand's desire to

attend the funeral. The request, said Izvolski, could not possibly be refused and the Russian Government could not receive him otherwise than as king, and give him royal honours. As Nicolson reported to Sir Edward Grey, Izvolski declared that 'if the Prince were not received as a King it would be an affront to Bulgaria and would throw that country into the arms of Austria, and would also run counter to public sentiment here'.[39] Sir Edward Grey instructed Nicolson to stand aside, and at the funeral to avoid any position likely to compromise the British Government. Nicolson was to represent King Edward at the funeral and told Izvolski that he did not want to find himself in a position where Ferdinand would take precedence over him. He was assured that the question would not arise since at the cathedral ceremony there would be no placing according to any order of precedence.

Ferdinand's train arrived at the station and he was received by one grand duke, three adjutant generals, three generals, three other officers and a guard of honour. When Ferdinand greeted the guard of honour with the customary 'Good Health, Brothers', the soldiers roared back in chorus: 'We wish good health to your Royal [in fact they used the Russian adjectival form of 'Tsar'] Majesty!' This was the 'surprise' which Tsar Nicholas had thought would captivate Ferdinand. In fact Bulgarian newspapers had already announced two days earlier that he would be received with royal honours on arrival in St Petersburg.

Despite Izvolski's assurances to Nicolson about the placing at the funeral, the latter wrote a note to Izvolski just before the ceremony to say that, 'if by chance' he found himself below Ferdinand in the distribution of places in the cathedral, he did not want to see this taken as a tacit recognition by him of Ferdinand as Tsar. Nicolson was right to take this precaution. This, as described by the German ambassador in his report to Berlin, is what actually took place:

> The Prince stood near the [Russian] Emperor, ahead of all the Grand Dukes and other Princes, throughout the ceremony. By means of very skilful stage-management things happened as if the Prince had only taken up his position by accident. After the court had entered the cathedral, he appeared, all on his own, as if he had been delayed, looked about apparently unsure of what to do and then placed himself next to the Emperor. The general opinion was that he had played his part in this obviously pre-arranged *mise en scène* in a masterly manner.[40]

Later Ferdinand stood by the open grave of his relative and threw little pink rosebuds upon the coffin. According to Sir Arthur's son, Sir Harold Nicolson, Ferdinand by this time 'no longer bore any resemblance to a fox, his hair and beard having changed to a wolf-like grey, his figure having swelled to regal proportions'.[41] He was extremely affable to the British Ambassador. Nicolson 'profited by the occasion to beg him in all earnestness to use his influence for the maintenance of peace in the Balkans. The King of Bulgaria placed one finger beside his enormous Coburg nose. *'Je serai doux,'* he said, *'comme un petit agneau.'*[42]

'Good trick of Izvolski's to annoy Aehrenthal and win over Bulgaria!' the German Kaiser wrote in the margin of the German ambassador's report about the funeral. Aehrenthal was indeed very put out and his ill-humour made him clumsy. Ferdinand had instructed the Bulgarian envoy in Vienna to ask Aehrenthal in what manner he would be received if he called on the Austrian Foreign Minister. Aehrenthal replied that he would gladly address Ferdinand as 'Your Majesty' in private, but that he could do nothing which would imply official recognition. Ferdinand seized on this and other expressions of Austrian 'ill-will' to encourage Russian hopes that he now felt committed to them.

In April the outstanding problems between Bulgaria and Turkey were settled and Bulgaria was recognized as an independent kingdom by the European powers. In Sofia, Maurice Paléologue wrote that Ferdinand,

> considers that it is the *chef-d'oeuvre* of his policy to have achieved his dream of royalty without enfeoffing himself to either Russia or Austria, and without losing any freedom of action. For twenty-one years, the courts of St Petersbourg and Vienna have in turn accused the Bulgarian sovereign of betrayal. In fact he never betrayed either of them since he never committed himself to either, and they were naive to think that he had done so. One may be certain that he will continue this see-saw policy at which he excels.[43]

When Ferdinand returned to his capital after his brilliant reception in St Petersburg, where the Emperor of all the Russias had treated him as his equal, he momentarily became acutely sensible of the modesty of his palaces and his country compared to the splendours he had just seen. As he entered the palace in Sofia, he was greeted by his Court officials. As each one saluted him gravely, Ferdinand could only repeatedly mutter one word in return: *'Merde! Merde! Merde!'*

His ill-humour was probably mainly due to the internal Bulgarian problems which he again had to face; above all the great national longing for Macedonia. Also, he was conscious of the sense of anti-climax that so often tarnishes the brilliance of achievement. At first it was a fleeting mood. The struggle that lay ahead was perilous and dark, but shot through with dazzling prospects.

A new full-length portrait of Ferdinand in the robes of a Byzantine Emperor already hung in the palace. He had only recently commissioned it from the Czech artist Mrkvicka, a disciple of Alphonse Mucha, who was in Sofia with other of Mucha's followers to decorate the new Sofia Cathedral of St Alexander Nevski, begun in 1904 and completed in 1912. The cathedral was the biggest in Bulgaria, and built in the neo-Byzantine style which, as Professor Mario Praz has written, was so beloved by the *fin de siècle* Decadents: 'The period of antiquity with which the artists of the *fin de siècle* liked best to compare their own was the long Byzantine twilight, that gloomy apse gleaming with dull gold and gory purple, from which peer enigmatic faces, barbaric yet refined, with dilated neurasthenic pupils....'[44]

This was the very stuff of Ferdinand's phantasies. At that time, a British officer, General Sir Ian Hamilton stopped over in Sofia on his way to Constantinople. Ferdinand received him at the palace and saw him looking at the new portrait. He put his hand on his heart and half-closed his eyes. '*Quand vous serez a Constantinople,*' he whispered, '*pensez à moi!*'[45] The general could only bow and murmur a polite assent.

CHAPTER 19

The Crusade

The royal crown, which Ferdinand saw as the vindication of his ancestry and intellectual gifts, brought no serenity, not even a restful pause. The new dignity, as he quickly realized, had merely allowed him to join the ranks of Europe's lesser royalty. He seemed even more of a *parvenu*. His self-regard and his acute self-consciousness rendered him more than ever vulnerable to slights, fancied or intended. Self-assertion, never faint, became dominant in his life and politics.

A number of incidents during his first years as Tsar of Bulgaria bore witness to this and amused a lot of people. In December 1909, Tsar Ferdinand and Tsaritsa Eleonore visited Germany. He had brought a pocketful of armaments contracts which he intended to give to Krupp of Essen. After a banquet in honour of Ferdinand, which Kaiser William held at the New Palace at Potsdam, the Bulgarian King was talking with other guests by a window. As he leant out of it, the Kaiser approached from behind and, unable to resist the tight expanse of uniform breeches which faced him, laughed loudly and delivered a stinging slap on the royal bottom. Ferdinand whipped round and demanded the Kaiser's apology in front of all the witnesses. William said no apologies were due for a good joke. At this Ferdinand immediately left the palace in a blind fury. In a letter describing the incident, Princess Radziwill wrote:

I fear the Germany's Balkan policy is going to feel this blow on the backside.
Unfortunately this has for long been a habit [of the Kaiser]; all the aides-de-camp and Bülow himself have experienced it and I cannot understand the Kaiser's failure to realize that when occupying the throne, one cannot behave like a lieutenant in the garrison.[1]

The Kaiser soon had cause to regret his exuberance when Ferdinand took his armanents contracts to the French firm of Schneider-Creusot.

233

This was particularly galling since William for years had been successfully using his contacts with Ferdinand to push Krupp artillery for the
Bulgarian army.

Later Ferdinand turned the incident into a good after-dinner story.
Mensdorff, the Austrian Ambassador in London, wrote that 'King
Ferdinand personally described the whole scene to me in a manner part
indignant, part humorous; altogether he was irresistibly amusing.'[2] In
serious vein, Ferdinand warned McGregor, the British Consul in Sofia,
against German ambition as a danger to the whole of Europe.

Ferdinand and the Kaiser met again five months later for the funeral
of Edward VII in London. At a dinner at Buckingham Palace on the
night before the funeral, President Theodore Roosevelt was talking to
Ferdinand, when William walked up to the American. He took him
aside and lowered his voice: 'That man is not worth knowing. I wouldn't
talk to him in your place. He is a miserable creature.'[3] He then
deliberately turned his back on Ferdinand and, as Roosevelt described it,
said aloud: 'Roosevelt, my friend, I want to introduce you to the King of
Spain,' (then with a sudden ferocious glance over his shoulder at the
Tsar) 'he is worth talking to!'[4]

In London the Kaiser went out of his way to goad Ferdinand. When
the latter told him that he was shortly due to preside at an international
congress of ornithologists in Berlin, the Kaiser flatly refused to let him
come on the pretext that Ferdinand had not yet paid a State visit to
Berlin since becoming Tsar. Ferdinand told William that this was an
infringement on personal liberty and turned his back on him. 'I shall
never again set foot in Berlin', he told the Austrian Ambassador in
London. 'All this is due to vanity and jealousy. He [the Kaiser] finds it
unbearable that someone else is able to address a conference, something
he couldn't do.'[5] In his report to Aehrenthal the Austrian Ambassador
made much of the fact that Ferdinand had dared turn his back on the
Kaiser after his previous experience at Potsdam.

The Kaiser supported without reserve the Archduke Francis Ferdin-
and, the heir to the Austrian throne, in his row with Tsar Ferdinand,
which broke out on their way to London. Roosevelt described what
happened in a letter to his friend, the American novelist David Gray:

Well, the Tsar and the Archduke came to London on the same
express train. The Tsar's private carriage was already on it, and the
Archduke had his put on at Vienna. Each wished to have his carriage
ahead of the other, but the Archduke triumphed and had his placed
nearest the engine, the Tsar's carriage coming next, and then the
dining carriage. The Archduke was much pleased at his success, and
rode next to the engine in purple splendour; and all went well until

dinner time, when he sent word to the Tsar saying that he should like
to walk through his carriage to the dining saloon, and the Tsar sent
back word that he could not! Accordingly, breathing stertorously, he
had to wait until a station came, get out and get into the dining saloon,
and after eating his dinner, wait until another station was reached,
get out again, and pop back into his own carriage. This struck all his
brother royalties as a most serious matter, and the German Emperor
heatedly sided with the Austrians![6]

In considering Ferdinand's sudden enmities, it is not always easy to
decide how much they were due to personal dislike and how much they
were a part of his balancing act between the Triple Alliance and the
Triple Entente. At this time he was veering towards the latter and two
months before his train row with the Archduke, he expressed his
feelings about Francis Ferdinand to Paléologue, the French representative of the entente in Sofia. The Austrian Archduke, he said had acted
towards him with 'unspeakable ill-will and hostility'. He went on:

> I cannot tell you everything about his offensive behaviour towards
> me; some of the facts are of too intimate a nature – it will suffice
> were I to tell you that I have been wounded to the quick. He even
> gave me open proof of his animosity by giving the Golden Fleece to
> the Crown Prince of Romania, that useless incompetent who has
> never done anything; the Golden Fleece, which they refuse to give me
> after twenty-one years on the throne, a reign which has been by no
> means an easy one – I am not one of those who are born with a crown
> attached to their umbilical cord.[7]

Here was the genuine accent of the self-made man.

Just as Ferdinand had worsted the Austrian Archduke on the train
journey to King Edward's funeral, he managed to have the last word
when his cousin, the King of Portugal, joined the others in baiting him in
London. Ferdinand turned on him savagely: *'Riez, riez mon cher cousin, je
suis en effet un roi d'hier, mais êtes-vous vien sûr d'être un roi de demain?'* [Laugh,
laugh away my dear cousin, I am indeed a King of yesterday, but are you
quite certain of being a King of tomorrow?][8] Five months later King
Manuel II was forced to flee to England when a revolution proclaimed
Portugal a republic.

Well before King Edward's funeral, Ferdinand had tried to ensure that
there would be no snubs for him in London by trying to find out in
advance what the order of precedence would be. The British Minister in
Sofia could not answer the Tsar's exhaustive questions. Would the
order of precedence at the funeral be established alphabetically,

according to seniority or according to degrees of kinship? The Minister
did not know and pathetically started his dispatch to the Foreign Office:
'I am suffering from moral exhaustion after an hour's conversational
fencing with, King Ferdinand.'[9]

When the funeral was over Ferdinand told the Minister that he was
more than satisfied with his reception. It had been, in the words of a
modern historian, the 'greatest assemblage of royalty and rank ever
gathered in one place and, of its kind, the last'.[10] Nine kings rode behind
the coffin and seventy nations were represented in the gorgeous funeral
cavalcade, clanking and glittering in the May sunshine. Tsar Ferdinand
startled the huge, crape-clad and hushed crowds along the route (some
six thousand people fainted in the crush and the heat) with his elaborate
uniform. He was on show; and he had the satisfaction, this time, of
riding just ahead of the Archduke Francis Ferdinand, and of preceding
the head of the House of Saxe-Coburg as well as his own eldest brother,
Prince Philip of Saxe-Coburg.

But there was nothing he could do about the fact that the German
Kaiser, equally dressed to kill, was in the leading row of the sovereigns,
at the right hand of the new King George V. Though their titles, Kaiser
and Tsar, were equivalent and both derived from the Latin *Caesar*, in the
eyes of the world, the Kaiser of Germany *was* an emperor; Ferdinand, on
the other hand, was a newly hatched king of a small country claiming a
long-defunct imperial dignity which only made sense to antiquarians.
But to Ferdinand, whose sense of history and whose ambition had
already achieved so much after such an unpromising start, the title of
Tsar meant much more than a nominal historical revival: it seemed a
gage of future greatness. Only recently Paléologue, ever ready to
please and amuse Ferdinand, had traced a somewhat shaky ancestral link
between the Tsar and the Crusader Pierre de Courtenay, who was Latin
Emperor of Constantinople in about 1216. Ferdinand was pleased
and impressed: a pre-destined pattern seemed to become clear. He had
got so far, and why not further; after all, the German Kaiser, that
unbalanced, arrogant, overgrown schoolboy, was only an emperor
because his grandfather had proclaimed himself Kaiser in 1871 – less
than fifty years before – at Versailles, which *his*, Ferdinand's, forebear
had built while William's ancestor was merely the King of barren, ugly
Prussia?

Ferdinand made his mark in London: King Edward's Private Secretary, Sir Frederick Ponsonby, wrote in his memoirs that of the large
gathering of kings at the funeral the German Emperor and the King of
Bulgaria were 'by far the greatest personalities'. Ferdinand, he wrote,
'had a strong but evil personality, and gave one the impression that he
could be capable of any crime; and history bore this out. The fact that he

had remained so long on the throne of Bulgaria proved that he was a man who would stick at nothing.'[11] Strangely enough this was the kind of hyperbolical and extravagant judgement Ferdinand himself was apt to pronounce, and he would not necessarily have minded it as a judgement against himself. It had the right decadent flavour and would have flattered the Machiavellian pose which he coyly affected.

His stay in London had been a personal success, but it was his state visit to Paris in June 1910, his first as Tsar of Bulgaria, that marked a high point in his life. He arrived with Tsaritsa Eleonore at the Bois de Boulogne railway station, where he was greeted by President Fallières and the French leaders, who included Aristide Briand, the Prime Minister. There was a royal gun salute, brilliant sunshine and a multitude of French and Bulgarian tricolours. He was loudly cheered by crowds of Parisians on his drive to the Ministry of Foreign Affairs, which was to be his residence. It had been transformed into a royal palace. His apartments were expressly filled with furniture from Fontainebleau and contained pieces which had been used by Louis XIV, Louis XV and Marie Antoinette. His bedroom was entirely furnished with objects and furniture which had belonged to his grandfather Louis Philippe. Paléologue who had come over from Sofia, had found a huge, hideous baluster vase with a central medallion portrait of Princess Clémentine as a young girl. He had it put in Ferdinand's bedroom.

Paléologue showed the Tsar his apartments and wrote later in his diary:

> When he saw his mother's portrait, the King cried out: 'Oh, mother, mother!' Then, with tears in his eyes and squeezing my hands, he added: 'What an unforgettable day, my dear minister! That drive down the Champs-Elysées! I, a Bourbon-Orléans, greeted with shouts of 'Long Live the King!' In this city of Paris which drove away my grandfather! Do you understand what I feel?'[12]

The extraordinary welcome in Paris for a foreign monarch surprised French politicians particularly as it coincided with a period of serious labour troubles and a strike on the French railways. It was not Ferdinand's gorgeous headgear – a blue toque bordered with white astrakhan fur – which he wore with his Bulgarian general's uniform that was the cause of his popularity. It was the French royal connection. At a municipal reception in his honour at the Hôtel de Ville the president of the Paris municipal council delivered a speech in 'purest monarchist vein'. The Prefect of the Department of the Seine declared: 'Your Majesty will forgive my boldness in saying that while we bow respectfully before the Tsar of Bulgaria, we also honour in his person the gallant son of our beloved France!'[13]

But the Tsar did not rely solely on his French ancestry to court popularity. The Third Republic was also to admire him as a democrat and workers' friend. Paléologue described Ferdinand's performance at the Paris railway station after his return from a military display at Chalons:

> A republican guard of honour awaits him on the platform. The adjoining platforms are crowded with travellers and railway workers. There is also a thick crowd in the rue d'Alsace, which runs above the station.
>
> The King, on the right of M. Fallières, slowly walks past the guard of honour. For some reason, I don't know what, he has put on his most arrogant, haughty expression and he returns the salute of the captain of the honour guard with a gesture that borders on insolence.
>
> 'What's the matter with the king?' Briand asks me. Like me, he is struck by the sudden change in his manner. 'I don't know. M. Fallières has perhaps offended him without knowing. He is so touchy!' On reaching the locomotive Ferdinand suddenly stops. His left hand, gloved in white, grasps the handrail leading to the footplate. He raises himself up and majestically holds out his hand to the engine driver. The latter, a good-looking lad with a russet beard and lively expression, looks stunned and then, as if to excuse himself, spreads out his hands which are coal-black. Ferdinand insists. The driver then takes off his cap, throws it on the ground and grasps the royal hand. A thunder of applause breaks out in the station. Thousands of workers shout: 'Long live the King! Long live the King!'[14]

Astride Briand, the Prime Minister, a Socialist and like Ferdinand, an expert political performer, took Paléologue's arm: 'What a find! Look, among the thousands of men here, you wouldn't find a single one who wouldn't be prepared to fight for him!'
Paléologue replied:

> Yes, he really is very good at it. But he would never have acted like this in Vienna. There he would have appeared more haughty, more monarchical, more autocractic than the proudest descendant of Charles V and Maria-Theresa. He excels at adapting. 'But why did he put on this haughty air when he got off the train?' 'To emphasize by contrast, his demonstration of democratic feeling.' 'What a ham!' From the railway station the shouts of 'Long Live the King!' spread to the place de Strasbourg and follow us along the boulevards; it seemed as if the monarchy had been restored in France.

Ferdinand was also playing to the smaller gallery of French bourgeois

liberal opinion. He refused all invitations from his numerous aristocratic relatives in the Faubourg Saint-Germain. The only private
invitation which he accepted was to a luncheon given by Joseph
Reinach, the French Jewish politician and writer and a leading supporter of Dreyfus. The Faubourg Saint-Germain was offended by
Ferdinand's behaviour and expressed its irritation in witticisms
linking Reinach, Ferdinand's nose and that of *Cyrano de Bergerac.*
Edmond Rostand, Cyrano's creator, had been one of the guests at the
luncheon.

The Tsar, Paléologue noticed, was 'radiant' with his success in Paris,
'flattered in the inmost fibres of his being.'[15] He had 'come over' as a
character. The writer Marcel Proust, was to use his impressions of
Ferdinand. It was, of course, Ferdinand's homosexual side that fascinated him. When in *A la Recherche du Temps Perdu,* Proust's great novel, the
Duchess de Guermantes, asked by Ferdinand if she was ever jealous, rep-
lies: 'Yes, sir, of your bracelets.'[16] In a later passage her brother-in-law
Charlus speaks of Ferdinand as 'a hussy through-and-through, really
gorgeous, but very intelligent, a remarkable man'.[17] Charlus explains the
fact that Bulgaria became Germany's ally in the Great War in terms of a
presumed homosexual affinity between Kaiser William and Ferdinand:
'Well, yes – fundamentally it makes sense, one just has got to indulge a
sister, one can't refuse her anything.'[18] In another scene Proust has the
Marquis de Norpois, the old diplomat, discussing the Dreyfus case with
Madame de Guermantes. Ferdinand, says Norpois, has too fine a
political judgement, inherited from the 'admirable Princess Clémentine', to be an anti-Dreyfusard and to 'embrace Major Esterhazy' (the
hero of Dreyfus's opponents). At this the Duchess murmurs: 'No, he
would have preferred a common soldier.'[19]

The Tsar was joined by his two sons and ended his French visit with a
week-long stay as the guest of Monsieur Schneider, the head of the
French armaments firm, at his Château de la Verrerie at Le Creusot. It
was an opportunity for Ferdinand to savour his revenge on Kaiser
William for his ill-judged horse-play at Potsdam. Schneider was
delighted with his pun about the 'stroke of luck' which had brought him
the arms contracts originally destined to go to his German rival Krupp
and never tired of telling the story.

Ferdinand enjoyed his success in France and his reception to the full,
although his habitual pessimism broke through on one occasion. As he
was watching the huge and dazzling military display in his honour at
Chalons, he said to Paléologue: 'Ah, my dear minister, look at all this,
look well, then close your eyes and remember Sofia, foul Sofia, my
depressing palace, my study, my mauve satin furniture!'[20] The minister
knew that the Tsar was striking a pose and that any commiseration at

this apparent appeal for sympathy would have been unwelcome; Ferdinand was well aware that his Court was one of the best-run and most luxurious in Europe. It was not the mauve satin upholstery that worried him but the mood of Bulgaria. A groundswell of feeling was gathering about Macedonia and Ferdinand's failure to bring about its liberation from Turkish rule. The familiar unfavourable comparisons between his predecessor's martial courage and his own aversion to war were being made and he was openly accused of cowardice. On his name-day, a Sofia newspaper extended the customary greetings and went on to say that his name would go down in history as that of a cowardly ruler were he not, now that he had assuaged his personal vanity by obtaining the royal crown, to apply all his energies to unite Bulgaria and Macedonia.

The new urgency of the Macedonian question was a direct outcome of the revolution of the Young Turks. Their coming to power was hailed in Western Europe as a miraculous end to Ottoman tyranny and the advent of young, enlightened idealists anxious to establish parliamentary democracy, a Turkish Westminster on the Bosphorus. The new régime's talk of constitutional reform, and of equal rights for all nationalities and religions in the Ottoman Empire was widely acclaimed, especially in Britain.

This was wishful thinking, a self-indulgent surrender to the illusion of inevitable progress, which could not fail to irritate Ferdinand. A British diplomat who saw Ferdinand in December 1909, reported home: 'He made no secret of his scepticism regarding the regeneration of the Ottoman Empire by the Young Turks and he is of the opinion that by blindly fostering the New Régime, Europe is cherishing a viper in her bosom, as the utmost that Young Turkey can achieve is the formation of an armed despotism even more reactionary and anti-Christian than the Turkey of Abdul Hamid.'[21]

Ferdinand was incensed by the initial uncritical, not to say enthusiastic welcome extended to the Young Turks. It deepened his pessimism about the future of the continent. He saw it as yet another symptom that 'Europe is profoundly demoralized,' a condition which, five years before the outbreak of the Great War, he predicted would lead to an '*écroulement général qui ebranlera bien de trônes* [a general collapse which will shake many a throne]'.[22] The major Powers were directly and morally responsible for the well-being of the Christian population of Macedonia. Already thirty years had passed since they signed the Treaty of Berlin which promised the introduction of reforms in the region. Yet no real improvements had been imposed due to rivalry between the Powers. The plight of the population had steadily worsened. It was not a state of affairs which the Balkan states adjoining Macedonia, especially

Bulgaria with its great number of Macedonian refugees, could contemplate with equanimity.

Ever since his arrival in Bulgaria, Ferdinand had appealed to the Powers to carry out the promised reforms. He pointed out that the condition of Macedonia was a constant threat to the stability of Bulgaria and south-eastern Europe as a whole. To him the general acclaim which greeted the Young Turks was simply another example of the European Powers' failure to act: they now lulled themselves with the hope that these 'modern' Turks would overnight turn the ramshackle remains of Ottoman despotism into a model of enlightened rule.

Ferdinand had few illusions. He was perfectly well aware that considerations of humanity, morality and altruism rarely played an essential role in determining international policy: his scorn and contempt for the first Hague Peace Conference showed that. Whatever illusions he might have had on this score he lost after the years during which he had tried to get the Powers to honour their commitment over Macedonia. It was unlike him to be shocked by their immorality in not doing anything effective to alleviate the sufferings in Macedonia, though at times he was indignant at powerful Christian nations doing nothing to help their oppressed co-religionists. Most of all he was incensed at their failure to act decisively to remove a constant threat to the peace and stability of Europe – and, of course, to his own throne.

The tortuous foreign policy that Ferdinand had to pursue in his peculiar and difficult position, the balancing between Austria and Russia, between the Triple Alliance and the Triple Entente, had given him a unique and disenchanted view of the weaknesses, foolishness, greed and cynicism as well as of the ambition and material strength of the major Powers of Europe. His pessimism about the future of Europe deepened as 1914 drew nearer. In 1912 he was only a few months out in predicting the exact date of the World War when speaking to an Austrian diplomat: 'A heavy, thick, oppressive atmosphere weighs upon Europe at the moment.... These are difficult times.... You will see, you will see, I have always predicted it; in a year, in at most a year and a half it will start and we shall be in it.'[23] The Austrian who reported his remarks to Vienna wrote that they were the result of a bad attack of gout.

By 1910 the Young Turks had abrogated the ancient rights of non-Turkish nationalities under Ottoman rule. The privileges of the Christian churches were interfered with, political clubs were suppressed, public meetings forbidden and every effort was made to extinguish the national sentiments of the various races. The British Ambassador in Constantinople described the present policy of 'Ottomanization' as one of 'pounding the non-Turkish elements in a Turkish mortar'.[24] The

disarmament of all Christian peasants was carried out with extreme
severity and the campaign, especially in Macedonia, was beginning to
assume the proportions of deliberate genocide. The various nationalities
of Macedonia, which the deposed Sultan Abdul Hamid had maintained
in a state of mutual hostility, began to discover that their only hope lay
in combining against their mutual enemy. For the first time a close
understanding between Greek and Bulgarian peasants came about and
the groundwork of the future Balkan Alliance was laid. The last
desperate fling of Ottoman imperialism in its decline resulted in what
had always been considered impossible: the healing of the deep centuries-old feuds in the Balkans.

Each new outrage by the Young Turks in Macedonia brought
increased popular pressure in Bulgaria on Ferdinand and the Government. He was blamed for having sacrificed Macedonia in order to
obtain the royal crown. On the first anniversary of the declaration of
independence a leading Bulgarian newspaper stated: 'The anniversary
which is being celebrated today merely commemorates Ferdinand of
Coburg's victory over his own people. But let us be patient: the people
will have their revenge!'[25] In October 1909, Ferdinand told Paléologue
that he felt a 'magic circle' enclosing him from all sides. 'My position has
never been more difficult. Soon it will become untenable, because my
Bulgarians will never forgive me for the collapse of their national
aspirations.'[26] In reporting these words to Pichon, the French Foreign
Minister, Paléologue commented: 'Unfortunately the Tsar is quite right
about this.... Recently Bulgarian opinion has been judging him harshly.
Grave symptoms of uneasiness and discontent can be observed in the
army.'[27] All Ferdinand's efforts to solve the Macedonian problem by
diplomatic means had failed. The major Powers simply did not want to
know and bombarded Sofia with stern warnings against military action.
Inside Bulgaria considerations of European diplomacy were mere
abstractions: the only reality was the suffering of the Macedonians and
the restoration of the Great Bulgaria of the Treaty of San Stefano.

The Macedonian cause was effectively kept alive in Bulgaria by the
IMRO, which maintained contact with successive Bulgarian governments through Macedonians who sat in practically every Bulgarian
Cabinet. The Revolutionary Organization was tolerated in Bulgaria but
was seldom actively supported by the Government. At times steps had
to be taken against it – but such was the strength of its influence on
Bulgarian public opinion that the Government at times was driven on to
the defensive. The most effective means used by the Macedonians to
keep their cause before the public was by terrorist acts in Macedonia
aimed at provoking the Turks to retaliate and by using the indignation at
resulting massacres to draw attention to the state of affairs.

The thought of these grim, determined and often desperate Macedonians, of the butchered bodies of Stamboloff and of other of his ministers who were considered to have harmed the Macedonians' cause, was never far from Ferdinand's mind. The fact that he was constantly aware of the danger of assassination was easily caricatured by his enemies as irrational terror. The unfairness of the accusation becomes apparent if it is turned on its head: it *would* have been irrational if he had not been aware of the danger of assassination. First, he was living in the heyday of the European political assassin. From early manhood he had seen one emperor, one empress, four kings, two presidents, one shah and dozens of prime ministers and ministers murdered. Second, Ferdinand's early years in Bulgaria had been dogged by the tenacity, however gauche, of Russia's would-be assassins. It can fairly be said that his appreciation of the threat presented by the political assassin was no sick fancy.

During a confidential talk between Paléologue and one of the leading Macedonian activists in Bulgaria, the French Minister told the Macedonian that he did not think that the Tsar supported his cause. The latter's reaction was a measure of the Macedonians' self-confidence: 'What? The Tsar not with us? He is far too afraid of us not to be with us. He knows very well what it would cost him to betray the national cause. Before six months are out, he would be dethroned or assassinated!'[28]

It was obvious to all that Ferdinand was going to have to make a move and choose between his dynastic aspirations and a potentially fatal military adventure. As it turned out, the dilemma was resolved for him. A number of complex political factors converged with seemingly effortless ease to reach their climax in October 1912, in war against Turkey by a Balkan League composed of Bulgaria, Greece, Serbia and Montenegro.

Apart from the arrogant nationalism of the Young Turks, the other factors which led to the formation of the Balkan League were a direct outcome of the annexation of Bosnia and Hercegovina by Austria and the consequent humiliation and defeat of Serbia and Russia. In his famous Christmas speech in the Russian Duma in 1908, the resentful Izvolski openly proclaimed the idea of a Balkan League. His sole aim in sponsoring the idea was to re-establish Russian prestige in the Balkan peninsula and to gain a diplomatic success over Austria. Russia's subsequent efforts to bring about such an alliance were governed by the thought that a Balkan League would stop any Austrian advance southwards.

Serbia's resentment of the annexation led her statesmen to expect, sooner or later, war against Austria-Hungary. Having hitched her political aspirations to Russia, Serbia also began to feel more and more that a rapprochement with Bulgaria was necessary. Bulgaria reacted cautiously to Serbia's preliminary advances. This circumspection was due to fears that an alliance with Serbia would be more of a hindrance than a help to her national aspirations in Macedonia; Bulgaria had no desire to be placed in a position which would imply recognition that Serbia had justifiable claims in Macedonia. The point was succinctly made by A.J.P. Taylor:

> The Bulgarians had regarded all Macedonia as theirs ever since the treaty of San Stefano – a view with which most ethnologists agreed. The Serbs could not claim the inhabitants of Macedonia as Serb, except in the extreme north; but they invented the theory that most of Macedonia was inhabited by neither Bulgarians nor Serbs, but by 'Macedo-Slavs'; and this invention of a nationality ultimately carried the day.[29]

In a footnote to the above he added: 'The theory of the 'Macedo-Slavs' did not prevent the Serbs treating the inhabitants of Macedonia as Serbs once they had been conquered.[30]

Serbia's pretensions in Macedonia were not the only obstacle to an alliance with Bulgaria. Ferdinand was reluctant to pledge himself to Serbia at this time, for it would have meant losing his free-lance status in a Europe which, by 1910, was already polarized into the Triple Entente and the Triple Alliance. The scales between the two power groups were very evenly balanced. This significantly increased the importance to Europe of the smaller powers. In the contest for allies between the Triple Entente and the Triple Alliance, the Balkan states, especially if grouped together, came to be regarded as a major prize.

While Russia, with the tacit encouragement of Britain, was trying to encourage the formation of a Balkan League, whose cornerstone would be Bulgaria and Serbia, and whose effect would be to prevent a further dangerous Austrian-German advance, Austria and her allies also had their ideas of a Balkan alignment. Excluding Serbia, they hoped to effect a concert of Bulgaria, Romania, Greece, and in some proposals Turkey, a combination which, Aenrenthal believed, would act as a check to Russian-Panslav expansion.

Ferdinand was determined to keep his options open as long as possible, or until the opportune moment came for choosing sides. More than ever before he travelled, criss-crossing Europe. Trusting no one, he became a one-man foreign office. Which way was the wind blowing? Or, as one cartoonist visualized it – alluding again to the vast nose – which scents did it bear?

He excelled at this game. No commitment and plenty of elbow room had become a *sine qua non* of survival and at best, of success. By playing hard to get, Ferdinand made it possible to raise loans for Bulgaria alternately from the Entente or the Triple Alliance.

There were personal prizes: in April 1911, the Austrian Emperor also presented him with the Golden Fleece. Ferdinand had coveted the golden chain and its pendant, the golden ram, for years. On receiving it he exclaimed: 'The highest order of Christianity for the first time sheds forth its radiance this side of the Balkans: it is an auspicious omen for the future![31] The cryptic wording was typical; it did not commit him in any way but could be interpreted as an implied backing of Austria. The Austrian Press greeted the new Knight of the Golden Fleece with unusual warmth. There were fulsome references to his past services as an officer in the Austro-Hungarian army.

Austria's wooing of Ferdinand turned into a game of dupes in which the Tsar kept always one step ahead. Following the bestowal of the Golden Fleece the question arose of when Ferdinand would pay an official visit to Vienna to thank the Emperor. At first the Austrians decided that it would be best if Ferdinand did not come to Vienna too soon, the idea being that during that time he would 'behave', for fear of the visit being called off by Austria. By contrast, a fortnight later Austrian diplomats were extremely worried that Ferdinand was trying to avoid paying an official visit to Austria by visiting the Emperor privately instead.

As it turned out, Ferdinand saw the Austrian Emperor privately in November 1911, and again, six months later, on a state visit. The private visit caused a considerable degree of uneasiness in St Petersburg and Belgrade, although Ferdinand was only sounding out Austria. Like a woman trying to be scrupulously fair to two suitors, he made a special gesture to Russia on his return to Sofia and for the first time since assuming the royal title accepted to lunch at the Russian Legation on the occasion of Tsar Nicholas's name-day. There he discussed the possibility of a marriage between his heir, Prince Boris and one of the Russian Tsar's daughters. Commenting on this latest gesture to Russia, the French *chargé d'affaires* reported: 'The King of Bulgaria's habitual see-saw policy is less inspired by bravery than by personal interest; but one must recognise that it represents the wisest discretion: all in all, it is a policy of which the most serious-minded people in this country approve.'[32]

As if to counterbalance the Austrian bestowal of the Golden Fleece and give Russia an opportunity to do him a favour, Ferdinand at this time requested a loan from the large financial houses in St Petersburg to help him out with a personal debt of 1,500,000 francs to a Viennese bank. The bank was making difficulties and so as to get much-needed cash, Ferdinand had been forced to sell short-dated Court bonds to the Sofia banks for trifling sums. Neklyudoff, the Russian Minister in Sofia, wrote later: 'In order to put an end to this humiliating state of things, the King begged me to arrange for a loan of 2 million francs as a mortgage on his property of Vrana.'[33] The Bulgarian Minister of Finance, who approached Neklyudoff on Ferdinand's behalf, explained that the Viennese bank was being difficult due to Austria's displeasure at the present Bulgarian policy. '*Ergo*,' Neklyudoff wrote, 'it entered into our calculations to liberate King Ferdinand from all pecuniary obligations to Vienna.'[34] After a few months' delay the two million were advanced to Ferdinand by a St Petersburg bank; but in reality the money was supplied out of the personal funds of Nicholas II at five per cent with repayment over several years.

The Russian Minister wrote to his chief about the requested loan and made a point of warning him against the idea that Ferdinand could be *bought* for two million francs. In fact, the money was repaid according to the terms of the loan. Ferdinand was quite well aware of the importance and power of money and he was shrewd in using it. But he was not venal; and those who imprudently thought that he might be, burnt their fingers in trying to approach him. When discussing the possibility of a French loan to Bulgaria in 1909, the French Ambassador in St Petersburg told Izvolski:

> One must not have an exaggerated idea of the hold which one would have on the King by means of financial or other services to Bulgaria. Neither Russia, nor France were able to prevent Prince Ferdinand from unleashing the 1908 crisis. Even now, despite the sacrifices made by the Russian government in order to get Turkey to recognize Bulgaria's independence, the King has managed to slip away from Russian or French control.[35]

Ferdinand had asked the Russians for the loan in the winter of 1911-12. By that time Bulgaria was involved in secret negotiations with her neighbours Serbia and Greece with a view to an alliance. Events had moved swiftly during 1911. In March a new Bulgarian cabinet headed by Geshoff and Daneff came to power. The new administration was distinctly Russophil and greatly welcomed by St Petersburg. Geshoff, the new Prime Minister, and Daneff, the President of the Sobranie, realized that in view of the worsening situation in Macedonia, Bulgaria could no longer remain inactive: the Great Powers were clearly not going to force reforms on Turkey; Bulgaria, despite her strong and well-equipped army, could not fight Turkey alone. There was only one other course of action: they came to the conclusion that in order to keep the Bulgarians from being exterminated in Macedonia, it would be necessary for Bulgaria to come to an understanding with Serbia and her other neighbours.

The new Government altered the constitution so that Tsar Ferdinand might enter upon political treaties without being forced to lay them before the Sobranie. This *carte blanche* for Ferdinand was an expedient to safeguard the secrecy of Bulgarian diplomacy.

There remained the task – by no means easy – of persuading Ferdinand that in view of the disquieting state of affairs in Bulgaria he had to decide once and for all to cast his country's lot with either Russia or Austria – the Entente Powers or the Triple Alliance. An unexpected development helped the Tsar make up his mind. On 29 September 1911, Italy, for reasons of national prestige and expansion, declared war on Turkey and invaded Tripoli, the sole remaining area administered by the Turks on the African shores of the Mediterranean.

The opportunity was too good to be missed. It was not only the fact that Turkey was now committed to a full-scale war against Italy, but also the circumstance that Turkey's opponent was a member of the Triple Alliance that made it easier for Ferdinand to come to a decision. It looked as if he would be having it both ways. In sanctioning an alliance with Serbia, Austria's enemy, he would be making a pro-Entente move and displeasing the Triple Alliance; but in waging war against Turkey, he would be fighting an opponent of Italy, a member of the Triple Alliance. The Triple Alliance, he may have hoped, would see it as a case of 'the enemy of my enemy is my friend'.

The secret talks about the alliance between Bulgaria and Serbia were under way when the celebration of Prince Boris's coming-of-age, on 2 February 1912, provided a splendid opportunity for a manifestation of Balkan feeling. The heirs-apparent of Serbia, Romania, Greece and Montenegro were invited to the festivities in Sofia, which lasted three days. Russia's Grand Duke Andrew represented Tsar Nicholas, Boris's godfather. The Austrian Emperor's representative was Archduke Charles Albert and Prince Frederick Leopold of Prussia represented the German Kaiser. Ferdinand stage-managed the occasion. It was less of a birthday party for Prince Boris than an opportunity for Tsar Ferdinand to show himself as the most important man in south-east Europe. The central event was a service of thanksgiving attended by the five young princes and celebrated, as *The Times* pointed out, 'in accordance with the ritual of their common faith'.[36] It was an unprecedented demonstration of Orthodox and Balkan unity. The leader writer discerned in the Balkan nations a 'growing disposition amongst them to renounce the jealousies and dissensions which have separated them in the past'.[37]

A further extract from *The Times* indicates Ferdinand's new stature:

No people have watched the progress of Bulgaria since she again became a nation with deeper interest than our own. That progress has indeed been wonderful, and it is only just to say that much of it must be attributed to King Ferdinand. There have been features in his policy which have not commended themselves to Englishmen, but we must acknowledge that, as a whole, it has proved beneficial to the land whose destinies he directs.

A generation ago Bulgaria was little more than a memory in the minds of a few scholars. To-day she is beyond question the second military state in the Balkan Peninsula. Her internal development has been rapid and continuous, and her fine army, as our Correspondent notes this morning, specially excited the admiration of the distinguished visitors who have just left Sofia.[38]

The show of Balkan unity in Sofia speeded up the Bulgarian-Serb negotiations about the terms of the proposed Alliance. The stumbling block, as in previous attempts at an alliance, was their respective claims on Macedonia. Serbia absolutely refused Bulgarian urgings that Macedonia should become an autonomous state, fearing, probably rightly, that Macedonia would eventually opt for union with Bulgaria, just as Eastern Rumelia had done in 1885. So there had to be an agreement as to division of spoils if there was to be any treaty. Definite allotments of territory were agreed on. But there remained an area of Macedonia, subsequently to be known as the 'contested zone', the partition of which was left to the arbitrament of the Tsar of Russia. The other important provisions of the agreement, which was finally signed on 14 March 1912, were the offensive clauses against Turkey, and also the Bulgarian promise to come to Serbia's assistance if she were attacked by Austria-Hungary. This last provision was the one Ferdinand was most loth to accept because it committed him, if only on paper and secretly, to the Entente powers against the Triple Alliance. He agreed to it in the end because he could not believe that Austria would attack a Christian nation in the back while she was fighting against Turkey. For Bulgaria the Alliance was simply a·weapon against Turkey – its provisions against Austria were a necessary evil. Serbia saw the Alliance as a double-edged weapon to be used against Vienna or Constantinople. Russia saw the alliance as a weapon against Austria and tried to ignore the obvious fact that it was primarily aimed against Turkey, at worst accepting it as a necessary evil.

The other Entente Powers also welcomed it as a means of weakening and containing the Triple Alliance, especially to stop Austria's and Germany's supposed *Drang nach Osten*. Whatever the plans and calculations of the foreign offices of the major European Powers, the most important aspect of the Bulgarian alliance with Serbia, to be followed shortly by Bulgarian alliances with Greece and Montenegro, was the fact that a Balkan League had come into being. Sofia was the hub of the whole, and as the hub turns, so does the wheel.

Unlike the Serbian-Bulgarian Alliance, the one between Greece and Bulgaria contained no territorial provisions. Privately, each side had allotted to itself Salonika and even, possibly, Constantinople. Just as Russia's diplomatic representatives in Sofia and Belgrade had worked assiduously to help bring about the Serbian-Bulgarian Alliance, the one between Greece and Bulgaria was to a large extent the result of the efforts of James Bourchier, the former assistant master at Eton who became the Balkans correspondent of *The Times*. Diplomats rightly marvelled at the secrecy with which he managed to conduct the negotiations between Athens and Sofia, since his notorious deafness and his friendship with the political leaders in the Balkans had earlier caused one diplomat to declare that whenever there was a great noise in the Balkans it was either Bourchier telling a secret to a Prime Minister or *vice versa*.

The alliance between Bulgaria and Montenegro took the form of a verbal agreement. The most important aspect of it was that Montenegro should start the ball rolling by an independent declaration of war against Turkey.

Up to the outbreak of the Balkan War the attitude of Russia remained ambiguous. On the one hand she had encouraged the formation of the Balkan League, with the active participation of Tsar Nicholas. The Russian idea had been to set up the Balkan bloc as a barrier to Austria's advance southwards. Yet, when it became obvious quite early on that the Alliance was primarily directed against Turkey, Russia did little except issue half-hearted warnings that she could not come to the Balkan nations' assistance if they got into difficulties. Essentially Russia felt that she was not sufficiently prepared to undertake a conflict. But the Balkan leaders had been given a distinct impression that Russia would support them if necessary. Sir Arthur Nicholson made the point in a letter to Lord Hardinge in October 1912:

> To my mind the primary cause of all that has happened is the secret alliance which Russia encouraged the four States to conclude. I imagine that Sazonoff [who replaced Izvolski as Russia's Foreign Minister] had in his mind in the first instance merely to gain a diplomatic success over Austria and to re-establish Russian prestige in the Balkan peninsula.

> He should, however, have foreseen that by encouraging and promoting the close understanding between the four Balkan powers he was practically raising hopes and aspirations which they had some grounds for thinking Russia would enable them to realize.[39]

Tsar Nicholas provided an instance of Russia's woolly thinking on the Balkan Question when he was visited in the Crimea by Dr Daneff, the President of the Bulgarian Sobranie. Daneff brought him the text of the Serbian alliance with Bulgaria, which explicitly named the Tsar as the arbitrator on the contested zone in Macedonia. The Tsar expressed his joy at agreements having been reached with Serbia, accepted to act as arbitrator – a role that would only be his as a result of a war against Turkey – and in the same breath advised the allies not to fight Turkey. The latter, he said, was too powerful an opponent for the Balkan countries to tackle alone and Russia was in no position to help.

Ferdinand had no illusions about Russian military help. But displays of pro-Russian sentiment could do no harm. Shortly after the signing of the treaty with Serbia he received Neklyudoff, the Russian Minister in Sofia. The carefully arranged setting did not fail to strike the Russian, who later described the scene:

His Majesty received me in his study; he was half lying on a wide leather sofa; one of his legs was wrapped in a plaid rug, testifying to an attack of gout [earlier Ferdinand had pleaded gout for not granting Neklyudoff an audience]. On a table next to the sofa a few art treasures were littered about: an antique Byzantine crucifix in carved wood set in silver – the gift, if I am not wrong, of the Metropolitan of Moscow; an old snuff-box in gold – the gift of the Empress Alexandra – a box with artistic miniatures – a souvenir of the Emperor Nicholas II. In his hands, white, dimpled and well cared for, the King held a crutch-stick with a gold knob in the old Russian style, similar to the one with which Ivan the Terrible was always armed; only the steel point which ended the stick of the Tsar of all the Russias and which the bloodthirsty autocrat sometimes dug into the foot of an undesirable questioner, was replaced on that of the Tsar of the Bulgarians – for the greater well-being of his visitors – by a common rubber end; the crutch had been given him by his cousin the Grand Duchess Vladimir.

'You see before you, Monsieur,' began the King, 'a poor invalid surrounded by a few of his treasures, valuable by reason of their associations. Here is my sole consolation in my sufferings,' he continued, pointing to the old crucifix, 'here...' and the king began to show me the artistic treasures which consoled him on his bed of sickness and to tell me about their Russian origins. This preamble over, Ferdinand came down to facts.[40]

Three months later, Ferdinand, Eleonore and his sons paid State visits to Berlin and Vienna, their first as monarchs. Right to the last minute

Ferdinand had feared that the Austrians, in particular the Emperor Francis Joseph, would learn of the clause in the treaty with Serbia which pledged Bulgaria to help the former in case of an Austrian attack. His fears were groundless, and, despite the great heat, Francis Joseph went in person to the railway station to greet Ferdinand on arrival. Princess Radziwill received a letter from a friend in Vienna which said that 'the King of Bulgaria, who is subtle and astute, had the wit to bring magnificent presents for the children of the Archduke [Francis Ferdinand, the heir to the throne], which had the effect of immediately changing his feelings about Bulgaria'.[41] Ferdinand talked to Count von Berchtold, the new Austrian Foreign Minister, about the memories of his youth which were 'inseparable from Vienna' and told him that the traditions of his family were 'tied to the Austrian Imperial House'.[42]

The State visit to Berlin was an even greater success and Kaiser William, on his very best behaviour, praised Ferdinand's twenty-five-year reign in Bulgaria in fulsome language. He made full amends for the notorious slap and appointed Ferdinand honorary colonel of a German regiment.

The visits to Germany and Austria were so successful that at least one member of the Entente, France, in the person of the Prime Minister Raymond Poincaré, expressed fears that Ferdinand had come to a secret arrangement with Germany and Austria. It was only after Russia assured Poincaré that Ferdinand had firmly committed Bulgaria on the side of the Entente that a major French loan to Bulgaria was sanctioned.

By the summer of 1912 Bulgaria had decided on war in the autumn. Until then the King and the Government had to lull Turkish suspicions so as to prevent Turkey from concluding peace with Italy before the Balkan League was ready. It was also essential to convince the chancelleries of Europe that the Bulgarian Government was being reluctantly pushed on to war by agitated public opinion.

The latter was not far from the truth. War fever had taken hold. A massacre of 150 Christians at Kochana in Macedonia at the beginning of August resulted in mass meetings all over Bulgaria demanding action. With great circumspection the government restricted itself to a single protest and influenced the newspapers to temper their anti-Turkish tirades. Ferdinand stayed abroad for most of the summer, and his absences were attacked in the newspapers. In fact he was keeping away so as to allay Turkish fears of an attack. He only came to Bulgaria briefly in August for the celebrations in Tirnovo of his Silver Jubilee. There he expressed his feelings about what lay ahead by confiding to a lady beside him after the great army parade: '*Ces pauvres jeunes gens...*'[43]

The die had been cast. By the end of September the Balkan Allies announced mobilization. As arranged, King Nikita of Montenegro set the ball rolling on 8 October and declared war on Turkey. A few days later, Bulgaria, Serbia and Greece jointly asked Turkey to take immediate measures to implement the reforms laid down, thirty-four years earlier, in the Treaty of Berlin. The European Powers made half-hearted, feeble diplomatic moves to try to prevent war. Turkey refused to answer the Balkan Note and declared war on Bulgaria and Serbia on 18 October. The same day Greece declared war on Turkey.

By then King Ferdinand was at his headquarters at Stara Zagora, close by the southern foothills of the Balkan range. From there he issued his war manifesto. In what he described as the 'just, great and sacred' task which faced Bulgaria and her Balkan allies, they would have the sympathy of all those who loved 'justice and progress'. The coming war would be waged in the interests of 'humanity and Christendom'. It would be a struggle of 'liberty against tyranny'. It would also be the 'struggle of the Cross against the Crescent'.[44]

In that idiosyncratic call to arms, he called on the progressive forces of the twentieth century to join hands with the atavic passions of a holy war. Within minutes the telegraph informed the world that a new Crusade had been proclaimed in the Balkans.

CHAPTER 20

The Dream of
Byzantium

—◦❧◦—

The rest of Europe watched anxiously. A general conflagration seemed inevitable. How could war in the Balkans, so directly affecting the interests of Austria and Russia, fail to bring about the long-dreaded military confrontation between the two great powers to decide their age-long rivalry for supremacy in south-eastern Europe?

Within one month of the beginning of the war, some 1,200,000 men were on active service in the war zone. This was a greater number than in the first month of hostilities in any other European war of the preceding century: twice as many as during the Franco-Russian war of 1812, three times as many as in the Crimean War; and more even than in the the Franco-Russian war of 1870.

The military objectives of the members of the Balkan Alliance had been determined by geography. Bulgaria was to concentrate her efforts down the valley of the River Maritza and on to Constantinople; Serbia was to push into Macedonia; Greece was to attack to the north and use her naval forces to intercept the transport of Turkish reinforcements from Asia Minor to European Turkey.

The rapidity and completeness of the successes of the Balkan armies took Austria and Russia by complete surprise. The latter, together with the rest of Europe, still thought of Turkey as the Ottoman Empire. Though a 'sick man', Turkey had routed Greece in the 'Thirty Days' War' of 1897 and had resisted Russia's armies with great determination during the Russo-Turkish War of 1877-8.

Within a fortnight of the start of the war every Turkish army in Europe was defeated except for the three fortresses of Adrianople, Yanina and Scutari. The advance of the Bulgarians towards Constantinople after overwhelming victories at Kirk-Kilissé and Lulé-Burgas,

seemed irresistible. The Turks attempted to make a stand at Lulé-
Burgas. They had to abandon it after four days of heavy Bulgarian
artillery bombardment and bayonet charges, and were forced to fall
back on the Chatalja line of fortifications, the last defence before
Constantinople. The city was only twenty miles to their rear. The
windows of the ancient capital rattled to the sound of the guns. The
Bulgarian victory at Kirk-Kilissé on 22-3 October was followed the
next day by a striking Serbian victory at Kumanovo. The Greek
forces, meeting little opposition, advanced rapidly.

The rout of the Turks seemed complete. They failed to score a single
tactical success. Political disturbances in Constantinople during the
summer of 1912 had led to a reorganization of the General Staff. The
consequent dismissal of officers and the reduction of trained troops had
meant that by the time the German-trained Turkish army was mobilized
for war in Europe, it was in disarray and consisted of many raw recruits.
The Austrian Military Attaché in Turkey reported that the Turkish
forces were worse off for communications than they had been a hundred
years before and that it took seven-to eight hours for generals' orders to
reach the troops. There were numerous cases of Turkish soldiers
invalided with broken noses – recruits so untrained as to aim their rifle
with the butt resting on the nose. The Turks' unpreparedness went some
way to explain their defeat. But there was no doubt in the minds of
military observers that the overwhelming reasons were the efficiency of
the military forces of the Balkan allies – especially of the Bulgarians
who bore the brunt of the fighting – and their morale, sustained by the
knowledge that they were at last settling a centuries-old score.

Europe had witnessed the first *Blitzkrieg*. In Britain, the public
greeted the spectacular Bulgarian victories with enthusiasm. The
French Ambassador in London, Paul Cambon, wrote to Poincaré:

> The successes, unforeseen by the English, of the Bulgarian, Serbian
> and Greek armies have influenced the spirit of a nation which respects
> strength. But these triumphs have not actually created but increased
> the sympathy which has always existed in religious England for the
> Christians of Macedonia. It is the sympathy awakened by Mr
> Gladstone during his famous campaign on the Bulgarian atrocities in
> 1877 and which created in 1894 a pro-Armenian movement.[1]

Sir Edward Grey told the Russian Ambassador that English opinion
was 'quite categorically in favour of Bulgaria'.[2]
Kaiser William's former sympathies for Turkey were effaced by his
enthusiasm for the brilliant Balkan victories. He turned a blind eye to
his own loss of prestige by the defeat of the German-trained Turks. His

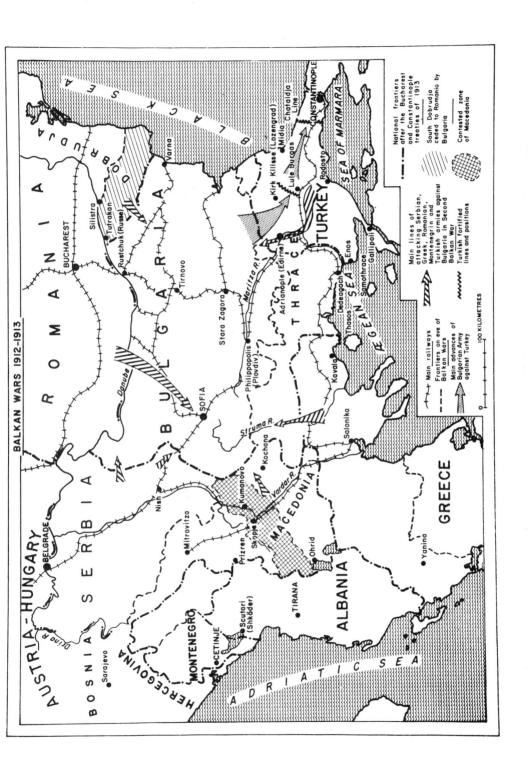

BALKAN WARS 1912-1913

National frontiers
after the Bucharest
and Constantinople
treaties of 1913

South Dobrudja
ceded to Romania by
Bulgaria

Contested zone
of Macedonia

Main lines of
attacking Serbian,
Greek, Romanian,
Montenegrin and
Turkish armies against
Bulgaria in Second
Balkan War

Turkish fortified
lines and positions

Main railways

Frontiers on eve of
Balkan Wars

Main advances of
Bulgarian Army
against Turkey

100 KILOMETRES

0

BLACK SEA

AUSTRIA-HUNGARY

BOSNIA

HERCEGOVINA

SERBIA

MONTENEGRO

ALBANIA

GREECE

ROMANIA

BULGARIA

MACEDONIA

THRACE

TURKEY

DOBRUDJA

AEGEAN SEA

SEA OF MARMARA

ADRIATIC SEA

Sarajevo

Drina R.

BELGRADE

Mitrovitza

Nish

Prizren

Skopje

Kumanovo

Vardar R.

Kochana

Ohrid

CETINJE

Scutari
(Shköder)

TIRANA

Yanina

Salonika

Struma R.

Kavala

Thasos

Samothrace

Dedeagach

Enos

Gallipoli

Radosto

CONSTANTINOPLE

Midia
Chataldja
Line

Lule Burgas

Kirk Kilisse (Lozengrad)

Adrianople (Edirne)

Maritza R.

Philippopolis
(Plovdiv)

SOFIA

Danube

Stara Zagora

Tirnovo

Varna

Silistra

Tutrakan

Rustchuk (Russe)

BUCHAREST

Kochana

opinion of Ferdinand changed with characteristic abruptness:

> The Bulgarians have been led in a masterly fashion and have
> engaged brilliantly. No conference of the Powers can take even a
> single village away from them. They have honestly conquered what
> they wanted and have forced their way into the Concert of Europe.
> That is what new blood and spirits needed! Perhaps we shall see
> Ferdinand I as Tsar of Byzantium? Or as supreme leader of the Balkan
> Confederation?[3]

Paléologue, by this time Director of Political Affairs at the Quai
d'Orsay, commented on these new sentiments of the Kaiser. (French
cryptographists had intercepted German diplomatic exchanges on the
Balkan War.) 'The Kaiser... is prepared to greet King Ferdinand as
Emperor of Byzantium.... And it is the same William who but lately
used to proclaim himself as the most faithful friend and staunch defender
of the Turks![4]

The French were equally enthusiastic, as Princess Radziwill reported
from Paris: 'All the talk here is of the Bulgarians, of the merits of their
King, of their excellent army and of the superiority of Schneider-
Creusot artillery over that of Krupp.'[5] She went on to retell the story of
Kaiser William's slap which resulted in Bulgaria's order from Le
Creusot. France, especially the Press, hailed the Bulgarian victories as
evidence of the superiority of the French Schneider-Creusot artillery
over the German Krupp guns with which the Turkish army was
equipped. For months a bitter, chauvinistic argument raged in the
German and French Press over the merits of their respective guns. Large
sections of the public in both countries saw the war in the Balkans in
terms of a trial of German against French artillery. The argument begun
in October 1912 was not to be finally settled until 1918. When Austria's
Foreign Minister Berchtold suggested the following April that it might
be politic for Ferdinand to pay Kaiser William some kind of military
courtesy, possibly by presenting him with a battle trophy, Ferdinand
had the quiet satisfaction of pointing out that this was out of the question
since all the captured Turkish equipment was of German origin.

By the beginning of November 1912, the fall of Constantinople to the
Bulgarians seemed imminent. George V told Mensdorff, the Austrian
Ambassador, that due to Ferdinand's 'ambition' and 'sense of history' –
which he also called 'vanity' and 'theatricality' – the Tsar would find
the temptation to celebrate Mass in St Sophia quite irresistible after
riding into the city in triumph.

King George took a very gloomy view, as Mensdorff reported to
Vienna:

Were the cross to be set up on the dome of St Sophia then' the Moslems would be certain to blow it up, be it church or mosque. There would be massacres of Christians in Asia Minor, and Moslems all over the world would start agitating. All countries with Moslem subjects – which include France and Russia – would suffer from this, but above all England, in India and the Sudan. 'I have 80 million Mohammedan subjects,' the King added.[6]

If King George's worries about a new Indian Mutiny as a result of the reconsecration of St Sophia were far-fetched, those of Britain's Entente partner, Russia, were solidly based. As early as 1908, when the Balkan League was but a pipe-dream, Russia's Izvolski told Germany's State Secretary for Foreign Affairs, Baron von Schoen, that Russia was totally opposed to Constantinople falling into Bulgarian or Greek hands. Alarmed by the victories and rapid advance of the Bulgarians, Izvolski's successor, Sazonoff, declared that on the Bosphorus there could only be the Turks or the Russians. Immediately after the first Bulgarian victories, Sazonoff wrote to Izvolski that if the Bulgarians entered Constantinople they would be attacked by Russia: 'The occupation of Constantinople could compel the appearance of our whole Black Sea fleet before the Turkish capital.'[7] It was ironic that the Russian Foreign Minister – that 'sad wobbler' as a British Foreign Office minute called him – who had tried so hard to bring about the alliance of the Balkan states, should contemplate military action against the leading member so soon after its formation.

With the Bulgarian armies only twenty miles away, Constantinople was on the verge of panic. The main concern inside the city was over probable riots and the massacre of Christians when the retreating Turkish troops reached the city. All the Powers dispatched warships for the protection of their various nationals, the embassies were put under guard and plans drawn up for the evacuation of foreigners.

In London Sir Arthur Nicolson voiced his fears to the Austrian Ambassador and wondered 'whether it would not be advisable in the interests of humanity to appeal to King Ferdinand's sense of magnanimity not to advance any further'.[8] The German Kaiser took a more sanguine view. In the margin of the German Ambassador's report from Constantinople describing how the Turkish Grand Vizier Kiamil Pasha had told the assembled ambassadors of the European powers that if the Bulgarians entered Constantinople their lives, and those of the Christians in the city, would be forfeit, while he, Kiamil, would await the enemy and die at his desk, Kaiser William wrote: 'Rubbish! The Bulgarians shall and must enter! Old Kiamil can die in peace; he is practically a hundred years old!'[9]

All this time King Ferdinand kept out of sight at his headquarters in a yellow stuccoed two-storey house at Stara Zagora. He avoided the crowd of Europe's war correspondents (Trotsky was among them), and only allowed occasional photographs of himself getting into a motor-car or train to visit the front. He especially avoided the diplomatic representatives of the Powers. The Russian Minister Neklyudoff hardly managed to see him at all and thought Ferdinand was right in refusing to see them. He and his diplomatic colleagues were straining to give him their respective governments' advice, to which Ferdinand was not at all inclined to listen.

An acquaintance of Neklyudoff, a Bulgarian lady who was Russian by birth, met the King at the railway station at Stara Zagora at this time:

> The King walked with her along the station where his headquarters were, and the incredible elasticity of his movements were a great contrast to his usual walk of a gouty and obese person; His Majesty bounded in the air like an india-rubber ball.
>
> 'Now then!' he exclaimed with a triumphant smile, 'what have you to say about it, madame? What do you say? *Bulgar-Vilayet!* Eh, what? *Bulgar-Vilayet?* Who would have thought it?' and the King went on repeating his *Bulgar-Vilayet,* accompanying the words with his most malicious smile aimed at the *Padishah.*
>
> At this moment he was evidently remembering his first journey to Constantinople, when the Sultan was holding an investiture; he remembered his meeting with the sly, obstinate old Abdul-Hamid, and how he had to bow before him and to kiss the hand of the *Padishah* [Emperor], his sovereign. Yes, he had gone through it all; he had done it in an insinuating manner, as if it cost him nothing; but in reality he had felt deeply humiliated, and the memory had never been effaced from his heart. It was at this period that at the Sultan's Court Bulgaria was always spoken of as *Bulgar-Vilayet* [the Bulgarian province].
>
> And now 'what a change of destiny by the grace of God!' The fate of Turkey seemed to be in Ferdinand's hands as it once had been in the hands of the Bulgarian Tsar Simeon, who approached the walls of Constantinople with his army, with the object of cutting a way through and being proclaimed Emperor of the East. And Ferdinand with his vivid and prompt imagination saw himself playing the part of Simeon.
>
> The objectives assigned to the war with Turkey seemed to him to have been left far behind, and all his thoughts, all his projects were centred now on the town so near at hand. He pictured himself making his entry into the Imperial City, having obliterated the last traces of Ottoman domination in Europe. And then on his skill, his subtle

diplomacy an unexpected solution of the Straits question might depend – a solution in favour of the Bulgarians, .this people who but forty years ago had been ignored by the whole world.[10]

The brilliance of the Bulgarian victories and the speed of the advance towards Constantinople had stunned King Ferdinand as they had amazed Europe. His unwarlike temperament had dreaded the coming conflict as strongly as his intelligence had convinced him that it was necessary. He had faced the prospect of war as reluctantly as he donned the khaki uniform which he wore throughout the war, and which did not suit him at all. The quick decisive victories were an immense relief.

A mere fortnight of warfare transformed his ideas about Byzantium. Hitherto Byzantium had been a romantic fancy, a *fin-de-siècle* historical pose in which he could indulge by having his portrait painted as emperor of Byzantium, a means of impressing his guests, a harmless exercise in home theatricals. He was too much of a realist and had far too much political sense to go beyond that. But now, with the applause of Europe ringing in his ears, the idea of Byzantium assumed what his French secretary, the poet Paul de Chèvremont, called 'a perilous consistency'.[11] Fancy was becoming reality. Like iron filings reacting to a magnetic field, Ferdinand saw his life as a definite pattern shaped by the magnet of Constantinople. Everything now seemed predestined, and the celebrated Parisian clairvoyante Madame de Thebes, whom he had consulted in his youth, less of a humbug than ever.

From his headquarters Ferdinand sent an immediate order to Sofia for the parade uniforms of the Royal Guard, the State coach and six white horses. According to the Russian Minister in Sofia, Ferdinand also asked for his Byzantine emperor's costume. Evidently, it was unthinkable for Byzantium's last conqueror to enter the city in triumph, in a motor-car and in khaki. A new best-selling chromolithograph in the Balkan countries at that time had captured the mood of the Allies. It showed a ghostly horse and rider (a diaphanous Constantine XI, the last Byzantine Emperor who was killed defending Constantinople against the Turks in 1453) guiding the four Balkan kings, riding side by side through a plain strewn with the bodies of fallen Turks, towards St Sophia in the distance, blue and yellow, its great dome glittering with an unearthly radiance.

The real obstacle, now that the Turks had collapsed, was Russia. For two centuries Russia had been aspiring to the possession of the Straits and dreamed of erecting the cross on the dome of St Sophia. Would she calmly sit back and allow her 'little Slav brother' to snatch the prize? There was a distinct taste of sour grapes in Nicholas II's answers to questions about Constantinople put to him by the German Kaiser's admiral brother, Prince Henry. What would happen if the Bulgarians insisted on entering the city? 'All right, let them go in, no one will stop them.'[12] Prince Henry asked if that would not be displeasing to the Russian Tsar. 'Why should it?' Prince Henry insisted and said that everyone including himself thought that the Tsar and the whole of Russia wanted to possess Constantinople.

At that the Tsar declared emphatically that neither he nor Russia had given the matter a moment's thought; that he wouldn't have Constantinople even as a present and that he couldn't care less if the Bulgarians went in. This display of indifference failed to convince Prince Henry. The whole thing was exceedingly awkward for Russia, as the German *chargé d'affaires* in London explained in a report to Berlin after a talk with Count Benckendorff, the Russian Ambassador. Benckendorff was convinced that King Ferdinand, who for many years had had a picture of St Sophia hanging in his room, would go to Constantinople to celebrate High Mass in the church-mosque. He said that the Russian Government would wish to use force to get the Bulgarians out of Constantinople; but Slav enthusiasm would be so great in Russia that the Government would not be able to use arms against Bulgaria.

> Ferdinand is a very experienced politician and knows this better than anyone, and he might well play this daring and adventurous gambit. That will be exceedingly difficult for Russia. Russia therefore considers it of urgent importance that the Powers should jointly inform Sofia that they would not stand for an occupation of Constantinople.[13]

Neklyudoff, Russia's Minister in Sofia, was convinced that one of the mainsprings which incited Ferdinand to the taking of Constantinople was the possibility this offered of reconciliation with the Vatican and the lifting of the ban of excommunication. Ferdinand, according to Neklyudoff, intended to celebrate a solemn mass in St Sophia strictly in accordance with the Orthodox rite, in the course of which the name of the Pope would be mentioned before and above that of the Patriarch of Constantinople. 'Then only would they understand in Rome that by consenting to his son's conversion to the Orthodox Church, Ferdinand had rendered one of the greatest services to Roman Catholicism. And then not only would his excommunication be rescinded, but also his name would be blessed and quoted side by side with those of the great isapostolic monarchs.'[14] There is no other evidence that Ferdinand really thought that the Western and Eastern Churches could be reconciled under his aegis. But he must have found the thought immensely attractive.

While Tsar Nicholas II was affecting insouciance about the Bulgarian threat to Constantinople, Russia's diplomats were urgently calling on Britain and France to help restrain the Bulgarians. The Bulgarian Cabinet was disposed to listen to the warnings and advice from the Entente countries, but Ferdinand and most of the army approved of continuing the advance. He turned down a Turkish request for negotiations towards an armistice after the initial Bulgarian victories and sent a telegram of reassurance to the Bulgarian army supreme command: 'In the name of the 500,000-strong victorious army I have protested to the government and forbidden it to negotiate. We shall dictate the peace in Constantinople.'[15]

Tsar Ferdinand and the army chiefs were firmly resolved to reap the utmost profit from the victories that had been won. The momentum of the advance brought the Bulgarians to the Chataldja line and, despite the unusually heavy rains which seriously impeded communications, turning the roads into rivers of mud, the Turkish fortifications and defence positions were attacked on 17 and 18 November. The Bulgarians were thrown back, with nearly 10,000 dead and wounded. When the Turks had been engaged in offensive operations in open country none of their officers had known how to direct properly. But now, in their entrenched positions along a high ridge running from the Black Sea in the north to the Sea of Marmara in the south, they were very different opponents. Another enemy, far more daunting than the Turks, played havoc with the Bulgarians in the unhealthy, marshy Chataldja region: cholera and dysentery. Less than a week after the assault on the Chataldja line nearly 20,000 Bulgarian soldiers were down with cholera. Another frontal attack against the Turkish defences was unthinkable. The area of the fighting was like a jetty: neither combatant, with sea on each side and a twelve mile front, could effect a turning movement – it all had to be straight slogging.

The ravages of cholera and the breakdown in supplies made the Bulgarians vulnerable. Their military commanders calculated that any Turkish attack with fresh forces at that moment could have catastrophic results and urged Ferdinand and the Government to agree to armistice negotiations to give the troops respite. The Tsar agreed and asked Dr Daneff, the President of the Sobranie, to head the Bulgarian delegation at the armistice talks near Chataldja. As a civilian, Daneff felt that it was not right for him to be the chief Bulgarian negotiator in working out the terms of an armistice, a purely military matter, and tried to turn down the appointment. He keenly felt the awkwardness of being formally in charge of the other two Bulgarian delegates: the Commander-in-Chief, General Savoff, and the Chief of the General Staff, General Fitcheff. Ferdinand begged him to accept the appointment and explained that he

was afraid the two generals were 'hypnotized' by the failure of the
Chataldja attack and might concede too much to the Turks. Daneff was
to act as a counterweight. When Daneff insisted that he had no desire to
meddle in purely military matters Ferdinand, on the verge of tears, put
his arms around him and asked: 'Do not refuse, go and save my fine
army.'[16] It was a rare display of spontaneous emotion and Daneff
accepted. The delegates met for several days in a wagon-lit dining-car
just outside the Chataldja line, only interrupting their discussions for
well-served luncheons sent up by rail from a Constantinople hotel. On 3
December an armistice was signed.

Peace negotiations were to begin in London on 13 December, while
the belligerent armies remained in their respective positions with a
neutral zone established between them.

Disease and exhaustion in the army were not the only reason the
Bulgarians were glad to conclude an armistice. From the beginning of
the war they began to realize that while they were bearing the brunt of
the attack in Thrace, their Allies, faced by considerably smaller Turkish
forces, were occupying territory in Macedonia and Albania. Military
considerations had compelled Bulgaria to make Constantinople her
objective and Thrace her campaigning ground. But her real political
objectives were Macedonia and the port of Salonika. The great military
successes in Thrace could not secure these political objectives. As the
war proceeded, Ferdinand and his ministers feared that at the coming
peace settlement Bulgaria's Allies would advance the argument that
'possession is nine-tenths of the law' and refuse to budge from Macedonia and Salonika.

The port of Salonika on the Aegean fell on 8 November in circumstances which already showed the first cracks in the Balkan alliance. No
definite agreement as to the future of Salonika had been reached in the
Greek-Bulgarian treaty. Each side had privately assigned it to itself,
with the result that when the war began there was an undignified race
for the city. The main Greek army advanced north across the Thessalian
plain, fully aware that a Bulgarian division was racing south down the
valley of the River Struma. The Greeks won and took the city from the
Turks. When the Bulgarians arrived less than twenty-four hours later,
only a token force was allowed in. Almost from the beginning there was
bad blood between the Greek and Bulgarian soldiers.

A few days later, King George of Greece moved his headquarters to
the city. On 19 December Tsar Ferdinand came to see his royal ally. He
was determined to show that he was not coming as a guest, and that he
had an equal right to Salonika.

Foreseeing an official reception which would have put him in the
unwelcome position of a guest, Ferdinand left the train at the station

before Salonika and drove rapidly by motor-car to the Bulgarian consulate in Salonika. The Greek royal reception party at the Salonika railway station only learnt what had happened when the train reached the city. They all raced to the Bulgarian consulate. There, to their chagrin, they saw Prince Ferdinand reviewing the token force of Bulgarian troops. The following day he called on the King of Greece and stayed for lunch. Ferdinand was at his best. Prince Nicholas of Greece wrote later, 'during the meal and after, King Ferdinand charmed us with the elegance of his speech, his wit and rare intelligence; both his erudition and historical knowledge are remarkable.'[17] Both Kings avoided the delicate question about who was to have Salonika. 'More forward than her husband, the Russian-born Queen Olga of Greece endeavoured to persuade Ferdinand that Salonika would have to form an integral part of the Greek dominions. Ferdinand parried, and replied that it was a question for future discussion between the two governments.'[18]

The day after the Greeks won the race to Salonika, Austria's Foreign Minister Berchtold received Dr Daneff in Budapest and taunted the Bulgarian statesman: 'Well, the Greeks have just beaten you to it and have entered Salonika. We believe that they are determined to hold on to it.'[19] Daneff would not rise to this. He explained that Bulgaria had gone to war for one reason only: the liberation of Macedonia, to which Berchtold immediately replied that the region was almost entirely occupied by the Serbian army. Daneff agreed: 'It could not be otherwise for strategic reasons; our armies had to destroy the main Turkish forces in Thrace. But I can assure you that we shall not quarrel with the Serbs over Macedonia.'[20]

Leopold, Count Berchtold, was not even trying to be subtle about his trouble-making. The victory of the Balkan Allies and Balkan nationalism was a disaster for the Habsburg monarchy. The disruption of the Balkan League, this new and apparently formidable obstacle between Central Europe and the Mediterranean, was now the prime objective of Austria and her partners in the Triple Alliance. Even more, it was essential to humble Serbia and reassert Austria-Hungary's 'prestige'.

How was this to be done, short of war? It did not take Vienna long to find the answer. Hardly had the Balkan states entered upon the path of victory when Serbia and the European Powers received Austria's warning that Serbia, whatever her territorial gains from Turkey, would absolutely be refused a port on the Adriatic. At the same time Austria would insist on setting up an independent Albania, which would block Serbian access to the Adriatic. It was a cruel blow to Serbia, for whom an Adriatic outlet meant economic independence and riches, after many

years of commercial disputes and customs wars with Austria. In
Austrian eyes, a Serbian port on the Adriatic would have boosted the
prestige of Belgrade and consequently increased the irredentist agitation among the Slavs of the Habsburg monarchy.

Despite the warning Serbian armies were advancing as rapidly as
possible to the Adriatic. Once again all Europe was anxious to discover
whether Austria's armies would intervene against Serbia, which would
bring in Russia on Serbia's side and so inevitably lead to the Great War.
Both Austria and Russia were arming when tension over Serbia was
increased by the so-called 'Consular Affair'. This blew up when the
Serbs complained that the Austrian Consul in Prizren had encouraged
the Turks and Albanians in the city to fight the Serbs, when the latter
captured the city. Shots had been fired from the roof of the consulate on
Serbian soldiers. The Serbs demanded the Consul's recall. Owing to the
war, there was a breakdown in communications and rumours reached
Vienna, fanned by the Press, that the Austrian Consul had been killed by
the Serbs. It was even believed that he had been castrated. Anti-Serb
feeling in Austria rose to fever pitch. Then news came that the Consul
was unharmed. By then Russia had increased her standing army by
about 400,000. The tension can be gauged by the instructions sent by
Vienna to Austria's representatives in Serbia, Russia and Montenegro as
to what they should do in case war broke out. Essential archives were to
be packed immediately, ready for collection at a minute's notice. When
Austria's representatives had to leave various capitals at the outbreak of
war in 1914, they were referred back to this very order.

An announcement by the Austrian Foreign Office on 17 December
1912, that its Consul in Prizren was safe and unharmed, coincided with
the opening in London of the peace negotiations between the Balkan
Allies and Turkey. The centre of interest now shifted from the Balkans
to St James's Palace, where the peace delegates held their meetings.
Simultaneously, at the Foreign Office sat a second conference composed
of the London Ambassadors of the five powers – Austria-Hungary,
Germany, Italy, Russia and France. Sir Edward Grey, quite naturally,
was chosen chairman of the latter conference, which saw itself as a kind
of diplomatic supreme court.

Equally naturally, the Ambassadors' conference represented a confrontation of the Triple Alliance and the Entente, though the British
Foreign Secretary managed as chairman to maintain an appearance of
strict neutrality which received full recognition. At the outset both
sides were worried by the fact that three of the Ambassadors were
cousins – Russia's Benckendorff, Austria's Mensdorff and Germany's
Lichnowsky. The relationship brought criticism in their respective
countries, where it was charged that family links jeopardized national

interests. In fact, the family links between the representatives of the opposing alliance groupings at the London ambassadors' conference had no more effect on events than the degree of cousinship between William II and George V had in preventing the Great War.

The Duchess of Sutherland gave culinary expression to the general European relief at a luncheon for the peace delegates with an optimistic menu:

Oeufs à la turque
Fillet de sole à la grecque
Faisan bulgare au blanc
Selle d'agneau Grande Bretagne
Salade espoir
Mousse de jambon de paix
Asperges
Crême Cardinal serbe
PâtisserieMonténégre

At the St James's Palace conference, the Bulgarian delegation headed by Dr Daneff was surprised by new instructions from Sofia, stipulating that Bulgaria was to insist that her new frontier with Turkey should be a line from Midia on the Black Sea to Rodosto on the Sea of Marmara.

Such a frontier was far in excess of what had been agreed before the Bulgarian delegates left for London. The new line would give Bulgaria half the northern shore of the Sea of Marmara as well as the Gallipoli Peninsula and its hinterland – in fact direct control of the Dardanelles. Daneff was amazed by this ambitious claim, one the major Powers were bound to veto. Later he realized that it expressed Tsar Ferdinand's desire to dominate the approaches to Constantinople. The Bulgarian military success had not only fired Ferdinand's territorial ambitions but his romantic fancy. Only the latter, according to Paléologue, could explain Ferdinand's insistent request to the Powers during the peace negotiations that they should cede to him, as a personal gift, the island of Samothrace in the northern Aegean, close to the Dardanelles. It had no tolerable harbour and barely sustained a population of some 2,000 sponge fishermen. Paléologue thought it an example of Ferdinand's 'insidious romantic imagination' at work even while his country was on a war footing. According to Paléologue, Ferdinand wanted the island not for any strategic or economic reasons but because, since the dawn of history, it had been famous for the orgiastic Samothracian Mysteries, 'le *culte effrayant des Cabires'* in Paléologue's words. Neklyudoff, on the other hand, thought that the island 'evidently tempted Ferdinand by the divine classic lines of its pearl-grey rocks rising out of the blue sea'.[21]

He may have wanted to own the island for quite another reason than its scenery or its mysterious past. According to Roger Peyrefitte, the French writer, Ferdinand was an assiduous and discreet visitor to Capri, whose complaisant young boatmen had turned it into the happy hunting ground of Europe's rich homosexuals. In 1902 Fritz Krupp, the head of the German armaments firm, took his life so as to avoid the exposure of his extravagant homosexual indiscretions on Capri. After the Krupp scandal Capri was never quite the same. Is it not possible that Ferdinand saw Samothrace as a possible and far more discreet substitute?

Towards the end of January 1913 the conference of the belligerents at St James's Palace seemed to be in its concluding stages, with a peace treaty in sight after prolonged wrangling. The Turks were resisting the Balkan Allies' demands to cede all territory north of the Enos-Midia line, which meant surrendering Adrianople, the most important city of the Ottoman Empire next to Constantinople. A collective note of the European powers advising Turkey to surrender Adrianople was handed to the Porte on 22 January 1913.

Five days later the Turkish Government decided to accept the allied demands and to conclude peace. But before the diplomatic note to this effect could be drawn up, a group of Young Turk army officers, led by Enver Bey, staged a coup in Constantinople. They burst into the chamber where the Cabinet was sitting, shot Nazim Pasha, the Turkish Minister of War, and gave out word that no such dishonourable peace would be concluded with the Balkan states. The Balkan League denounced the armistice. Hostilities were resumed on 3 February 1913. The Bulgarians concentrated on capturing Adrianople which had been besieged since the early weeks of the war. Serbia, already master in Macedonia and Albania, had no special war objective and supplied Bulgaria with some troops and weapons for the offensive at Adrianople.

Adrianople surrendered on 26 March after a fierce bombardment followed up by a night attack with bayonets. There was no time to cut the thick barbed wire entanglements defending the main fort and the Bulgarians threw their greatcoats over the wires and broke through by clambering over lines of thick felt.

The battle and siege of Adrianople involved the first really extensive use of war techniques, such as barbed wire, which were to become familiar in the Great War. Among the 'firsts' of modern warfare during the Balkan Wars were 'bombs' – in fact grenades – dropped from a Bulgarian aeroplane. (During a later phase of the Balkan Wars water-melons were dropped with considerable psychological effect as their pink flesh burst on impact.) Pilots were also shot down by fire from the ground for the first time in warfare.

The news of the fall of Adrianople was greeted with immense enthusiasm in Bulgaria. Popular demonstrations in St Petersburg were as enthusiastic, and the alarmed Russian authorities ordered the crowds to be broken up by mounted police armed with whips. At the same time a *Te Deum* was celebrated in the Russian capital with Rodzianko, the President of the Duma, leading a choir formed by the deputies. It was a day for the Panslavs. In France, too, the victory was greeted with rejoicing; it was seen as an additional proof of the superiority of the Schneider-Creusot gun over that of Krupp.

Tsar Ferdinand, accompanied by his sons, arrived in Adrianople twenty-four hours after its capture. His joy was such as to overcome his deep fear of cholera infection. He entered the town by motor-car through long lines of Turkish prisoners of war. After reviewing his troops, he received Shukri Pasha, the captive Turkish commander of Adrianople. The defeated Turkish general handed Ferdinand his sword. Ferdinand returned it. The following day Shukri was sent to Sofia, where a great crowd awaited him at the railway station. He was officially greeted with the words: 'A welcome to your Excellency. The whole world admires both victors and vanquished. Bulgaria cherishes profound respect towards the illustrious hero of Adrianople. Your Excellency may rest assured of our sincere sympathy and admiration.' He was then lodged in the best hotel in Sofia where sumptuous apartments, with every luxury and comfort had been prepared for him and his staff. In this way, Ferdinand was showing magnanimity in victory.

After Ferdinand had seen Shukri Pasha, he drove to the great mosque of Sultan Selim. With its four great minarets stabbing the Adrianople skyline, it is one of the masterpieces of Ottoman art. Eyes shining, Ferdinand told Emile Dard, a French diplomat who was with him, that the mosque was as beautiful as St Sophia. He took him round the white marble court and showed him where he intended to group oleanders and other plants to harmonize with the architecture.

Just as Ferdinand was about to be driven away from the mosque, there was a small incident. Emile Dard described the scene to Paléologue:

At the exact moment that the car began to move I suddenly saw his great nose at the window. Looking upset and tragic he murmured briefly to his servant, the Croat who has his fullest confidence and whom you know. Without any hesitation and as if he needed no further instructions, the man leapt from his seat, rushed over to one end of the court where a black cat was prowling about. With one blow of his cane he broke the animal's back. Two policemen ran up at the same moment and finished off the poor animal with their boots.[22]

When Paléologue heard this, he asked if the cat had been on Ferdinand's left side. Dard confirmed this. Paléologue: 'A black cat on his left! That is so bad an omen that he cannot speak of it without a shudder. I have no doubt that he instantly told himself: "a black cat, on my left, in Selim's mosque!... I shall lose Adrianople!"'

It was not the mere appearance of the unfortunate animal that blighted Ferdinand's joy in the aftermath of the victory at Adrianople. The feline ill omen did no more than bring to his mind a latent anxiety. This anxiety was increased by the second failure of the Bulgarian troops at Chataldja to pierce the lines guarding Constantinople after a week-long battle. Certainly, for Ferdinand the dream of Byzantium, its 'perilous consistency' and compelling charm, was dissolving in the blood and miasma of sickness before the Chataldja fortifications.

To be sure, this was a great disappointment, but not the root cause of his unease; he was too much of a realist not to understand the romantic nature of the urgings within himself that drove him to Constantinople, notions which he had found it easy to invest with political substance and validity in the first headlong victories. If Constantinople was not to be, so be it. But what of Macedonia, the object of the war and of Bulgaria's desire?

While the main Bulgarian forces had been busy before Adrianople, at Chataldja and in Thrace, the Greeks transferred the weight of their army to Macedonia after capturing the fortress of Yanina on 6 March. So now Macedonia was occupied by Serbian and Greek troops. It was daily becoming clearer that the Serbs, at least, were not intending to honour the treaty with Bulgaria regarding the division of Macedonia. James Bourchier of *The Times* wrote on 20 April 1913, from Sofia to a friend in London:

> I am horrified by the state of feeling I find here and at Belgrade. At Belgrade they are more demonstrative; here 'still waters run deep'. The Serbians cynically say they will not keep their treaty with Bulgaria, because 'the balance of power must be preserved in the Peninsula'.
>
> The Bulgarians are very indignant, and say they will give them 'a taste of the bayonet'. There is, of course, an end to all treaties if they are to be broken in this way; the truth is that the Serbian officers, finding themselves in possession at Monastir, etc., don't see why they should go out, and they regard treaties as waste paper. At Belgrade they coolly talk of a Serbo-Greek attack on Bulgaria, though under

the Treaties of Alliance both Serbia and Greece are bound to Bulgaria
for terms of years.[23]

Serbia, denied access to the Adriatic by Austria and the Powers, was
determined to have fitting compensation in Macedonia at Bulgaria's
expense. Greek chauvinists were determined to hold on to Greek-
occupied territory. As early as January 1913, Crown Prince Alexander
of Serbia and Prince Nicholas of Greece discussed the possibility of an
alliance against Bulgaria. That month the Serbian Government officially requested Bulgaria for a redefinition of the Macedonian frontiers
fixed by the Alliance. Bulgarian statesmen easily refuted the reasons
given by Serbia for her claims – legally, the Bulgarian position was
strong. The Serbs reiterated their claims during the following months.
No settlement was reached and relations between the two allies steadily
grew worse. By that time the Serbian and Greek occupying forces in
Macedonia openly started a campaign to grecize and serbicize the
Bulgarians in Macedonia. The Bulgarian schools were closed and used
as lodgings for the occupying troops. The priests and bishops were
forbidden to perform services in Bulgarian and members of IMRO were
persecuted. As news of all this reached Bulgaria, public feeling in Sofia
was hardening against Ferdinand and the Government for their failure
to deliver the prizes for which the nation had made such great sacrifices.
    In May 1913, Serbia and Greece signed a protocol providing for a
common policy towards Bulgaria and, as a supplement to it, a preliminary military convention. By then, several reports of local skirmishes
with Bulgarian forces had reached Belgrade and Athens.
    All this time the peace negotiations in London between the Balkan
states and Turkey, which had resumed following the fall of Adrianople,
were going on. The essence of the negotiations no longer concerned the
differences between the Balkan states and Turkey, but between the
'Allies'. Bulgaria's delegates, led by Daneff, now desired a rapid
conclusion of an armistice so that the Bulgarian armies, still tied down
in Thrace, might be transferred to Macedonia. This was exactly what
the Serbians and Greeks were trying to prevent, by delaying as much as
possible the signing of a peace treaty. The Powers grew impatient. The
chairman of the ambassadors' conference, Sir Edward Grey, saw the
chief delegates in his room at the Foreign Office and, as Sir Harold
Nicolson described the scene, he 'advanced towards them with his eagle
eye: he pointed towards them with an outstretched and imperative
finger: he summoned to his assistance the total resources of his
Wykhamist French. *"Ou signer"*, he shouted at them *"Ou partir!"'*[24]
    Three days later the peace preliminaries were signed in London. The
following day Serbia and Greece secretly concluded an alliance treaty

and military convention against Bulgaria. In regard to Macedonia the principle of 'effective occupation' was to be followed. Not only did Serbia and Greece negotiate an anti-Bulgarian alliance between themselves but they also tried to recruit Romania. The latter preferred to keep her hands free for the time being, but received the advances from Belgrade and Athens with cordiality and expressed her anti-Bulgarian attitude.

The attitude of the Romanians troubled Ferdinand as much as those of Bulgaria's other neighbours. Before the war against Turkey, the Balkan allies had invited Romania to join them. Bucharest declined, chiefly because King Carol and his ministers did not believe that a coalition of Balkan states could beat Turkey. But when it became clear that the Turks were losing and that Bulgaria's territory was bound to increase, Romania demanded territory from Bulgaria across the Danube as compensation for what she alleged was a change in the balance of forces in the Balkans. Romania threatened to use force if her demands were not satisfied at a moment when the Bulgarian forces were concentrated in Thrace. With a heavy heart and under pressure from Austria and Russia, both anxious to prevent a conflict which would involve them, Ferdinand agreed to some changes in the frontier between the two countries, which included ceding the town of Silistra. For consenting to this sacrifice, King Ferdinand received official thanks from the Powers. But he was aware that the thanks were meaningless and that Romania, emboldened by this success, was greedy for more and biding her time.

Ferdinand and the Bulgarians were increasingly playing a lone hand, not only in the Balkans but in the wider context of Europe. While Austria was now trying to win over Bulgaria, Austria's senior partner Germany was becoming distinctly anti-Bulgarian. The change in attitude was entirely due to Kaiser William. His enthusiasm about Bulgaria's early victories and his new admiration of Ferdinand did not last long. In a characteristic change of face, he recovered his old antipathy towards the Bulgarian Tsar. He became an ardent and active supporter of the Greek and Romanian claims on Bulgaria, not least due to family reasons; the Romanian royal family were Hohenzollerns and the new King of Greece, Constantine (he succeeded his father George in March 1913, after the latter's assassination by a madman), was married to William's sister Sophia.

In May that year Paléologue, on being told of the Kaiser's new and extreme Bulgarophobia, replied:

> I must admit that this brusque new volte-face of William II towards Bulgaria does not surprise me.
> He is so impulsive, so changeable! During the five years I spent in

Sofia, I saw the Kaiser and Ferdinand switch, frequently and all of a sudden, from mutual love to hatred, from admiration to contempt. They are two ham actors, too intelligent not to recognise each other's talents, but also far too vain not to allow their charlatanism to set them against each other all the time.[25]

Usually, Paléologue expressed himself with greater clarity. His tone, however, is reminiscent of that used by Proust's Charlus when he refers, with a smirk, to William and Ferdinand's homosexual tendencies.

The aura of martial success which surrounded King Ferdinand eventually soured not only the Kaiser's feelings towards him but those of the other sovereigns as well. In May 1913, Nicholas II and George V were together in Berlin as guests of honour for the marriage of Kaiser William's only daughter Victoria to Duke Ernest-Augustus of Brunswick. During this, the last great family ceremony of the Hohenzollerns, Kaiser William received a telegram from his sister, Queen Sophia of Greece. In alarmist terms she accused Bulgarian troops of encroaching on the neutral zone which had been established between the Greek and Bulgarian armies. So far there had been only a vague rumour of a minor incident between Bulgarians and Greeks, with each side accusing the other of having caused it. The Kaiser discussed his sister's telegram with King George and Tsar Nicholas and within hours, without obtaining any details or confirmation of the reported incident far away in the south of Macedonia, William and Nicholas sent accusatory telegrams to Ferdinand. The Russian Tsar went so far as to warn Ferdinand that if the incident should result in war, the responsibility would rest on Bulgaria. King George did not send a telegram but 'expressed himself very sharply about Ferdinand'.[26]

The personal dislike of Ferdinand shown then by the three sovereigns had, whatever the political considerations, the characteristics of the mixed contempt and disquiet with which older members tend to view the successful *parvenu*. Kaiser William was well aware of Nicholas's feelings towards Ferdinand and the Russian's fury on hearing that the Bulgarian had styled himself *Tsar* in 1908. In the margin of a German diplomatic dispatch reporting secret anti-Bulgarian agreements between Serbia, Greece and Romania, the Kaiser wrote: 'What does Russia say about all this? Is it because Ferdinand has become too great and independent for Russia's liking?'[27] Certainly, at least in so far as Kaiser William was concerned, there was an element of personal jealousy. It was galling to see the effete Ferdinand bathed in military glory after a campaign which had amazed Europe, while he, William, the sovereign of one of the most powerful countries in the world, could only express his military ambitions and keep up with the ghost of

Frederick the Great by posing for Court painters and photographers in
ever-more grandiose Wagnerian, eagle-topped helmets. Who can say
how much William's latent yen for war was stimulated in that last
fretful year of near-total peace by the lightning military campaigns in
the Balkan Peninsula?

Tsar Nicholas's attitude, and that of his ministers and diplomats
towards Ferdinand, was more complex, uncertain and contradictory.
Russia had worked hard to promote the formation of the Balkan League
as a barrier to Austro-German expansion and as a means of increasing
her prestige in the Balkan Peninsula. In promoting the Balkan bloc, the
Russians managed to avert their eyes from the most obvious outcome of
such an alliance: that it would wage war against the decrepit and
tyrannical remains in Europe of centuries of Turkish rule.

The Russian public greeted the Balkan victories with enthusiasm,
while official Russia, at least Tsar Nicholas and his diplomats, became
fearful when it seemed that the advance of the Bulgarian armies would
take them into Constantinople and Ferdinand on to the Byzantine
throne. This fear remained with the Russians despite the repeated
failure of the Bulgarian attempts to storm the Chatalja defences.
Already in the autumn of 1912, Sazonoff, Russia's Foreign Minister,
threatened that if Constantinople was captured Russia would be ready
to go to war within twenty-four hours. In Constantinople the Bulgarians would be faced by the whole of Russia's Black Sea fleet.

It seems that neither Ferdinand nor his ministers were aware of just
how greatly Russia's leaders had been alarmed by a possible Bulgarian
takeover of Constantinople and how insistently their fear would linger.
'I know that your Tsar hates me. But why?'[28] Ferdinand asked Pavel
Milyukoff, a leading member of the Duma, who visited Sofia in April
1913. It was a rhetorical question; Ferdinand carried on talking and
Milyukoff wrote in his memoirs: 'His speech flowed in cascades, sparkled
with flashes of wit, antithesis and unexpected *saillies* in the style of
French eloquence, in brilliant French. I remember that somebody once
told me that should Ferdinand want to charm somebody, he would
certainly know how to do it.'[29]

The failure of Ferdinand and his advisers to gauge the extent to which
St Petersburg was now beginning to turn against Bulgaria is excusable,
since the Russians themselves were unsure of their own attitude to the
situation in the Balkans.

Bulgaria seemed well on the way to achieve her ambition by realizing
the frontiers of Great Bulgaria as drawn – by Russia – in the abortive
Treaty of San Stefano in 1878. This would make Bulgaria the biggest of
the Balkan states; Romania, it seemed to Sazonoff, was sure to gravitate
towards Bulgaria. Possibly Turkey would eventually do likewise. It

then only needed for them to associate with Austria for a powerful new bloc of nations, hostile to Russia, to appear in the Balkans. As serious differences between Bulgaria and Serbia emerged in the beginning of 1913, would it not be better policy for Russia to reduce the chances of a Great Bulgaria coming into being and, instead, give a discreet push in the direction of creating a Great Serbia? No one could have any doubts that opposition to Austria was a constant of Serbian national policy; whereas there was no basic clash of interest between Bulgaria and Austria.

Sazonoff, the 'sad wobbler', did not formulate a firm policy on the basis of these considerations, although they formed part of the anti-Bulgarian prejudices of Russian diplomats in Belgrade, Athens and Bucharest. The most significant of these men was Hartwig, the Russian Minister in Belgrade, who actually encouraged Serbia to hold on to Macedonia.

In April 1913, Bulgaria asked Russia to arbitrate the difference with Serbia over Macedonia as provided for in the original treaty between the two countries. Tsar Nicholas immediately agreed, but urged Bulgaria not to stand on a 'formal' interpretation of her treaty with Serbia; rather, the Russians advised the Bulgarians to give the Serbs some additional territory from their share of Macedonia, over and above that area described in the treaty as the 'contested zone'. Thus, in the eyes of Ferdinand and his subjects, the Russian Tsar seemed to be spoiling the fruits of arbitration already. Now he seemed to be supporting Serbia in her demands, backed by the Serb military presence in the whole of Macedonia, for a revision of the original treaty and the cession by Bulgaria of those parts of Macedonia which the treaty assigned to her outright. Confidence in Russian impartiality was severely shaken. But Ferdinand's Russophil ministers persisted in the belief that the final arbitration of the Russian Emperor would solve the Serbian-Bulgarian difference.

On 30 May 1913 Prime Minister Geshoff resigned because he felt unable to fulfil his policy of keeping the Balkan alliance intact and believed war inevitable. He was replaced by Dr Daneff, an international lawyer fresh from the London negotiations. Daneff was determined to stick to the spirit and letter of the treaty with Serbia: a treaty was a treaty and its provisions were there to be fulfilled. A Russophil, he trusted Russia's assurances of arbitration and her desire to keep the Balkan alliance intact. But even he began to be discouraged by the lack of clarity of Russian diplomacy, and Sazonoff's 'wobbling' and inconsistency. In her desire to preserve the Balkan Alliance and in her indecisive half-measures to achieve this, Russia was in fact doing the work of her rival Austria, who wanted nothing better than to break it up.

On 1 June 1913, the day after the signing in London of the peace treaty between the Balkan Allies and Turkey, Serbia and Greece gave final treaty form to their agreement to act against Bulgaria and divide Macedonia between themselves. They also began separate secret negotiations with Turkey aimed against Bulgaria. Greece was especially concerned to have a large Turkish army concentrated at Chatalja to bring pressure on Bulgaria. Although no definite treaty resulted from these talks, the Turks were able to see for themselves how their victorious enemies had fallen out.

In Bulgaria tension was rising daily as evidence showed that the Serbian and Greek occupiers of Macedonia intended to remain there. The more moderate Macedonian elements in Bulgaria were demanding the territory guaranteed by the treaty. This demand often turned into a cry for 'Macedonian autonomy', the old cry which in effect implied the eventual union of Macedonia with Bulgaria. The extremists were afraid that the Bulgarian Government would accept a Russian arbitral award dividing Macedonia, and both Tsar Ferdinand and Dr Daneff were threatened with assassination if they resorted to Russian arbitration.

The situation in the Balkans was so obviously explosive that even Sazonoff felt that Russia had to act in some way to bring about a settlement. On 8 June 1913, Nicholas II sent personal messages to Tsar Ferdinand and to King Peter of Serbia, advising them to ask for arbitration as foreseen in the treaty.

In his answer Ferdinand pointed out that Bulgaria had already asked for arbitration under the terms of the treaty in April and that he still stood by this position.

The Serbian King's reply, full of expressions of pro-Russian sentiment, contained not one word about arbitration on the basis of the treaty. Instead, King Peter argued for a revision of the treaty. In essence this was the Serbian position: Serbia, while accepting the idea of 'arbitration', was not prepared that this should be restricted to the 'contested zone' as specified in the treaty. It was to cover the whole of Macedonia, including those parts which had been guaranteed outright to Bulgaria. It amounted to a bid for Macedonia.

CHAPTER 21

The Firebrand

In his despatches to *The Times*, James Bourchier, probably the best informed foreign observer in the Balkans, was full of alarm:

> The psychological moment seems not far off when the Powers, if they are to avert the catastrophe of another Balkan war, must display some energy in the assertion of their authority, and give evidence of their determination to maintain peace at all costs....
> The most dangerous feature of the situation is the Serbo-Bulgarian dispute. Whatever concessions Bulgaria may be induced to make in other directions, it is certain she will never abandon her claims to the districts in Western Macedonia already assigned to her by the Treaty with Serbia. On this point the whole nation is unanimous, from the King to the humblest peasant. The districts in question are the most thoroughly Bulgarian portion of Macedonia, and were recognized as such by the Turks.... They were the scenes of the Bulgarian insurrection of 1903, and have sent thousands of volunteers to the Bulgarian army in the present war.
> It is felt that no Bulgarian Government could hand over these regions to another nation without dishonour, and should Serbia persist in occupying them, an armed conflict will become inevitable.[1]

With his deep knowledge of the Balkans and the centuries-old enmities between its nationalities, Bourchier was convinced that catastrophe was almost inevitable. He saw only one hope of preventing it: firm and decisive action by the major European Powers. A fortnight before war broke out between the Balkan Allies he wrote in *The Times*: 'Those who wish well to all the young States can only hope that Europe will help them to arrange their differences. They have covered themselves with glory: let them beware lest a sordid quarrel should tarnish their laurels.'[2]

As Bourchier must have known, Europe, as a whole, could do nothing in a situation that involved the conflicting interests of Austria and Russia. Ferdinand certainly entertained no such illusions. During more than a quarter of a century as Bulgaria's ruler he had gained the absolute conviction that Europe was profoundly demoralized. It was a conviction, not a pessimistic pose, borne in upon him by the insights he had gained of power politics from his perch on the fence between the Triple Entente and the Triple Alliance.

By the third week of June 1913, the Bulgarian Government was fully aware of the secret Serbian-Greek agreement for the partition of Macedonia. General Savoff, the Commander-in-Chief of the Bulgarian army, pressed for the Bulgarian occupation of those territories definitely ceded to Bulgaria in her treaty with Serbia. Unless this was done, he wrote to one of his army commanders, these territories 'will remain in the hands of the Greeks and Serbians, since it is difficult to suppose that they will be peacefully handed over to us'.[3] He was equally anxious about the mood of the Bulgarian army, which was becoming increasingly restless.

On 22 June 1913, a ministerial council was held in Sofia. Savoff confronted the ministers with a demand based upon his estimate of the army's mood. He said that he could not guarantee its discipline for longer than ten days. The alternatives were either action or demobilization within that period. The picture he drew was as black and alarming as he could make it; he had been urging action against Serbia and Greece ever since April when the armies under his command were tied down in Eastern Thrace, while the Greeks and Serbians were consolidating their hold on Macedonia. He was absolutely convinced that the Bulgarian army could easily deal with them. As veteran of the 1885 war in which Bulgaria had defeated the Serbian invaders, and now flushed with the recent Bulgarian victories against the Turks, he had no doubts whatsoever.

Despite Savoff's strong arguments in favour of action, the ministerial council adopted a policy of peace. That same day Prime Minister Daneff, who was also Minister of Foreign Affairs, Savoff and another member of the Cabinet, went to see the Tsar in his palace at Vrana. There it was decided to ask Russia to make an arbitral award on the basis of the original treaty. Because of the temper of the army it was essential that the award be made as soon as possible. Daneff immediately informed Sazonoff that he was prepared to go to St Petersburg if Tsar Nicholas should find it possible to make an arbitral award between Bulgaria and Serbia within seven days.

Sazonoff was in one of his low moods, due in part to a severe gastric attack complicated by kidney troubles. He gave no indication to Daneff that he took cognizance of the request for a decision within a limited time. He seemed to be ignoring the critical situation in Bulgaria. His dilatoriness irritated Daneff who telegraphed to the Bulgarian Minister in St Petersburg:

> I instruct you to inform the Imperial Government that the formula of arbitration and the seven-day period for the awarding of the decision were our final proposal, made as an ultimate concession and permitting us to control the situation on the frontier which constitutes a great danger and does not permit of any delay. Sazonoff's answer is a definite refusal because he does not fix a limited period for the awarding of the decision. Under such circumstances we are forced to stop any further negotiations. Tomorrow Tosheff [the Bulgarian Minister at Belgrade] will be recalled.[4]

Daneff had purposely used sharp language in order to goad Russia into action. The effect of his words on Sazonoff, still suffering from stomach pains, was devastating. In a fit of pique and choler, he told the Bulgarian Minister in St Petersburg that he washed his hands of Bulgaria:

> You are acting on the advice of Austria. You are free. Thus the Serbs with their folly and you with your incorrect attitude have rejected Russia and Slavdom.
> The Russian Emperor did not expect an ultimatum with a time limit in which to declare his decisions concerning the Serbian-Bulgarian difference. However, he would have fulfilled his difficult mission with expedition. Now, after your declaration I communicate ours to you! Do not expect anything from us, and forget the existence of any of our engagements from 1902 until today![5]

The intemperance of the outbursts shook Daneff, a confirmed Russophil. The accusation of acting under Austrian influence he saw as a gratuitous insult, against which he immediately protested. But the Russian's reply had shaken his belief in the soundness of Russian policy-makers. Sazonoff, on the spur of the moment, had gone back on Russia's original promise to act as arbitrator when required. Russian arbitration was the keystone which had made the treaty. Its removal at that moment could only precipitate the disintegration of the Balkan Alliance, the edifice Russia had been so eager to build, and Austria to destroy. Despite Sazonoff's outburst, Daneff insisted on the necessity of having the arbitral award within the specified time. The Bulgarian Government, he explained, had used the promise of immediate settlement as a bribe in restraining the army. He pleaded that the Russian Government should notify him as quickly as possible as to when he could expect Tsar Nicholas's decison. Daneff still could not believe that Russia would do nothing to preserve the Balkan Alliance.

Sazonoff's rancour was characteristic of the attitude of Russian statesmen and diplomats towards the young Slav states of south-east Europe. The tone had been set by Alexander III. It was an assumption of paternalism towards 'the young Slav brothers'. Whenever the latter refused to act the role which Russia had quite irrationally assigned to them, they were taxed with 'ingratitude'. These politics of sentiment drew sustenance from what little remained of the old Panslav dream. Like any parent, Russia could turn nasty at what she chose to see as 'filial ingratitude'. Sazonoff's pique was preceded by a strikingly similar display of rancour a few days earlier by Izvolski, Sazonoff's predecessor as Foreign Minister, and now Russian Ambassador in Paris. Izvolski met Stancioff, the Bulgarian Minister in Paris, in Paléologue's office, and the three discussed Tsar Nicholas's original telegrams to the rulers of Bulgaria and Serbia, proposing to act as arbiter. Stancioff mentioned a town in Macedonia which, as he pointed out, was Bulgarian outright by the terms of the treaty. Paléologue described how, at these words, Izvolski interrupted the Bulgarian Minister and, 'while adjusting his monocle with an air of supreme insolence', said: 'My dear Stancioff, I think it very... discourteous of you to seek to limit the action of His Majesty the Emperor when he deigns to arbitrate between people of the Balkans.' The snub upset Stancioff and he left the room. Paléologue wrote in his diary that evening: 'He [Stancioff] must have left full of hatred which he will no doubt pour out in a telegram to the King. The Russians do not realize what harm they have been doing to themselves in the Balkans for over twenty years by their quite unwarranted arrogance!'[6]

Russia's attitude had by now seriously shaken Bulgarian confidence in Tsar Nicholas as arbitrator. It was inevitable that Russia's impartiality came to be doubted after she tried to press Bulgaria to cede to Serbia territory which was already allocated to Bulgaria in the treaty. It was as if during the course of the game, the umpire, before giving his decision, tried to alter the agreed rules in favour of one of the contestants. Even to Bulgaria's Russophil statesmen it seemed that Russia was trying to make up to Serbia at Bulgaria's expense in order to regain the prestige she had lost in Serbia by allowing Austria to frustrate her desire for an Adriatic outlet.

While Ferdinand and his ministers had their own doubts about Russia's reliability, the leading Macedonian activists in Bulgaria were convinced that arbitration and its acceptance would mean a sell-out.

Ferdinand and Daneff were still being threatened with assassination if they resorted to arbitration at St Petersburg.

Public opinion in Bulgaria, with few exceptions, was in favour of war. It seemed unthinkable that after the victories and sacrifices the prize, Macedonia, should elude Bulgaria. The entire Press called on the Tsar and Government to act, with opposition newspapers accusing the Government of 'treason' and 'defeatism'. 'We must take everything the Serbs have grabbed in Macedonia.... Forward to Belgrade!' was a typical headline. Ferdinand was under very great pressure. The Commander-in-Chief Savoff, the army commanders and the officers under them were urging on him the necessity to attack. Evidence reached them daily of new Serbian and Greek troop concentrations opposite the Bulgarian positions.

During the night of 29-30 June 1913, Bulgarian forward units attacked Serbian and Greek advance positions in Macedonia. The order to attack was given by General Savoff on 28 June, after he himself had obtained it from Tsar Ferdinand. The mood of the Bulgarian army on the eve of the attack can be gauged from an exchange of telegrams between the chiefs of staff of two Bulgarian armies on 29 June. From Sofia, Colonel Zhostoff, of the Third Army, sent an appeal to Colonel Zhekoff, of the Second Army near Macedonia: 'Daneff is off to Petersburg for arbitration.... Timidity has gained everyone.... The eyes of the nation and the army are on you. Save the nation. Tomorrow it will probably be too late. To do this you will receive no order and no carte blanche. You must act on your own. It is essential to act at once.'[7]

A few hours later Zhekoff replied: 'Set your mind at rest. We start today.' Not very long after he received a message from Sofia: 'We are all delighted. All Sofia without exception is jubilant.... I conjure you by all that is sacred to press forward and even to disregard any orders trying to stop you.'[8]

Zhostoff was right to anticipate such orders. He must have known that the order to attack by Tsar Ferdinand and General Savoff was given behind the back of the Bulgarian Cabinet. The Cabinet as a body never authorized or even sanctioned the attack. The Bulgarian ministers only heard officially of the advance of the armies at a meeting on 1 July. There and then, under threat of resignation, the Cabinet forced through a decision to halt the attack. Accordingly, Daneff gave General Savoff a written order to stop the attack on the morning of 1 July. One hour later, Ferdinand sent one of his confidants with an oral order to continue the attack. The bewildered Commander-in-Chief refused to change the command to stop the advance, which he had already given on the basis of Daneff's written order. Two days later King Ferdinand summoned General Savoff and relieved him of his command, 'because you did not fulfil my order to continue the attack'.[9] General Dimitrieff, a Russophil, took over his duties.

On the day that Daneff issued the Government's order to stop the attack Sazonoff, in St Petersburg, received a Bulgarian appeal to use his influence to stop counter-action by Serbia and Greece as Bulgaria had ordered her troops to halt. Sazonoff made a feeble attempt to do this but his representations were ignored as the Serbian and Greek troops began scoring successes against the Bulgarians.

From the point of view of Serbia and Greece the situation was perfect. For months, as their secret treaties now show, they had been anticipating war with Bulgaria. Even before the Bulgarian attack, troops from Montenegro had joined the Serbian forces for the war on Bulgaria. Now Bulgaria had put herself in the wrong as the aggressor. Weeks before, the French Minister in Sofia, Panafieu, had made a shrewd assessment of the intractable and provocative behaviour of Serbia: 'One would think that the Serbian government, relying on some support based on some arrangement, desires war with the responsibility of war to fall on Bulgaria.'[10] The Frenchman was hinting that the 'support based on some arrangement' came from the Russian minister in Belgrade, Hartwig, who advised the Serbian government that if the war must come, Serbia must see that Bulgaria provoked it. On 7 July, James Bourchier wrote in his diary in Sofia: 'Poor people. Hartwig has much to answer for. We are only at the beginning of this horrid tragedy.'[11]

The Second Balkan War was Bulgaria's disaster and a moment of supreme humiliation. The blows came hard and fast. Within a fortnight of Ferdinand's order to attack, Bulgaria was encircled by enemies. In the west the Bulgarian armies were defeated by the Serbs after a week of furious fighting on the left bank of the River Vardar. To the south the Greeks were winning. Reassured by their success, on 5 and 6 July, Greece and Serbia made formal declarations of war.

Romania, who had already mobilized her army and watched developments, declared war on Bulgaria on 10 July and immediately crossed the Danube with 150,000 men. Northern Bulgaria was denuded of troops and the Romanians, meeting no opposition, swept on towards Sofia. 'Their advance was more like manoeuvres on a large scale than a military campaign,'[12] in the words of one historian. The final blow came two days later when Turkey advanced into Thrace and recaptured Adrianople within ten days.

Attacked on all sides, Bulgaria's débâcle was complete. Bourchier wrote in his diary on 15 July: 'These days remind me of *Job*, Chapter 1. Calamity upon calamity.' That day Bourchier met the Russian Minister in Sofia, Neklyudoff, who blamed St Petersburg for what was happening. Neklyudoff 'expressed great disgust at his own Government; said it had "no policy"'.[13] That day also saw the resignation of Daneff and his Cabinet. The Prime Minister told the Sobranie that his policy was bankrupt. It was Daneff's admission that he had been wrong to rely on Russian help, an admission that coincided with a deep revulsion against Russia among the majority of Bulgarians. Russia had failed to stop the disastrous Romanian advance despite Daneff's repeated appeals. Many Bulgarians shared the opinion of the British Ambassador in St Petersburg that Russia had actually encouraged Romania to attack Bulgaria. The new Government that came to power two days later under Dr Vassil Radoslavoff was, inevitably, pro-Austrian.

The extent of the Bulgarian disaster was measured out at the Treaty of Bucharest on 10 August 1913, signed six weeks after Ferdinand had sanctioned the order to attack. Macedonia went to Serbia and Greece; Romania received the region between the lower reaches of the Danube and Black Sea, known as Southern Dobrudja. At the subsequent Treaty of Constantinople, Turkey regained Adrianople and much of Thrace. All that Bulgaria was allowed to retain for her military effort was an eighty-mile stretch of the Aegean coast with the poor port of Dedeagach, an area of the Rhodope mountain range, and a small triangle of land along the Black Sea: in all a net gain of 9,663 square miles. For this, Bulgaria had sustained the heaviest losses both in men (140,000 killed and wounded) and money, of all the combatants in both Balkan wars (the total estimated for all killed and wounded in the two wars, a period of some ten months, was 348,000 killed and wounded). Serbia and Greece had each nearly doubled their territories for far smaller sacrifices, amounting respectively to 70,000 and 30,000 killed and wounded.

The scale of the Bulgarian defeat was enormous. In *The World Crisis, 1911-1914,* published in 1923, Winston Churchill wrote:

It is possible that no nation ever contemplated its fortunes with more profound and desperate resolve than the Bulgarians at this juncture. All their sacrifices had been useless and worse than useless. All the fruits of their conquests had gone to aggrandize their rivals. They had been, as they considered, stabbed in the back and blackmailed by Romania, to whom they had given no provocation of any kind. They saw the great Powers, England in the van, forbid the return of the Turk to Adrianople without offering the slightest attempt to make their word good. They saw not only Salonika, but even Kavala, seized by the Greeks.

They saw large districts inhabited largely by the Bulgarian race newly liberated from the Turks pass under the yoke – to them scarcely less odious – of Serbians and Greeks. It was in these circumstances that the Bulgarian army, in the words of King Ferdinand, 'furled its standards' and retired to wait for better days.

This warlike and powerful Bulgaria, with its scheming King and its valiant peasant armies brooding over what to them seemed intolerable wrongs, was the dominant factor in the Balkans in 1914 and 1915.[14]

The magnitude of the Bulgarian disaster caught the imagination of Europe. The newspapers and the public who had closely followed the fighting in the Balkans, the biggest war on European soil within recent memory, were struck by the swiftness of Bulgaria's fall from triumph to disaster. Few believed that Tsar Ferdinand would manage to keep his throne. It was widely reported that he was a broken man and was preparing to abdicate. People like Paléologue, who knew him personally, believed these reports and considered that his high-strung temperament would not take the strain or his vanity the humiliation. Those who had known him as a foppish young man considered the end of his royal career a foregone conclusion. To nearly everyone's surprise, Ferdinand proved tough and resilient. James Bourchier was received by the King on 23 July, the day after the Turks and retaken Adrianople. He had expected to see a broken man, but later wrote in his diary:

July 23rd. Miserable days these; have no heart to do anything. Historic interview with King in Palace, 10.30 - 1. He was far less depressed than I expected, and even spoke of the scenery of Macedonia he has seen on his journey from Salonika by motor to Vrana. His description of his interviews with Savoff was thrilling; also his account of the nocturnal visit of Khristoff to Vrana *en route* to take Salonika.[15]

Five days before seeing Bourchier, Ferdinand received Count Tarnowski, the Austrian Minister in Sofia. Tarnowski, who had not seen the King for nearly a year, reported to Vienna that Ferdinand was 'mentally and physically unchanged' and 'did not appear at all broken'.[16]

Five days after the Treaty of Bucharest was signed, Tsar Ferdinand, accompanied by his two sons, entered Sofia on horseback at the head of the returning Bulgarian armies. Large crowds watched their arrival and greeted them with flowers. The Russian Minister Neklyudoff was there:

The Bulgarian soldiers, in their brown service uniforms, spoilt by sun and rain, bore traces of extreme fatigue on their emaciated and sunburnt faces, but nevertheless they marched with spirit and pride.

Behind the infantry ghost-like horses dragged the guns. Most of the generals whose names had become so popular in 1912 were with their troops. And the population of the town greeted them calmly and sympathetically, recognizing that they had done their whole duty, and had deserved well of their country.

Most of the soldiers taking part in the march were adorned with flowers, and so were King Ferdinand and his two sons, who headed the procession on horseback, and were greeted by the crowd without the slightest sense of hostility.[17]

During the march past and a *Te Deum* service in the cathedral, the Russian minister could not rid himself of the feeling that, whatever the responsibility of Ferdinand and his ministers for all that had occurred, 'each of the Bulgarian soldiers passing before me had, by his ardent patriotism and undaunted courage, earned a less piteous result for his country, and deserved a really triumphant entry into his home'.[18] Neklyudoff felt bitterly about his country's and his own failure 'to prevent this melancholy ending to our influence in Bulgaria'.[19]

In a subsequent proclamation to the Bulgarian army Ferdinand with effect struck a note of mingled resignation and defiance: 'The Bulgarian people, as proudly tempered as a steel blade, stand erect in the tempest, braving calumny as they defied death on the field of battle. At the voice of their leaders, they have furled their glorious standards for the days to come and taken up once more the patient work of reorganization, meditating on the ancient Eastern saying: "All things pass".'[20]

It was the Russians who were most of all surprised that the defeats and disasters of Bulgaria did not serve as the signal for Ferdinand's downfall. Neklyudoff was irritated by those of his countrymen who tried to explain the fact that Ferdinand remained in power by the theory 'that the Bulgarian nation had become so accustomed to servitude that Ferdinand could lead it whither he would'.[21] Russians who thought so had got hold of the wrong end of the stick, wrote Neklyudoff. The truth was that throughout the two Balkan wars the majority of Bulgarians had been completely at one with their King in their ardent desire to realize the frontiers of Bulgaria as promised by the Treaty of San Stefano. Before the wars, Ferdinand had not been able to achieve real popularity in Bulgaria mainly because Russian disapproval of him was seen by many Bulgarians as the stumbling block to better relations with Russia. This Bulgarian objection to Ferdinand lost its strength with the general revulsion against Russia in 1912-13.

However excruciating to Tsar Ferdinand the consciousness of his enormous error in sanctioning the Bulgarian attack of the night of 29-30

June, he was determined to show to Europe that the tragedy had not broken him. In this he was not unsuccessful. Only seven weeks after the Treaty of Bucharest had set the seal on Bulgaria's defeat, Germany's Kaiser William was expressing the fear that Ferdinand was preparing to 'erupt into Thrace' and attack Constantinople. It hardly needs saying that Ferdinand had no such plans. But the Kaiser's fear was a measure of Ferdinand's success in concealing his real state of mind.

He only really dropped his guard once, at the end of December 1913, when he received Neklyudoff who was leaving Sofia to take up a new post in Stockholm. The outgoing Russian Minister was stung by Ferdinand's bitter reproaches against Russia for deserting Bulgaria in her hour of need, and replied: 'Sir, the Bulgarians have drawn their misfortunes on themselves, and have forced Russia to give up all attempts to come to their assistance. And Your Majesty knows better than anyone when the irreparable blow was struck at Bulgaria's interests: it was on the 29th of June last. Your Majesty knows as well as I do that I had nothing to do with that day of misfortune, of which I was the first dupe.'[22]

At this, as Neklyudoff recalled in his memoirs, 'Ferdinand cast his most evil glance at me, but restrained himself, and after a short silence, without raising his eyes, he said: "Yes, that was a great mistake." Then he rose and took leave of me.'[23]

It is hard to say what specifically caused King Ferdinand to give the fateful order to attack. He never answered the question which intrigued his contemporaries. They could not understand how a man of his undoubted gifts, intelligence and ability, who not only had managed to keep his seat on the Bulgarian throne for twenty-six years against such heavy initial odds, but had made such a striking success of his tenure, could suddenly make such a catastrophic mistake. King George V expressed this sarcastically to the Austrian Ambassador in October 1913: 'Your friend Ferdinand, with all his cleverness and intrigues, has made a fine mess of it!'[24]

Among the factors that influenced Ferdinand's decision, fear of assassination at the hands of the Macedonians cannot be discounted. It would have been foolish to disregard their threats at the best of times, let alone at a moment when, as they saw the situation, the future of Macedonia seemed to depend entirely on Ferdinand's willingness to act. It was open season for political assassins. King George of Greece was murdered in March in Salonika; just over a year later Archduke Francis Ferdinand was to be shot in Sarajevo.

At the time Ferdinand cannot have been untouched by the mood of euphoric chauvinism in Bulgaria. A mood which was further inflamed by anger at the unwarranted and disloyal behaviour of the Serbs and

Greeks in Macedonia. No Bulgarian doubted the superior fighting ability of the Bulgarian soldier against the Serbs and Greeks. The Greeks in particular, were not to be taken seriously: hadn't they let themselves be ignominiously beaten by the *Turks* in the brief war of 1897? Such was the language of the Press and people. More important, as far as influencing Ferdinand was concerned, it was also the language of the Bulgarian army commanders.

However, as always, Ferdinand's decision to sanction the advance of the army, was based not on military, but on diplomatic considerations. Nearly everything points to the fact that he sanctioned the advance because he saw it merely as a demonstration, a tactical move, a mere rattle of the sabre, based on 'the idea that through a threat of force Russia might be brough to show more favour to the Bulgarian cause'[25] in making the arbitral award.

Ferdinand, knowing how keen Russia was to keep the Balkan League intact, may well have hoped to compel Russian diplomacy to make a speedy settlement. The advance of the Bulgarian army was not accompanied by a declaration of war. The argument that was possibly uppermost in his mind was that the Bulgarian forces were only ordered into that part of Macedonia occupied by Serbs and Greeks which, according to the treaty, Bulgarian troops had the right to occupy conjointly with the former. According to the historian Ernst Helmreich:

> Military action was thus intended as a means of strengthening Bulgaria's position in the settlement which was to come through the mediation of Russia. The policy of arbitration was never abandoned at Sofia in these days. On 30 June Daneff handed to the Russian legation the requested memoir stating Bulgaria's position at length, and announced his readiness to leave for St Petersburg. A Russian steamer lay at Varna ready to take him to Russian soil. The immediate outbreak of war through the refusal of Serbia and Greece to countermand the order to attack dashed these hopes of arbitration. Daneff did not have to sail the Black Sea.[26]

If Ferdinand had decided on a policy of war it seems likely that he would have first reached an understanding with Romania and Austria to make sure of the neutrality of the former and at least a demonstration of active support from the latter. As it was, he walked into a Serbian-Greek trap by providing them with the *casus belli*. But the greatest miscalculation was the Bulgarian failure to gauge to what extent Russia was pursuing an anti-Bulgarian policy at the time, and how seriously the spectre of Bulgaria in possession of Constantinople and in control of the

Straits had alarmed Russia. Only a weakened, humbled Bulgaria could exorcize it.

By striking the first overt blow, Ferdinand inevitably incurred general odium. He was accused of treachery towards his allies and of greed for conquest. The charge of treachery seemed obvious enough, since Bulgaria had made the first military move. That plain fact quite obscured the evidence, then only scanty, that Serbia and Greece had secretly concluded their anti-Bulgarian alliance aimed at denying Bulgaria the possession of her agreed share of Macedonia. As for the other charge, that of greed for conquest, it can be said in Ferdinand's defence that he had merely tried to secure territory which had been assigned, by prior agreement, as Bulgaria's rightful share. But only a few people in Europe at the time were prepared to listen to Ferdinand's side of the case; for he had not only openly put himself in the wrong, he had also been unsuccessful. The prevalent image of Ferdinand as a man who alone had brought punishment on himself by his own duplicity and greed was a morally satisfying one.

Ferdinand's fatal decision, however, had had a far more personal motive: to make up for his earlier error, the error that had resulted in the disposition of the Balkan armies on the eve of the Second Balkan War. That initial error must have weighed heavily on the Tsar for it stemmed directly from his own nature and temperament: it was due to his bedazzlement by the vision of Byzantium. This infatuation had resulted in the bloody Bulgarian onslaughts against the Chataldja line, the modern wall of Byzantium, while the Serbs and Greeks were occupying Macedonia. The thought that Bulgaria had entered the war for Macedonia, only to find that she had sacrificed tens of thousands of men for a historical vision, cannot have been easy for him to bear.

This dream of Byzantium had not been Ferdinand's alone. King Constantine I and Queen Sophie of Greece, the German Kaiser's sister, were excited by an old prophecy that claimed that when 'Constantine and Sophia' reigned, Constantinople would become Christian again – naturally, it was assumed, under their aegis. The beautiful Queen Marie of Romania also dreamed of being crowned in St Sophia. The *fin de siècle* artists and writers of the Decadent movement had done much to popularize the idea of Byzantium. The actress Sarah Bernhardt, the painters Gustav Klimt, Alphonse Mucha and other artists, the writers Stefan George, Gabriel d'Annunzio and many lesser writers, all helped to create a Byzantine vogue which spread into the decorative arts. In 1910, even Paris took on a Byzantine appearance with the completion of the basilica of the Sacre-Coeur. Ferdinand, however, was not impelled solely by this current fashion for Byzantium, although it was certainly a seductive aspect of the 'perilous consistency' which the dream of

Byzantium assumed for him in the first weeks of the war against
Turkey.

Nearly all Ferdinand's critics have accused him of forfeiting his
country's prospects for the sake of a romantic illusion. Indeed, it is
undeniable that in the first flush of the Bulgarian victories of 1912 there
came for him a moment when the vision of Byzantium overwhelmed
him, swamping his natural caution. But Ferdinand's delusion seems less
eccentric and extravagant when it is recalled that, at the time, the rest
of the world expected his appearance in Constantinople. It seemed the
natural, logical, and in the opinion of some – including the Kaiser –
well-merited outcome of the war.

The humiliation of having failed twice, of turning mistake into
disaster, was unbearable. In a rare moment of weakness he complained
to his Foreign Minister: 'I have bcome the laughing stock of the entire
world. I dare not show myself in Europe.'[27] The latter worry loomed
large as he was already impatient to go abroad.

His fear of ridicule and of being snubbed abroad was by no means
fanciful. While in Vienna that autumn he met King Alphonso of Spain.
The twenty-seven-year-old Spaniard, Ferdinand's junior by twenty-
five years, later boasted to Paléologue in Paris:

> In Vienna I also saw your august friend Ferdinand of Bulgaria....
> What a scoundrel!...A real scoundrel....I made no bones of telling
> him what I thought about his conduct during the second Balkan war.
> But he swore by the Gods that it was not he who had opened fire
> against his old allies, that he had simply defended himself....At that I
> gave him such a look that he got entangled in all kinds of vague
> explanations of which I could make neither head nor tail....
>
> What I did understand only too well were his last words, which I
> quote to you exactly: 'I have made mistakes; I know all the
> reproaches that can be made against me. But I won't leave it at
> that!...My hour will come. I shall have my revenge; I shall set fire to
> the four corners of Europe!'[28]

CHAPTER 22

The Wrong Horse

—◦❦◦—

The effect of the Balkan Wars was to increase the tension amongst the major European powers and their preparations for war. A new German army bill in the first quarter of 1913 enormously increased the nation's armed forces and brought into being the mass-army. The breathtaking swiftness and decisiveness of the battles in the Balkans encouraged the deep-rooted predilection of Europe's military planners for frontal attack with superior forces. The fighting in the Balkans obscured for them the lessons of the Russo-Japanese War of 1904-5 in which the paralysing power of machine guns against frontal attacks foreshadowed the trenches of the First World War. They overlooked the fact that even the Balkan fighting provided a foretaste of the 1914-18 War pattern when the Bulgarians were bogged down outside Constantinople.

The Germans, who gave the signal in what became a race for preparedness, had no doubt that war was near. In February 1913, Germany's Chief-of-Staff General von Moltke wrote to his Austrian counterpart: 'a European war must come sooner or later in which ultimately the struggle will be one between Germanism and Slavism.'[1] This was written just before the outbreak of the Second Balkan War from which emerged a Serbia greatly grown in arrogance, territory and ambition. Serbia's plans were summed up by her Prime Minister Nikola Pašić when he declared: 'The first round is won; now we must prepare for the second round, against Austria.'[2]

Now that the Serbs living under Turkish rule had been liberated, the time had come to liberate those under Habsburg rule in Bosnia-Hercegovina, Croatia, and southern Hungary. Serbia's bitterness over Austria's 1908 annexation of the former was deepened by Vienna's later refusal to allow her access to the Adriatic. The British Ambassador in Vienna privately summed up the situation in a prophetic letter to Sir Arthur Nicolson in May 1913:

288

As soon as peace is restored in the Balkans, the Austrian authorities anticipate that Serbia will begin a far-reaching agitation in the Serb-inhabited districts of the Dual Monarchy, and as this country cannot allow any dismemberment of her provinces without incurring the danger of the whole edifice crumbling down, we have all the elements in the near future of another violent crisis in this part of the world, which may not unlikely end in the final annexation of Serbia by the Dual Monarchy. That, however, will lead to a war with Russia, and possibly to a general conflict in Europe.[3]

The conflict between little Serbia, brimming over with self-confidence, and the exasperated and anxious Austro-Hungarian giant nearly broke out in the autumn of 1913, when Serbian troops infiltrated into Northern Albania. In what could later be seen as a dress rehearsal for July 1914, Austria sent an ultimatum on 18 October, demanding Serb withdrawal from Albania within a week. On this occasion Serbia complied to the letter and announced on 25 October that the troops had been withdrawn.

Though safely weathered on that occasion, the Austrian-Serbian crisis of October 1913 had fateful consequences. It allowed Austria's statesmen to feel that in future they could count on Germany's full support in a conflict with Serbia and therefore, inevitably, with Russia. At a tea party given in the German embassy in Vienna in his honour on 26 October, Kaiser William II told Berchtold, the Austrian Foreign Minister, that,

Panslavism and with it Russia have played their role in the Balkans, but simultaneously the Slavic states have been strengthened in a fashion that gives Germany and Austria pause to think. The war between East and West cannot be avoided indefinitely and if Austria-Hungary is then open to an attack in the flank by a respectable military power, this could have a fateful influence on the struggle of the nations.... The Slavs were not born to rule but to serve. This they must be taught....

Lest Berchtold should have any doubts about the full import of his words, the Kaiser added: 'You can be certain I stand behind you and am ready to draw the sword whenever your action makes it necessary... whatever comes from Vienna is for me a command.'[4]

Tsar Ferdinand was resting at his estate in Austria-Hungary at the time of the 1913 Austrian ultimatum to Serbia. Stancioff, who was with him, later told Paléologue that the Tsar was 'sad and tired but not at all discouraged; his only care is to help us to reconstruct our moral and material damage; he is full of hope for the future'.[5] Just before his departure from Sofia, Ferdinand had seen Tarnowski, the Austrian minister, and told him: 'I merely want to rest in the solitude of my forests where, for a time, I can try to forget the many enemies who conspired against me and against whom I am full of hatred.'[6] He singled out the Kaiser, whose 'contemptible' policy had harmed Bulgaria even more than Russia had done. Even at the height of the Second Balkan War Ferdinand had already complained to Tarnowski about Kaiser William's 'irony and insults'.[7] On that occasion, back in July, he taunted the Austrian for his country's failure to attack Serbia: 'How is it possible that Vienna is not seizing this opportunity to finish off the Serbs? Germany is doing you a great disservice by preventing you from going to war. One kick would knock out Serbia.'[8] Austria's chances were excellent, as Russia was not yet ready for war. A few days later he again saw Tarnowski and once more blamed Kaiser William for preventing an Austro-Hungarian attack against Serbia. A perfect opportunity to 'wipe Serbia off the map' had been missed. In any case war between Austria-Hungary and Russia was 'unavoidable'. He said he wanted an alliance with Vienna and added: 'The purpose of my life is the destruction of Serbia.'[9]

Ferdinand was keenly aware that the outcome of the Second Balkan War had severely limited the efficacy of his chief diplomatic weapon, his flexibility. Bulgaria now had one fixed determination: to reverse the hated Treaty of Bucharest, 'this cruel butchery' as Ferdinand called it. Russia's patronage of Serbia made it inevitable that Ferdinand, however he might hate it, should turn towards Austria. Once again it was a case of 'the enemy of my enemy is my friend'.

It was mortifying enough for Ferdinand, after years of being the object of the rival wooing of Austria and Russia, to be forced into the distasteful role of a suitor for Vienna's favour. He now also had to put up with the reserve which the Austrians affected when receiving his advances. Perhaps the hardest to bear was the frosty irony of the elegant Berchtold.

On 6 November 1913, Ferdinand was in Vienna to press his suit on the Austrians. However unpalatable, he worked hard at it: he had a meeting with Berchtold at the Coburg Palace in the morning, next drove to Schönbrunn where he was received by Emperor Francis Joseph; and then returned to the Austrian Foreign Ministry for a second meeting with the Foreign Minister. Berchtold's own account of his two meetings with the King on that day show how relentlessly Ferdinand tried to obtain Austria's help. Berchtold played hard to get and tried not to show his contentment at the Bulgarian offers of help against Serbia, the thorn in Austria's flesh. Both Bulgaria and Austria, Ferdinand told him, had reasons to be dissatisfied with the result of the Balkan wars. The Great Serbia that had come into being was as full of hate against Austria as against Bulgaria; the entire Serbian army now thought of nothing but war against Austria. There was not a single Serb who did not consider that the conquest of Bosnia-Hercegovina should be the next goal of Serbian policy; the Serbs were determined to extirpate the Albanian race and destroy Albania, Austria's protégée.

At one point Ferdinand evidently got carried away. He told Berchtold that, in fighting Serbia, Bulgaria had not only fought for herself but also for Austria-Hungary. This gave Berchtold an irresistible opening: if, as Ferdinand had just said, Bulgaria had fought on Austria's behalf, how could it be explained that Bulgaria had concluded the 1912 treaty with Serbia which contained an anti-Austrian clause? The Tsar had known that, sooner or later, the Austrians would bring up this most awkward of points. He exclaimed: 'I know from where this comes and I am well aware of the infamous calumnies which all come from the same source. It is the vengeance of Russia who cannot forgive me for having destroyed her Panslav dreams.'[10]

Ferdinand could not deny outright the anti-Austrian provisions in the Bulgarian-Serbian treaty. Indeed it would have been risky to do so. Although the treaty was secret, he was aware that the Austrians, at the least, knew of its existence and he could not know how detailed a knowledge they had of its text.

It was just as well that he did not go too far. A fortnight later the French newspaper *Le Matin* published the full text of the treaty while Ferdinand was still in Austria. It is not known who gave the text to the newspaper, but the intention was clearly to sabotage a *rapprochement* between Bulgaria and Austria-Hungary. The Tsar's talks in Vienna had considerably worried Serbia and her patron Russia, and there were rumours of a military agreement between Vienna and Sofia. After the revelations in *Le Matin*, Russia put out a diplomatic feeler via the French embassy at St Petersburg and got the French to put it about that Ferdinand had abdicated, that Prince Boris would succeed him and would marry a Russian grand duchess. An official denial had to be put out in Sofia.

As was to be expected, public opinion in Austria was indignant to learn that Tsar Ferdinand had pledged himself the previous year to back Serbia with arms against Austria-Hungary. Ferdinand told one of his Bulgarian advisers that his position *vis-à-vis* the Viennese public had become 'impossible'. Nevertheless, on 27 November, only three days after the appearance of *Le Matin,* he nerved himself to face the eighty-three-year-old Francis Joseph at Schönbrunn. There is no detailed record of their meeting but a few days later in Sofia the Bulgarian

official in charge of the Tsar's political Cabinet told the counsellor of
the Austrio-Hungarian legation that the Tsar had been deeply grateful
and touched by the 'exceptionally gracious' way in which the Emperor
had received him.

It was only politic for the Bulgarian Tsar to try to appear satisfied
with his reception in Vienna. But in fact the strain of the visit showed
once he was back in Sofia. 'According to my private informant,' wrote
Paléologue in his diary, 'he was in extreme ill-temper, railing against
"that idiot, that old dotard of a Francis Joseph", against his heir the
Archduke, against Berchtold, hustling and jumping down the throat of
anyone who came near him, and as usual in such a mood, giving full vent
to foul abuse.'[11]

His bad mood was only in part due to the fact that he was forced by
circumstances to pay court to Vienna. More galling was the realization
that his advances brought no'tangible result. His offers to Austria of an
alliance had been sympathetically received, but both the Emperor and
Berchtold objected that a closer relationship between Vienna and Sofia
depended on improved relations between Bulgaria and Romania.
Romania had had links with the Triple Alliance for thirty years. Thus
Bulgaria would have to make her alliance not only with Austria but
with Austria's allies as well. Berchtold would gladly have accepted
Ferdinand's offer were it not for the strong objections of the German
Kaiser. William II was going through a phase of intense dislike of
Ferdinand and liked and trusted the aged King Carol of Romania. He
was also on good terms with both Greece and Turkey.

Ferdinand knew a rapprochement with Romania would prove
impracticable, for Bulgaria's deep resentment against the Romanian
'stab in the back' during the Second Balkan War was too great and no
Bulgarian could accept the Bucharest Treaty as final. He was infuriated
by the Kaiser's failure to see that Romania, who was casting an
increasingly covetous eye on the Austro-Hungarian region of Transylvania, was moving ever closer to the Entente. The coming world war in
which Romania eventually fought against the Central Powers, proved
him right.

Apart from Bulgaria's foreign difficulties, Ferdinand and the Government were faced with the urgent need for money at home; after the
two Balkan wars the State coffers were almost empty. A foreign loan
was an absolute necessity. Ferdinand wanted to obtain the credits in
France. A loan from an Entente Power would have acted as a counter-
poise to his diplomatic approaches to the Central Powers. But the
political balancing act was no longer easy in the Europe of early
1914. Russia was well aware of Bulgaria's financial need and determined
to use it as a means of regaining her previous influence in Sofia. She

imposed a virtual veto on a French loan without the implied condition of Bulgaria's political vassalage to herself.

At the beginning of 1914 Savinsky, the new Russian Minister, arrived to take up his post in Sofia with secret orders to assist in the downfall of the pro-Austrian Government of Radoslavoff. Bulgaria, he told Ferdinand, could obtain a French loan with ease: it merely needed the replacement of the present Government by a Russophil one. This was both blatant and inept. Russia's attitude led to redoubled efforts by the Bulgarian Government to obtain the money elsewhere and in July 1914 a massive loan was contracted with Germany. Austria's Berchtold had worked hard to arrange it and overcome the Kaiser's objections. While the terms of the loan gave Germany important economic concessions in Bulgaria, it involved no political engagements of the kind Russia had been trying to impose as a condition for a French loan. Thus when war came to Europe in July 1914, Bulgaria was still technically uncommitted to either party and Ferdinand's hands were free.

One day in mid-June 1914, Ferdinand was crossing Serbia on his way back to Sofia from Austria when he heard raised voices and a commotion outside the door of the compartment in which he was sitting. He was told that the Serbian *chef de train* on the Orient Express had appeared in the Tsar's carriage and demanded that the compartment in which he was sitting be opened. 'I must see the Coburger!' he shouted and told Ferdinand's adjutant who was trying to dissuade him, that he was acting on orders from Belgrade and would stop the train if the door of the compartment was not opened. Only after the train stopped did Ferdinand's entourage succeed in making the *chef de train* retreat.

Ferdinand was outraged. On arriving in Sofia, he sent Dobrovich, the head of his political Cabinet, to Count Tarnowski, the Austrian Minister, to inform him of this most recent Serbian affront. Ten days later the assassination of Archduke Francis Ferdinand at Sarajevo supplied him with far more powerful anti-Serb ammunition. Again, Dobrovich was dispatched to Count Tarnowski. On this occasion he brought a document which could not fail to strengthen the resolve of the war party in Vienna to crush Serbia once and for all. It was a report by the Bulgarian Minister in Belgrade describing Serbian reactions to the Sarajevo murders. Ferdinand's decision to let Vienna see the report made his boast to the King of Spain of the previous autumn appear less theatrical. It is worth quoting as an example of one of the sparks that went into the blowing-up of Europe: 'The news of the assassination of the Archduke Francis Ferdinand was an agreeable surprise for all Serbians. Rejoicing was all the greater due to the outrage having been committed on the anniversary of the battle of Kossovo [in 1389 between the Serbians and the invading Turks]. Everyone in Belgrade sees it as a new victory for the Great Serbian idea and as a step towards the realization of their ideal: the union of all Serbians.'

The Archduke, wrote the Minister, had been considered as an obstacle towards realizing that ideal. The report continued:

> The editor of 'Balkan' [a Belgrade newspaper] came to see me at the Legation and to tell me that the assassination had delighted all Serbians and that their only regret is that the shot had not also killed the old Emperor, after whose death Serbians expect the monarchy to fall and rich plunder for themselves. The general impression is that the assassination had been expected.
>
> From my conversations with several Serbians I gathered the impression that consciences here are not clear, for it is evident that the assassination was the result of a plot hatched in Belgrade. The two assassins had been in Belgrade for several weeks.
>
> The secretary of the Russian Legation said to me that the assassination was a fortunate thing for Austria and for Europe, as the Archduke Francis Ferdinand had been solely interested in personal glory and would have hurled the State into the abyss. He went on to abuse Austria and her dynasty.[12]

Sarajevo not only provided Ferdinand with welcome fuel for the fire-brands in Vienna. At the same time it eliminated the Archduke Francis Ferdinand as the next Habsburg emperor. King Ferdinand had been convinced that the Austrian Archduke regarded him as an enemy and had dreaded the moment when he would succeed to the throne. It was ironic that both men were targets for Serbian assassins. After Sarajevo, an Austrian consul in Serbia reported to Vienna about Serbian reactions to the assassinations and quoted one Serbian official as exclaiming, 'Now, it's the turn of the other Ferdinand [meaning the Tsar of Bulgaria] and then we can quietly complete our work!'[13]

After Sarajevo, an Austrian-Bulgarian alliance appeared to be much more attractive to Vienna. As it happened, Count Berchtold had completed a memorandum urging such an alliance four days before the assassination. He took it out, added a postscript blaming Serbia for the murder and sent it to Berlin together with a letter from Francis Joseph to William II. In it the old Emperor declared that peace could only be assured if 'Serbia, which at present constitutes the focus of Panslav policy, is eliminated as a political factor in the Balkans'.[4] William received the messages in Potsdam on 5 July and there and then, without any serious consultations, encouraged Austria to start a war against Serbia and promised Germany's backing if Russia threatened to support Serbia. The Kaiser did not think then that he was making a decision for

war; he was envisaging a diplomatic confrontation which would bring
prestige to Germany and humiliate Serbia. But his promise to back
Austria, whatever her decision, was one of the major steps towards war.
At Potsdam he also told the Austrian Ambassador that he considered a
treaty between Austria and Bulgaria 'by no means congenial'[15] but
would in no way object to its conclusion.

Having received Kaiser William's sanction, the Austrians lost little
time in trying to obtain a Bulgarian alliance. The roles were reversed:
Ferdinand, until only recently the suitor of Vienna, became the object of
Austrian wooing. Count Tarnowski, Austria's Minister in Sofia, was to
find to his chagrin and growing frustration that far from falling into
Austria's arms, the Tsar had become the most elusive of quarries. The
Minister kept trying without success to obtain an audience. On 16 July
he anxiously cabled Berchtold that he had been informed that Ferdinand
was intending to leave for Bayreuth. Berchtold was horrified at the
threatened Wagnerian interference in his plans and immediately
ordered Tarnowski to 'do everything' to prevent Ferdinand from
leaving Bulgaria at that moment. He left it up to Tarnowski's 'skill' how
to achieve this. The Austrian Minister urged Ferdinand at least to delay
his departure until the expected Austrian *démarche* in Belgrade.

On 23 July, the day of the Austrian ultimatum to Serbia, Radoslavoff,
the Prime Minister, told a nearly frantic Tarnowski that the reasons
why the Tsar did not want to see him were personal and not political: he
had been wounded by the 'unfriendly' way in which Tarnowski had
behaved to him the previous autumn in Vienna. Tarnowski denied this
and objected that Ferdinand had been friendly towards him on several
occasions since then. Radoslavoff then said that Ferdinand was in 'one of
his moods'.[16]

By 31 July, three days after Austria had declared war on Serbia, the
Austrian Minister had still not seen Ferdinand. The Tsar, he cabled
Vienna, was on 'an autombole excursion'. It was, he added, a case of
'characteristic nonchalance'.[17]

Unlike the German Kaiser who went on a three-week Norwegian
cruise on his yacht *Hohenzollern* after giving Austria the 'go-ahead' on 5
July, Tsar Ferdinand's nonchalance was feigned. The great European
crisis which he and others had expected so long was at hand. Despite the
recent loan from the Central Powers, he remained uncommitted to
either side in Europe. He was determined to remain so as long as
possible, until it became clear which way the wind was blowing. Now
was not the moment to decide for one or the other side. In a string of
telegrams to Vienna the frustrated Tarnowski bewailed the fact that
'Bulgaria, whose attitude will be of decisive significance for us, is today
quite uncommitted. It is by no means impossible that her King will be in

a position to upset the calculations on which our plan is founded.'[18] Had it not been for Germany's opposition to an alliance with Bulgaria, Ferdinand by now would have been firmly committed to Austria and not open to probable bids for support from the Entente.

The Austrian declaration of war on Serbia on 28 July had been greeted with joy in Bulgaria. It was generally seen as the first step in a process that would at last lead to the union of Bulgaria and Macedonia. Madame Petroff was on her way to Bulgaria by Danube steamer from Vienna when she heard the news:

> On the steamer there was a crowd of Bulgarian students returning to their country. They had sensed the coming storm and had chosen to return to their homes.... It was announced that Austria-Hungary had declared war on Serbia. A tremendous 'hurrah' went up from the steamer. The Bulgarian students and we trembled with joy. At last! 'La revanche', that word which had so often been pronounced with enthusiasm by all true Frenchmen, was at last sounding for us! Although mere spectators, we were going to see our treacherous and cowardly allies vanquished and humbled.[19]

Her artless *Schadenfreude* was no doubt shared by the majority of her compatriots, whose feelings about their former Balkan allies were given expression in a popular song opening with the words 'Allies, robbers'. The instinctive reaction was to see the war against Serbia as punishment for her successful plot to rob Bulgaria of the fruits of victory of the war against Turkey. But whatever the popular mood, Ferdinand and the Government, despite its pro-Austrian orientation, determined to stay on the side-lines. From the very beginning of the European war both sides made offers to Bulgaria to coax her from the strict neutrality she had declared; but Ferdinand made it clear from the outset that his price was the revision of the Treaty of Bucharest. Above all, this meant Macedonia. The assassination at Sarajevo had brought the chance to recoup his losses much sooner than he could have expected. He was determined that this time there would be no mistakes.

The auction for Bulgaria's support was to last well over a year. The rivalry in Sofia between the representatives of the Allies and the Central Powers was explicit. An instance of this was recounted by H.D. Napier, the British Military attaché in Sofia, on the occasion of the State funeral in July 1915 of the Bulgarian Exarch:

> The procession in which all the diplomats took part, was most imposing. On leaving the building from whence the procession started I noticed that the German and Austrian Legation Staffs with a

formidable array of military uniforms, had obtained a leading place in the procession just behind the Ministers of the various foreign countries. They were followed by the staffs of the Entente Legations. The Ministers of all the foreign nations were leading, the British and Austrian being side by side.

From a spectacular point of view this did not signify as regards the Ministers who were all in much the same diplomatic uniform, but I thought the effect of the German and Austrian military uniform strutting along in front of the British, French and Italian all through the town was most undesirable. So, as soon as a favourable bend in the road came in sight, by gradually edging up we were able to insert ourselves in front of the Germans and Austrians, which must have annoyed them considerably. This manoeuvre was, however, not in time to stop several cinematograph operators who photographed the procession at the start and doubtless only those samples reached Berlin.[20]

Turkey's entry into the war on the side of the Central Powers in the autumn of 1914 considerably increased the value of Bulgarian participation. The importance of Bulgaria to both sides increased even more with the opening of the Dardanelles campaign in April 1915. The Central Powers needed Bulgaria's goodwill to transport to Turkey much needed arms and ammunition. Conversely, for the Allies, a Bulgarian attack against Constantinople could have ensured success at Gallipoli and opened up the Straits to war supplies for Russia. As First Lord of the British Admiralty, Winston Churchill had from the outset anticipated the importance of seizing the Gallipoli Peninsula if Turkey entered the war on the side of the Central Powers. Together with Lloyd George he backed a visit to the Balkans in September 1914, of Noel Buxton, an influential Liberal MP. Through Buxton, and his talks with the leaders of the Balkan states, Churchill was working towards the goal of a new league of all the Balkan states built upon their common hatred of Turkey. In his enthusiasm, Churchill overlooked the fact that the divisions between the Balkan states were now greater than their hatred of Turkey.

By June 1915, Churchill was insisting that Britain's main diplomatic effort in south-east Europe should be to bring Bulgaria into the war on the side of the Allies. He wrote to Lloyd George on 25 June: 'I am all for playing the game right out to get Bulgaria. She is the real prize, & it is only if and when we know she will not come that we should consider Greek & Serbian interests.'[21] Churchill was increasingly annoyed by what he considered the dilatoriness and lack of initiative on the part of the Foreign Office in making concrete offers to Bulgaria. On 26 June he wrote to Lord Edgar Cecil, Under-Secretary of State for Foreign Affairs, and insisted that the Foreign Office should not 'whittle away the definite offers which have been made to her.... For the present we are in the Bulgarian camp: let us stay there. She is worth all the rest put together, and she would bring all the rest in too.'[22]

The essential difficulty that faced Allied diplomacy was the nature of the prize Bulgaria wanted: the unconditional promise of Macedonia at the end of the war. With Serbia as their ally, the Allies could only promise Macedonia to Bulgaria with Serbian consent. Serbia, fighting the Austrians, adamantly refused to make such a concession. In his memoirs, Sir Edward Grey expressed his frustration and irritation with the Serbian ally:

> Never were dice so heavily loaded against anything as against Allied diplomacy in 1915.... Serbia was under obligation to the Allies for help given; but for their presence in the war Serbia must be crushed; her only hope of survival lay in an Allied victory. In that event Serbia would not only survive intact, but would get large acquisitions of Slav territory at present held by Austria. These gains would have been made possible only by the efforts and sacrifice and victory of the Allies. We were, therefore, entitled to press Serbia to make concessions to Bulgaria that were essential to the safety of Serbia and the common cause.
>
> Serbia was quite intractable. In vain I pointed out that France, Britain, and Russia had no troops to spare and could send none to help Serbia; that an attack by Bulgaria must be fatal to her; that if she would only concede what was necessary to secure Bulgaria's friendship there was every prospect of a victory in which Serbia would gain far more than she was now being asked to concede.... It was all in vain. The Serbian Minister closed on conversation with me by saying they would all rather die than let Bulgaria have Monastir. A preference for death put an end to all argument, and I became respectfully silent.[23]

There were those among the Allies who believed that Serbia should be forced to cede Macedonia so as to bring in Bulgaria and shorten the war. Churchill expressed his annoyance that Serbia 'refused to give Bulgaria Bulgarian country even against heavy compensation elsewhere'.[24] The reluctance of the Allies to force Serbia was partly due to embarrassment and partly to plain decency: it was not easy to compel a small ally to make sacrifices while it was fighting bravely against the powerful common enemy.

The competing promises of territory by the two sides were by themselves not enough to sway Ferdinand. Of even greater importance was the question of which side was likely to be in a position to honour them at the end of the war. During the spring and summer of 1915, the decisive period in the wooing of Bulgaria, the Central Powers scored spectacular victories against Russia and achieved a massive break-through. The Russians were forced to abandon Galicia, then most of Poland. In prisoners alone the Russians lost three-quarters of a million men and more territory than the whole of France. At the same time, on the Western Front, the Allies had not done anything to distract the Germans while the Russians were being mauled.

Against the background of these Allied defeats came the failure of the British at Gallipoli. This made even more of an impression on Bulgaria, due to its proximity and the fact that the Turks, so easily defeated in 1912 by the Bulgarians themselves, were actually able to check the British.

While the Allied offers of Macedonia were only partial and condi-tional on Serbia's compliance, the Central Powers were able to make far larger unreserved offers of Serbian territory without consulting any-body. Sir Edward Grey, as keen an ornithologist as Ferdinand, put it like this: 'Our bird offered to Bulgaria was not only a smaller and duller bird, but it was receding more and more into the bush. The bird offered by Germany was not only a bigger and brighter bird, but seemed to be coming nearer and nearer to the hand.'[25]

Both sides set great store on personal approaches to Ferdinand and a string of visitors came to Bulgaria, all intent on swaying him to one or the other. Among them was the Duc de Guise, Ferdinand's relative. He had been sent in secret by Delcasse, the French Foreign Minister, and with the agreement of the other Allies. Guise, as a Prince of Bourbon-Orléans, was to do his utmost to lay stress on Ferdinand's French blood and to persuade him of his duty to France. Ferdinand no doubt enjoyed the irony of a republican government sending a member of the royal family on an official mission.

The arrival of the Duc de Guise in February 1915 took Ferdinand unawares. He had to wait for a whole week in a hotel in Sofia before the Tsar could make up his mind to send for him. When Guise referred to Ferdinand's French family, he interrupted: 'Keep sentiment out of this and remember the French press in 1913.'[26] After the Duc de Guise had finished speaking to him at some length about his duties as a grandson of Louis Philippe, Ferdinand said: 'And now that you have discharged your mission, you must again become my nephew.'[27] After that he would not discuss the war. Several years later Ferdinand told the Infanta Eulalia of Spain: 'The France of my ancestors calls me a traitor. She insists that as a grandson of Louis Philippe, I ought not to have fought against her. This I find somewhat amusing, since France herself gave Louis Philippe his *congé* and would have none of him or his family.'[28]

Ferdinand was rightly irritated by such appeals to his ancestry and the consequent French accusations of 'treason'. As Tsar of Bulgaria, it was his duty to act solely in what he considered his country's best interests. In any case, he would point out, was the English King to be reproached for 'betraying' his German ancestry, the Empress of Russia her German blood, and so on? There is no doubt that his eventual decision to join the ranks of France's enemies was not taken without bitterness. After Bulgaria entered the war, he avoided seeing Madame Stancioff, his mother's one-time, French-born, lady-in-waiting. Princess Clémen-' tine was the last person of whom he wished to be reminded at that time.

Ironically, the year 1915 which brought these accusations of treason was also the year in which Ferdinand was forgiven for his religious apostasy nineteen years earlier. On Easter Sunday Ferdinand received the sacrament of communion after Pope Benedict XV lifted the ban of excommunication imposed when the infant Boris was converted to the Orthodox Church. In January Boris had reached the age of twenty-one and his continued adherence to the Orthodox Church could henceforth be considered by Rome as a free choice rather than an imposition by his father.

Bulgaria joined the Central Powers on 6 September 1915, with the signing of a secret treaty and a military convention. Ferdinand had waited more than a year before committing himself. The Tsar and his immediate advisers had come to the conclusion that Germany was going to win after the disastrous defeats of the Russians and the failure of the fresh Allied landings at Suvla Bay, Gallipoli, in August. From the moment Ferdinand came to that conclusion, there was no other way of securing Macedonia than by joining the Central Powers. The fate of Macedonia, it was clear to Ferdinand, depended on his decision.

Under the terms of the treaty, Bulgaria was to take the offensive against Serbia and was guaranteed in return both zones of Macedonia as well as parts of eastern Serbia. In case Greece or Romania, who were then still neutral, entered the war on the side of the Allies, Bulgaria was promised rectifications at the expense of either or both countries. Only two years after the disastrous Treaty of Bucharest Ferdinand was being presented with the opportunity to wipe the slate clean of that humiliation and to regain the fruits of the victories of the First Balkan War.

He was only seen very rarely at this time and those who saw him found him much depressed. There was talk that he was becoming a 'morbid recluse'. There is little doubt that his mood was not only due to the familiar and intense hesitations which he experienced before making a decision. He was at the same time aware that external circumstances were compelling him to commit Bulgaria and himself to a course of action – joining the Central Powers – which went against his basic inclinations. Twenty years after Bulgaria entered the First World War, Dr Daneff wrote that it was quite wrong to suppose that Ferdinand became Germany's ally due to his personal feelings about the Central Powers: 'If the former King's personal relations with anyone were ever subject to severe strain, then doubtless this was above all true of his relations with the German emperor.'[29]

Despite the secrecy of the treaty with the Central Powers, by mid-September there were clear signs of which way the wind was blowing, including the arrival of German and Austrian officers at Bulgarian military headquarters. On 17 September, Bulgaria's opposition leaders were received by Ferdinand at the Sofia palace. In a stormy meeting the former Prime Ministers Daneff and Geshoff, and Alexander Stamboliski, the huge burly peasant leader and head of the Agrarian Party, warned the Tsar against the dangers to the country and to himself if Bulgaria entered the war against the Allies. The rugged Stamboliski threatened him: 'I see that you intend to go your own way. Follow it and I will follow mine. The nation will oppose your order of mobilization and unite in revolution.' Ferdinand remarked: 'I have made my decision.' Stamboliski answered heatedly, 'If you carry it out you will risk losing your head.' The Tsar went pale and looking at him steadily, replied: 'Do not trouble yourself about my head; I am old. Think of your own. You are young.'[30] Two days later Stamboliski was arrested and put in prison where he was to remain for three years. Shortly afterwards Ferdinand ordered general mobilization which the Government described as a state of 'armed neutrality'. On 4 October an Allied ultimatum asked Bulgaria to break off relations with the Central Powers and to expel all their officers present in Bulgaria.

The Bulgarian reply to the ultimatum gave no satisfaction. The diplomatic representatives of the Allies broke off relations with Bulgaria and asked for their passports. O'Beirne and Panafieu, the British and French Ministers, were astonished to receive a summons to the palace on the day of their departure. To the Frenchman, Ferdinand said: 'You are the last Frenchman I am seeing, my dear Minister. I might well disappear during this war and I strongly desired to say "goodbye" to an old friend of Bulgaria. I cannot forget that French blood flows in my veins and you may believe me when I tell you how painful it is for me that France and I should have come to such a pass!'[31] O'Beirne was equally astonished when Ferdinand, on parting, expressed the hope that the war would not affect his good personal relations with King George V. Ferdinand then gave them a special train.

The Russian Minister Savinsky was unable to leave with the others due to a violent attack of appendicitis which kept him in bed for several days. Tsar Ferdinand's *aide-de-camp* called at the Russian Legation every day to inquire after his health. When his doctor pronounced him fit to travel he received a letter from the Tsar giving him his personal train consisting of a drawing-room carriage, a carriage for the accompanying staff and a luggage van, for his journey to the frontier. Ferdinand's *aide-de-camp* was to accompany Savinsky and see to his every need. The day before the Minister's departure, Tsar Ferdinand, to the former's great surprise, personally called at the Russian Legation. Savinsky wrote later: 'Extraordinary, almost incredible visit! A visit much commented upon and just as complex in itself as the entire personality of King Ferdinand!'[32]

By his appearance at the Russian Legation in Sofia on the eve of Bulgaria's entry into the war as Russia's enemy, he was making one more attempt to have a second string to his bow. He told Savinsky: 'Well, they [the Russians] got what they wanted! It is I who have destroyed with my own hands the bridge that connected the two countries [Russia and Bulgaria], but it is still I who can rebuild it!'[33] It was a hopeless attempt to get the old see-saw in motion once more.

Ferdinand complained to the Minister of Russia's hostility towards himself: when he visited St Petersburg in 1910, Russia, he said 'cut me and insulted me' and 'now it is me they hate in Russia; yes they do hate me. I have been deprived of my regiment, of my Honorary Colonel's uniform, they have struck me off the lists of the order of St Andrew....'[34]

On leaving, Ferdinand turned to Savinsky: 'There is a question I want to ask you. What have you done with my big portrait in oils I gave you? If you intend taking it with you to Russia, I shall ask you not to, because in their hatred, they will rip it to pieces, trample upon it....'[35] Savinsky allayed his fears; the portrait was to remain in Bulgaria, together with the rest of his belongings. Mindful as ever of occult forces, Ferdinand at least had the satisfaction of knowing that there would be one effigy less for his enemies to stick pins in.

The day diplomatic relations between the Allies and Bulgaria were broken a British-French expeditionary force landed in Salonika in response to Serbia's appeal for help against the expected Bulgarian attack. The Serbs had asked for 150,000 troops, but only some 13,000 landed on 5 October, a scratch force gathered together by diverting units from Gallipoli. A few days later the First and Second Bulgarian Armies launched their offensive against the Serbs in Macedonia.

The loss of Bulgaria to the Allies was seen as a major failure of British and French diplomacy. In two successive leading articles, *The Times* castigated the Foreign Office. One on 9 October, read: 'Great Britain had a unique position in the Balkans and especially in Bulgaria.... Great Britain alone could speak in the Balkans with force and weight and achieve an attentive hearing. That priceless advantage has been somehow frittered away in the last few months largely as a result of inattention, half-heartedness and a want of definite policy.'

Lloyd George said in the House of Commons on 20 December 1915: 'Too late in moving here, too late in arriving there, too late in coming to this decision, too late in preparing! In this war the foot-steps of the Allied forces have been dogged by the mocking spectre of "too late", and unless we quicken our movements damnation will fall on the sacred cause for which so much gallant blood has flowed.'[36] After quoting the above Lloyd George added in his memoirs: 'That summed up my considered opinion at the time of the muddled campaign of 1915. This is my judgement today after a careful perusal of all the documents and histories written on the subject from every point of view.'[37]

In France the loss of Bulgaria, and the consequent criticisms of the French Government, led to the fall of the Prime Minister, Viviani and the Foreign Minister, Delcassé.

In St Petersburg the British Ambassador, Sir George Buchanan, formerly Minister in Sofia, felt strongly that Serbia should have been forced by the other Allies to cede territory to Bulgaria. In his memoirs he wrote: 'Could we but have won Bulgaria to our side, Romania would almost certainly have cast her lot in with us in the autumn of 1915. Turkey's fate would have been sealed and the whole course of the war would have been changed.'[38] Had Serbia been forced to give up Macedonia, 'the war would have been considerably shortened and Russia might have been spared the horrors of the Bolshevik revolution'.[39]

In his war manifesto, issued on 12 October, Tsar Ferdinand gave himself a hearty pat on the back for hard work by beginning: 'Bulgarians! You have all witnessed my incredible efforts during a whole year since the outbreak of the European war to preserve peace in the Balkans and tranquillity in our land.'[40] He pointed out that since the outbreak of the war both warring sides had conceded that the greater part of Macedonia should belong to Bulgaria.

Only our treacherous neighbour Serbia remained stubborn in the face of the advice given her by her friends and allies.

Bulgarians! The national ideals which we all treasure made it our duty in 1912 to call our heroic army to battle, a battle in which it unfolded the banners of freedom and broke the chain of slavery.

Our Serbian allies then became the main cause of our loss of

Macedonia. Tired and exhausted, though undefeated, we had to furl
our standards in the expectation of better days. The good days arrived
much sooner than we could have expected. The European war is
nearing its end. The victorious armies of the Central Powers are in
Serbia and advancing rapidly.... Our cause is just and holy!

As a nation Bulgaria greeted the news of general mobilization and the
entry into the war with none of the fervour that had been seen in
London, Paris or Berlin in the previous year. The memories of the two
Balkan wars were too recent. On the other hand, there was no sign of
the revolution with which Stamboliski had threatened the Tsar. The
desire for revenge and of at last achieving union with Macedonia was
still strong. To most Bulgarians going to war this time seemed not like a
new adventure but the completion of an unfinished task.

The Bulgarian plan of campaign was to advance with two armies
westwards into Serbia towards the towns of Nish, to the north, and
Skopje, further south. This would cut the links between central Serbia
and Salonika along the valleys of the Morava and Vardar. The Bulgarians were to join German and Austrian units which would cross the
Rivers Sava and the Danube under the command of General von
Mackensen.

Caught between the Germans and Austrians moving down from the
north and the Bulgarians advancing from the east, the Serbian army was
destroyed. By the end of November the remnants of the Serbian troops
were on the plateau of Kossovo, known as the Plain of Blackbirds,
where the medieval Serbian kingdom had fought its final valiant battle
against the Turks in 1389. There, in a last bid for safety, the Serbian
troops, accompanied by civilian refugees, took to the blizzard-swept
Albanian mountains so as to force their way to the Adriatic where they
hoped to find Allied vessels to evacuate the survivors. It was an epic
retreat and no one knows for certain how many tens of thousands died
from famine, frost, typhus and attacks by Albanian tribesmen in the
narrow defiles between the mountain peaks. Among the refugees who
eventually reached Corfu was Serbia's King Peter, aged seventy-one,
who tried to trudge along beside his peasant soldiers until, too sick to
continue, they bore him to the coast in a litter. A few weeks later Tsar
Ferdinand toured Macedonia and near Prizren saw the carriage which
King Peter had abandoned in his flight.

The advancing Bulgarians were greeted as liberators. By 12 December the Bulgarian army reached the Greek frontier and, having strict
instructions not to penetrate into Greece, ceased its pursuit. That date
may be taken as the moment when the whole of Serbian Macedonia
came under Bulgarian administration and thus de facto united with

Bulgaria. Among the total of prisoners captured during the campaign were some 50,000 Serbs and 1,200 French and British from the Salonika expeditionary force. The latter, arriving too late, had been unable to do anything to help the Serbs. Its advance northwards to the Bulgarian border had been pushed back. The force, which eventually reached nearly a quarter of a million men, was to remain in Salonika for most of the rest of the war and earn Clemenceau's contemptuous nickname, 'The Gardeners of Salonika'.[41]

In his speech from the throne at the Sobranie on 27 December 1915, Ferdinand praised the army which 'in less than two months completely destroyed the cunning enemy'. But, he said, even more glorious than the defeat of Serbia was the fact that it had chased out of Macedonia 'the troops which two great powers, England and France, to civilization's and to their own shame, sent against the martyred Bulgarian nation in order to maintain Serbian tyranny'.[42]

Bulgaria greeted 1916 in a mood of optimism. The liberation of Macedonia had set to rights the grievances caused by the Treaty of Bucharest in 1913. Almost the entire Opposition in the Sobranie voted the budget and the war credits, although it still emphasized its disagreement with the manner in which the Government of Radoslavoff had elected to solve the Macedonian problem.

On 18 January 1916, Ferdinand arrived in Nish, the temporary seat of the Serbian Government, which the Bulgarians had captured on 5 November. Here he received an official visit by Kaiser William. The Kaiser arrived aboard the new German Balkan Express, 'probably the handsomest train in Europe' according to the enterprising and resourceful correspondent of the London *Daily Mail*, who had somehow managed to witness the ceremonious meeting. The train ran from Berlin to Constantinople and back twice weekly and was intended as an impressive symbol of the political unity of the Central Powers and their allies which now extended from Antwerp to Baghdad. Earlier the meeting between the Bulgarian and German forces in Serbia was celebrated by a zeppelin which landed in Sofia after crossing Serbia.

At Nish Ferdinand greeted the Kaiser with a speech in Latin which began: '*Ave Imperator, Caesar et Rex. Victor et Gloriosus* es....'[43] The latter epithet provoked amused speculation among the Allies. The accepted sense of *gloriosus* is 'vainglorious' or 'braggart'. Was Ferdinand being malicious or was his Latin shaky?

Arm in arm the royal pair walked up and down the railway platform. According to the *Daily Mail*'s correspondent: 'The Kaiser is not the tall man he is represented to be in photographs, and beside the great, massive figure of the hawk-nosed Ferdinand, who has a curious duck-like waddle, the great War Lord seemed almost diminutive.'[44] In the

evening the Kaiser was Ferdinand's guest at a royal banquet for forty
guests at the town-hall of Nish. The Bulgarian Tsar, who had already
been awarded the Iron Cross First Class, was made a field-marshal in the
Prussian army. A month later he returned William's visit and also called
on the Emperor Francis Joseph, from whom he received the baton of an
Austrian field-marshal.

As far as Bulgaria was concerned, she had achieved her war aim with
the occupation of Macedonia. All that remained now was to await the
end of the European war. The average Bulgarian was reasonably sure
that the Central Powers would win.

On 27 August 1916, Romania abandoned neutrality and declared war
on Austria-Hungary. In 1915 she had kept out of the war for the same
reason which made Bulgaria join it: the massive defeats of the Russian
armies. This time the apparent and temporary success of the offensive
by Russia's General Brusiloff in Galicia determined the Romanians to
throw in their lot with the Allies. Any further delay in joining, they
feared, might cost them the chance of claiming their spoils, above all
Transylvania, from Austria-Hungary.

Romania's commitment was greeted with acclamation by the Allies;
but what appeared as a blessing turned out in the event to be a disaster.
Romania's forces struck north, invaded Transylvania and at first carried
all before them, capturing the capital of Transylvania in early September. It was an illusory success. On 1 September Bulgaria had declared
war on Romania and together with some German units attacked the
Southern Dobrudja, the province which Bulgaria had lost to Romania in
1913. By 5 January 1917, the whole of the Dobrudja, north and south,
was cleared of the Romanians. The Bulgarian army distinguished itself
in storming and capturing the fortified town of Tutrakan, which was
considered impregnable, with an artillery preparation of only one
hour's duration and forts attacked and taken in hand-to-hand fighting.
The number of captured Romanian soldiers—28,000—outnumbered the
number of captors. Years later Ferdinand recalled the fall of the fortress
with the words: 'I know of nothing more beautiful than my army.'[45]

The victories in the Dobrudja greatly raised the morale of the
Bulgarian army. In fact the campaign against Romania proved far more
popular than that against Serbia. It was an opportunity to avenge the
unjustifiable invasion of Bulgaria in 1913: the 'stab in the back' at a time
when Bulgaria was engaged in a life-and-death struggle with her
quondam allies. The hard-pressed Romanians had asked for and
obtained the help of Russian troops. The Bulgarian commanders had
been apprehensive about their troops' possible reaction to being faced
by a Russian enemy. There was, however, no sign of indiscipline and
Russian units were defeated by the Bulgarians in several engagements.

The attack on Romania from the south, together with a German attack in Transylvania, finished the Romanian army for the time being. Bucharest fell on 6 December. Romania's entry into the war had turned out to be a blessing for the Central Powers; the opulence of the country, her natural wealth in corn and other foodstuffs, now lay at their disposal. Only her rich oilfields were denied to the Germans due to the timely destruction of the surface workings by British agents.

Apart from bringing Romania into the war, General Brusiloff's offensive of 1916 had marked the moment when the armies of Austria-Hungary lost their fighting spirit. Loyalty and unity suddenly went. War weariness and demoralization deepened with the death in Vienna of the Emperor Francis Joseph, at the age of eighty-six, on 21 November 1916, only two years short of the seventieth anniversary of his accession.

Ferdinand was determined to be present at the coronation in Buda of his successor Charles, the old Emperor's twenty-nine-year-old great-nephew. The new Emperor wanted to keep the ceremony as simple as possible but war or no war, Ferdinand was going to see him crowned as King of Hungary with the fabulous Crown of St Stephen. Charles's Empress, Zita (as the sister of Princess Marie-Louise she was Ferdinand's sister-in-law), quite recently told of King Ferdinand's persistence:

> The Emperor Charles wanted to keep it [the coronation] as a small family affair. King Ferdinand of Bulgaria – who loved these occasions – wanted however to come at all costs 'just to have a look', pleading that legally he after all counted as one of the magnates of Hungary.
> At first the Emperor protested on the lines: 'Look, I shall be swearing an oath to get back all the lost territories of historic Hungary and your Bulgaria was once part of it.' But King Ferdinand persisted, saying, 'No one will know', and got his way in the end, though he was kept pretty much out of sight.[46]

At the coronation on 30 December 1916, Ferdinand saw the Crown of St Stephen slip, coming down over Charles's eyes and covering half his face. The significance of the incident as an omen of the end of the reigning House of Habsburg was probably not lost on Ferdinand.

Though the year 1916 closed with Bulgaria in occupation of a territory beyond the dreams of her most extreme chauvinists, Tsar Ferdinand and many of his people were becoming increasingly apprehensive about the future. Used as they were to the nature of war as it had been waged in the Balkans, with rapid campaigns, decisive victories and swift peace settlements, the nature of what was happening on the Western Front only dawned on them slowly. Ferdinand, who as early as

1916 told the Bulgarian Minister at Vienna that Bulgaria would lose the war but that it was too late to repair the error, was greatly upset by the Allies' rejection of Germany's peace note of December 1916. It was then that he realized that the war would only end with the 'knock out blow', the complete defeat of one of the combatants. He knew that his troops, the majority of them peasants who worried about what was happening to their land in their absence, could not possibly sustain a campaign lasting several years.

In January 1917, a special envoy from Berlin informed Ferdinand of the impending German announcement of unrestricted submarine warfare. Deeply disturbed, Ferdinand expressed the opinion that it would be far better if the advent of peace could be hastened with concessions over Alsace-Lorraine. But, on 31 January, Germany duly announced unrestricted naval warfare and brought the United States into the war.

Ferdinand was by now looking for a way out. His name was associated with the new Austrian Emperor's muddled and abortive offer of a separate peace offer to the Allies, in which Prince Sixtus of Bourbon-Parma, a brother-in-law of both the Emperor and of Tsar Ferdinand, acted as go-between for the Emperor Charles and France's President Poincaré. There were equally abortive and obscure negotiations with representatives of the Allies in Switzerland carried on by several Bulgarians without official status, possibly with Ferdinand's tacit consent. The Bulgarian Minister in Berlin, Rizoff, a son-in-law of the Bulgarian Prime Minister Radoslavoff, attempted to enter into negotiations with Russia's diplomatic representatives in Norway and Sweden in early 1917. These attempts of course achieved nothing. Prince Sixtus's 'peace-offer' was, in the words of the historian A.J.P. Taylor, 'a last splutter of secret diplomacy'.[47] When the enraged Germans learned of these negotiations they made Emperor Charles put his signature to agreements which would have made Austria practically a satellite of Germany. While looking for a way out, Tsar Ferdinand was also well aware that a separate peace for Bulgaria, had it been possible, would have been promptly and ruthlessly suppressed by the Germans who could flood the country with their troops quartered in Turkey, Romania, the Ukraine and the Black Sea coast. Ferdinand's see-saw was well and truly stuck.

By June 1918, friction between the Bulgarian Government and Berlin was acute. There were bitter squabbles concerning the administration and future boundaries of Dobrudja. The food shortage in Bulgaria had become very serious; during the winter of 1917-18 large sections of the population were nearly starving. Helped by the cupidity and corruptibility of functionaries of the Radoslavoff Government, the Germans daily conveyed secret truck-loads of foodstuffs out of the country while groups of German soldiers drove entire herds of livestock across the Bulgarian frontiers. Having captured Belgrade and Bucharest, and being well entrenched in Sofia and Constantinople, Germany considered herself the mistress of the Balkan Peninsula and was treating Bulgaria as her colony. In addition to all this there was growing tension due to Germany's failure to honour her treaty obligations by providing sufficient troops for the protection of the Macedonian Front, where the Bulgarians had to face increasing pressure from the growing Allied army in Salonika. Instead of the promised twelve German divisions, there were only three battalions. To make matters worse, Germany ceased to extend the promised financial assistance to the Bulgarian Government and from 1 March 1918, refused to provide the Bulgarian Army with munitions and clothing.

The Bulgarian peasant was tired of war. The country's manhood had been almost continually at war since 1912. In all, four per cent of the population had been killed and another seven per cent severely wounded. The Bulgarians had occupied all the territory they wanted before the end of 1916, and the continuing burden of war came to be regarded as senseless. There was widespread belief in a popular rumour that they were still fighting because Tsar Ferdinand had hired them out to Germany for three years. As the third anniversary of Bulgaria's entry in the war approached, the soldiers were announcing their determination not to allow a renewal of this imaginary contract.

The most demoralizing factor for the troops was President Wilson's statement at the beginning of 1918, in which he outlined his Fourteen Points and the additional Four Principles. It is impossible to overrate their tremendous effect on the Bulgarian soldier, who implicitly believed Wilson's assurances that after the war the principle of the free determination of peoples would prevail. Most effective of all was the last of Wilson's Principles, which has been summarized as follows: 'All well-defined national elements shall be accorded the utmost satisfaction that can be accorded to them without introducing new, or perpetuating old elements of discord and antagonism.'

As the Bulgarian soldier saw it, this meant that the pre-eminently Bulgarian character of Macedonia would be recognized and guaranteed by the Powers. It was for this very principle that Bulgaria had gone to war. The impact of Wilson's promises was especially great in Bulgaria because the United States had not declared war on Bulgaria. The American Minister in Sofia arranged for the speeches to be translated in full and widely distributed throughout the country and among the troops.

Bulgaria's growing suspicions and apprehensions prompted William II to visit the country in October 1917. By flattery, cajolery and a liberal dispensation of promises and decorations he managed to calm the atmosphere for a while, and consolidate temporarily the tottering fabric of the pro-German Government of Radoslavoff. His visit came a month after the death of Queen Eleonore at the end of a long illness. She was greatly mourned by the Bulgarian people, who knew of her devoted hospital work during the war. At her wish she was buried at a small twelfth-century church at Boyana near Sofia. The year of her death also marked the thirtieth anniversary of Ferdinand's accession. Due to the war and the Queen's illness, there were no celebrations.

By June 1918, the clamour for peace, and dissatisfaction with the Radoslavoff administration decided Ferdinand to bring about a change of Government under Alexander Malinoff, the leader of the Democratic Party, who had strong Western leanings. Yet a mere change of Government could do nothing to save the situation. The prospect of coming to terms with the Allies would no doubt have attracted the new Prime Minister; but it was too late. The Allies themselves no longer seemed disposed to make advances to Bulgaria; Malinoff and Ferdinand wavered about facing the risk of German retaliation in case of an independent Bulgarian move; and, ill informed as they were about the position on the Western Front, neither Ferdinand nor his ministers seemed to have lost all belief in the invincibility of Germany until the very end.

Ferdinand was in his mid-fifties and, despite the anxieties of the war, his passion for blond, blue-eyed young men seemed to grow. His Arcadian automobile jaunt with his two young chauffeurs at the height of the crisis of 1918 has been described in an earlier chapter. There were other incidents. While inspecting a military unit Ferdinand noticed a good-looking officer cadet. Ferdinand insisted that he should be appointed his orderly. This caused considerable trouble as, according to army regulations, the young man would have had to be promoted to full officer rank before he could take up his duties. Ferdinand was so insistent that eventually, under protest, the Commander-in-Chief and the Chief of the General Staff had to agree to the promotion, but they insisted on the appointment not being gazetted. The young officer clearly disappointed Ferdinand, for after two or three months the Tsar began to find fault with him and asked for his removal from the palace. This presented a new headache; the young man could not be returned to his regiment because his fellow officer-cadets were bound to find out about his irregular promotion. Eventually he was found work in the Ministry of War.

Some time later Ferdinand took a fancy to a young courier of the German Military Attaché. He had noticed the young German during a sight-seeing tour arranged for some visiting members of the Reichstag.

Back in Sofia he sought him out, invited him frequently to the palace and eventually appointed him as his official reader of German newspapers. The question that agitated Ferdinand's entourage was: who was spying on whom? Was Ferdinand spying on the German Military Attaché, General von Massow, or the other way round?

As early as July 1918, Bulgarian commanders along the southern Macedonian Front were disquieted by clear signs of preparations by the Allied troops. The repeated and insistent appeals to Germany by Malinoff, the new Prime Minister, for the promised auxiliary troops remained unanswered.

All that Bulgaria received were two successive visits from King Ludwig III of Bavaria (first cousin of 'Mad Ludwig'), nick-named 'the dairyman' for his simple, pastoral tastes, and from King Frederick August III of Saxony. The latter was the divorced husband of Luisa of Tuscany whom Ferdinand had wooed operatically and without success in 1890 and who ended up by marrying the Italian singer Enrico Toselli. The two visitors were hardly equivalent to twelve divisions. It was during the presence in Sofia of the King of Saxony that, on 14 September, five hundred Allied guns began to pour shells on the Bulgarian positions along eighty miles of mountain and ravine in Macedonia. It was nothing compared to the standards of the Western Front; but it was without precedent in the Balkans. Ironically, the Allied offensive in Macedonia started on the eve of 15 September, the day on which large sections of Bulgarian troops had previously decided to down weapons and return to their fields. At this, the decisive Battle of Dobro Pole – the name of a broken ridge more than 7,000 feet above sea-level – the Bulgarians were faced by French, Serbian and Senegalese infantry and outnumbered by two to one in number of troops and five to one in artillery power. Though demoralized, ill-fed and ill-clothed, the Bulgarians put up a determined resistance and the French were forced to use flame-throwers against their emplacements along the ridge. After three days of fierce fighting the Bulgarian line was broken. Fifty miles to the east, the British and Greeks (who had entered the war at the end of June) launched their assault at eight minutes past five on the morning of 18 September after receiving their orders by telephone in a somewhat rudimentary code: '508 bottles of beer will be sent to you.'[48]

With the Bulgarian Front broken, there followed days of hectic pursuit. The Bulgarian retreat through the grim mountainous terrain turned into a rout when the British RAF poured bombs on enemy columns trapped in rocky ravines. This, according to the historian Alan Palmer, constituted 'the first real victory of air power'.[49]

As news of the defeat arrived in Bulgaria the latent unrest broke into open acts of defiance and mutiny, encouraged by Communist agitators. Soviets were proclaimed in several villages and messages reached Sofia that mutinous armed troops were making their way to the capital. On 25 September Ferdinand ordered the release of Stamboliski from the prison in which he had spent three years. The peasant leader was summoned to the palace, where the King requested him to use his influence to pacify the troops. One body of mutineers reached the outskirts of Sofia with the intention of sacking the capital. The few remaining loyal troops in Sofia, together with the cadets and some German troops who had just arrived from Odessa, met the mutineers and dispersed them after both sides had lost some 1,500 men.

With the whole structure of Bulgarian society challenged, Ferdinand agreed with his ministers to seek an armistice from the Allies. The Bulgarian peace delegates reached Salonika on 28 September and negotiated with the Allied Commander Franchet d'Espérey. The armistice was signed the following day and provided for all hostilities between the Allies and Bulgaria to cease at noon on 30 September. During the negotiations General Franchet d'Espérey (the British soldiers in Macedonia simplified his tricky name to 'Desperate Frankie') remarked to the chief Bulgarian delegate that the Allies would find it easier to deal with Crown Prince Boris. When the armistice delegation returned, Ferdinand asked its head: 'Was anything said about me?' To which the Bulgarian, a member of the Cabinet, diplomatically replied: 'I did not wish to discuss that subject. But the Allies spoke in terms of admiration about the Crown Prince.'[50]

During the next few days Ferdinand remained in the palace and granted no audiences. On 3 October he summoned his two sons and his secretaries and told them that he had decided to abdicate in favour of Prince Boris. A document was drawn up and he signed. Ferdinand then summoned the Prime Minister, handed him the paper, and without any other explanation said: 'My abdication! Accept it!'[51] As Prince Boris drew near to Malinoff, Ferdinand came up and said to the Prime Minister: 'Let us two be the first to swear allegiance to the new Tsar.' A moment later Ferdinand embraced his twenty-four-year-old son and said: 'From now on I am your subject, but I am Your Majesty's father.'[52]

He left Sofia and Bulgaria by train next evening, accompanied by a small suite. Boris went with him as far as the frontier. Before departure, Ferdinand paid a last visit to his beloved Vrana and walked through the gardens, the hot-houses and the farm. According to one witness he was delighted to see a rare butterfly which had not been seen at Vrana for some years and even more pleased when he caught it in his net.

The news of Bulgaria's collapse was the unmistakeable signal for which the world had so long been waiting. Winston Churchill, who was in Paris at once recognized that the end had come. It helped Germany to accept the unacceptable and to recognize her defeat. The news was discussed by Hindenburg and Ludendorff on the afternoon of 28 September. They admitted to each other that they had lost the war. The next day they went together to see Kaiser William to tell him that an armistice had to be concluded immediately. The Bulgarian defeat had severed the link between Berlin and Constantinople and had put at risk the German supplies of Romanian oil. Together with Foch's great attack on the Western Front, started on 26 September, the victory of the Salonika force, which left southern Europe wide open, seemed like a great pincer movement extending over the whole continent. On the day Ferdinand signed his abdication, Germany asked for an armistice.

CHAPTER 23

The Survivor

Ferdinand was fifty-seven when his reign of thirty-one years ended. He boarded his train with the intention of travelling to Ebenthal, near Vienna, where his two daughters were staying. When the train reached Budapest, it was met by the city commandant who informed him that he had received orders not to allow him to go to his Murany properties in Hungary. Ferdinand explained that he was travelling to his Ebenthal residence. The royal train reached Marchegg, on the border between Austria and Hungary, on 5 October. Although Ebenthal was only a few hours' journey away, Ferdinand decided to sleep on the waiting train.

At about 2 a.m., Ferdinand's adjutant, General Gancheff, was woken up and summoned to the ex-Tsar's carriage. There he found Ferdinand in bed and before him Count Berchtold. Berchtold, who in 1915 had been dismissed as Austria's Foreign Minister for showing 'weakness' and now acted as Minister in the new Emperor's Household, was asking Ferdinand to leave Austrian territory forthwith. He said that he was acting on the orders of the Emperor Charles. Ferdinand was indignant and furious that Austria, who owed so much to him, was refusing him asylum. Most of all he was infuriated by Berchtold's ironical expression (which, in fact, was natural to him) and too correct, over-polished French, which sounded like sarcasm to his ears. He later explained his feelings about Berchtold: 'It was cowardly of him to accept such a mission; but the shame falls equally on my brother-in-law Charles!'[1]

Emperor Charles feared that Ferdinand's presence in Austria would lead to popular demonstrations and demands for his own abdication. With or without Ferdinand, that is exactly what happened: Charles lost his throne and a republican government came to power the following month.

General Gancheff managed to calm down Ferdinand and pointed out to Berchtold that Austria could hardly refuse asylum to Ferdinand who was a victim of his alliance with the Central Powers and had lost his throne because of it. Berchtold insisted that his orders were strict but finally consented that Ferdinand should spend the rest of the night with his daughters at Ebenthal.

The following day, after Ferdinand had seen his daughters, the train left for Coburg. The German Government, after a series of frantic telegrams, had agreed that Ferdinand could live there. Kaiser William, whose abdication was to follow shortly, could afford to be generous to his old enemy and recent ally. He refused to accept Ferdinand's renunciation of his rank as a German field-marshal.

In Coburg, Ferdinand was offered the Ehrenburg Castle for his residence. Instead, he chose to live in a villa which he had bought some years before the war. He wanted to keep his head down. He was also feeling his way into his new role. It did not take him long to find it: it was to be a kind of whimsical elegaic dignity. By the early 1920s he was dedicating photographs of himself, uniformed, bemedalled and white-bearded, the Bourbon nose jutting from his profile, with the bold handwritten inscription underneath: '*Le vieil Exilé! J'expie tout le bien et le bon de mon passé!* [The old Exile! I expiate all the good in my past!]' Each photograph was framed in a neo-Classical mounting decorated with laurel-like foliage.

He had the satisfaction of knowing that by his abdication he had managed to safeguard the dynasty he had founded. The new Tsar Boris III was behaving with great tact and judgement under tremendous difficulties. He had the advantage of having been born a Prince of Bulgaria and of belonging to the Bulgarian Orthodox Church, but it was his frank simplicity of behaviour that captured the hearts of his subjects. Ferdinand soon developed an embellished and dramatized version of his own abdication, which put him in a heroic light. He described the scene to a Viennese journalist in 1931:

When I had decided to give up my throne I summoned the Prime Minister: 'It is my agreeable duty,' I told him, 'to present you to the new King, the former Crown Prince. We shall be the first subjects to pay homage to him.' He took this for a joke and it took some time to convince him. At last he left the drawing-room, his hands raised to heaven repeating: 'Ah, these Coburgers, such willpower, what a breed!'[2]

The image of himself as the '*pauvre exilé*' was a pose he enjoyed as much as that of the '*pauvre excommunié*' in the past. A correspondent of *The Times* who visited him in Coburg in 1920 found him looking ten years younger, surrounded by his two daughters, Prince Cyril and a suite of about a dozen Bulgarians.

The comptroller of the household was the Austrian Weich, whom Ferdinand years before had brought to Bulgaria from Wiener Neustadt. Weich, who as a young man looked like Lohengrin, began his career as one of Ferdinand's chauffeurs and was later promoted to supervise the running of Ferdinand's palaces in Bulgaria. Ferdinand had insisted that Weich be in his official suite during a State visit to Germany, much to the disgust of Kaiser William's Master of the Ceremonies.

Ferdinand was rich compared to the other European ex-royals. Less than a year after his abdication, he tried to get hold of his securities, which had remained invested in the Bank of England throughout the war. In 1919 an English court decided that they were forfeit as enemy property; but a year later he successfully appealed against that decision, arguing that the money and securities had been deposited by Princess Clémentine since about 1850 and were therefore not subject to sequestration. By 1921 he was a sterling millionaire. A few years later, again through the courts, he forced the German Government to pay him large sums of money. This money had been guaranteed to Ferdinand by Germany in 1915, when Bulgaria entered the war, in the event of an unfavourable outcome. He also succeeded in releasing for the benefit of his family the greater part of his property which was situated in what was formerly Hungary, and which had been assigned to and confiscated by the new Czechoslovakia. His successful claim against the German Government led to strong attacks in the German Press. One German newspaper wrote that 'the future historian will have to place Ferdinand by the side of those German princes of the past who sold their subjects to England as soldiers, for he only risked the blood and property of his beloved Bulgarians after he had made sure – by private treaty – that this hazardous enterprise would cost him nothing'.[3]

In exile Ferdinand indulged, undisturbed, his life-long interest in natural history. At Coburg he built large aviaries, feeding the birds daily and observing them for hours. He made a point of attending international ornithological congresses. His butterfly collection and love of flowers also occupied much of his time. His frequent travels took him to South America, East Africa and, above all, to Egypt which had always fascinated him. Coburg is only some thirty miles away from Bayreuth and he hardly missed a performance during the Wagner festival, frequently calling at the Villa Wahnfried where the composer's widow, Cosima, presided over her husband's relics. In 1929 he was given the freedom of Bayreuth.

In 1923 Maude ffoulkes, the English writer who specialized in ghosting the memoirs of aristocrats and royalty, was given an intorudction to Ferdinand by his cousin, the Infanta Eulalia of Spain. The Infanta paved the way for Mrs ffoulkes's first meeting with Ferdinand and told her that she had many qualities which would appeal to him, especially her love of the occult, her sense of humour and her intelligence.

At the time Ferdinand was staying in the royal suite at Munich's Regina Palast Hotel. He received Mrs ffoulkes in the mauve and white salon:

> The King, who greeted me, was tall and finely built, with a face recalling the portraits of the death mask of Louis XIV. Here was the same sensitive, arrogant, long nose, the superb carriage, the thoroughbred slender feet, and the eyes were the smallish, shrewd, blue ones of so many French monarchs. As King Ferdinand took both my hands in his own, I noticed he was wearing chamois leather gloves, and I remembered the Infanta had told me her cousin invariably wore gloves to preserve his hands from adverse influences.[4]

Mrs ffoulkes had arrived from Paris, and he asked her about the then unsettled state of affairs there:

> Is not France *tiresome*? She is most tiresomely drunk with victory, forgetting she might have been annihilated if America had not come in. And how France hates me. Like my ancestor, Philippe Égalité, my papers are not quite in order. You must understand I refuse to meddle in politics; as a political power I am completely negligible. I went into the Monarchy to benefit mankind, but I was too progressive for Europe. My relative, the late King Leopold II of Belgium, who also worked for the advancement of his country, did not receive adequate recognition during his lifetime – but his domestic discords did much to alienate popular sympathy.[5]

At a later meeting Mrs ffoulkes, at Ferdinand's request, brought a manuscript copy of the memoirs of 'Boni',the Marquis de Castellane, or as she called him, 'the Splendid Spendthrift'. Boni de Castellane, who it is thought may have provided Marcel Proust with the pattern on which to build Saint Loup's earliest appearance, had married Anna, the daughter of Jay Gould, the American railroad millionaire. For ten years he had entertained the world with her money until the marriage broke up and he found himself nearly penniless.

Ferdinand insisted on going through the typescript with her. Mrs ffoulkes was in an agony of apprehension and embarrassment about his reactions to passages in the memoirs concerning himself. He was only upset by one which read: 'Ferdinand took part in the celebration of Mass with apparent devotion, and, holding his missal in his long fingers with their painted nails, he seemed absorbed in his prayers.'[6] Ferdinand turned to Mrs ffoulkes. 'Boni has no right to describe my nails as being painted. I don't like this at all. Look for yourself.'[7] At that he placed his ungloved right hand in hers.

He read on until he reached a page which she knew contained something 'unpleasant' about him. She begged him to skip the reference when she noticed that he was looking at her with 'kindly amusement'. When he asked her why he should not read the page, she replied that it contained something unkind and prejudiced. 'Excellent reason for reading it', Ferdinand said, 'Let us have it at once.'

In her own memoirs Mrs ffoulkes described how his 'charming voice' read slowly and carefully over the following passage: 'That year I made the acquaintance of Tsar Ferdinand, whom I met later at Dampierre and Maintenon. I thought him clever and refined, possessing all the virtues and vices of the Valois. His malicious little eye resembled that of an elephant, in fact his whole appearance was that of a rakish Italian brigand.'

At this point he took off his glasses with great deliberation and, putting down the typescript, patted her hand, saying: 'Why are you so upset? I am not in the least angry. Boni speaks the truth. I *have* the eyes of an elephant: all my family say so. I am certainly a wicked old white elephant, but the brain behind the eye of the elephant has known how to deal with my opponents. Let us talk of something more cheerful.'[8]

At another meeting Ferdinand delivered a homily on his personal feelings as an exile:

> Kings in exile are more philosophic under reverses than ordinary individuals; but our philosophy is primarily the result of tradition and breeding, and do not forget that pride is an important item in the making of a monarch. We are disciplined from the day of our birth and taught the avoidance of all outward signs of emotion. The skeleton sits forever with us at the feast. It may mean murder, it may mean abdication, but it serves always to remind us of the unexpected. Therefore we are prepared and nothing comes in the nature of a catastrophe. The main thing in life is to support any condition of bodily and spiritual exile with dignity. If one sups with Sorrow, one need not invite the world to see you eat.[9]

Such talks 'were a continual delight' to Mrs ffoulkes. She wrote:

> Imagine the thrill of meeting someone who told you he 'adored' earthquakes!
> I said: 'Well, Sire, you are the first person I've met who likes earthquakes. I am certain it must be an acquired taste.'

'It is true, I assure you, and once when I happened to be in the
Rhodope mountains, we had an earthquake every day for a week. We
heard them coming – a distant rumble, a kind of whistle, then the
great rocks crumbled and slid downwards with incredible swiftness,
as if pushed by the unseen hand of a giant. The valleys diappeared –
the black and hungry mouth of the inmost earth gaped – her hot
breath devastated Nature—she spoke, and her voice came from the
nethermost De Profundis. One always sensed an earthquake in the
Rhodope mountains some time before it took place. The sun became
obscured, all dumb creatures trembled, except the cats, who were not
in the least perturbed.'[10]

Mrs ffoulkes lapped this up. She experienced her greatest thrill
shortly before she had to leave Munich:

One afternoon King Ferdinand sent for me, he had motored over
from Wiessi, expressly to give me what he described as a personal
souvenir of our friendship.
  'It would be easy,' he said, 'to offer you the usual cypher brooch, or
some shop-bought trinket – I prefer something connected with
myself, something I have constantly worn.' As he said these words the
King drew a magnificent cat's-eye and diamond pin from his tie and
held it towards me.
  'Oh, Sire,' I stammered, 'I cannot accept such a present.'
  'It is because the associations of this pin are purely personal that I
offer it to you. But, before it becomes actually yours we must
perform a certain mystic rite of friendship. Will you humour me?'
  'Willingly, Sire,' I answered.
  'Then draw your chair close to mine. That is well. Now give me
your hand.'
  I did so, and placing my right-hand palm downward in his left,
Ferdinand slowly traced a triangle on the back of my hand with the
point of the pin. He then asked me to do the same and, with much
inward trepidation, I obeyed. The King next produced a minute file
and carefully dulled the point. I did not question him on the whys and
wherefores of this ritual. That he took himself seriously, and believed
in the efficacy of the charm, was evident. It would be impossible and
presumptuous to ridicule King Ferdinand's occult beliefs when one
knows how inseparable they are from his mentality.[11]

In a letter written a few days later he told her that he had found the
cat's eye in Constantinople in 1910 and had worn it for more than twelve
years.

The last time she saw Ferdinand he spoke to her with 'tremendous pathos' and said: 'A lost wind walks with me in the night. But I have found sanctuary in the Kingdom of the Mind. There I find my true friends, unchangeable, incorruptible, free from the taint of intrigue. Here – I am still a king.'[12]

He had clearly enjoyed spoofing and impressing the impressionable Mrs ffoulkes. But she failed to obtain any literary return. Any hopes that she may have had of inducing him to allow her to ghost his memoirs were forlorn. Ferdinand pleaded ill-health. He had already turned down a considerable American publisher's offer for his memoirs. He also turned down a subsequent offer for an autobiography to be published after his death.

In the autumn of 1930 he emerged from retirement into the limelight for an occasion that, in his eyes, amply justified his abdication: the wedding of Tsar Boris to Princess Giovanna of Savoy, the third daughter of King Victor Emmanuel of Italy. His son's marriage to a member of a reigning royal house meant the consolidation of his own dynasty. The wedding was celebrated with much pomp at Assisi. With Italy's Queen Helena on his arm he led the royal procession, a figure of enormous dignity. His enjoyment was only marred by a small incident. Among the guests was Prince Christopher of Greece with his wife, the French-born Princess Françoise of Orléans, sister of the Comte de Paris. When Ferdinand assured his spirited young kinswoman that he felt 'more Orléans than Coburg' she tartly answered: 'So, Uncle, you have already forgotten the war?'[13]

Two years later Ferdinand appeared at a Coburg wedding between Princess Sybilla of Saxe-Coburg-Gotha and Prince Gustavus-Adolphus, the son of the Crown Prince of Sweden. Despite his gout and his seventy-one years, Ferdinand was determined to keep his position in the van of the mass of competitive wedding guests. His particular rival for precedence was the Grand Duchess Cyril of Russia, the wife of the Romanoff pretender to the Russian throne. When the procession emerged from the church, Ferdinand used his stick – something between a sceptre and a field-marshal's baton – to brush aside anyone who tried to take precedence, including the Grand Duchess.

According to another guest, Gerald Hamilton, Ferdinand was 'gaily attired in black breeches, a shimmering gold tunic and a large black beret surmounted by a gold and jewelled aigrette'. Hamilton asked him what uniform it was. Ferdinand claimed it was the uniform of a Bulgarian Field-Marshal, adding: 'I designed it myself for myself. I was the first Bulgarian field-marshal in the history of the world. And, my dear Gerald, the last.'[14]

Not long after Tsar Boris's wedding, Ferdinand told a visitor at

Coburg: 'For the past thirteen years I have only known one duty: to prevent my shadow from falling on Bulgaria and not to disturb my son's work there.'[15] Boris paid private visits to his father, but there was no question of a return visit by Ferdinand. From afar Ferdinand had watched Tsar Boris's early years of rule during which, despite internal political upheaval, *coups d'état,* and several assassination attempts, he managed by the mid-1930s to bring a measure of calm, economic prosperity and progress. His undoubted popularity reached its height with the birth of a son and heir, Prince Simeon of Tirnovo, in 1937 (a daughter, Princess Marie-Louise, was born in 1933).

Boris's early reign began under the shadow of the peace treaty imposed on Bulgaria in 1919. The Treaty of Neuilly was the punishment for backing the wrong horse in 1915. In addition to a crushing indemnity, the Treaty confirmed the uneven 1913 division of Macedonia, with some additional territorial awards to Serbia, and handed back the Southern Dobrudja to Romania in total defiance of every ethnical consideration. The hardest blow was the loss of Western Thrace to Greece, which cut off Bulgaria from her vital commercial outlet to the Aegean Sea. The treaty in effect sanctioned the subjugation of about a third of the Bulgarian race to foreign dominion. This amputation of Bulgarian-inhabited regions resulted in an army of refugees from the Dobrudja, Thrace and above all Macedonia. They not only confronted the country with a major economic problem but troubled and envenomed its political life with their irredentist aims.

As Bulgaria's Prime Minister from 1919 until 1923, Alexander Stamboliski was the country's virtual peasant dictator. His original, single-minded and arbitrary régime united his opponents, the most violent of whom were the Macedonians in the terrorist organization IMRO. He was killed during a *coup d'état* in June 1923 by IMRO terrorists, who could not forgive him his policy of reconciliation with Yugoslavia. In September that year, the Communists tried to take advantage of circumstances following Stamboliski's fall to foment an uprising which was quickly suppressed. On 14 April 1925, there was an unsuccessful attempt to assassinate Boris while he was being driven to Sofia. Two days later an infernal machine concealed in the roof of the old cathedral of Sveta Nedelja exploded during a funeral service for a Bulgarian general who himself had been assassinated. The bombing was hideously successful, but Boris, the chief target of the Communist terrorists, escaped unhurt. This Comintern outrage brought such fearful retribution that Communism ceased for some years to be an active force in Bulgaria, or anywhere in the Balkans.

The growing influence of the Macedonians in Bulgaria's political life after the fall of Stamboliski, their single-minded devotion to liberating their people from Yugoslavia, regardless of the cost or means and their use of violence against Bulgarians or against each other, led to the fall of the Government in 1934 and the establishment of an authoritarian régime that put an end to Macedonian terrorism.

The new régime, headed by Colonel Damian Velcheff, soon alienated many military and civilian leaders. In 1935 Tsar Boris, with army assistance, installed a more moderate government which calmed the political climate. Boris had ridden the political storms shrewdly and cautiously, without committing himself in any direction. Now he established a royal dictatorship which governed through civilian experts, with a limited participation of minor political leaders. New economic policies were elaborated which soon brought a new prosperity to the country: during the five years between 1934 and 1939, industrial production rose by sixty-four per cent while the per capita consumption of cereals rose by over a quarter.

Ferdinand had watched the years of turmoil with anxiety, but adhered to his resolve not to discuss political matters or to give any opinion on the domestic problems of Bulgaria. In 1928, the millennium of the reign of Bulgaria's Tsar Simeon and the fiftieth anniversary of the liberation of Bulgaria from Turkish rule, he wrote down a sort of brief personal and private apologia which concluded:

Tired by a long and unequal struggle, vanquished but unconquered, the Bulgarian nation has accepted its painful fate and has again returned to its peaceful occupations. In the Bulgarian people's capacity for diligent work I see the guarantee of a brighter future. May it find consolation for its present sufferings in its peaceful and productive labours. The fiftieth anniversary of the new Bulgaria coincides with the tenth anniversary of my exile. I have always wanted the good of the Bulgarian people and it appears to me that I have not merited my fate for having, as the head of the State, twice led it on the road towards the realization of its ideal; but evil people or enemy forces destroyed that road and prevented the reunification of the Bulgarian people of which I dreamed and for which, in the end, I sacrificed myself!

Now that the Bulgarian people is celebrating its fiftieth anniversary, may it know that though far away, a heart full of pain and suffering is also filled with the most ardent wishes for its bright and happy future![16]

Ferdinand expressed his joy at the birth of his grandson, Prince Simeon, in a letter to Konstantin Kalcheff, the delegate of the Bulgarian Sobranie whom he had first approached in the Vienna Opera in 1886. At the same time the letter was a manifestation of his desire to be recognized as the head of the Bulgarian dynasty. He reminded Kalcheff that he was writing to him exactly fifty years after a deputation of the Sobranie had arrived at Ebenthal with the official announcement of his unanimous election as Bulgaria's ruler:

At that time the Grand Sobranie voted unanimously for an unknown youngster who, despite his youth, was filled with the desire to devote himself to the service of the Bulgarian people....

Today, half a century after the day on which I picked up the reins of authority, my thoughts are centred on my beloved Bulgaria which is now full of joy following the birth of the heir to the throne in whom I see the guarantee for the nation's well-being and for the consolidation of the dynasty, whose head is the ruler elected on 7 July 1887.

He ended with the words:

Sharing in the joy of the Bulgarian nation, I am also filled with deep sorrow that I am unable to be present in Tirnovo, my beloved royal city in which I received my Bulgarian baptism, for this fiftieth anniversary. If the last twenty years of exile were accompanied by great sorrow and suffering, then my sorrow increases at the thought that my hope of seeing once more the country to which I devoted and sacrificed my youth, is disappearing.

My dear Konstantin Kalcheff, tell all those from whose memory the historic date of 7 July 1887 has not yet disappeared and who still remember and feel for their old Ruler, that He loves and longs for Bulgaria and will carry that love to his grave.[17]

Kalcheff, who was surprised to receive the letter, may well have wondered if, with the reference to his disappearing hope of revisiting Bulgaria, Ferdinand was not putting out a feeler to find out whether in the stabler climate of Bulgaria a visit might be possible. Significantly, a year later Tsar Boris told George Rendel, the newly arrived English Minister in Sofia, of his fears that Ferdinand might try to stage a comeback. Rendel later wrote that Boris 'was much upset, and even asked my advice as to how best to reduce the risk of this happening'.[18]

Rendel recorded his impression that

King Ferdinand had not been a kindly parent. He seems to have taken a peculiar pleasure in bullying his two sons. A Bulgarian friend of mine of the same age as King Boris had often been invited as a boy to the family lunch at the palace. He used to tell me how at these meals King Ferdinand would spend his time baiting Boris, comparing him adversely to my friend, and making his life a misery. '*Regarde donc ton ami,*' he would say, '*il n'est pas un imbécile comme toi. Il passe ses examens, lui!*'

On one occasion we were looking at an exhibition of butterflies together and King Boris was complimented by the Director on the gentle way in which he handled some new species that had just been brought from the tropics. The King turned to me and said: 'I learnt that from my father. If my brother or I ever disturbed a scale on one of his specimens, we were made to pay for it for a fortnight.'[19]

According to Rendel, Tsar Boris spoke of his father with no affection or respect, though with obvious nervousness'. Yet when the Minister called on the Tsar at the country palace of Vrana in 1938, he was surprised to see set on an easel next to Boris's desk,

> a horribly sinister life-size full-length portrait of King Ferdinand – fairly recently painted, for it showed the old man with white hair and a white beard. The figure in the portrait had a queer penetrating expression, and the dominating personality of the old King seemed to brood like an evil spirit over the room. It was a curious paradox that with such unhappy youthful memories, King Boris should still wish in this odd way to perpetuate this association.[20]

But according to other witnesses Ferdinand, albeit a strict parent, was not an unkind one. In 1921 Tsar Boris spoke to a visiting Englishman, Colonel Repington, about his debt to his father:

> The King's manner at once changed and he displayed deep feeling. He told me how much statecraft he had learnt from him [Ferdinand]. He had been allowed to see all that went on from the *coulisses*, and it had been a great education to him. When the break came he felt that the only course in Bulgaria's interest was to make it a real break, and had consequently had no more direct relations with his father. This had been a great grief to him but he felt that F. understood.[21]

Three days after Ferdinand's abdication the Austrian Minister in Sofia, Count Czernin sent to Vienna an epitaphic report about him which was mainly hostile. For example, he wrote: 'During the first twenty-five years of his reign he ceaselessly encouraged the rivalry between Austria-Hungary and Russia and so prepared the ground for the world war.'[22] But this is what he had to say of Ferdinand's personality:

'As a private person, King Ferdinand is quite extraordinarily gifted. He is deeply learned in numerous subjects, can be captivatingly kind and charming when he thinks it is worth his while. He is an appalling husband, yet a loving father who has conducted his children's education with extraordinary skill.'[23]

In 1938 Bulgaria was prospering under Tsar Boris's rule. Political life was stabler than at any time during his twenty years on the throne. But, with some of the pessimistic insight he had inherited from his father, he was only too well aware of the precariousness of Bulgaria's position. Rendel has described Boris's fears in his memoirs published in 1957:

> Looking back it is easy to see how fundamentally precarious the position really was of the whole line of independent States lying between the Slav and Teuton giants, from the Baltic to the Mediterranean and the Black Sea. Most of them had only come into being in their modern form when the neighbouring empires had been in eclipse. With the resurgence of Germany and the growth of the new dynamism in Russia, the future of most of these border countries became dark indeed. King Boris, always inclined to pessimism, was the first to recognise these perils. He more than once told me that, unless peace could be preserved, he thought the days of small independent countries were numbered.
>
> But to him the alternatives were always Germany or Russia. Western Europe was, in his view, too far away and too pre-occupied with its own anxieties to be able effectively to intervene. The choice of sides in fact presented itself in the Balkans in a form quite different from that in which we were accustomed to think of it in the West.[24]

In 1938 Tsar Boris's dominating object was to help to avert war. In August, as the Munich crisis loomed over Europe, he spent a weekend at Balmoral with King George VI. At the end of August he was due to return to Bulgaria via Germany where he had a long-standing engagement to shoot with Goering. Before he left London he had a meeting with Neville Chamberlain at Downing Street, at the latter's request, during which the Prime Minister left him under no illusion as to the temper of the British people. At his subsequent meetings with Hitler and Goering, Tsar Boris tried to convince them that they were wholly mistaken in their belief in British weakness. If pushed too far, he told them, Britain would react sharply and with increasing effectiveness. He reminded them that she had a 'well-known way of winning the final battle'.[25]

Sir George Rendel was instructed by Chamberlain to thank King Boris for what he had done and to tell him 'that it was felt that he had

acted as a 'great European'.'[26] Rendel wrote later: 'The word 'appeaser'
had not then become a term of abuse, but came nearer in meaning to the
evangelical word 'peacemaker'. He [Boris] turned to me, and asking me
to thank Mr. Chamberlain for his message, said rather sadly, *"Nous deux,
nous sommes les seuls, vrais pacifistes, lui et moi* [We two, we are the only true
pacifists, he and I]".'[27]

When war came, Bulgaria was only too anxious to remain neutral.
But whatever slim hopes Tsar Boris may have had of maintaining
neutrality were already vitiated before war broke out by the Nazi-
Soviet Pact of 23 August 1939. Its effect in Bulgaria was electrical. The
large proportion of Bulgarians who were Russophil by tradition –
irrespective of Russia's political colour – and the pro-Germans found
themselves united in their attitude to the events in Europe. As the war
developed, the full weight of Russian influence in Bulgaria was thrown
exclusively on the German side. Bulgaria's Communists and other
Russian-orientated leftists did not raise any objections when, in early
1941, Tsar Boris was forced to yield to Hitler's demands for passage
through the country of German troops en route to invade Greece. It
was only after the Germans attacked the Soviet Union on 22 June 1941,
that they began to protest against Bulgarian collaboration with Germany.

By this time Germany had gained for herself considerable popularity
in Bulgaria by inducing Romania to give up the province of the
Southern Dobrudja, her ill-gotten gain of 1913. The transfer of the
province in September 1940, was the result of peaceful negotiations
according to international law, and was recognized not only by its
initiator, Germany, but also by Great Britain, France and the Soviet
Union. Tsar Boris was in a unique position when, at the height of the
war in Europe, he tactfully thanked both warring sides for the return of
the province. It was largely his tact that assured the possession of the
Southern Dobrudja for Bulgaria to the present day.

The return of the Southern Dobrudja was in part the result of Tsar
Ferdinand's last political act. On 7 July 1940, shortly before the Germans
induced the Romanians to open negotiations with Sofia, he wrote to
Hitler and asked him to put right the 'injustices' suffered by Bulgaria
after the First World War: 'I beg you on behalf of the brave Bulgarian
soldiers who fell under my command during the World War and on
behalf of my Bulgarian people who suffered heavily in those days and
who see me as the sole culprit for the catastrophe which befell them at
that time, and for its consequences, to right the injustice inflicted on
Bulgaria by the Entente.'[28]

Hitler's brief reply contained the phrase: 'I must say that I have
always regarded with sympathy the Bulgarian demands for revision [of

the 1919 Peace Treaty of Neuilly]. Perhaps the moment is not far distant when they can be satisfied.'[29]

In 1941 Bulgaria was neutral but the Government under the pro-German Prime Minister Bogdan Filoff was certainly 'neutral for Germany'. Bulgaria, despite mounting Nazi pressure, did not join in the German military offensive against Yugoslavia and Greece. King Boris limited Bulgaria's military participation in the war to occupation of those territories of Yugoslavia and Greece – Macedonia and Western Thrace – which were described as 'Bulgarian lands liberated by the German Army'. Thus, for the third time this century, Bulgaria had almost achieved the frontiers awarded to her by the Treaty of San Stefano of 3 March 1878, and then denied her some three months later by the Congress of Berlin.

One of the intriguing 'might-have-beens' of recent European history is what would have happened if the Congress of Berlin had not reversed the Treaty of San Stefano. In *The Struggle for Mastery in Europe*, A.J.P. Taylor wrote:

> Macedonia and Bosnia, the two great achievements of the congress, both contained the seeds of future disaster. The Macedonian question haunted European diplomacy for a generation and then caused the Balkan war of 1912. Bosnia first provoked the crisis of 1908 and then exploded the World War in 1914, a war which brought down the Habsburg monarchy. If the treaty of San Stefano had been maintained, both the Ottoman empire and Austria-Hungary might have survived to the present day.[30]

On 1 March 1941, the Bulgarian Government signed the Tripartite Pact under pressure from Hitler, but also under equal pressure from the Bulgarian nationalists who felt that this was the time to fulfil their old territorial aspirations. Bulgaria was still officially neutral and Germany and the Soviet Union were not yet at war. After the outbreak of the Nazi-Soviet war, the Bulgarian Government made an official declaration of neutrality. Despite German insistence, Bulgaria neither declared war on the Soviet Union nor sent troops to the Eastern Front. However, as a sop to Germany, the Filoff government declared war on Britain and the USA on 14 December 1941. Filoff tried to minimize the importance of that act and to describe it as purely 'symbolic', since no direct Bulgarian military involvement was either likely or possible.

Tsar Boris was thoroughly unhappy with these developments and the increasing German pressure. As early as January 1942, according to Goebbels's diary, he was looking for a way out.

He was deeply distressed by German insistence that Bulgaria should

introduce anti-Jewish legislation. While the Filoff Government passed
legislation forbidding Jews to live in Sofia and requiring them to wear
the yellow star of David, Boris succeeded in saving Bulgaria's Jews
from deportation for extermination. In 1943 he instructed the Bulgarian
Minister in Berlin to inform Ribbentrop, Germany's Foreign Minister,
that the Bulgarian Government had already introduced measures
against the Jews. He added that Bulgarian subjects of Jewish descent
were serving in the Bulgarian army, and it was impossible for him, as
Tsar and Commander-in-Chief of the armed forces, to send his own
soldiers or their relatives out of the country. His firm stand combined
with protests by the Opposition in the Sobranie and by the Synod of the
Bulgarian Orthodox Church, saved the Bulgarian Jews from Hitler's
'Final Solution'.

Unlike other parts of Central and East Europe there was no tradition
of anti-semitism in Bulgaria. Tsar Boris was not only reflecting
his country's distinct lack of racial or religious prejudice, but
equally giving expression to his father's abhorrence of intolerance on
grounds of race or creed. In a rare interview which he gave to an
Austrian journalist in 1931, Ferdinand said:

> I consider tolerance as one of the ruler's first duties. I have always
> tried to be tolerant and to respect and treat with consideration all
> kinds of religious beliefs. In this respect the ruler must not permit any
> discrimination. During my long reign in Bulgaria there was no
> persecution of those belonging to another faith, of Mohammedans or
> Jews. Had there been any I would have punished those responsible
> with the greatest severity.[31]

By the beginning of 1943 Boris's relations with Hitler were deterio-
rating rapidly. Apart from the Tsar's attitude to the Jews and his
increasing resentment of the activities of Gestapo agents in Bulgaria, he
had many personal grudges against the Nazis, including the persecution
of his sister Nadejda, Duchess of Wurttemberg (she had married Duke
Albrecht-Eugen of Wurttemberg in 1924), for bringing up her children
as Catholics. Later the Nazis' brutal ill-treatment of Boris' sister-in-law
Princess Mafalda of Italy, the favourite daughter of King Victor
Emmanuel III, led to her death in a German concentration camp.

In August 1943 Tsar Boris, who had just been on a visit to Hitler in
Germany. died mysteriously shortly after his aeroplane landed in
Sofia. The cause of death was given out as heart failure, but the exact
circumstances have never been cleared up. His brother, Prince Cyril,
later stated publicly his belief that Boris had been murdered on Hitler's
orders during his return flight from Germany by forcing excessively

strong oxygen into his flying mask. The explanation of his death most generally believed was that the aeroplane flew unusually and unnecessarily high and that the Tsar's breathing equipment was purposely faulty. Sir George Rendel gave this explanation for the events leading up to Boris's death:

> Some years later I was told by a foreign friend who had exceptionally close contacts in Bulgaria and whose story I am inclined to believe, that, at this point [the summer of 1943] Hitler decided to summon Boris to Berlin. It seems that the King was injudicious enough to have a long telephone conversation with his unmarried sister, Princess Eudoxia, on the eve of his departure, and to have referred not only to his determination not to send Bulgarian troops against Russia, but also to his intention, if King Victor Emmanuel should agree to an armistice with the Allies, of immediately trying to follow his example. The line seems to have been tapped by the Germans and the story runs that King Boris was greeted by Hitler with one of his hysterical bursts of fury. King Boris then arranged to return to Sofia by air.[32]

Ferdinand received the news of his son's death in Bratislava, the capital of the short-lived, 'independent' Slovakia, where he was staying as the guest of the Bulgarian Minister. The Minister's wife interpreted Ferdinand's stoical reaction to the news as evidence of his 'egoism'. The ex-Tsar was then aged eighty-two but still carried himself well.

As Ferdinand's grandson, the new Tsar Simeon, was only six years old, a three-man Regency was set up, including Prince Cyril. The three regents brought about a change of Government in June 1944. The new non-party Government's task was to find a way out of the war. Failing in this, it was replaced by a Government uniting the pro-Western political parties. The Government tried to negotiate an armistice with Britain and the United States and denounced the pro-Axis policies of its predecessors. On 5 September 1944, it broke off diplomatic relations with Nazi Germany. Only a few hours later, the Soviet Union declared war on Bulgaria and, unopposed, invaded the country. It was an unexpected blow, a striking example of Soviet hypocrisy and aggression. In the words of an American historian, L.A.D. Dellin: 'The Soviet Government, which did not declare war on any of the former pro-German Bulgarian governments, suddenly declared war on an anti-German government which was about to sign an armistice with the Western Allies.'[33] The Russian invasion supported a Soviet-backed Communist coup, and so Bulgaria finally lost her independence and became a Russian satellite. Stalin had succeeded where Tsar Alexander III had failed.

The new Communist regime's first task was the establishment of so-called 'People's Courts'. Among their earliest victims was Prince Cyril, who was shot during the night of 1 February 1945. He was first made to dig his own grave.

There was a historical symmetry in the death of Ferdinand's two sons: Tsar Boris murdered by the Nazis and Prince Cyril murdered by the Communists. That symmetry was an extension of the balancing act which Ferdinand had so long maintained between the national ambitions and resentments of the Teutonic and Slav worlds. In 1887 Ferdinand had ventured out to occupy the vacant Bulgarian throne, at a moment when it was the focal point of Austro-Russian rivalry. At that time it was still possible for him to survive and even to consolidate his position, despite attempts to oust or assassinate him. He had manoeuvred between the ramshackle graces of two dynastic empires on the eve of their dissolution. Necessity, in the form of Bulgaria's precarious position between Hitler and Stalin – the ruthless totalitarian successors of the Habsburgs and the Romanoffs – compelled Ferdinand's sons to try to repeat the performance. But whereas a defeated Ferdinand went on to live a life of luxurious exile for thirty years, Tsar Boris choked to death thousands of feet above wartime Europe and his brother was shot in the base of the skull.

In its first two years of rule, the Communist régime eliminated thousands of Bulgarians in all walks of life. Then it was the turn of the monarchy. A plebiscite on 8 September 1946 produced the predictable majority in favour of a republic and the nine-year-old Tsar Simeon, together with his mother and his sister, went into exile.

Ferdinand died peacefully during the night of 10 September 1948, at Coburg, in the presence of his two daughters. He was eighty-seven and had survived the end to all his ambitions. His reported words at hearing that Prince Cyril had been shot were a fitting epitaph for himself: 'Everything is collapsing around me!'

References

—◦❦◦—

The full title of the book and the name of the author is repeated in each chapter where subsequent references occur. The name of the publisher and date of publication are given only once, the first time that a work is mentioned.

Abbreviations:

GP   *Die grosse Politik der Europäischen Kabinette,* quoted by document number.
OUA   *Oesterreich-Ungarns Aussenpolitik,* quoted by document number.
BD   *British Documents on the Origins of the War 1898-1914,* quoted by page number.
DDF   *Documents Diplomatiques Français 1871-1914,* quoted by document number.

Chapter 1   **A Night at the Opera**

1 Konstantin Kalcheff, private papers in the author's family.
2 Idem.

Chapter 3   **The Soldier Hero**

1 Count Egon Corti, *Alexander von Battenberg*, Cassell, London 1954. p.39.
2 *The Letters of Queen Victoria 1886-1901* (ed. Buckle), Third Series, Vol 1, John Murray, London 1930. p. 179.
3 Idem, p. 180.
4 Corti, op. cit., p. 43.
5 B.H. Sumner, *Russia and the Balkans*, O.U.P., Oxford 1937, p. 575.
6 Corti, op. cit., p. 181.
7 Simeon Radeff, *Stroitelite na Suvremenna Bulgaria*, Vol. 1, Sofia 1973, p. 731
8 Idem, p. 778.
9 Idem, Vol. 2, p. 27.
10 Idem, p. 188.

11 Corti, op. cit., p. 239.
12 Idem, p. 241.
13 Radeff, op. cit., Vol. 2, p. 201.
14 *Avantyuri Russkovo Tsarizma v Bolgarii* (ed. P. Pavlovich), Moscow 1935, p. 30.

Chapter 4 **My Effeminate Cousin**

1 *The Letters of Queen Victoria 1886-1901,* (ed. Buckle), Third Series, Vol. 1, John
    Murray, London 1930, p. 229.
2 Idem, p. 230.
3 J. V. Königslöw, *Ferdinand von Bulgarien*, Südosteuropäische Arbeiten, Vol. 69. Munich
    1970, p. 34.
4 Idem.
5 Idem, p. 17.
6 Hans Roger Madol, *Ferdinand de Bulgarie*, Plon, Paris 1933, p. 10.
7 Lady Paget, *The Linings of Life*, Vol. 2, Hurst & Blackett, London 1928, p. 432.
8 A. Neklyudoff, *Diplomatic Reminiscences*, John Murray, London 1920, p. 7.
9 Bresnitz von Sydacoff, *Bulgarien und der Bulgarische Fürstenhof*, Berlin and Leipzig 1896,
    p. 41.

Chapter 5 **A Mother's Ambition**

1 Anonymous, *Ferdinand of Bulgaria—The Amazing Career of a Shoddy Czar*, Melrose,
    London 1916, p. 27.
2 *The Letters of Queen Victoria* (ed. Benson and Esher), Vol. 2, John Murray, London
    1907, pp. 184 and 194.
3 *Neue Freie Presse*, Vienna 22.2. 1931.
4 Nadejda Muir, *Dimitri Stancioff*, John Murray, London 1957, p. 30.
5 Cecil Woodham Smith, *Queen Victoria*, Vol. 1, Hamish Hamilton, London 1972,
    p.114.
6 Idem, p. 115.
7 Queen Marie of Romania, *Story of My Life*, Cassell, London 1934, pp. 251-2.
8 *Neue Freie Presse*, Vienna, 22.2.1931.
9 J.V. Königslöw, *Ferdinand von Bulgarien*, p. 14.
10 Princess Louise of Belgium, *My Own Affairs*, Cassell, London 1921, pp. 119-20.
11 Meriel Buchanan, *Diplomacy and Foreign Courts*, Hutchinson, London 1928, p.65.
12 Ghislain de Diesbach, *Secrets of the Gotha*, Chapman & Hall, London 1964, p. 31.
13 Stephen Bonsal, *Heyday in a Vanished World*, Allen & Unwin, London 1938, pp. 263-4.

Chapter 6 **Public Relations**

1 Anonymous, *Ferdinand of Bulgaria – The Amazing Career of a Shoddy Czar*,
    p. 15.
2 The account of the first meeting between Prince Ferdinand and the Sobranie
    delegates in this chapter is based on Konstantine Kalcheff's private papers in the
    author's family.
3 Königslöw, *Ferdinand von Bulgarien*, p. 33.
4 Idem, p. 48.
5 Idem, p. 34.
6 Radeff, *Stroitelite na Suvremenna Bulgaria*, Vol 2, p. 516.
7 Oskar Freiherr von Mitis, *Das Leben des Kronprinzen Rudolf*, Leipzig 1928, p. 156.
8 Radeff, op. cit., p. 515.
9 Kalcheff, op. cit.
10 Königslöw, op. cit., p. 33.

11 Idem, p. 30.
12 Idem, p. 37.
13 *The Spectator*, London, 18.12. 1886.

Chapter 7 **Bismarck's Rebuff**

1 *Schulthess Europäischer Geschichtskalender*, Vol. 27, p. 257.
2 Königslöw, *Ferdinand von Bulgarien*, pp. 44–5.
3 Idem, p. 48.
4 Idem, p. 49.

Chapter 8 **The Hesitant Suitor**

1. Königslöw, *Ferdinand von Bulgarien*, p. 54.
2 James Samuelson, *Bulgaria Past and Present*, London 1888, p.175.
3 Muir, *Dimitri Stancioff*, p. 36.
4 Königslöw, op. cit., p.56.
5 Idem, p. 55.
6 Idem, p. 56.
7 Idem.
8 Idem.
9 Idem.
10 *The Letters of Queen Victoria* (ed. Buckle), Third Series, Vol. I, John Murray, London
    . 1930. p.337.
11 John Macdonald, *Czar Ferdinand and his people*, T.C. & E.C. Jack, London 1913, p.108.
12 Königslöw, op. cit., p.58.
13 Macdonald, op. cit., p.110.
14 GP, Vol. 5, No. 1046.
15· Idem.

Chapter 9 **A Secret Journey**

1 *Schulthess Europäischer Geschichtskalender*, 1887, p.472.
2 *Punch*, 20.8.1887, p.82.
3 *Avantyuri Russkovo Tsarizma v Bolgarii*, No. 63, p.59.
4 Will S. Monroe, *Bulgaria and her People*, Boston 1914, p.69.
5 A. Hulme Beaman, *Stambuloff*, Bliss, Sands & Foster, London 1895.
6 Virginia Cowles, *The Russian Dagger*, Collins, London 1969, p.195.
7 Königslöw, *Ferdinand von Bulgarien*, p.9.
8 Monroe, op. cit., p.73.
9 *The Cambridge Modern History*, Vol. 12, Cambridge 1910, p.410.
10 Königslöw, op. cit., pp.62–3.
11 Idem, p.63.
12 Baron Rosen, *Forty Years of Diplomacy*, London 1922, p.63.
13 Königslöw, op. cit., p.60.
14 Idem, p.63.
15 Idem, p.65.
16 Sir Frederick Ponsonby, *Recollections of Three Reigns*, Eyre & Spottiswoode, London
    1951, p.234.
17 Sir Robert Graves, *Storm Centres of the Near East*, Hutchinson, London 1933, p.100.
18 Anna Stancioff, *Recollections of a Bulgarian Diplomatist's Wife*, Hutchinson, London
    1930, pp.32–3.
19 Königslöw, op. cit., p.66.
20 Idem, p.67.

21 Graves, op. cit., pp.100–101.
22 Queen Marie of Romania, *Story of My Life*, p.250.
23 *Punch* 10.9.1887, p.117.

Chapter 10   **Settling In**

1 Dobri Gancheff, *Spomeni za Kniazhevskoto Vreme*, Sofia 1973, p.20.
2 Meriel Buchanan, *Queen Victoria's Relations*, Cassell, London 1954, p.141.
3 Gancheff, op. cit., pp.20-1.
4 Idem, p.22.
5 Königslöw, *Ferdinand von Bulgarien*, p.79.
6 Samuelson, *Bulgaria Past and Present*, p.134.
7 Sydacoff, *Bulgarien und der Bulgarische Fürstenhof*, p.47.
8 Königslöw, op. city., p.64.
9 Sydacoff, op. cit., p.45.
10 Gancheff, op. cit., p.89.
11 Anonymous, *Ferdinand of Bulgaria—The Amazing Career of a Shoddy Czar*, p.53.
12 Idem.
13 Alexadre Hepp, *Ferdinand de Bulgarie Intime*, Paris 1910, p. 196.
14 Gancheff, op. cit., p.143.
15 Idem, p.144.

Chapter 11   **The Thorn in Russia's Flesh**

1 *Ferdinand de Bulgarie Intime*, p.193.
2 Oskar von Mitis, *Das Leben de Kronprinzen Rudolf*, pp.367-8.
3 *Neue Freie Presse*, Vienna, 22.2.1931.
4 Stancioff, *Recollections of a Bulgarian Diplomatist's Wife*, p.25.
5 Idem, pp.25-6.
6 Königslöw, op. cit., pp.198-9.
7 Idem, p.86.
8 GP, Vol. 5, Nos 1144-9.
9 Idem.
10 Königslöw, op. cit., pp. 198-9.
11 Idem.
12 Stancioff, op. cit., p.29.
13 Idem.
14 Königslöw, op. cit., p.103.
15 Gancheff, op. cit., p.65.

Chapter 12   **'This Impure Spring'**

1 Königslöw, *Ferdinand von Bulgarien*, pp.116–17.
2 Gancheff, *Spomeni za Kniazhevskoto Vreme*, p.55.
3 *Schulthess Europäischer Geschichtskalender*, Vol. 29, p.381.
4 Hulme Beaman, *Stambuloff*, pp.152-3.
5 Idem.
6 GP, Vol. 6, No. 1352.
7 Königslöw, op cit., p.123.
8 Sydacoff, *Bulgarien und der Bulgarische Fürstenhoff*, p.31.
9 Königslöw, op. cit., p.155.
10 Idem, p.155-6.
11 Idem, p.126.
12 Hulme Beaman, op. cit., p.227.

Chapter 13 **Courtships**

1 *Avantyuri Russkovo Tsarizma v Bolgarii,* p.69.
2 Hans Roger Madol, *Ferdinande de Bulgarie,* pp.44–5.
3 Königslöw, *Ferdinand von Bulgarien,* p.128.
4 *The Letters of Queen Victoria 1886-1901* (ed. Buckle), Third Series, Vol. 2, pp.122-3.
5 Louisa of Tuscay, *My Own Story,* London 1911, pp.65-8.
6 Lady Grogan, *The Life of J.D. Bourchier,* Hurst & Blackett, London 1926, p.43.
7 Königslöw, op. cit., p.155.
8 *The Times,* 19.7.1895
9 *The Letters of Queen Victoria 1886-1901* (ed. Buckle), Third Series, Vol.2,p.122.
10 Hepp, *Ferdinand de Bulgarie Intime,* p.212.
11 *The Letters of Queen Victoria 1886-1901* (ed. Buckle), Third Series, Vol.2, pp.123-4.
12 Idem, pp.124-5
13 Königslöw, op. cit., p.144.
14 Madol, op. cit., p.53.
15 Königslöw, op. cit., p.146.
16 Idem.
17 *The Letters of Queen Victoria 1886-1901* (ed. Buckle), Third Series, Vol. 2, p.226.
18 Idem, p.229.
19 *Lettres de la Princesse Radziwill au General de Robilant 1889-1915.* Bologna 1934, Letter dated 1.5.1893.
20 Königslöw, op. cit., p.147.
21 Stancioff, *Recollections of a Bulgarian Diplomatist's Wife,* p.68.
22 Stancioff, op. cit., p.67.
23 Gancheff, *Spomeni za Kniazhevskoto Vreme,* p.121.
24 *Lettres de la Princesse Radziwill,* etc., Letter dated 13/14. 3. 1893.
25 Gancheff, op. cit., p.117.
26 A.G. Drandar, *La Bulgarie sous le Prince Ferdinand,* Brussels 1909, p.106.

Chapter 14 **Severed Hands**

1 *The Letters of Queen Victoria 1886-1901* (ed. Buckle), Third Series, Vol 2, John Murray, London 1931, p.356.
2 Idem, p.327.
3 Richard von Mach, *Aus Bewegter Balkanzeit,* Berlin 1928, p.82.
4 Idem, pp.83-4.
5 Königslöw, *Ferdinand von Bulgarien,* p.163.
6 Königslöw, op. cit., p.164.
7 Mach, op. cit., p.89.
8 Königslöw, op. cit., p.174.
9 Mach, op. cit., pp.85-6.
10 Königslöw, op. cit., p.165.
11 Sydacoff, *Bulgarien und der Bulgarische Fürstenhof,* p.42.
12 Königslöw, op. cit., p.160.
13 Hulme Beaman, *Stambuloff,* p.206.
14 Idem.
15 Hulme Beaman, op. cit., p.207.
16. *The Times,* 28.8.1894.
17 Idem.
18 Hulme Beaman, op. cit., pp.224-5.
19 Mach, op. cit., p.104.
20 Idem, pp.144-6.
21 Idem, pp.133-4.

22 Harold Nicolson, *Lord Carnock,* Constable, London 1930, pp.106-7.
23 Idem.
24 Mach, op. cit., pp.132-3.
25 *Svoboda,* 16.7.1895.
26 Lady Grogan, *The Life of J.D. Bourchier,* p.46.
27 Sir George Buchanan, *My Mission to Russia,* Cassell, London 1923, p.63.
28 *Lettres de la Princesse Radziwill,* etc., Letters dated 3/4.7.1895 and 30/31.7.1895.
29 Mach, op. cit., 145.
30 Idem, pp.110-111.
31 *Deutsche Allgemeine Zeitung* 27.2.1931.
32 Prince von Bülow, *Memoirs 1897-1903,* Berlin 1931, pp.33-4.
33 Hepp, *Ferdinand de Bulgarie Intime,* p.185.
34 Neklyudoff, *Diplomatic Reminiscences,* pp. 12-13.

Chapter 15 Anathema and Recognition

1 Königslöw, *Ferdinand von Bulgarien,* p.181.
2 Idem, p.186.
3 Idem, p.182.
4 Idem, p.187.
5 Anna Stancioff, *Recollections of a Bulgarian Diplomatist's Wife,* p.111.
6 GP, Vol. 10, No. 2488.
7 Königslöw, op. cit., p.187.
8 *Lettres de la Princesse Radziwill,* etc., letter dated 21/23.2.1896.
9 Gancheff, *Spomeni za Kniazhevskoto Vreme,* p.121.
10 *Lettres de la Princesse Radziwill,* etc. letter dated 21/22.7.1896.
11 Gancheff, op. cit., p.113.
12 Idem.
13 Königslöw, op. cit., p.188.
14 Idem.
15 Stancioff, op. cit., p.118.
16 Sydacoff, *Bulgarien und der Bulgarische Fürstenhof,* p.130.
17 Sydacoff, op. cit., pp.130-31.
18 Ernest Daudet, *Ferdinand Ier,* Paris 1917, p.161.
19 Sydacoff, op. cit., p.131.
20 Idem, pp.133-4.
21 *Lettres de la Princess Radziwill,* etc., letter dated 14/15.2.1896.
22 Princess Louise of Belgium, *My Own Affairs,* p.125.
23 Idem.
24 Stancioff, op. cit., p.119.
25 *The Times,* 15.2.1896.
26 Idem.
27 Sydacoff, op. cit., p.135.
28 Idem.

Chapter 16 Cannon and Flowers

1 Maurice Paléologue, *The Tragic Empress: Intimate Conversations with the Empress Eugénie,* Thornton Butterworth, London 1928, pp.174-5.
2 Paul Cambon, *Correspondence 1870-1924,* Vol. 1, Paris 1940, p.402.
3 Idem.
4 GP, Vol. 12, No. 2680.
5 Idem, No. 2956 (footnote).
6 Idem, No. 2949.

7 Idem.
8 Idem, No. 2948.
9 Daudet, *Ferdinand Ier*, p.167.
10 Michael Balfour, *The Kaiser and his Times*, Pelican Books, London 1975, p.146.
11 David Duff, *Hessian Tapestry*, Muller, London 1967, p.154.
12 Gancheff, *Spomeni za Kniazhevskoto Vreme*, p.109.
13 Martin Page, *The Lost Treasures of the Great Trains*, Weidenfeld & Nicolson, London 1975, p.93.
14 Hepp, *Ferdinand de Bulgarie Intime*, p.196.
15 Captain Walter Christmas, *The Life of King George of Greece*, London 1914, p.154.
16 Anonymous, *Ferdinand of Bulgaria—The Amazing Career of a Shoddy Czar*, p.163.
17 Gancheff, op. cit., 196.
18 Idem, pp.193-4.
19 *The Amazing Career*, etc., pp.265-6.
20 Muir, op. cit., p.121.
21 Meriel Buchanan, *Diplomacy and Foreign Courts*, Hutchinson, London 1928, p.81.
22 Madol. *Ferdinand de Bulgarie*, pp.96-7.
23 Meriel Buchanan, *Queen Victoria's Relations*, pp.155-6.
24 Idem, p.150.
25 Hepp, op. cit., p.249.
26 Violet Powell, *A Substantial Ghost*, Heinemann, London 1967, p.152.
27 Muir, op. cit., p.114.
28 Hepp, op. cit., p.291.
29 Stancioff, *Recollections of a Bulgarian Diplomatist's Wife*, pp.138-9.
30 Idem.
31 Idem, p.152.
32 Idem, p.149.
33 Gancheff, op. cit., p.125.
34 Idem.
35 Idem, p.127

Chapter 17 **Macedonian Sickness**

1 Nadejda Muir, *Dimitri Stancioff*, p.87.
2 DDF, Second Series, Vol. 12, No. 435.
3 Idem.
4 Elizabeth Barker, *Macedonia: Its Place in Balkan Power Politics*, London, 1950.
5 Muir, op. cit., p.79.
6 GP, No. 2960.
7 A. Neklyudoff, *Diplomatic Reminiscences*, p.10.
8 Sir Sidney Lee, *King Edward VII*, Vol. 2, London 1925-7, p.267.
9 Idem, p.269.
10 Idem, p.267-8.
11 Queen Marie of Romania, *Story of My Life*, pp.249-250.
12 Sir George Buchanan, *My Mission to Russia*, Vol.1., pp.62-63.
13 Lee, op. cit., p.299.
14 BD, Vol. 5, p.114.
15 Maurice Paléologue, *Journal 1913-1914*, Paris 1947, p.48.
16 BD, Vol. 5, p.114.
17 GP, Vol. 18, No. 5422.
18 Dr S. Daneff, *Rodina*, Sofia, June 1941.
19 Madol, *Ferdinand de Bulgarie*, pp.98-9.
20 Idem.
21 DDF, Second Series, Vol. 2, No. 9.

22 Idem.
23 BD, Vol. 5, p.356.
24 Idem.
25 Muriel Buchanan, *Queen Victoria's Relations*, p.156.
26 Idem.
27 Muir, op. cit., p.123.
28 Daudet, *Ferdinand Ier*, p.126.
29 Idem.
30 Madol, op. cit., p.108.
31 Idem, p.100.

Chapter 18 **The Other Tsar**

1 Madol, *Ferdinand de Bulgarie*, pp.94–5.
2 Idem, p.103
3 Idem.
4 Idem, p.104
5 Idem.
6 Idem, p.105.
7 Idem.
8 Nicolson, *Lord Carnock*, p.216.
9 Idem, p.265.
10 H.A.L. Fisher, *A History of Europe*, Arnold, London 1936, p.1086.
11 OUA, Vol 1, No. 1.
12 Idem.
13 Idem, No. 27.
14 GP, Vol. 26, No. 8952.
15 Muir, *Dimitri Stancioff*, pp.127–8.
16 Madol, op. cit., p.110.
17 Hardinge, *Old Diplomacy*, p.167.
18 Madol, op. cit., p.111.
19 OUA, Vol.2, No. 1318 (footnote C).
20 BD, Vol. 9, No. 42.
21 Madol, op. cit., p.115.
22 Hardinge, op. cit., p.167.
23 Madol, op. cit., p.116.
24 GP, No. 9199.
25 Sir Valentine Chirol, *Fifty Years in a Changing World*, London 1927, p.132.
26 DDF, Vol. 2, No. 574.
27 Lord Redesdale, *Memories*, Vol. 1, Hutchinson, London 1916, pp.178–9.
28 GP, Vol. 26, No. 8939.
29 Idem, No. 8992.
30 Stancioff, *Recollections of a Bulgarian Diplomatist's Wife*, p.237.
31 *Lettres de la Princesse Radziwill*, etc., letter dated 28.1.1909.
32 OUA, Vol. 1, No. 781.
33 Idem.
34 *National Review*, London, December 1908, No. 310.
35 GP, Vol. 26, No. 8977.
36 Idem, No. 9004.
37 *Schulthess Europäischer Geschichtskalender*, Vol.50, p.713.
38 OUA, Vol. 1, 1040.
39 BD, Vol. 5, 584.
40 GP, Vol. 26, No. 9340.
41 Nicolson, op. cit., p.295.

42 Idem.
43 Madol, op. cit., pp.134–5.
44 Philippe Jullian, *Dreamers of Decadence,* Phaidon Press, London 1974, p.149.
45 Buchanan, *Diplomacy and Foreign Courts,* p.119.

Chapter 19 **The Crusade**

1 *Lettres de la Princesse Radziwill,* etc., letter dated 26/30.12.1909.
2 OUA, Vol. 1, No. 2185.
3 André Maurois, *Edouard VII et son Temps,* Paris 1933, p.367.
4 Theodore Roosevelt, *Cowboys and Kings,* Harvard 1954, p.111.
5 OUA, Vol. 1, No. 2185.
6 Roosevelt, op. cit., p.111.
7 DDF, Second Series, Vol. 12, No. 331.
8 Chirol, *Fifty Years in a Changing World,* p.132.
9 BD, Vol. 9, p.150.
10 Barbara Tuchman, *August 1914,* Constable, London 1952, p.13.
11 Ponsonby, *Recollections of Three Reigns,* p.272.
12 Madol, *Ferdinand de Bulgarie,* p.144.
13 Idem, p.145.
14 Idem, pp.147–8.
15 Idem, p.145.
16 Marcel Proust, *A la Récherche du Temps Perdu,* Vol. 2, Bibliothéque de la Pléiade, Paris
    1954, p.243.
17 Idem, Vol. 3, p.787.
18 Idem, Vol. 3, p.788.
19 Idem, Vol. 2, p.243.
20 Madol, op. cit., p.146.
21 BD, Vol. 9, No. 86 (enclosure).
22 Idem.
23 OUA, Vol. 4, No. 3492.
24 *History of the 20th Century* (ed. A.J.P. Taylor and J.M. Roberts), Purnell, London.
    p.205.
25 DDF, Second Series, Vol. 12, No.331.
26 Idem.
27 Idem.
28 Idem, Vol. 13, No. 21.
29 A.J.P. Taylor, *The Struggle for Mastery in Europe,* Oxford 1954, p.485.
30 Idem.
31 OUA, Vol. 3, No. 2502.
32 DDF, Third Series, Vol. 1, No. 376.
33 A. Neklyudoff, *Diplomatic Reminiscences,* pp.59–60.
34 Idem.
35 DDF, Second Series, Vol. 12, No. 390.
36 *The Times,* 6.2.1912.
37 Idem.
38 Idem.
39 Harold Nicolson, *Lord Carnock,* p.377.
40 Neklyudoff, op. cit., p.62.
41 *Lettres de la Princesse Radziwill,* etc., letter dated 10/11.6.1912.
42 Madol, op. cit., p.160.
43 Muir, *Dimitri Stancioff,* p.147.
44 John Macdonald, *Czar Ferdinand and His People,* pp.333–4.

Chapter 20 **The Dream of Byzantium**

1 Muir, *Dimitri Stancioff,* p.154.
2 Madol, *Ferdinand de Bulgarie,* p.168.
3 GP, Vol. 33, No. 12297.
4 Paléologue, *Journal 1913-1914,* entry for 31.3.1913.
5 *Lettres de la Princesse Radziwill* etc., letter dated 4.11.1912.
6 OUA, Vol. 4, No. 4321.
7 Taylor, *The Struggle for Mastery in Europe,* p.492.
8 Madol, op. cit., p.170.
9 GP, Vol. 33, No. 12342.
10 Neklyudoff, *Diplomatic Reminiscences,* p.116.
11 Madol, op. cit., p.174.
12 Idem, p.172.
13 GP, Vol. 33, No. 12318.
14 Neklyudoff, op. cit., pp.117-9.
15 Dr S.Daneff, *Primirieto v Chataldja na 20 Noemvrii 1912,* Vol. 3, Rodina, Sofia 1939, p.94.
16 Idem, p.98.
17 Prince Nicholas of Greece, *My Fifty Years,* Hutchinson, London 1926, pp.234-5.
18 BD, Vol. 9, p.330.
19 Dr S. Daneff, *Aktziata mi v Peshta prez Oktomvrii 1912,* Vol. 1, *Rodina,* Sofia 1940, p.72.
20 Idem.
21 Neklyudoff, op. cit., pp.125-6.
22 Paléologue, op. cit., p.152.
23 Lady Grogan, *The Life of J.D. Bourchier,* Hurst and Blackett, London 1926, pp.146-7.
24 Nicolson, *Lord Carnock,* p.388.
25 Paléologue, op. cit., entry for 20.5.1913.
26 GP, Vol. 34, No. 13331.
27 Madol, op. cit., p.183.
28 Pavel Milyukov, *Political Memoirs 1905-1917,* University of Michigan Press 1967, p.253.
29 Idem.

Chapter 21 **The Firebrand**

1 *The Times,* 22.5.1913.
2 Idem, 16.6.1913.
3 Ernst Helmreich, *The Diplomacy of the Balkan Wars,* Harvard 1938, p.480.
4 Idem, p.360.
5 Idem, pp.360-1.
6 Madol, *Ferdinand de Bulgarie,* pp.195-6.
7 Dr S. Daneff, *Ocherk na Diplomaticheskata Istoria na Balkanskite Durzhavi,* Sofia 1931, p.127 (footnote).
8 Idem.
9 Helmreich, op. cit., p.364.
10 Muir, *Dimitri Stancioff,* p.161.
11 Grogan, *Life of J.D. Bourchier,* p.149.
12 Helmreich, op. cit., p.380.
13 Grogan, op. cit., p.150.
14 Winston Churchill, *The World Crisis 1911-1914,* Thornton Butterworth, London 1923, pp.484-5.
15 Grogan, op. cit., 150.
16 OUA, Vol. 6, No. 7838.
17 Neklyudoff, *Diplomatic Reminiscences,* pp.217-8.

18 Idem.
19 Idem.
20 Muir, op. cit., p.166.
21 Neklyudoff, op. cit., pp.216-17.
22 Idem, pp.232-5.
23 Idem.
24 OUA, Vol. 7, No. 8818.
25 Helmreich, op. cit., p.366.
26 Idem, p.367.
27 OUA, Vol. 7., No. 8673.
28 Paléologue, *Journal 1913-1914*, p.255.

Chapter 22 The Wrong Horse

1 Taylor, *Struggle for Mastery in Europe*, p.496.
2 C.A. Macartney and A.W. Palmer, *Independent Eastern Europe*, Macmillan, London 1962, p.33.
3 Nicolson, *Lord Carnock*, p.390.
4 GP, Vol. 36, No. 14161.
5 Paléologue, *Journal 1913-1914*, p.216.
6 OUA, Vol. 7., No. 8792.
7 OUA, Vol. 6, Nos 8072, 8074.
8 Idem, No. 7838.
9 Idem, Nos. 8072, 8074.
10 Idem, Vol. 7, No. 8969.
11 Paléologue, op. cit., entry for 10.12.1913.
12 OUA, Vol. 8, 10019.
13 Idem, No. 10064.
14 Taylor, op. cit., p.521.
15 OUA, Vol. 8., 10058.
16 Idem, Nos 10555, 10556.
17 Idem, Vol. 9, Nos 11105, 11185.
18 Idem, Vol.8, No. 10422.
19 Sultane Petroff, *Trente Ans à la Cour de Bulgarie*, Paris 1927, p.171.
20 HD. Napier, *Experiences of a Military Attaché in the Balkans*, Drane, London 1924, pp.516-17.
21 Martin Gilbert, *Winston S. Churchill 1914-1916*, Vol.3, Heinemann, London 1971, p.505.
22 Idem, p. 506.
23 Lord Grey of Fallodon, *Twenty-five Years*, Hodder & Stoughton, London 1925, pp.195-6.
24 Gilbert, op. cit., p.597.
25 Grey of Fallodon, op. cit., 198.
26 Madol, *Ferdinand de Bulgarie*, p.227.
27 Idem.
28 Infanta Eulalia of Spain, *Courts and Countries after the War*, Hutchinson, London 1925, p.223.
29 Dr S. Daneff, *Nai Nova Diplomaticheska Istoria*, Sofia 1936, p.116.
30 Muir, *Dimitri Stanicoff*, p.189.
31 Madol, op. cit., pp.237-8.
32 A. Savinsky, *Recollections of a Russian Diplomat*, London 1927, p.307.
33 Idem.
34 Idem.

35 Idem.
36 Muir, op. cit., p.190.
37 Idem.
38 Buchanan, *My Mission to Russia*, pp.234–5.
39 Idem.
40 Konstantin Katzaroff, *60 Godini Zhivyana Istoria*, Montreux 1970, p.205.
41 Alan Palmer, *The Gardeners of Salonika*, Andre Deutsch, London 1965, p.70.
42 *Schulthess Europäischer Geschichtskalender*, Vol. 56, p.1188.
43 Anonymous, *Ferdinand of Bulgaria—The Amazing Career of a Shoddy Czar*, p.276.
44 *The Times*, 27.1.1916.
45 Petroff, *Trente Ans à la Cour de Bulgarie*, p.208.
46 As told to Mr Gordon Brook-Shepherd by the ex-Empress Zita of Austria.
47 A.J.P. Taylor, *War Weariness and Peace Overtures*, No. 30, History of the 20th Century, Purnell, London p.817.
48 Palmer, *The Gardeners of Salonika*, p.205.
49 Palmer, *Collapse of Germany's Allies*, No. 31, History of 20th Century,, Purnell, p.846.
50 Madol, op. cit., pp.262–3.
51 Idem, p.264.
52 Idem, p.265.

Chapter 23   The Survivor

1 Madol, *Ferdinand de Bulgarie*, p.267.
2 *Neue Freie Presse*, Vienna 2.2.1931.
3 Madol, op. cit., pp.238–9.
4 Maude ffoulkes, *All This Happened to Me*, Grayson & Grayson, London 1937, pp.63–64.
5 Idem, p.64.
6 Idem, p.74.
7 Idem.
8 Idem, p.75.
9 Idem, p.80.
10 Idem, p.81.
11 Idem, pp.83–4.
12 Idem, p.84.
13 *Memoirs of Prince Christopher of Greece*, Hurst & Blackett, London 1938, pp.259–60.
14 Gerald Hamilton, *Blood Royal*, Anthony Gibbs & Phillips, London 1964, p.26.
15 Madol, op. cit., p.287.
16 Idem, pp.285–6.
17 Letter in the author's family.
18 Sir George Rendel, *The Sword and the Olive*, John Murray, London 1957, p.153.
19 Idem, p.152.
20 Idem, pp.152–3.
21 Colonel C. Repington, *After the War*, Constable, London 1922, p.371.
22 Königslöw, *Ferdinand von Bulgarien*, p.194.
23 Idem.
24 Rendel, op. cit., p.142.
25 Rendel, op. cit., p.157.
26 Idem.
27 Idem.
28 Konstantin Katzaroff, *60 Godini Zhiviana Istoria*, p.557.
29 Idem.
30 Taylor, *The Struggle for Mastery in Europe*, p.570
31 *Neue Freie Presse*, Vienna, 26.2.1931.

32 Rendel op. cit., pp.180-1.
33 L.A.D. Dellin (editor), *Bulgaria*, Praeger, New York 1957, p.118.
34 Buchanan, *Queen Victoria's Relations*, p.164.

Select Bibliography

Anonymous: *Ferdinand of Bulgaria: The Amazing Career of a Shoddy Czar*, London, 1916.

Anonymous: 'The Lesser Tsar' (*National Review*, London, December 1908).

Anonymous: *The Near East from Within*, London 1915.

Anonymous: 'La Reconaissance du Prince Ferdinand par l'Europe' (*Revue Hebdomadaire*, Paris, 22 July 1908).

Baldick, Robert: *The Life of J. K. Huysmans*, Oxford, 1955.

Balfour, Michael: *The Kaiser and His Times*, London, 1964.

Barker, Elizabeth: *Macedonia: its Place in Balkan Power Politics*, London, 1950.

Beaman, A. Hulme: *Stambuloff*, London, 1895.

Belgium, Princess Louise of: *My Own Affairs*, London, 1921.

Bing, E.J. (Ed.): *The Letters of Tsar Nicholas and Empress Marie*, London, 1937.

Bittner, Srbik, Pribram, and Übersberger: *Österreich-Ungarns Aussenpolitik*, Vienna and Leipzig, 1930.

Blunt, Wilfrid: *The Dream King*, London, 1970.

Bonsal, Stephen: *Heyday in a Vanished World*, London, 1938.

Buchan, John (Ed.): *Bulgaria and Romania*, London, 1924.

Buchanan, Sir George: *My Mission to Russia*, London, 1923.

Buchanan, Meriel: *Diplomacy and Foreign Courts*, London 1928; *Queen Victoria's Relations*, London, 1954; *Ambassador's Daughter*, London, 1958.

Bülow, Prince von: *Memoirs*, Berlin, 1921.

Cambon, Paul: *Correspondence 1870-1924*, Paris, 1940.

Cammaerts, Emile: *Albert of Belgium*, London, 1935.

Castellane, Marquis de: *Confessions*, London, 1924.

Chirol, Sir Valentine: *Fifty Years in a Changing World*, London, 1927.

Christmas, Capt. Walter: *The Life of King George of Greece*, London, 1914.

Churchill, Winston S.: *The World Crisis 1911-1914*, London, 1923.

Cowles, Virginia: *The Russian Dagger*, London, 1969.

Daneff, Dr S.: *Ocherk na Diplomaticheskata Istoria na Balkanskite Durzhavi*, Sofia, 1931; *Nai Nova Diplomaticheska Istoria*, Sofia, 1936; 'Primirieto v Chataldja na 20 Noemvrii 1912' (*Rodina*, series I, vol. 3, Sofia, 1939); 'Balkanskiut Suyuz' (*Rodina*, series 2, vol. 2, Sofia, 1940); 'Londonskata Konferentsia prez 1912-

1913' (*Rodina*, series I, Vol. 4, Sofia, 1939); 'Aktsiata mi v Peshta prez Oktomvrii 1912' (*Rodina*, series 3, vol. I, Sofia, 1940).
Daneva (Brisby), Liliana: 'Les relations russo-bulgares 1878-1886' (*Etudes de Lettres*, Lausanne, 1945).
Daudet, Ernest: *Ferdinand Ier*, Paris, 1917.
Dellin, L.A.D. (Ed.): *Bulgaria*, New York, 1957.
Diesbach, Ghislain de: *Secrets of the Gotha*, London, 1967.
Dillon, E.J.: *The Eclipse of Russia*, London, 1918.
Documents Diplomatiques Français, 1871-1914, Paris, 1929 et seq.
Drandar, A.G.: *La Bulgarie sous le Prince Ferdinand, 1887-1908*, Brussels, 1909.
Duff, David: *Hessian Tapestry*, London, 1967.
Erlanger, Philippe: *Louis XIV*, London, 1970.
Ernst, Dr Otto: *Kings in Exile*, London, 1933.
ffoulkes, Maude: *All This Happened to Me*, London, 1937.
Fox, Frank: *Bulgaria*, London, 1915.
Gancheff, Dobri: *Spomeni za Kniazhevskoto Vreme*, Sofia, 1973.
Gooch, G.P.: *Recent Revelations of European Diplomacy*, London, 1930.
Gooch, G.P. and Temperley, H.: *British Documents on the Origin of the War*, London, 1927 et seq.
Gorce, Pierre de la: *Louis-Philippe*, Paris, 1931.
Graves, Sir Robert Windham: *Storm Centres of the Near East*, London, 1933.
Greece, Prince Christopher of: *Memoirs*, London, 1933.
Greece, Prince Nicholas of: *My Fifty Years*, London, 1926.
Grey of Fallodon, Lord: *Twenty-Five Years*, London, 1925.
Grogan, Lady: *The Life of J.D. Bourchier*, London, 1926.
Gueshoff, I.E.: *The Balkan League*, London, 1915.
Hamilton, Gerald: *Blood Royal*, London, 1964.
Hardinge of Penshurst, Lord: *Old Diplomacy*, London, 1947.
Helmreich, Ernst: *The Diplomacy of the Balkan Wars*, Harvard, 1938.
Hepp, Alexandre: *Ferdinand de Bulgarie Intime*, Paris, 1910.
Jullian, Philippe: *Dreamers of Decadence*, London, 1971.
Kalcheff, Konstantin: *Memoirs* (private papers in the author's family).
Katsaroff, K.: *60 Godini Zhiviana Istoria*, Montreux, 1960.
Königslöw, Joachim von: 'Ferdinand von Bulgarien' (*Sudosteuropäische Arbeiten*, vol. 69, Munich, 1970).
Lamsdorff, V.N. Count: *Dnevnik 1886-1890*, Moscow and Leningrad, 1926.
Launay, L. de: *La Bulgarie*, Paris, 1907.
Lee, Sir Sidney: *King Edward VII*, London, 1925-7.
Lindenberg, Paul: *Ferdinand I - König der Bulgaren*, Berlin, 1911.
Logia, George: *Bulgaria Past and Present*, Manchester, 1936.
Ludwig, Emil: *July 1914*, London, 1929; *Kaiser Wilhelm II*, London 1926.
Macartney, C.A. and Palmer, A.W.: *Independent Eastern Europe*, London, 1962.
MacDonald, John: *Czar Ferdinand and his People*, London, 1913.
Mach, Richard von: *Elf Jahre Balkan*, Berlin, 1889; *Aus bewegter Balkanzeit 1879-1918*, Berlin, 1928.
Mackenzie, Compton: *Gallipoli Memories*, London, 1929; *First Athenian Memories*, London, 1931.

Madol, Hans Roger: *Ferdinand de Bulgarie*, Paris, 1933.
Manchester, William: *The Arms of Krupp 1587-1968*, London, 1969.
Martin, Gilbert: *Winston S. Churchill*, Vol. 3, (1914-1916), London, 1971.
Maurois, Andre: *Edouard VII et son Temps*, Paris, 1933.
Mendelssohn-Bartholdy, A., Lepsius, I., and Thimme, F. (Eds): *Die Grosse Politik der Europäischen Kabinette 1871-1914*, Berlin, 1922-6.
Miliukov, Paul: *Political Memoirs 1905-1907*, University of Michigan, 1967.
Mitis, Oskar Freiherr von: *Das Leben des Kronprinzen Rudolf*, Leipzig, 1928.
Monroe, Will S.: *Bulgaria and Her People*, Boston, 1914.
Muir, Nadejda: *Dimitri Stancioff*, London, 1957.
Napier, H.D.: *Experiences of a Military Attaché in the Balkans*, London, 1924.
Neklyudoff, A.: *Diplomatic Reminiscences*, London, 1920.
Nicolson, Harold: *Lord Carnock*, London, 1930; *Peacemaking, 1919*, London, 1943.
Page, Martin: *The Lost Treasures of the Great Trains*, London, 1975.
Paléologue, Maurice: *The Tragic Empress, Intimate Conversations with the Empress Eugénie 1901-1911*, London, 1928; *Journal 1913*, Paris, 1947.
Palmer, Alan: *The Gardeners of Salonika*, London, 1965.
Papancheff, A.: *Edno Prestupno Tsaruvane*, Sofia, 1923.
Pavlovich, P. (Ed.): *Avantyuri Russkovo Tsarisma v Bolgarii*, Moscow, 1935.
Petroff, Sultane: *Trente Ans à la Cour de Bulgarie, 1887-1918*, Paris, 1927.
Peyrefitte, Roger: *L'Exile de Capri*, Paris, 1959.
Poincaré, Raymond: *Les Balkans en Feu*, Paris, 1926; *Memoirs (1912)*, London, 1926.
Ponsonby, Sir Frederick (Ed.): *Letters of Empress Frederick*, London, 1928; *Recollection of Three Reigns*, London, 1951.
Radeff, Simeon: *Stroitelite na Suvremenna Bulgaria*, Sofia, 1973.
Radziwill, Princesse de: *Lettres de la Princesse Radziwill au General de Robilant, 1889-1915*, Bologna, 1934.
Rankin, Lt-Col. Sir Reginald: *The Inner History of the Balkan War*, London, 1914.
Rendel, Sir George: *The Sword and the Olive*, London, 1957.
Repington, Lt-Col C. à Court: *After the War*, London, 1922.
Roosevelt, Theodore: *Cowboys and Kings*, Harvard, 1954.
Romania, Queen Marie of: *The Story of My Life*, London, 1934.
Rosen, Baron: *Forty Years of Diplomacy*, London, 1922.
Runciman, Steven: *A History of the First Bulgarian Empire*, London, 1930; *The Fall of Constantinople, 1453*, Cambridge, 1965.
Samuelson, James: *Bulgaria - Past and Present*, London, 1888.
Savinsky, A.: *Recollections of a Russian Diplomat*, London, 1927.
Schmitt, Bernadotte E.: *The Annexation of Bosnia 1908-1909*, Cambridge, 1937.
Schwering, Axel von: *The Berlin Court under William II*, London, 1915.
Sellers, Edith: 'Tsar Ferdinand of Bulgaria' (*The Fortnightly Review*, London, 1910).
Seton-Watson, Hugh: *The Russian Empire 1801-1917*, Oxford, 1967.
Spain, Infanta Eulalia of: *Courts and Countries after the War*, London, 1925.

Stancioff, Anna: *Recollections of a Bulgarian Diplomatist's Wife*, London, 1930.
Sumner, B.H.: *Russia and the Balkans*, Oxford, 1937.
Sydacoff, Bresnitz von: *Bulgarien und der Bulgarische Fürstenhoff*, Berlin and Leipzig, 1896.
Szilassy, J. von: *Der Untergang der Donaumonarchie*, Berlin, 1921.
Taylor, A.J.P.: *The Struggle for Mastery in Europe*, Oxford, 1954.
Tuscany, Louisa of: *My Own Story*, London, 1911.
Wagner, Lt Hermengild: *With the Victorious Bulgarians*, London, 1913.
Wheeler-Bennett, Sir John: *Knaves, Fools and Heroes*, London, 1974.
Wolff, Robert Lee: *The Balkans in our Time*, Harvard, 1956.

Index

348

matricaria, Rila, 194
Maximilian, Duke, 43
Mayerling, 59, 105, 183
Mecklenburg-Schwerin, Marie von, *see* Vladimir, Grand
 Duchess
Menini, Monsignor, (Archbishop of Sofia and
 Philippopolis), 147
Menrad Laaba von Rosenfeld, *see* Laaba, Major von der
Mensdorff, Count von, 226, 234, 256, 264
Midia, 265-6
Milan, King of Serbia, 27-8
Milford Haven, Marquis of, *see* Louis of Battenberg,
 Prince
Milford Haven, Marchioness of, *see* Victoria, Princess of
 Battenberg
Milyukoff, Pavel, 272
Mincho (chauffeur to Ferdinand), 188
Misérables, Les, 116
Moltke, General Count Helmuth J.L. von, 288
Mondian, Foucault de, 109
Montenegro, 224, 243, 247-9, 264, 280
Montespan, Marquise de, 216
Mrkvička, Jan, 232
Mucha, Alphonse, 232, 286
Munich, 1938 Crisis, 325-6
Murany, Count of (Ferdinand's incognito), 47, 121, 314

Nabokoff, Captain, 29, 34-5, 112-4, 125, 180
Nachovich, Dr Grigoryi. 74, 77, 158
Nadejda, Princess of Bulgaria, Duchess of Württemberg,
 (daughter of Ferdinand), 195, 315, 328
Napier, Lieut-Col, The Hon. H.D., 296
National Review, 226-7
Nazi-Soviet Pact 1939, 326
Nazim Pacha, 266
Nazis, 326-9
Nechayeff, S., 64
Neisser, Dr, 75
Neklyudoff, A., 38, 166, 203, 245-6, 250, 258, 260, 266,
 280, 282-4
Nelidoff, Alexander, 112, 135, 180
Neuilly, Treaty of, 1919, 321, 326
Nicholas, Prince of Greece, 263-269
Nicholas I, Tsar of Russia, 112
Nicholas II, Tsar of Russia, 148, 169, 176, 205, 220, 225,
 228-9, 245, 247, 250, 259-61, 272-3, 276-8; Ferdinand
 and, 168-9, 175-6, 184, 195-6, 205-6, 223, 230-1, 246,
 272, 274
Nicholas of Russia, Grand Duke (brother of Alexander
 II), 17
Nicolson, Sir Arthur (later Lord Carnock), 158-62 *passim*,
 229-31, 249, 257, 288
Nicolson, Lady, 160
Nicolson, Sir Harold, 158, 161, 216, 230, 269
Nietzsche, Friedrich, 166, 226
Nikiforoff, 226
Nikita, King of Montenegro, 251
Nish, 304-5
Norway, 308
Novikoff (Russian merchant), 113
Novoie Vremia, 52

O'Beirne (British diplomat), 301
O'Connor (Britsh diplomat), 87
Olga, Queen of Greece, 263
Orient Express, 76, 106, 120, 123, 127, 187, 193, 222, 293
Orpheus, 195
Orpheus (opera by Gluck), 191
Orth, Johann, *see* Salvator, Archduke Johann
Ottoman Empire, *see* Turkey

Paget, Lady Walburga, 38
Paléologue, Maurice, 181, 190, 199, 205, 207-8, 212-6, 222,
 224-5, 231, 235-9, 242-3, 256, 265, 267-8, 270-1, 278,
 282, 287, 289, 292
Pall Mall Gazette, 87
Palmer, Alan, 311
Panafieu, H.A. de (French diplomat), 280, 301
Panitza, Major Kosta, 124-30, 160-1, 164, 202
Panslavism, *see* Russia
Paris, Comte de, 75, 320
Parsifal (opera), 184, 191
Pašić, Nikola (Serbian politician). 288

Pedro II, Emperor of Brazil, 43, 49
Peter, King of Serbia, 274, 304
Petkoff, Dimitr, 154, 160-1
Petroff, Col Racho, 97, 99-100, 145, 150-1, 225
Petroff, Madame, 97-100, 225, 296
Peyrefitte, Roger, 266
Philip of Macedon, 83
Philip of Saxe-Coburg-Gotha, Prince (brother of
 Ferdinand), 43, 105, 236
Philippopolis, 26, 80, 83, 140, 147, 194, 197
Pichon, Stéphane (French politician), 242
Pius IX, Pope, 170
Plevna, siege of, 17
Pobedonostseff, Konstantin, 60, 169
Poincaré, Raymond, 251, 254, 308
Ponsonby, Sir Frederick (later Lord Sysonby), 84, 236
Popoff, Major Khristo, 73, 99, 104
Portugal, 49, 212, 235
Praz, Professor Mario, 232
Proust, Marcel, 239, 271, 317
Punch, 77, 90

Radoslavoff, Dr Vassil (Bulgarian politician), 281, 293,
 295, 305, 308, 310
Radziwill, Princess, 142, 144, 163, 172, 176, 183, 226, 233,
 251, 256
Rasputin, Grigori. 196
Redesdale, Lord, 224
Reinach, Joseph, 239
Reinsurance Treaty 1887, 63, 71
Rendel, Sir George, 323-6, 329
Repington, Lieut-Col C., 324
Reuss, Prince of (German Ambassador in Vienna), 69, 109
Reuss, Prince Henry of, 211
Ribbentrop, Joachim von, 328
Rila Monastery, 97, 116, 198
Rizoff, M.D. (Bulgarian diplomat), 308
Robert of Bourbon-Parma, Duke, 140-1, 145, 147, 170-2,175
Rodosto, 265
Rodzianko, M.V., 267
Rolls, The Hon. Charles Stewart, 189
Romania, 30, 44, 58, 64, 88, 134, 139, 189, 203, 212, 229,
 271, 285, 300, 308, 313; Austria and, 244; Buchanan
 quoted on, 303; Bulgaria invaded by, 280-1; Bulgarian
 resentment against, 292; Bulgarian territory acquired
 by, 270, 281, 321; cedes South Dobrudja, 326; defeated
 in First World War, 306-7, Germany and, 292; Russia
 and, 272
Roosevelt, Theodore, 234-5
Rostand, Edmond, 239
Royal Air Force, 311
Rudolf of Austria, Crown Prince, 53, 59, 83, 103-6
Rumelia, 20, 26-7, 71, 104, 248
Russia, 13, 36-8, 53, 62, 72-3, 76, 79-80, 94, 117, 122, 137,
 139, 142, 193, 202, 290, 300, 325-6; Alexander of
 Battenberg, attitude to, 23-33, 50-1; annexation of
 Bosnia and Hercegovina, *see* Bosnia and Hercegovina;
 Austria-Hungary and, *see* Austria-Hungary; Balkan
 League, policy towards by, 243-4, 249, 257, 259-60,
 272-91 *passim*; Bolshevik *coup* in, 303; Britain and, *see*
 Britain; Bulgaria, relations with, 35, 63, 74; Bulgaria
 threatened by, 13, 33-5, 62-5, 71, 85, 88-9, 101;
 Congress of Berlin and, 18-21, 25, 27-8, 53, 201, 218,
 229; Constantinople, designs on, *see* Constantinople;
 Ferdinand, early illusions about, 54-5, 58, 70-1, 75;
 Ferdinand loan to, by, 245-6; Ferdinand, recognition of,
 by, 148-9, 152, 156, 168-9; Ferdinand 1896 visit to, 183-
 5; Ferdinand 1898 visit to, 195-6; Ferdinand 1909 visit
 to, 229-31; First World War and, 294, 297-300, 302,
 306-7; France and, 101, 109, 111, 169, 251, 261, 292-3;
 Germany and, *see* Germany; Japan, war with, *see*
 Russo-Japanese War; Macedonia and, 205-6; Panslavism
 in, 15-18 *passim*, 24-5, 53, 169, 289, 291; Press denounces
 bullying of Bulgaria by, 33, 35; Second World War
 and, 327, 329; subversive activities against Bulgaria by,
 63-5, 78, 80, 85, 89-90, 97, 99, 104, 112-3, 125, 127-31,
 134-5, 139, 243; Treaty of San Stefano and, 18, 21;
 Turkey, war with, *see* Russo-Turkish War
Russo-Japanese War 1904-5, 204, 206, 211, 217, 288
Russo-Turkish War 1877, 15-18, 22, 24, 53, 160

St Alexander Nevski, Cathedral of, 232
St Cloud, Palace of, 193